A Note to Readers

Although the 1st edition of this book was written to address the interim interface, anyone working with Office 365 knows the interface and options have changed much more extensively than anyone planned for. Thus, while it was my intent to revise and make available a general update for readers, this text required a complete revision from start to finish to address the substantive changes. As the new work represents a significant investment of time and resources, I hope readers will purchase, read and support this 2nd edition so that I can continue to write about Office 365 and Exchange Server.

Acknowledgments

To my readers—The *IT Pro Solutions* series is a new adventure. Thank you for being there with me through many books and many years.

To my wife—for many years, through many books, many millions of words, and many thousands of pages she's been there, providing support and encouragement and making every place we've lived a home.

To my kids—for helping me see the world in new ways, for having exceptional patience and boundless love, and for making every day an adventure.

To everyone I've worked with at Microsoft—thanks for the many years of support and for helping out in ways both large and small.

Special thanks to my son Will for his extensive contributions to this book. You've made many contributions previously, but now I can finally give you the cover credit you've earned and deserved for so long.

—William R. Stanek

Office 365 & Exchange Online:

Essentials for Administration

2nd Edition

IT Pro Solutions

William R. Stanek
Author & Series Editor

William R. Stanek, Jr.
Contributor

Office 365 & Exchange Online: Essentials for Administration 2nd Edition

IT Pro Solutions

Published by Stanek & Associates, PO Box 362, East Olympia, WA, 98540-0362, www.williamrstanek.com.

2nd Edition Copyright © 2017 William R. Stanek. Seattle, Washington. All rights reserved.

No part of this book may be reproduced, stored in a retrieval system or transmitted in any form or by any means, electronic, mechanical, photocopying, recording, scanning or otherwise, except as permitted by Sections 107 or 108 of the 1976 United States Copyright Act, without the prior written permission of the publisher Requests to the publisher for permission should be sent to the address listed previously.

Stanek & Associates is a trademark of Stanek & Associates and/or its affiliates. All other marks are the property of their respective owners. No association with any real company, organization, person or other named element is intended or should be inferred through use of company names, web site addresses or screens.

This book expresses the views and opinions of the author. The information contained in this book is provided without any express, statutory or implied warranties.

LIMIT OF LIABILITY/DISCLAIMER OF WARRANTY: THE PUBLISHER AND THE AUTHOR MAKE NO REPRESENTATIONS OR WARRANTIES WITH RESPECT TO THE ACCURACY OR COMPLETENESS OF THE CONTENTS OF THIS WORK AND SPECIFICALLY DISCLAIM ALL WARRANTIES, INCLUDING WITHOUT LIMITATION WARRANTIES OF FITNESS FOR A PARTICULAR PURPOSE. NO WARRANTY MAY BE CREATED OR EXTENDD BY SALES OR PROMOTIONAL MATERIALS. THE ADVICE AND DISCUSSION IN THIS BOOK MAY NOT BE SUITABLE FOR EVERY SITUATION. THIS WORK IS SOLD WITH THE UNDERSTANDING THTAT THE PUBLISHER IS NOT ENGAGED IN RENDERING PROFESSIONAL SERVICES AND THAT SHOULD PROFESSIONAL ASSISTANCE BE REQUIRED THE SERVICES OF A COMPETENT PROFESSIONAL

SHOULD BE SOUGHT. NEITHER THE PUBLISHERS, AUTHORS, RESELLERS NOR DISTRIBUTORS SHALL BE HELD LIABLE FOR ANY DAMAGES CAUSED OR ALLEGED TO BE CAUSE EITHER DIRECTLY OR INDIRECTLY HEREFROM. THE REFERENCE OF AN ORGANIZATION OR WEBSITE AS A SOURCE OF FURTHER INFORMATION DOES NOT MEAN THAT THE PUBLISHER OR THE AUTHOR ENDORSES THE INFORMATION THE ORGANIZATION OR WEBSITE MAY PROVIDE OR THE RECOMMENDATIONS IT MAY MAKE. FURTHER, READERS SHOULD BE AWARE THAT WEBSITES LISTED IN THIS BOOK MAY NOT BE AVAILABLE OR MAY HAVE CHANGED SINCE THIS WORK WAS WRITTEN.

Stanek & Associates publishes in a variety of formats, including print, electronic and by print-on-demand. Some materials included with standard print editions may not be included in electronic or print-on-demand editions or vice versa.

Country of First Publication: United States of America.

Cover Design: Creative Designs Ltd.
Editorial Development: Andover Publishing Solutions
Technical Review: L & L Technical Content Services

You can provide feedback related to this book by emailing the author at williamstanek @ aol.com. Please use the name of the book as the subject line.

Version: 2.1.2.3b

> **Note** I may periodically update this text and the version number shown above will let you know which version you are working with. If there's a specific feature you'd like me to write about in an update, message me on Facebook (http://facebook.com/williamstanekauthor). Please keep in mind readership of this book determines how much time I can dedicate to it.

Table of Contents

About This Book 1
    Print Readers 1
    Digital Book Readers 1
    Support Information 2
    Conventions & Features 2
    Share & Stay in Touch 3

PART 1 Office 365 & Exchange Online Overview 5

Chapter 1. Working with Office 365 & Exchange Online 7
Getting Started with Office 365 & Exchange Online 7
    Navigating Office 365 7
    Getting Started with Exchange Admin Center 11
    Understanding Office 365 Licensing 15
Using Windows PowerShell with Office 365 & Exchange Online 17
    Getting Started with Windows PowerShell 17
    Understanding the Default Working Environment 19
    Learning About Cmdlets and Functions 21
Connecting to Exchange Online Using PowerShell 22
    Exploring How the Shell Uses Remote Sessions 22
    Establishing Remote Sessions 24
        Using an Interactive Remote Session 24
        Creating and Importing a Remote Session 26
Connecting to Windows Azure and the Office 365 Service 28
    Cmdlets for Windows Azure Active Directory 29
Working with Exchange Online Cmdlets 32
    Cmdlets Specific to Exchange Online 32
    Using the Exchange Online Cmdlets 36

Chapter 2. Getting Started with Users and Contacts 39
Working with Users and Contacts 39
How Email Routing Works: The Essentials 41
Managing Recipients: The Fundamentals 41
Finding Existing Mailboxes, Contacts, And Groups 45
Finding Unlicensed, Inactive and Blocked Users 48

PART 2 Management Essentials for Users, Contacts & Mailboxes 51

Chapter 3. Managing Users 53
Creating Mailbox-Enabled and Mail-Enabled User Accounts 53
    Working with Logon Names and Passwords 53
    Mail-Enabling New User Accounts 54
    Removing Mail-Enabled User Accounts 59
    Creating Office 365 User Accounts with Mailboxes 59
Setting or Changing Contact Information for User Accounts 62
Changing Logon ID or Logon Domain for Online Users 63
Changing a User's Exchange Alias and Display Name 64
Adding, Changing, and Removing Email and Other Addresses 66
Setting a Default Reply Address for a User Account 67
Changing A User's Web, Wireless Service, And Protocol Options 68
Requiring Users to Change Passwords 70
Deleting Mailboxes from User Accounts 71
Deleting User Accounts and Their Mailboxes 72

Chapter 4. Managing Contacts 75
Creating Mail-Enabled Contacts 75
Setting or Changing a Contact's Name and Alias 78
Setting Additional Directory Information for Contacts 79
Changing Email Addresses Associated with Contacts 80
Deleting Contacts 82

Chapter 5. Adding Special-Purpose Mailboxes 85
Using Room and Equipment Mailboxes 85
Adding Room Mailboxes 90
Adding Equipment Mailboxes 93
Working with Archive Mailboxes 95
    Adding Archive Mailboxes 95
    Managing Archive Settings 98
Adding Arbitration Mailboxes 104
Adding Discovery Mailboxes 105
Adding Shared Mailboxes 106
Adding Public Folder Mailboxes 109

Chapter 6. Managing Mailboxes 113
Managing Mailboxes: The Essentials 113
    Viewing Current Mailbox Size, Message Count, and Last Logon 114

Configuring Apps for Mailboxes 114
Hiding Mailboxes from Address Lists 117
Defining Custom Mailbox Attributes for Address Lists 118
Restoring Online Users and Mailboxes 119
Repairing Mailboxes 122
Managing Delivery Restrictions, Permissions, and Storage Limits 123
Setting Message Size Restrictions for Contacts 123
Setting Message Size Restrictions on Delivery to and from Individual Mailboxes 123
Setting Send and Receive Restrictions for Contacts 124
Setting Message Send and Receive Restrictions on Individual Mailboxes 124
Permitting Others to Access a Mailbox 126
Forwarding Email to a New Address 130
Understanding Storage Restrictions on Mailbox and Archives 131
Understanding Deleted Item Retention 133

PART 3 Managing Groups, Clients & Security 135

Chapter 7. Configuring Groups for Exchange Online 137
Using Exchange Groups 137
Group Types, Scope, And Identifiers 137
When to Use Dynamic Distribution Groups 139
Working with Exchange Groups 140
Group Naming Policy 141
Understanding Group Naming Policy 141
Defining Group Naming Policy for Your Organization 143
Defining Blocked Words in Group Naming Policy 144
Creating Security and Standard Distribution Groups 145
Creating a New Group 146
Mail-Enabling Universal Security Groups 150
Assigning and Removing Membership for Individual Users, Groups, and Contacts
.... 151
Adding and Removing Managers 153
Configuring Member Restrictions and Moderation 155
Working with Dynamic Distribution Groups 158
Creating Dynamic Distribution Groups 158
Changing Query Filters and Filter Conditions 163
Modifying Dynamic Distribution Groups Using Cmdlets 164
Previewing Dynamic Distribution Group Membership 166
Other Essential Tasks for Managing Groups 167

Changing a Group's Name Information 167
Changing, Adding, or Deleting a Group's Email Addresses 168
Hiding Groups from Exchange Address Lists 170
Setting Usage Restrictions on Groups 171
Creating Moderated Groups 173
Deleting Exchange Groups 175

Chapter 8. Configuring Groups for Office 365 177

Getting Started with Groups in Office 365 177
Creating Security Groups in Office 365 179
Working with Security Groups in Office 365 181
Managing Security Group Membership in Office 365 182
Creating Distribution Lists in Office 365 183
Managing Distribution List Membership in Office 365 187
Adding and Removing Distribution List Owners 189
Creating Office 365 Groups 190
Managing the Properties of Office 365 Groups 193
Modifying the Membership and Ownership of Office 365 Groups 194
Changing the Naming Information for Groups and Lists 195
Controlling Group Creation 196
Deleting Groups in Office 365 Admin Center 198

Chapter 9. Working with Exchange Clients 201

Mastering Outlook Web App essentials 201
Getting started with Outlook Web App 202
Accessing Mailboxes and Public Folders 204
Working with Outlook Web App 205
Enabling and Disabling Web Access for Users 209
Configuring Mail Support for Outlook 211
Understanding Address Lists, Offline Address Books, and Autodiscover 211
Configuring Outlook for the First Time 212
First-Time Configuration: Connecting to Exchange Online 213
First-Time Configuration: Connecting to Internet Email Servers 216
Configuring Outlook for Exchange 218
Adding Internet Mail Accounts to Outlook 219
Repairing and Changing Outlook Mail Accounts 219
Leaving Mail on the Server with POP3 223
Checking Private and Public Folders with IMAP4 and UNIX Mail Servers 224

Managing the Exchange Configuration in Outlook 226
    Managing Delivery and Processing Email Messages 226
        Using Server Mailboxes 226
        Using Personal Folders 227
    Repairing .pst data files 230
    Repairing .ost data files 233
    Accessing Multiple Exchange Mailboxes 234
        Logging on to Exchange as the Mailbox Owner 235
        Delegating Mailbox Access 235
        Opening Additional Exchange Mailboxes 238
    Granting Permission to Access Folders Without Delegating Access 240
Using Mail Profiles to Customize the Mail Environment 243
    Creating, Copying, and Removing Mail Profiles 243
    Selecting a Specific Profile to use on Startup 245

Chapter 10. Customizing & Configuring Exchange Security 249
Configuring Standard Exchange Permissions 249
    Assigning Permissions 249
    Understanding Exchange Management Groups 250
    Assigning Management Permissions 253
Configuring Role-Based Permissions for Exchange 257
    Understanding Role-Based Permissions 258
    Working with Role Groups 263
    Managing Role Group Members 268
    Assigning Roles Directly or Via Policy 270
    Configuring Account Management Permissions 276
Index **281**
About the Author **289**

About This Book

William Stanek has been developing expert solutions for and writing professionally about Microsoft Exchange since 1995. In this book, William shares his extensive knowledge of the product, delivering ready answers for day-to-day management and zeroing in on core commands and techniques.

As with all books in the IT Pro Solutions series, this book is written especially for architects, administrators, engineers and others working with, supporting and managing a specific version of a product or products. Here, the products written about are Exchange Online and Office 365.

Because Exchange Online and Office 365 are online products, the features and options for these products can be updated from time to time by Microsoft. As this book was being written Microsoft was preparing to release a new version of Office 365 and this book is written to this new version.

This book, based on *Exchange Server 2016 and Exchange Online: Essentials for Administration*, is designed for those who work exclusively with Office 365 and Exchange Online. If you work with on-premises Exchange Server or a hybrid implementation, you'll want to use *Exchange Server 2016 and Exchange Online: Essentials for Administration* instead.

Print Readers

Print editions of this book include an index and some other elements not available in the digital edition. Updates to this book are available online. Visit http://www.williamrstanek.com/exchangeserver/ to get any updates. This content is available to all readers.

Digital Book Readers

Digital editions of this book are available at all major retailers, at libraries upon request and with many subscription services. If you have a digital edition of this book that you downloaded elsewhere, such as a file sharing site, you should know that the author doesn't receive any royalties or income from such downloads. Already downloaded this book or others? Donate here to ensure William can keep writing the books you need:

https://www.paypal.com/cgi-bin/webscr?cmd=_s-xclick&hosted_button_id=CPSBGLZ35AB26

Support Information

Every effort has been made to ensure the accuracy of the contents of this book. As corrections are received or changes are made, they will be added to the online page for the book available at:

http://www.williamrstanek.com/exchangeserver/

If you have comments, questions, or ideas regarding the book, or questions that are not answered by visiting the site above, send them via e-mail to:

williamstanek@aol.com

Other ways to reach the author:

Facebook: http://www.facebook.com/William.Stanek.Author

Twitter: http://twitter.com/williamstanek

It's important to keep in mind that Microsoft software product support is not offered. If you have questions about Microsoft software or need product support, please contact Microsoft.

Microsoft also offers software product support through the Microsoft Knowledge Base at:

http://support.microsoft.com/

Conventions & Features

This book uses a variety of elements to help keep the text clear and easy to follow. You'll find code terms and listings in `monospace`, except when I tell you to actually enter or type a command. In that case, the command appears in **bold**. When I introduce and define a new term, I put it in *italics*.

The first letters of the names of menus, dialog boxes, user interface elements, and commands are capitalized. Example: the New Mail Contact dialog box. This book also has notes, tips and other sidebar elements that provide additional details on points that need emphasis.

Keep in mind that throughout this book, where William has used click, right-click and double-click, you can also use touch equivalents, tap, press and hold, and double tap. Also, when using a device without a physical keyboard, you are able to enter text by using the onscreen keyboard. If a device has no physical keyboard, simply touch an input area on the screen to display the onscreen keyboard.

Share & Stay in Touch

The marketplace for technology books has changed substantially over the past few years. In addition to becoming increasingly specialized and segmented, the market has been shrinking rapidly, making it extremely difficult for books to find success. If you want William to be able to continue writing and write the books you need for your career, raise your voice and support his work.

Without support from you, the reader, future books by William will not be possible. Your voice matters. If you found the book to be useful, informative or otherwise helpful, please take the time to let others know by sharing about the book online.

To stay in touch with William, visit him on Facebook or follow him on Twitter. William welcomes messages and comments about the book, especially suggestions for improvements and additions. If there is a topic you think should be covered in the book, let William know.

PART 1
Office 365 & Exchange Online Overview

Chapter 1. Working with Office 365 & Exchange Online

Exchange Online is available as part of an Office 365 plan and as a standalone service. Microsoft offers a variety of Office 365 plans that include access to Office Web Apps, the full desktop versions of Office, or both as well as access to Exchange Online. If you don't want to use Office 365, Microsoft offers plans specifically for Exchange Online. The basic plans are the cheapest but don't include in-place hold and data loss prevention features that large enterprises may need to meet compliance and regulatory requirements.

In Office 365 and Exchange Online, user accounts, email addresses, groups, and other directory resources are stored in the directory database provided by Active Directory for Windows Azure. Windows Azure is Microsoft's cloud-based server operating system. Exchange Online fully supports the Windows security model and by default relies on this security mechanism to control access to directory resources. Because of this, you can control access to mailboxes and membership in distribution groups and perform other security administration tasks through the standard permission set.

As you get started with Office 365 and Exchange Online, it's important to keep in mind that available features and options can change over time. Why? Microsoft releases cumulative updates for Windows Azure, Office 365 and Exchange on a fixed schedule and applies these cumulative updates to their hosted servers.

Getting Started with Office 365 & Exchange Online

With Office 365 and Exchange Online, the tools you'll use most often for administration are Office Admin Center and Exchange Admin Center. Regardless of whether you use Office aps with Exchange Online, you'll use Office Admin Center as it's where you manage service-level settings, including the Office tenant domain, subscriptions, and licenses.

Navigating Office 365

When you sign up for Office 365 and Exchange Online, you'll be provided an access URL, such as https://portal.microsoftonline.com/admin/default.aspx. You use this

URL to access Office Admin Center. After you log in by entering your username and password, you'll see the Office Admin Center dashboard, shown in Figure 1-1.

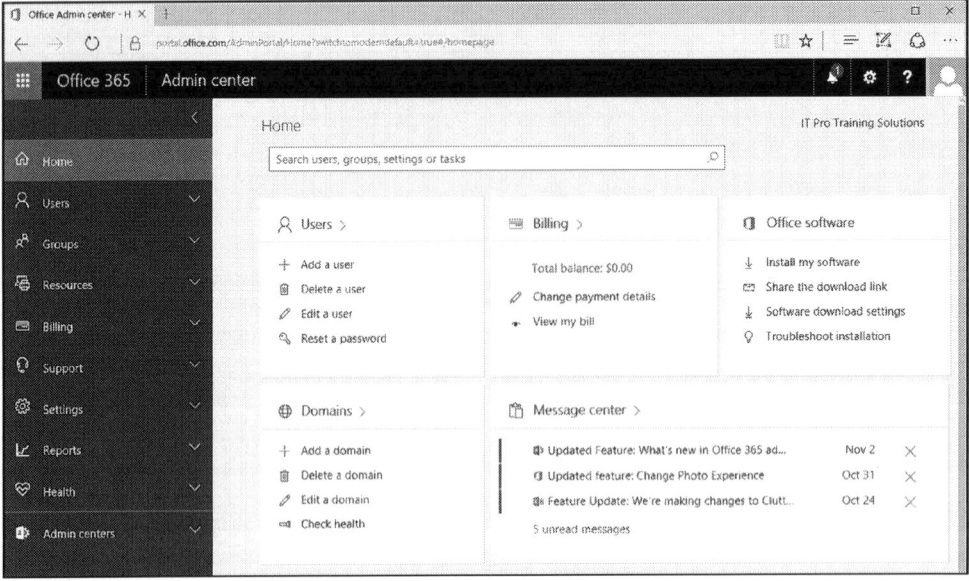

FIGURE 1-1 Use Office Admin Center to manage users and accounts.

As with Exchange Admin Center, Office Admin Center has a horizontal Navigation bar with several options:

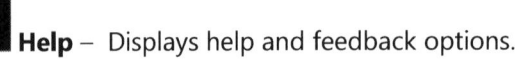 **Apps** – Displays a list of the available apps you can switch to, including Office Admin Center.

Notifications – Displays notifications, such as alerts regarding licensing or subscription issues.

Help – Displays help and feedback options.

8

 **Settings** – Displays options for accessing account settings.

Account – Displays the name of the currently logged in user and provides options for accessing the account's profile page and signing out.

Below the horizontal Navigation bar, you'll find the Navigation menu, shown in Figure 1-2.

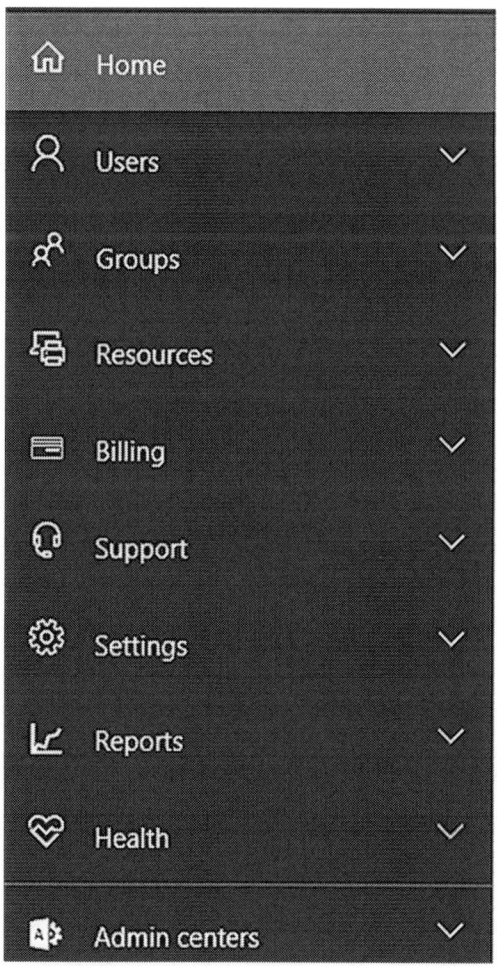

FIGURE 1-2 The Navigation menu in Office 365 Admin Center

Just as the Navigation menu can be expanded by clicking:

Or collapsed by clicking:

Each item on the menu can be expanded by clicking:

Or collapsed by clicking:

When you expand a menu item, you see a list of related options.

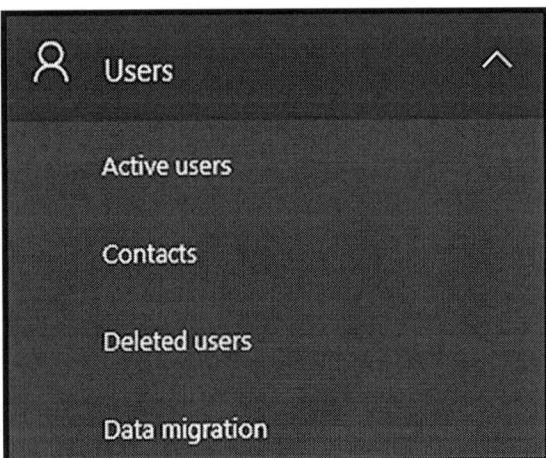

The same options are available when you hover over or point to a menu item with the Navigation menu collapsed.

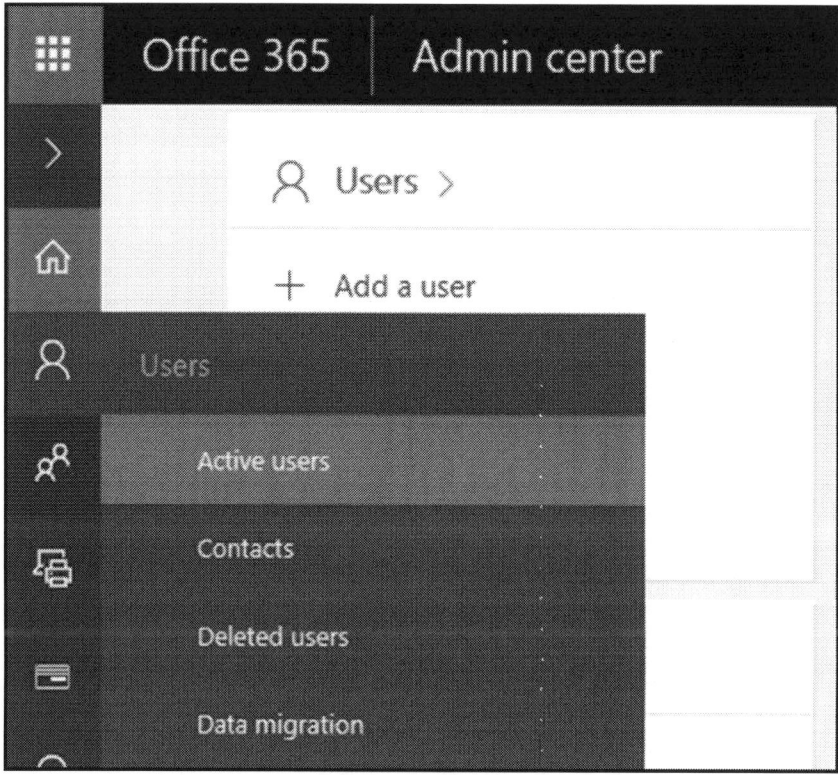

From the Office Admin Center dashboard, you have full access to Office 365 and Exchange Online. Like Office Admin Center, Exchange Admin Center for Exchange Online is a web application. You use Exchange Admin Center for Exchange Online to manage:

- **Organization configuration data.** This type of data is used to manage policies, address lists, and other types of organizational configuration details.
- **Recipient configuration data.** This type of data is associated with mailboxes, mail-enabled contacts, and distribution groups.

Getting Started with Exchange Admin Center

You access Exchange Admin Center through the Exchange servers hosted by Microsoft. Although Exchange Admin Center for on-premises installations and Exchange Admin Center for Exchange Online are used in the same way and have many similarities, they also have many differences. These differences include limitations that apply to the online environment but do not apply to on-premises environments.

The easiest way to access Exchange Admin Center for Exchange Online is via Office Admin Center:

1. If the Admin Centers (![icon]) panel is closed, click or hover over it in the Navigation menu to see the related options.
2. Click Exchange under the Admin Centers heading. This opens the Exchange Admin Center dashboard, shown in Figure 1-3.

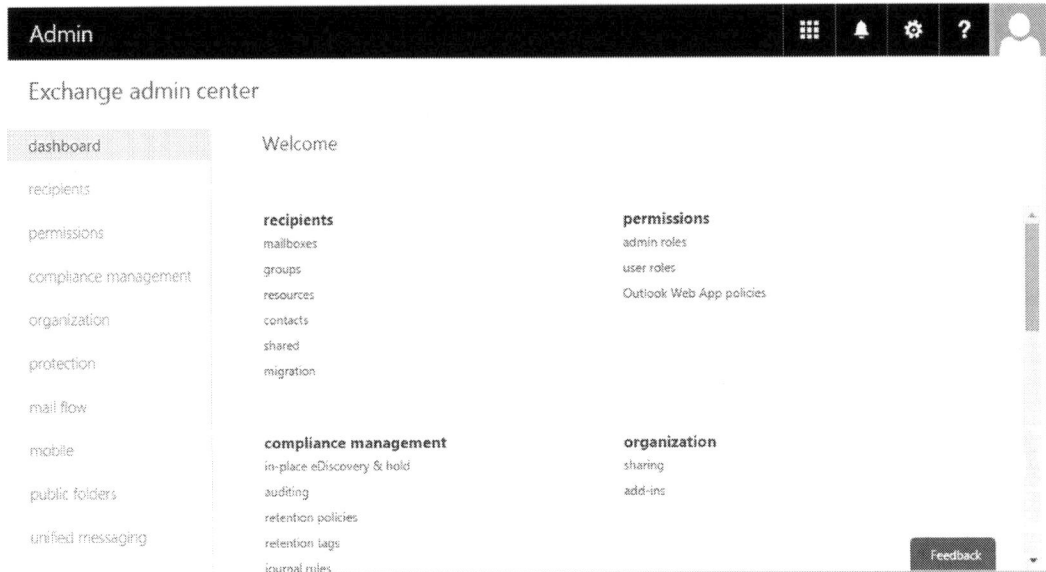

FIGURE 1-3 The dashboard in Exchange Admin Center for Exchange Online

The dashboard is unique to Exchange Admin Center for Exchange Online and serves to provide quick access to commonly used features. These features are also available via the Navigation menu and the related tabs. Other than the dashboard, the interface for Exchange Admin Center when working with Exchange Online works just like Exchange Admin Center for on-premises installations.

After you access Exchange Admin Center, you'll see the list view with manageable features listed in the left pane, also called the Navigation menu (see Figure 1-4). When you select a feature in the Navigation menu, you'll then see the related topics or "tabs" for that feature. The manageable items for a selected topic or tab are displayed in the main area of the browser window. For example, when you select

Recipients in the Navigation menu, the topics or tabs that you can work with are: Mailboxes, Groups, Resources, Contacts, Shared and Migration.

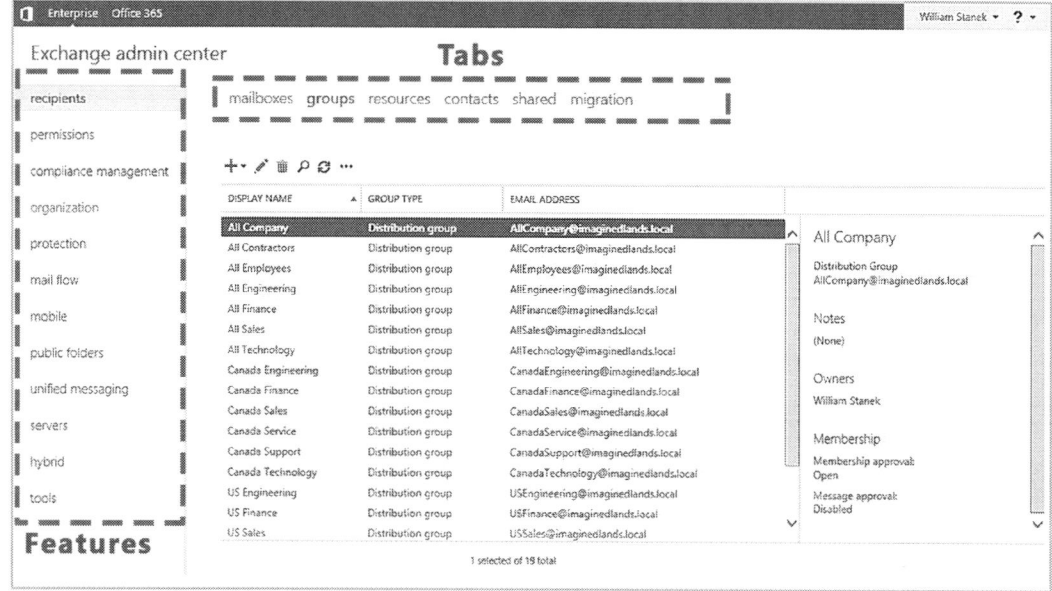

FIGURE 1-4 Exchange Admin Center features and tabs

As shown in Figure 1-5, the navigation bar at the top of the window has several important options. You use the Enterprise and Office 365 options for cross-premises navigation.

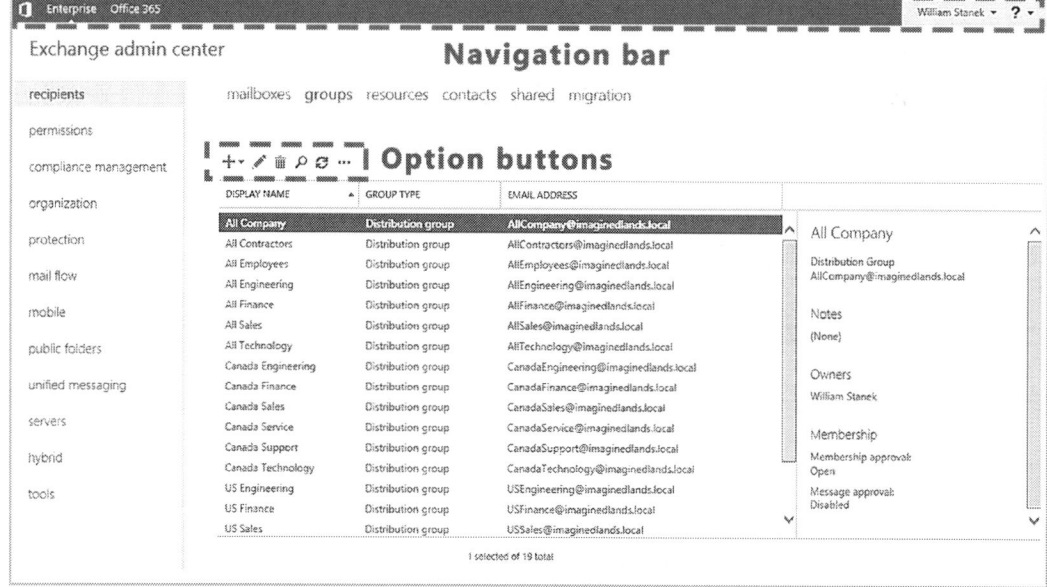

FIGURE 1-5 The Navigation bar in Exchange Admin Center

13

If there are notifications, you'll see a Notification icon on the Navigation bar. Clicking this icon displays notifications, such as alerts regarding automated or batch processes. The User button shows the currently logged on user. Clicking the User button allows you to logout or sign in as another user.

Below the tabs, you'll find a row of Option buttons:

New – Allows you to create a new item.

Edit – Allows you to edit a selected item.

Delete – Deletes a selected item.

Search – Performs a search within the current context.

Refresh – Refreshes the display so you can see changes.

More – If available, displays additional options.

When working with recipients, such as mailboxes or groups, you can click the More button (•••) to display options to:

- Add or remove columns
- Export data for the listed recipients to a .csv file
- Perform advanced searches

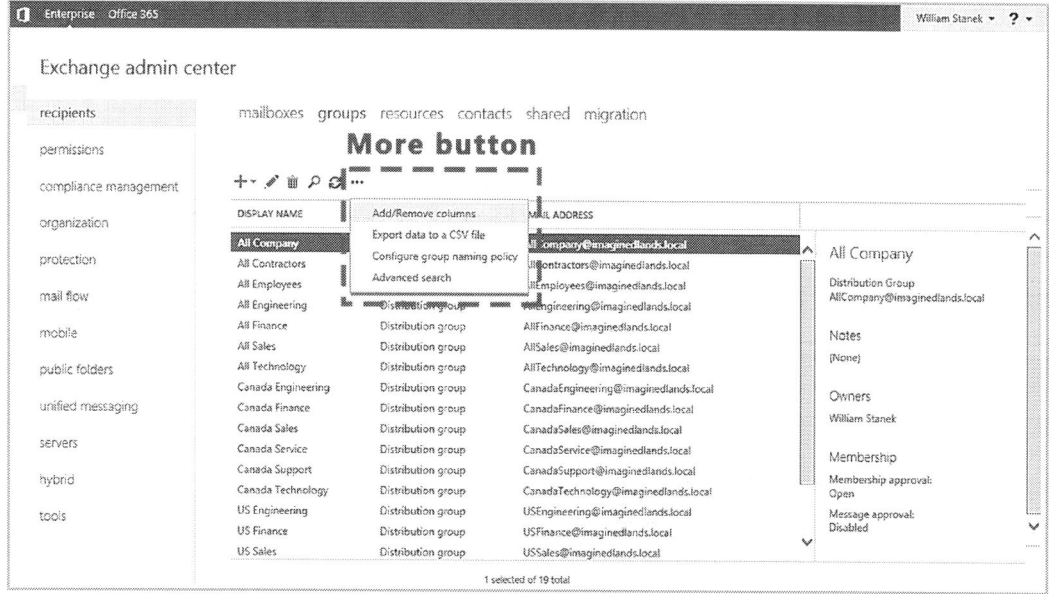

FIGURE 1-6 The More button in Exchange Admin Center

If you customize the view by adding or removing columns, the settings are saved for the computer that you are using to access Exchange Admin Center. However, because the settings are saved as browser cookies, clearing the browser history will remove the custom settings.

When working with recipients, you typically can select multiple items and perform bulk editing as long as you select like items, such as mailbox users or mail-enabled contacts. Select multiple items using the Shift or Ctrl key and then use bulk editing options in the Details pane to bulk edit the selected items.

Understanding Office 365 Licensing

With Exchange Online, you perform administration using either Exchange Admin Center or Windows PowerShell—not Exchange Management Shell, which is meant to be used only with on-premises installations of Exchange. Regardless of which approach you use to create new users in Exchange Online, you must license mailbox users in Office 365. You do this by licensing mailbox plans and associating a mailbox plan with each mailbox user.

Using Exchange Admin Center, you can associate mailbox plans when you create mailbox users or afterward by editing the account properties. In PowerShell, you use the New-Mailbox cmdlet with the –MailboxPlan parameter to do the same.

When you assign mailbox plans, you need to ensure you have enough licenses. You purchase and assign licenses using Office 365 Admin Center:

1. If the Billing options aren't currently displayed in the Navigation menu, expand Billing ( ) by clicking or hovering over it in the Navigation menu and then click Licensing to see the number of valid, expired and assigned licenses.

2. Click Subscriptions under Billing in the Navigation menu to display subscription and licensing options.

3. Click Add Subscriptions to purchase additional services. For example, if you scroll down the list of purchasable services, you'll see the Exchange Online plans.

4. While viewing plans, click Buy Now to purchase a particular plan. As shown in Figure 1-7, you'll have the option to specify how many user licenses you want for the selected plan before you check out.

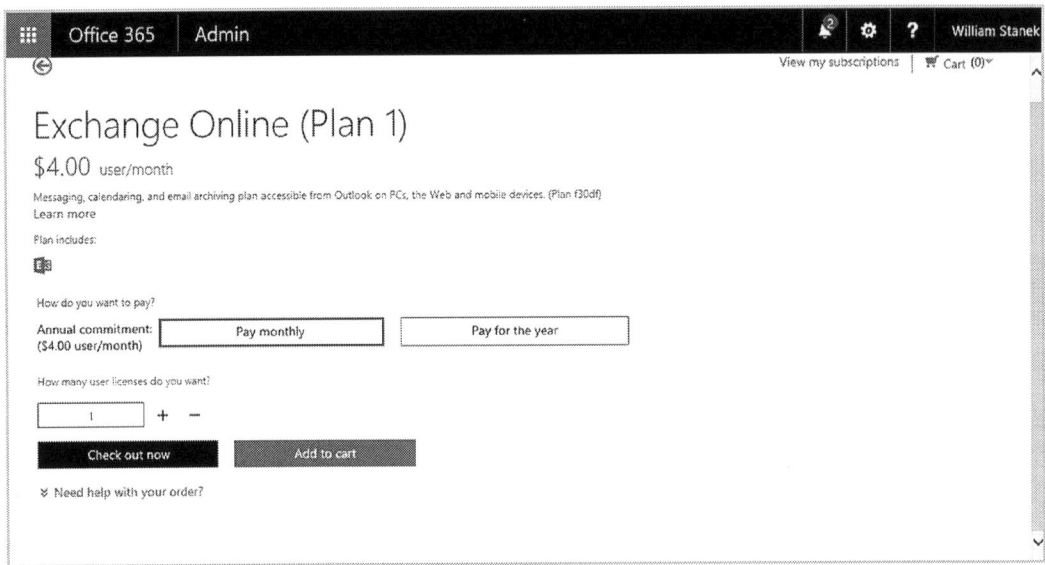

FIGURE 1-7 Select a plan and purchase licenses.

Although Office 365 will allow you to assign more mailbox plans than you have licenses for, you shouldn't do this. After the initial grace period, problems will occur. For example, mail data for unlicensed mailboxes may become unavailable. Remember, the number of valid licenses shouldn't exceed the number of assigned licenses.

You activate and license synced users in Office 365 as well. Under Users And Groups > Active Users, select the check boxes for the users you want to activate and license and then select Activate Synced Users. Next, specify the work location for the users, such as United States. Under Assign Licenses, select the mailbox plan to assign. Finally, select Activate.

Using Windows PowerShell with Office 365 & Exchange Online

Although Office Admin Center and Exchange Admin Center provide everything you need to work with Exchange Online, there may be times when you want to work from the command line, especially if you want to automate tasks with scripts. Enter Windows PowerShell.

Getting Started with Windows PowerShell

Windows PowerShell is built into Windows and Windows Server. Windows PowerShell supports cmdlets, functions and aliases. Cmdlets are built-in commands. Functions provide basic functionality. Aliases are abbreviations for cmdlet names. As cmdlet, function and alias names are not case sensitive, you can use a combination of both uppercase and lowercase characters to specify cmdlet, function and alias names.

Although Windows PowerShell has a graphical environment called Windows PowerShell ISE (powershell_ise.exe), you'll usually work with the command-line environment. The PowerShell console (powershell.exe) is available as a 32-bit or 64-bit environment for working with PowerShell at the command line. On 32-bit versions of Windows, you'll find the 32-bit executable in the %SystemRoot%\System32\WindowsPowerShell\v1.0 directory.

On 64-bit versions of Windows and Windows Server, a 64-bit and a 32-bit console are available. The default console is the 64-bit console, which is located in the %SystemRoot%\System32\WindowsPowerShell\v1.0 directory. The 32-bit executable in the %SystemRoot%\SysWow64\ WindowsPowerShell\v1.0 directory and is labeled as Windows PowerShell (x86).

With Windows 8.1 or later, you can start the PowerShell console by using the Apps Search box. Type **powershell** in the Apps Search box, and then press Enter. Or you can select Start and then choose Windows PowerShell. From Mac OS X or Linux, you can run either Windows 7 or later in a virtual environment to work with Windows PowerShell.

In Windows, you also can start Windows PowerShell from a command prompt (cmd.exe) by typing **powershell** and pressing Enter. To exit Windows PowerShell and return to the command prompt, type exit.

When the shell starts, you usually will see a message similar to the following:

```
Windows PowerShell
Copyright (C) 2012 Microsoft Corporation.
All rights reserved.
```

You can disable this message by starting the shell with the –Nologo parameter, such as:

```
powershell -nologo
```

By default, the version of scripting engine that starts depends on the operating system you are using. With Windows 8.1 and Windows Server 2012 R2, the default scripting engine is version 4.0. With Windows 10 and Windows Server 2016, the default scripting engine is version 4.0. To confirm the version of Windows PowerShell installed, enter the following command:

```
Get-Host | Format-List Version
```

Because you can abbreviate Format-List as FL, you also could enter:

```
Get-Host | fl Version
```

> **NOTE** Letter case does not matter with Windows PowerShell. Thus, Get-Host, GET-HOST and get-host are all interpreted the same.

Figure 1-8 shows the PowerShell window. When you start PowerShell, you can set the version of the scripting engine that should be loaded using the –Version parameter. In this example, you specify that you want to use PowerShell Version 3.0:

```
powershell -version 3
```

> **NOTE** Windows can only load available versions of the scripting engine. For example, you won't be able to run the version 5.0 scripting engine if only PowerShell Version 4.0 is available.

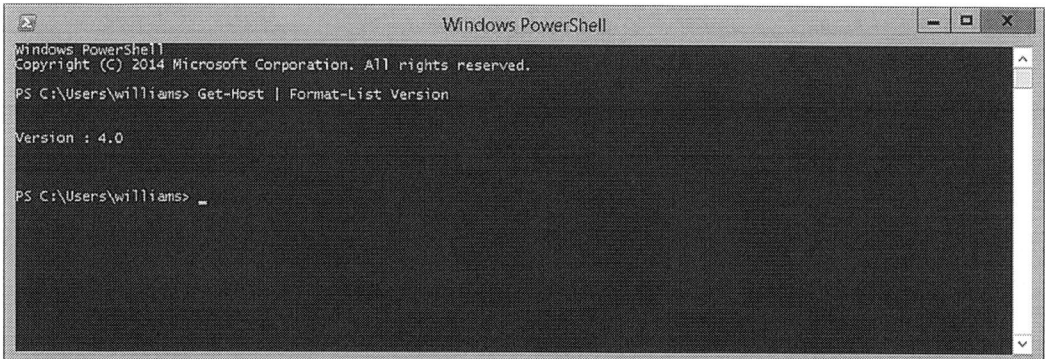

FIGURE 1-8 Use the PowerShell console to manage Exchange remotely at the prompt.

By default, the PowerShell window displays 50 lines of text and is 120 characters wide. When additional text is to be displayed in the window or you enter commands and the PowerShell console's window is full, the current text is displayed in the window and prior text is scrolled up. To temporarily pause the display when a command is writing output, press Ctrl+S. You can then press Ctrl+S to resume or Ctrl+C to terminate execution.

Understanding the Default Working Environment

When you run Windows PowerShell, a default working environment is loaded automatically. The features for this working environment come primarily from profiles, which are a type of script that run automatically whenever you start PowerShell. The working environment also is determined by imported snap-ins, providers, modules, command paths, file associations, and file extensions.

To start Windows PowerShell without loading profiles, use the –Noprofile parameter, such as:

```
powershell -noprofile
```

Whenever you work with scripts, you need to keep in mind the current execution policy and whether signed scripts are required. Execution policy is a built-in security feature of Windows PowerShell that controls whether and how you can run configuration files and scripts. Although the default configuration depends on which operating system and edition are installed, policy is always set on either a per-user or per-computer basis in the Windows registry.

You can display the execution policy currently being applied, using the Get-ExecutionPolicy cmdlet. The available execution policies, from least secure to most secure, are:

- **Bypass.** Bypasses warnings and prompts when scripts run. Use with programs that have their own security model or when a PowerShell script is built into a larger application.
- **Unrestricted.** Allows all configuration files and scripts to run whether they are from local or remote sources and regardless of whether they are signed or unsigned. When you run a configuration file or script from a remote resource, you are prompted with a warning that the file comes from a remote resource before the configuration file is loaded or the script runs.
- **RemoteSigned.** Requires all configuration files and scripts from remote sources to be signed by a trusted publisher. However, configuration files and scripts on the local computer do not need to be signed. PowerShell does not prompt you with a warning before running scripts from trusted publishers.
- **AllSigned.** Requires all configuration files and scripts from all sources—whether local or remote—to be signed by a trusted publisher. Thus, configuration files and scripts on the local computer and remote computers must be signed. PowerShell prompts you with a warning before running scripts from trusted publishers.
- **Restricted.** Prevents PowerShell from loading configuration files and scripts. Effects all configuration files and scripts, regardless of whether they are signed or unsigned. Because a profile is a type of script, profiles are not loaded either.
- **Undefined.** Removes the execution policy that is set for the current user scope and instead applies the execution policy set in Group Policy or for the LocalMachine scope. If execution policy in all scopes is set to Undefined, the default execution policy, Restricted, is the effective policy.

By default, when you set execution policy, you are using the LocalMachine scope, which is applied to all users of the computer. You also can set the scope to CurrentUser so that the execution policy level is only applied to the currently logged on user.

Using Set-ExecutionPolicy, you can change the preference for the execution policy. Normally, changes to execution policy are written to the registry. However, if the Turn On Script Execution setting in Group Policy is enabled for the computer or user, the user preference is written to the registry, but it is not effective. Windows

PowerShell will display a message explaining that there is a conflict. Finally, you cannot use Set-ExecutionPolicy to override a group policy, even if the user preference is more restrictive than the policy setting. For example, you can set the execution policy to run scripts regardless of whether they have a digital signature and work in an unrestricted environment by entering:

```
set-executionpolicy unrestricted
```

When you change execution policy, the change occurs immediately and is applied to the local console or application session. Because the change is written to the registry, the new execution policy normally will be used whenever you work with PowerShell.

Learning About Cmdlets and Functions

When you are working with Windows PowerShell, you can get a complete list of cmdlets and functions available by entering **get-command**. The output lists cmdlets and functions by name and associated module.

Another way to get information about cmdlets is to use Get-Help. When you enter **get-help *-***, you get a list of all cmdlets, including a synopsis that summarizes the purpose of the cmdlet. Rather than listing help information for all commands, you can get help for specific commands by following Get-Help with the name of the cmdlet you want to work with, such as:

```
get-help clear-history
```

Because Windows PowerShell V3 and later use online and updatable help files, you may see only basic syntax for cmdlets and functions when you use Get-Help. To get full help details, you'll have to either use online help or download the help files to your computer. For online help, add the –online parameter to your Get-Help command, such as:

```
get-help get-variable -online
```

You can use the Update-Help cmdlet to download and install the current help files from the Internet. Without parameters, Update-Help updates the help files for all modules installed on the computer. When you are working with Update-Help, keep the following in mind:

- Update-Help downloads files only once a day
- Update-Help only installs help files when they are newer than the ones on the computer
- Update-Help limits the total size of uncompressed help files to 1 GB

You can override these restrictions using the –Force parameter.

Connecting to Exchange Online Using PowerShell

The way you use Windows PowerShell to manage Exchange Server and Exchange Online are different. With Exchange Server installations, you manage Exchange using Exchange Management Shell, which is a command-line management interface built on Windows PowerShell that you can use to manage any aspect of an Exchange Server configuration that you can manage in the Exchange Admin Center. With Exchange Online installations, you manage Exchange using a remote session and the built-in functions and capabilities of Exchange Management Shell are not available.

Exploring How the Shell Uses Remote Sessions

The Exchange Management Shell is designed to be run only on domain-joined computers and is available when you have installed the Exchange management tools on a management computer or server. Whether you are logged on locally to an Exchange server or working remotely, starting Exchange Management Shell opens a custom Windows PowerShell console that runs in a remote session with an Exchange server.

A remote session is a runspace that establishes a common working environment for executing commands on remote computers. Before creating the remote session, this custom console connects to the closest Exchange server using Windows Remote Management (WinRM) and then performs authentication checks that validate your access to the Exchange server and determine the Exchange role groups and roles your account is a member of. You must be a member of at least one management role.

Because the Exchange Management Shell uses your user credentials, you are able to perform any administrative tasks allowed for your user account and in accordance with the Exchange role groups and management roles you're assigned. You don't need to run the Exchange Management Shell in elevated, administrator mode, but you can by right-clicking Exchange Management Shell, and then selecting Run As Administrator.

By examining the properties of the shortcut that starts the Exchange Management Shell, you can see the actual command that runs when you start the shell is:

```
C:\Windows\System32\WindowsPowerShell\v1.0\powershell.exe -noexit -command
". 'C:\Program Files\Microsoft\Exchange Server\V15\bin\RemoteExchange.ps1';
Connect-ExchangeServer -auto -ClientApplication:ManagementShell "
```

Here, the command starts PowerShell, runs the RemoteExchange.ps1 profile file, and then uses the command Connect-ExchangeServer to establish the remote session. The –Auto parameter tells the cmdlet to automatically discover and try to connect to an appropriate Exchange server. The –ClientApplication parameter specifies that client-side application is the Exchange Management Shell. When you run the shell in this way, Windows Powershell loads a profile script called RemoteExchange.ps1 that sets aliases, initializes Exchange global variables, and loads .NET assemblies for Exchange. The profile script also modifies the standard PowerShell prompt so that it is scoped appropriately and defines Exchange-specific functions, including:

- **Get-Exbanner.** Displays the Exchange Management Shell startup banner.
- **Get-Exblog.** Opens Internet Explorer and accesses the Exchange blog.
- **Get-Excommand.** Lists all available Exchange commands.
- **Get-Pscommand.** Lists all available PowerShell commands.
- **Get-Tip.** Displays the tip of the day.
- **Quickref.** Opens Internet Explorer and accesses the Exchange Management Shell quick start guide.

All of these processes simplify the task of establishing an interactive remote session with Exchange server. As implemented in the default configuration, you have a one-to-one, interactive approach for remote management, meaning you establish a session with a specific remote server and work with that specific server whenever you execute commands.

Establishing Remote Sessions

When you are working with PowerShell outside of Exchange Management Shell, you must manually establish a remote session with Exchange. As the RemoteExchange.ps1 profile file and related scripts are not loaded, the related cmdlets and functions are not available. This means you cannot use Get-Exbanner, Get-Exblog, Get-Excommand, Get-PScommand, Get-Tip or Quickref. Further, when you are working with an online installation of Exchange, the cmdlets available are different from when you are working with Exchange Server.

PowerShell provides several cmdlets for establishing remote sessions, including Enter-PSSession and New-PSSession. The difference between the two options is subtle but important.

Using an Interactive Remote Session

You can use the Enter-PSSession cmdlet to start an interactive session with Exchange or any other remote computer. The basic syntax is Enter-PSSession ComputerName, where ComputerName is the name of the remote computer, such as the following:

```
enter-pssession Server58
```

When the session is established, the command prompt changes to show that you are connected to the remote computer, as shown in the following example:

```
[Server58]: PS C:\Users\wrstanek.cpandl\Documents>
```

While working in a remote session, any commands you enter run on the remote computer just as if you had typed them directly on the remote computer. Generally, to perform administration, you need to use an elevated, administrator shell and pass credentials along in the session. Establishing a connection in this way uses the standard PowerShell remoting configuration.

However, you cannot connect to Exchange Online using the standard PowerShell remoting configuration. You must go through a PowerShell application running on ps.outlook.com or another appropriate web server. Typically, when you work with Exchange Online, you use the connection URI https://ps.outlook.com/powershell/

and the actual session is redirected to your specific online server. To ensure redirection doesn't fail, you must add the –AllowRedirection parameter.

As shown in the following example, you use the –ConnectionURI parameter to specify the connection URI, the –ConfigurationName parameter to specify the configuration namespace, and the –Authentication parameter to set the authentication type to use:

```
Enter-PSSession -ConfigurationName Microsoft.Exchange
-ConnectionUri https://ps.outlook.com/powershell/
-Authentication Basic -AllowRedirection
```

Here, you set the configuration namespace as Microsoft.Exchange, establish a connection to the Exchange Online URL provided by Microsoft, and use Basic authentication. As you don't specify credentials, you will be prompted to provide credentials.

You also can pass in credentials as shown in this example:

```
Enter-PSSession -ConfigurationName Microsoft.Exchange
-ConnectionUri https://ps.outlook.com/powershell/
-Authentication Basic -Credential wrstanek@imaginedlands.onmicrosoft.com
-AllowRedirection
```

Here, you pass in credentials and are prompted for the associated password.

Alternatively, you can store credentials in a Credential object and then use Get-Credential to prompt for the required credentials, as shown here:

```
$Cred = Get-Credential

Enter-PSSession -ConfigurationName Microsoft.Exchange
-ConnectionUri https://ps.outlook.com/powershell/
-Authentication Basic -Credential $Cred -AllowRedirection
```

When you are finished working with Exchange Online, you can end the interactive session by using Exit-PSSession or by typing exit. Although Enter-PSSession provides a quick and easy way to establish a remote session, the session ends when you use

Exit-PSSession or exit the PowerShell prompt and there is no way to reestablish the original session. Thus, any commands you are running and any command context is lost when you exit the session.

Thus, as discussed in this section, the basic steps for using a standard interactive remote session are:

1. Open an administrator Windows PowerShell prompt.
2. Use Enter-PSSession to establish a remote session.
3. Work with Exchange Online.
4. Exit the remote session using Exit-PSSession or by exiting the PowerShell window.

Creating and Importing a Remote Session

Instead of using a standard interactive session, you may want to create a session that you disconnect and reconnect. To do this, you establish the session using New-PSSession and then import the session using Import-PSSession. The basic syntax:

```
$Session = New-PSSession -ConfigurationName
Microsoft.Exchange -ConnectionUri https://ps.outlook.com/powershell/
-Authentication Basic -Credential wrs@imaginedlands.onmicrosoft.com
-AllowRedirection
```

In this example, you use New-PSSession to create a session and store the related object in a variable called $Session. You create the session by setting the configuration namespace as Microsoft.Exchange, establishing a connection to the Exchange Online URL provided by Microsoft, which typically is https://ps.outlook.com, and using HTTPS with Basic authentication for the session. You also allow redirection. Allowing redirection is important as otherwise the session will fail when the Microsoft web servers redirect the session to the actual location of your Exchange Online installation.

To establish the connection, you must always pass in your Exchange Online user name and password. In the previous example, you specify the user name to use and are prompted for the related password. You also could specify the credentials explicitly, as shown here:

```
$Cred = Get-Credential
$Session = New-PSSession -ConfigurationName Microsoft.Exchange
-ConnectionUri https://ps.outlook.com/powershell/
-Authentication Basic -Credential $Cred -AllowRedirection
```

Here, you store credentials in a Credential object and then use Get-Credential to prompt for the required credentials.

After you establish a session with Exchange Online, you must import the server-side PowerShell session into your client-side session. To do this, you enter the following command:

```
Import-PSSession $Session
```

Where $Session is the name of the variable in which the session object is stored. You can then work with the remote server and Exchange Online.

When you are finished working remotely, you should disconnect the remote shell. It's important to note that, beginning with Windows PowerShell 3.0, sessions are persistent by default. When you disconnect from a session, any command or scripts that are running in the session continue running, and you can later reconnect to the session to pick up where you left off. You also can reconnect to a session if you were disconnected unintentionally, such as by a temporary network outage.

Exchange Online allows each administrative account to have up to three simultaneous connections to sever-side sessions. If you close the PowerShell window without disconnecting from the session, the connection remains open for 15 minutes and then disconnects automatically.

To disconnect a session manually without stopping commands or releasing resources, you can use Disconnect-PSSession, as shown in this example:

```
Disconnect-PSSession $Session
```

Here, the $Session object was instantiated when you created the session and you disconnect while the session continues to be active. As long as you don't exit the PowerShell window in which this object was created, you can use this object to reconnect to the session by entering:

```
Connect-PSSession $Session
```

Later, when you are finished working with Exchange Online, you should remove the session. Removing a session stops any commands or scripts that are running, ends the session, and releases the resources the session was using. You can remove a session by running the following command:

```
Remove-PSSession $Session
```

Thus, as discussed in this section, the basic steps for working with an imported session are:

1. Open an administrator Windows PowerShell prompt.
2. Use New-PSSession to establish the remote session.
3. Import the session using Import-PSSession.
4. Work with Exchange Online. Optionally, disconnect from the session using Disconnect-PSSession and reconnect to the session using Connect-PSSession.
5. Remove the remote session using Remove-PSSession.

Connecting to Windows Azure and the Office 365 Service

You can manage the Office 365 service, its settings and accounts using either Office Admin Center or Windows PowerShell. Every account you create in the online environment is in fact created in the online framework within which Office 365 and Exchange Online operate. This framework is called Windows Azure, and like Windows Server, it uses directory services provided by Active Directory.

Before you can manage Office 365, its settings, and accounts from Windows PowerShell, you must install the Windows Azure Active Directory module (which is available at the Microsoft Download Center: http://go.microsoft.com/fwlink/p/?linkid=236297). Any computer capable of running Exchange or acting as a management computer can run this module. However, there are several prerequisites, including .NET framework 3.51 and the Microsoft Online Services Sign-in Assistant version 7.0 or later. At the time of this writing, the sign-in assistant was available at http://go.microsoft.com/fwlink/?LinkId=286152. Be sure to download and install only the 64-bit versions of the module and the sign-in assistant.

After you download and install the required components, the Windows Azure Active Directory module is available for your use in any PowerShell window. This module also is referred to as the Microsoft Online module. Although Windows PowerShell 3.0 and later implicitly import modules, you may need to explicitly import this module in some configurations. After you import the module, if necessary, you can connect to the Windows Azure and Microsoft Online Services using the Connect-MSOLService cmdlet.

Because you'll typically want to store your credentials in a Credential object rather than be prompted for them, the complete procedure to connect to Microsoft Online Services by using Windows PowerShell is:

```
import-module msonline
$cred = get-credential
connect-msolservice -credential:$cred
```

Or, with Windows PowerShell 3.0 or later, use:

```
$cred = get-credential
connect-msolservice -credential:$cred
```

After connecting to the service, you can use cmdlets for Windows Azure Active Directory to manage online settings and objects. For example, if you want to get a list of user accounts that have been created in the online service along with their licensing status, enter **get-msoluser**. The results will be similar to the following:

```
UserPrincipalName            DisplayName      isLicensed
-----------------            -----------      ----------
wrstanek@imaginedlands.onm... William Stanek    True
tonyv@imaginedlands.onm...   Tony Vidal        False
```

Cmdlets for Windows Azure Active Directory

Exchange Online runs on Windows Azure rather than Windows Server. As the two operating environments have different directory services, you must use cmdlets specific to Active Directory for Windows Azure if you want to work with users, groups and related objects.

You'll find complete information about these cmdlets online at http://msdn.microsoft.com/library/azure/jj151815.aspx. The available cmdlets include:

- **Cmdlets for managing groups and roles**

Add-MsolGroupMember
Add-MsolRoleMember
Get-MsolGroup
Get-MsolGroupMember
Get-MsolRole
Get-MsolRoleMember
Get-MsolUserRole
New-MsolGroup
Redo-MsolProvisionGroup
Remove-MsolGroup
Remove-MsolGroupMember
Remove-MsolRoleMember
Set-MsolGroup

- **Cmdlets for managing licenses and subscriptions**

Get-MsolAccountSku
Get-MsolSubscription
New-MsolLicenseOptions
Set-MsolUserLicense

- **Cmdlets for managing service principals**

Get-MsolServicePrincipal
Get-MsolServicePrincipalCredential
New-MsolServicePrincipal
New-MsolServicePrincipalAddresses
New-MsolServicePrincipalCredential
Remove-MsolServicePrincipal

Remove-MsolServicePrincipalCredential
Set-MsolServicePrincipal

- **Cmdlets for managing users**

Convert-MsolFederatedUser
Get-MsolUser
New-MsolUser
Redo-MsolProvisionUser
Remove-MsolUser
Restore-MsolUser
Set-MsolUser
Set-MsolUserPassword
Set-MsolUserPrincipalName

- **Cmdlets for managing the Azure service**

Add-MsolForeignGroupToRole
Connect-MsolService
Get-MsolCompanyInformation
Get-MsolContact
Get-MsolPartnerContract
Get-MsolPartnerInformation
Redo-MsolProvisionContact
Remove-MsolContact
Set-MsolCompanyContactInformation
Set-MsolCompanySettings
Set-MsolDirSyncEnabled
Set-MsolPartnerInformation

- **Cmdlets for managing domains**

Confirm-MsolDomain
Get-MsolDomain
Get-MsolDomainVerificationDns
Get-MsolPasswordPolicy
New-MsolDomain
Remove-MsolDomain

Set-MsolDomain
Set-MsolDomainAuthentication
Set-MsolPasswordPolicy

- **Cmdlets for managing single sign-on**

Convert-MsolDomainToFederated
Convert-MsolDomainToStandard
Get-MsolDomainFederationSettings
Get-MsolFederationProperty
New-MsolFederatedDomain
Remove-MsolFederatedDomain
Set-MsolADFSContext
Set-MsolDomainFederationSettings
Update-MsolFederatedDomain

You also can enter **get-help *msol*** to get a list of commands specific to Microsoft Online Services.

Working with Exchange Online Cmdlets

When you work with Exchange Online, the operating environment is different from when you are working with on-premises Exchange Server installations. As a result, different cmdlets and options are available.

Cmdlets Specific to Exchange Online

Because the operating environment for Exchange Online is different from on-premises Exchange, Exchange Online has cmdlets that aren't available when you are working with on-premises Exchange. You'll find complete information about these cmdlets online at https://technet.microsoft.com/library/jj200780(v=exchg.160).aspx. The additional cmdlets include:

- **Cmdlets for working with online recipients**

Add-RecipientPermission
Get-LinkedUser
Get-RecipientPermission

Get-RemovedMailbox
Get-SendAddress
Import-ContactList
Remove-RecipientPermission
Set-LinkedUser
Undo-SoftDeletedMailbox

- **Cmdlets for working with connected accounts**

Get-ConnectSubscription
Get-HotmailSubscription
Get-ImapSubscription
Get-PopSubscription
Get-Subscription
New-ConnectSubscription
New-HotmailSubscription
New-ImapSubscription
New-PopSubscription
New-Subscription
Remove-ConnectSubscription
Remove-Subscription
Set-ConnectSubscription
Set-HotmailSubscription
Set-ImapSubscription
Set-PopSubscription

- **Cmdlets for working with antispam and anti-malware**

Disable-HostedContentFilterRule
Enable-HostedContentFilterRule
Get-HostedConnectionFilterPolicy
Get-HostedContentFilterPolicy
Get-HostedContentFilterRule
Get-HostedOutboundSpamFilterPolicy
Get-QuarantineMessage
New-HostedConnectionFilterPolicy
New-HostedContentFilterPolicy

New-HostedContentFilterRule
Release-QuarantineMessage
Remove-HostedConnectionFilterPolicy
Remove-HostedContentFilterPolicy
Remove-HostedContentFilterRule
Set-HostedConnectionFilterPolicy
Set-HostedContentFilterPolicy
Set-HostedContentFilterRule
Set-HostedOutboundSpamFilterPolicy

- **Cmdlets for working with connectors**

Get-InboundConnector
Get-OutboundConnector
New-InboundConnector
New-OutboundConnector
Remove-InboundConnector
Remove-OutboundConnector
Set-InboundConnector
Set-OutboundConnector

- **Cmdlets for working with messaging policy and compliance**

Get-DataClassificationConfig
Get-RMSTrustedPublishingDomain
Import-RMSTrustedPublishingDomain
Remove-RMSTrustedPublishingDomain
Set-RMSTrustedPublishingDomain

- **Cmdlets for organization and perimeter control**

Enable-OrganizationCustomization
Get-PerimeterConfig
Set-PerimeterConfig

- **Cmdlets for online reporting**

Get-ConnectionByClientTypeDetailReport
Get-ConnectionByClientTypeReport
Get-CsActiveUserReport
Get-CsAVConferenceTimeReport
Get-CsConferenceReport
Get-CsP2PAVTimeReport
Get-CsP2PSessionReport
Get-GroupActivityReport
Get-MailboxActivityReport
Get-MailboxUsageDetailReport
Get-MailboxUsageReport
Get-MailDetailDlpPolicyReport
Get-MailDetailMalwareReport
Get-MailDetailSpamReport
Get-MailDetailTransportRuleReport
Get-MailFilterListReport
Get-MailTrafficPolicyReport
Get-MailTrafficReport
Get-MailTrafficSummaryReport
Get-MailTrafficTopReport
Get-MessageTrace
Get-MessageTraceDetail
Get-MxRecordReport
Get-OutboundConnectorReport
Get-RecipientStatisticsReport
Get-ServiceDeliveryReport
Get-StaleMailboxDetailReport
Get-StaleMailboxReport

Although cmdlets specific to Windows Azure Active Directory and Exchange Online itself are available, many of the cmdlets associated with on-premises Exchange continue to be available as well. Primarily, these cmdlets include those that are specific to recipients and mailboxes and do not include those specific to Exchange on-premises configurations or to Exchange server configurations. For example, you can continue to use cmdlets for working with mailboxes, including Disable-Mailbox,

Enable-Mailbox, Get-Mailbox, New-Mailbox, Remove-Mailbox, and Set-Mailbox. However, you cannot use cmdlets for working with mailbox databases. In Exchange Online, mailbox databases are managed automatically as part of the service.

Using the Exchange Online Cmdlets

When you work with the Exchange Online, you'll often use Get, Set, Enable, Disable, New, and Remove cmdlets. The groups of cmdlets that begin with these verbs all accept the –Identity parameter, which identifies the unique object with which you are working. Generally, these cmdlets have the –Identity parameter as the first parameter, which allows you to specify the identity, with or without the parameter name.

For identities that have names as well as aliases, you can specify either value as the identity. For example, to retrieve the mailbox object for the user William Stanek with the mail alias Williams, you can use any of the following techniques:

```
get-mailbox Williams
get-mailbox -identity williams
get-mailbox "William Stanek"
get-mailbox -identity 'William Stanek'
```

Typically, Get cmdlets return an object set containing all related items when you omit the identity. For example, if you enter get-mailbox without specifying an identity, PowerShell displays a list of all mailboxes available (up to the maximum permitted to return in a single object set).

Cmdlets can display output is several different formats. Although all cmdlets return data in table format by default, there are often many more columns of data than fit across the screen. For this reason, you might need to output data in list format.

To output in list format, redirect the output using the pipe symbol (|) to the Format-List cmdlet, as shown in this example:

```
get-mailbox "William Stanek" | format-list
```

Because fl is an alias for Format-List, you also can use fl, as in this example:

```
get-mailbox "William Stanek" | fl
```

With a list format output, you should see much more information about the object or the result set than if you were retrieving table-formatted data.

Note also the pipe symbol (|) used in the examples. When you are working with Windows PowerShell, you'll often need to use the pipe symbol (|) to redirect the output of one cmdlet and pass it as input to another cmdlet. For example, access to remote PowerShell is a privilege for an online user that can be viewed with Get-User and managed with Set-User. To determine whether a particular user has remote shell access, you can enter:

```
Get-User UserID | fl RemotePowerShellEnabled
```

where UserID is the identity of the user to view, such as:

```
Get-User WilliamS | fl RemotePowerShellEnabled
```

If the user should have remote PowerShell access but doesn't currently, you can enable access using the –RemotePowerShellEnabled parameter of Set-User, as shown in this example:

```
Set-User WilliamS -RemotePowerShellEnabled $true
```

If the user has remote PowerShell access but shouldn't, you can disable access by setting the –RemotePowerShellEnabled to $false, as shown in this example:

```
Set-User TonyG -RemotePowerShellEnabled $false
```

When you work with list- or table-formatted data, you may want to specify the exact data to display. For example, with Get-User, you can display only the user name, display name and remote PowerShell status using:

```
Get-User | Format-Table Name, DisplayName, RemotePowerShellEnabled
```

If your organization has a lot of users you can prevent the result set from getting truncated by allowing an unlimited result set to be returned, as shown in this example:

```
Get-User -ResultSize Unlimited | Format-Table
Name,DisplayName,RemotePowerShellEnabled
```

With cmdlets that have many properties, you may want to filter the output based on a specific property. For example, to display a list of all users who have remote PowerShell access, you can filter the result set on the RemotePowerShellEnabled property, as shown in the following example:

```
Get-User -ResultSize unlimited -Filter {RemotePowerShellEnabled -eq $true}
```

Alternatively, you may want to see a list of users who don't have remote PowerShell access. To do this, filter the results by looking for users who have the RemotePowerShellEnabled property set to $False:

```
Get-User -ResultSize unlimited -Filter {RemotePowerShellEnabled -eq $false}
```

Chapter 2. Getting Started with Users and Contacts

User and contact management is a key part of Exchange administration. User accounts enable individual users to log on to the network and access network resources. In Windows Azure Active Directory, users are represented by User objects and can have mailboxes associated with them.

User objects represent standard user accounts. In contrast, contacts, are people who you or others in your organization want to get in touch with. Contacts can have street addresses, phone numbers, fax numbers, and email addresses associated with them. Unlike user accounts, contacts don't have network logon privileges.

Working with Users and Contacts

Users can be mailbox-enabled or mail-enabled. A *mailbox-enabled* user account has an Exchange mailbox associated with it. Mailboxes are private storage areas for sending and receiving mail. A user's display name is the name Exchange presents in the global address list.

Another important identifier for mailbox-enabled user accounts is the Exchange alias. The alias is the name that Exchange associates with the account for addressing mail. When your mail client is configured to use Exchange Online, you can type the alias or display name in the To, Cc, or Bcc text boxes of an email message and have Exchange Online resolve the alias or name to the actual email address.

Although you'll likely configure most user accounts as mailbox-enabled, user accounts don't have to have mailboxes associated with them. You can create user accounts without assigning a mailbox. You can also create user accounts that are *mail-enabled* rather than mailbox-enabled, which means that the account has an off-site email address associated with it but doesn't have an actual mailbox. Mail-enabled users have Exchange aliases and display names that Exchange Online can resolve to actual email addresses. Internal users can send a message to the mail-enabled user account using the Exchange display name or alias, and the message will be directed to the external address. Users outside the organization can use the Exchange alias to send mail to the user.

It's not always easy to decide when to create a mailbox for a user. To better understand the decision-making process, consider the following scenario:

1. You've been notified that two new users, Elizabeth and Joe, will need access to Office 365.

2. Elizabeth is a full-time employee who starts on Tuesday. She'll work on site and needs to be able to send and receive mail. People in the company need to be able to send mail directly to her.

3. Joe, on the other hand, is a consultant who is coming in to help out temporarily. His agency maintains his mailbox, and he doesn't want to have to check mail in two places. However, people in the company need to be able to contact him, and he wants to be sure that his external address is available.

4. You create a mailbox-enabled user account for Elizabeth. Afterward, you create a mail-enabled user account for Joe, ensuring that his Exchange information refers to his external email address.

Mail-enabled users are one of several types of custom recipients that you can create in Exchange Online. Another type of custom recipient is a *mail-enabled* contact. You create a mail-enabled contact so that users can more easily send email to that contact. A mail-enabled contact has an external email address.

Exchange Online has in-place archiving for user mailboxes, which is designed to replace the need for personal stores in Outlook. An in-place archive is an alternative storage location for historical message data that is seamlessly accessible to a user in Microsoft Outlook 2010 or later and Outlook Web App.

The in-place archive is created as an additional mailbox and is referred to as an archive mailbox. Users can easily move and copy mail data between a primary mailbox and an archive mailbox. Because in-place archiving is a premium feature, an enterprise license is required for each user with an archive mailbox. For more information, see "Working with Archive Mailboxes" in Chapter 5 "Adding Special-Purpose Mailboxes."

How Email Routing Works: The Essentials

Exchange uses email addresses to route messages to mail servers inside and outside the organization. When routing messages internally, Exchange servers use mail connectors to route messages to other Exchange servers, as well as to other types of mail servers that your company might use.

Connectors use Simple Mail Transfer Protocol (SMTP) as the default transport and provide a direct connection among Mailbox servers in an Exchange organization. When routing messages outside the company, Exchange servers use mail gateways to transfer messages. The default gateway is SMTP.

Exchange uses directory-based recipient resolution for all messages that are sent from and received by users throughout an Exchange organization. The Exchange component responsible for recipient resolution is the Categorizer. The Categorizer must be able to associate every recipient in every message with a corresponding recipient object in Windows Azure Active Directory.

All senders and recipients must have a primary SMTP address. If the Categorizer discovers a recipient that does not have a primary SMTP address, it will try to determine what the primary SMTP address should be.

In addition to primary SMTP email addresses, you can configure alternative recipients and forwarding addresses for users and public folders. If there is an alternative recipient or forwarding address, redirection is required during categorization. You specify the addresses to which messages will be redirected, and redirection history is maintained with each message.

Managing Recipients: The Fundamentals

a remote session with Exchange Online provides many commands for working with mailbox-enabled users, mail-enabled users, and contacts. The main commands you'll use are shown in the following table:

MAILBOX-ENABLED USER	MAIL-ENABLED USERS	CONTACTS
Connect-Mailbox	Disable-MailUser	Disable-MailContact
Disable-Mailbox	Enable-MailUser	Enable-MailContact
Enable-Mailbox	Get-MailUser	Get-MailContact
Get-Mailbox	New-MailUser	New-MailContact
New-Mailbox	Remove-MailUser	Remove-MailContact
Remove-Mailbox	Set-MailUser	Set-MailContact
Set-Mailbox		

If a mailbox was created in the online Exchange organization, you connect to the online organization and work with the mailbox using the online implementation of Exchange Admin Center or a remote session with Exchange Online. Regardless of which approach you use to create new mailbox users in Exchange Online, you must license these mailbox users in Office 365.

You license users by associating a mailbox plan with each mailbox user. Using Exchange Admin Center, you can associate mailbox plans when you are creating mailbox users or afterward by editing the account properties. In a remote session with Exchange Online, you can use the -MailboxPlan parameter with the New-Mailbox cmdlet to do the same. However, at the time of this writing, there are no mailbox plan parameters for any of the RemoteMailbox cmdlets. (Hopefully, this oversight will be corrected by the time you read this.)

When you assign mailbox plans, you need to ensure you have enough licenses. You purchase and assign licenses using the billing and subscription options in Office 365 Admin Center. Select **Billing** on the dashboard or click **Subscriptions** under the Billing heading in the Navigation menu to see the subscription and licensing options.

Office 365 will allow you to assign more mailbox plans than you have licenses for. However, after the initial grace period, problems will occur. For example, mail data for unlicensed mailboxes may become unavailable. Remember, the number of valid licenses shouldn't exceed the number of assigned licenses.

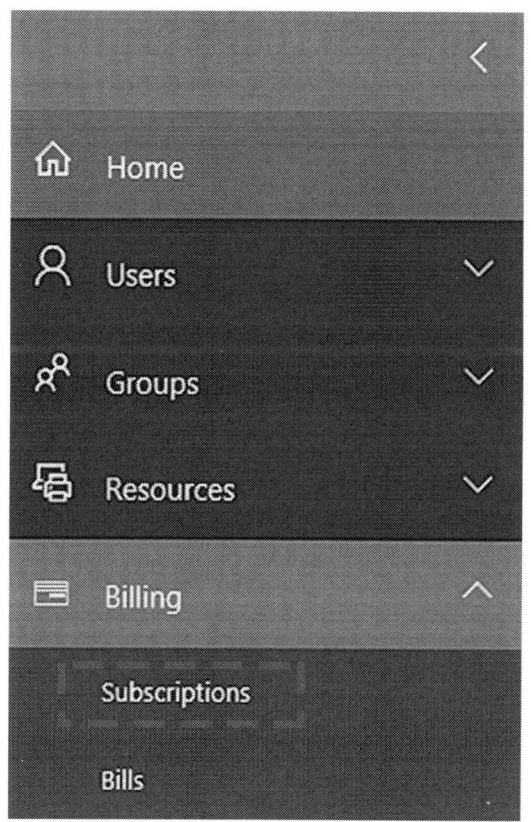

FIGURE 2-1 Accessing subscriptions in Office 365 Admin Center.

You activate and license synced users in Office 365 as well:

1. Select **Users** on the dashboard or click **Active Users** under the Users heading in the Navigation menu to display active users.

2. On the Users page, click a user that you want to activate and license to display account settings.

3. Click **Edit** on the Product Licenses panel.

4. As shown in Figure 2-3, specify the work location for the user, such as United States.

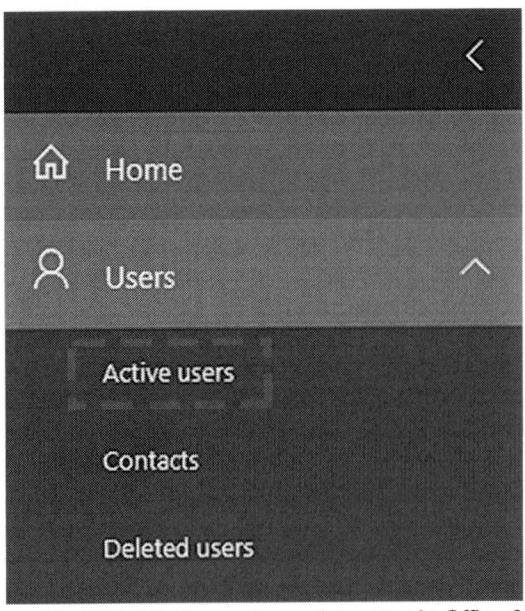

FIGURE 2-2 Accessing active users in Office 365 Admin Center.

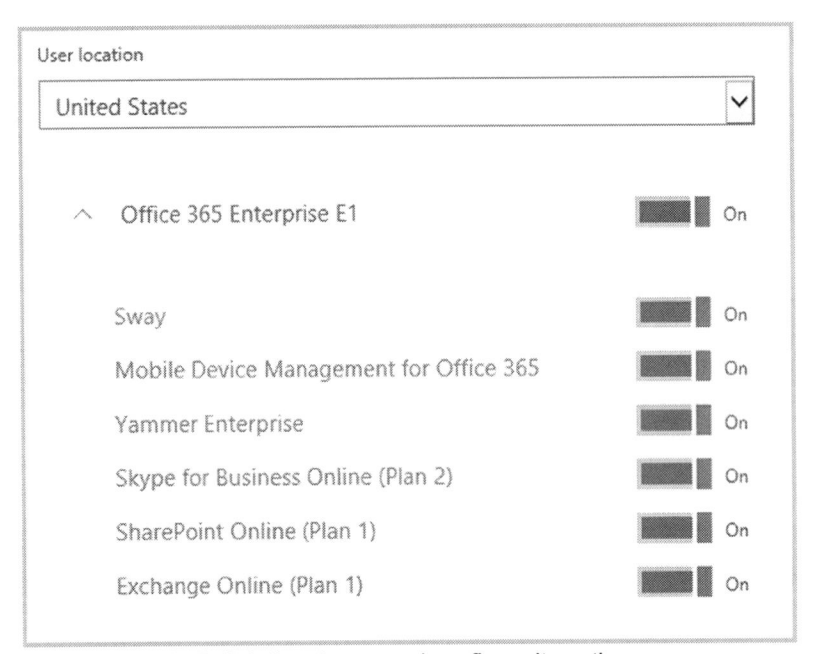

FIGURE 2-3 Switch the plan on and configure its options.

5. Select the mailbox plan to assign by clicking it to the On position.
6. Optionally, click to switch individual plan options on or off.

7. Select **Activate** or **Save** as appropriate.

The Office 365 service, its settings and accounts are all manageable from Windows PowerShell. Every account you create in the online environment is in fact created in the online framework within which Office 365 and Exchange Online operate. This framework is called Windows Azure, and like Windows Server, it uses Active Directory to provide its directory services. You can manage Office 365 from Windows PowerShell as discussed in "Connecting to Windows Azure and the Office 365 Service" in Chapter 1.

Finding Existing Mailboxes, Contacts, And Groups

You work with recipients in the Exchange organization where they were created. You can view current mailboxes, mail-enabled users, contacts, and groups by:

1. Open Exchange Admin Center. To do this, open your Web browser and then enter the secure URL for Office 365 Admin Center, such as *https://portal.microsoftonline.com/admin/default.aspx*. In Office 365 Admin Center, click **Exchange** under the Admin Centers heading on the Navigation menu. This opens the Exchange Online version of Exchange Admin Center.

2. As shown in Figure 2-4, select **Recipients** in the Navigation menu and then select the related Mailboxes, Groups, or Contacts tab, as appropriate for the type of recipient you want to work with.

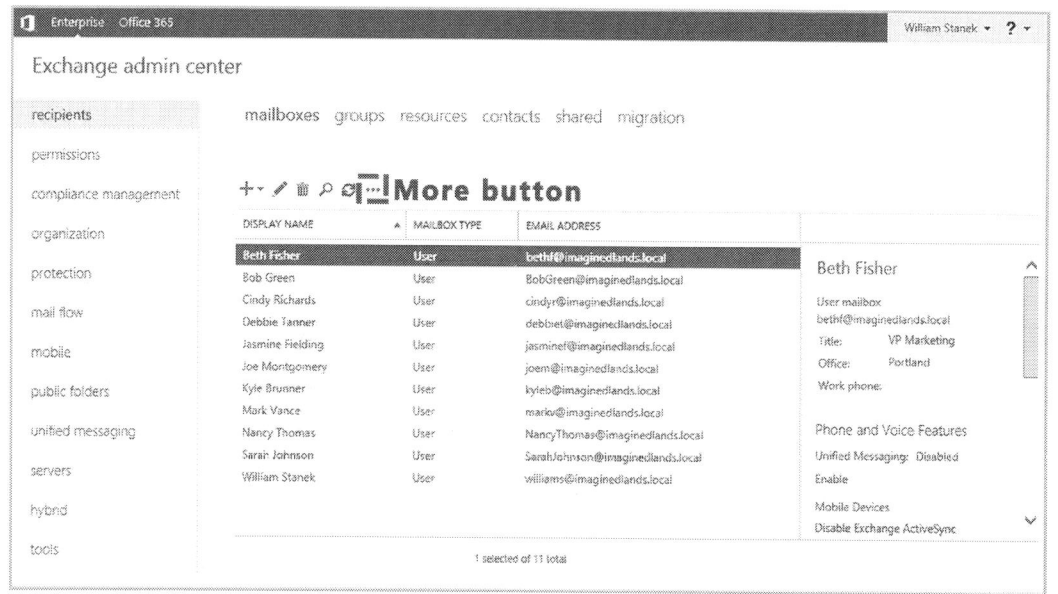

FIGURE 2-4 Accessing the Recipient node.

By default, all recipients of the selected type are displayed. With mailboxes this means that user mailboxes, linked user mailboxes, legacy user mailboxes, and remote user mailboxes are displayed.

By default, Exchange Admin Center displays only three columns of information for each recipient, including the display name, mailbox type, and email address. To customize the columns of information displayed, click the More button (•••) and then select **Add/Remove Columns**. Use the options provided in the Add/Remove Columns dialog box, shown in Figure 2-5, to configure the columns to use, and then click **OK**.

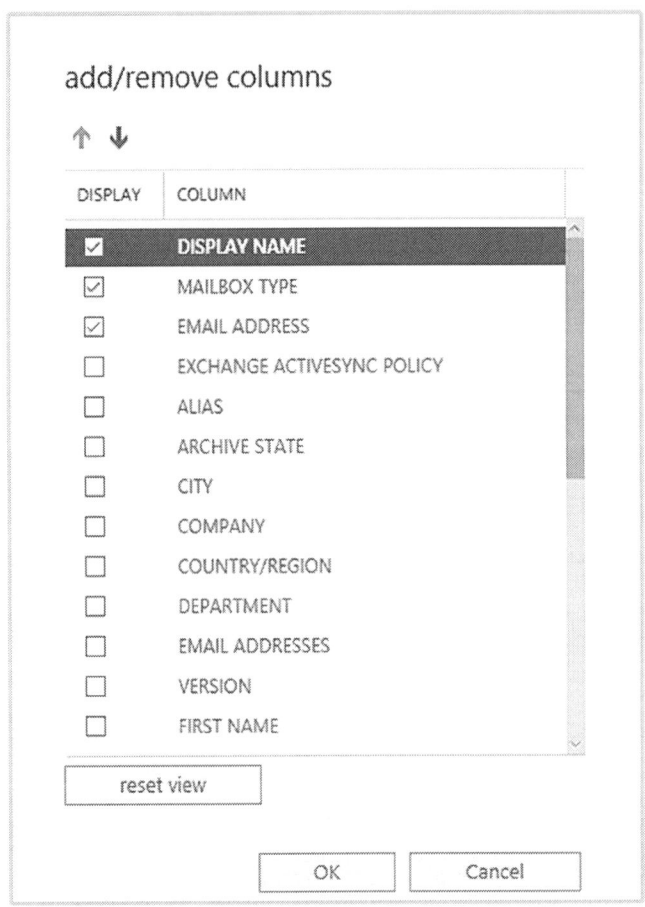

FIGURE 2-5 Customizing the list of columns to display using the options provided.

In large organizations, you may need to filter based on attributes to locate recipients you want to work with. To do this, click the More button (•••) and then select

Advanced Search. Next, use the Advanced Search dialog box, shown in Figure 2-6 to filter by alias, display name, department, email addresses, first name, last name, and recipient type. The Recipient Types condition allows you to filter the results for specific recipient subtypes, such as only remote mailbox users.

You can add conditions that allow you to filter results based on city, state, country, office, title, group membership, and more:

1. Select **More Options** and then select **Add Condition**.
2. Click in the selection list and then select the condition, such as City.
3. Type the search word or phrase and then click **OK**.
4. Repeat this process to add other conditions.

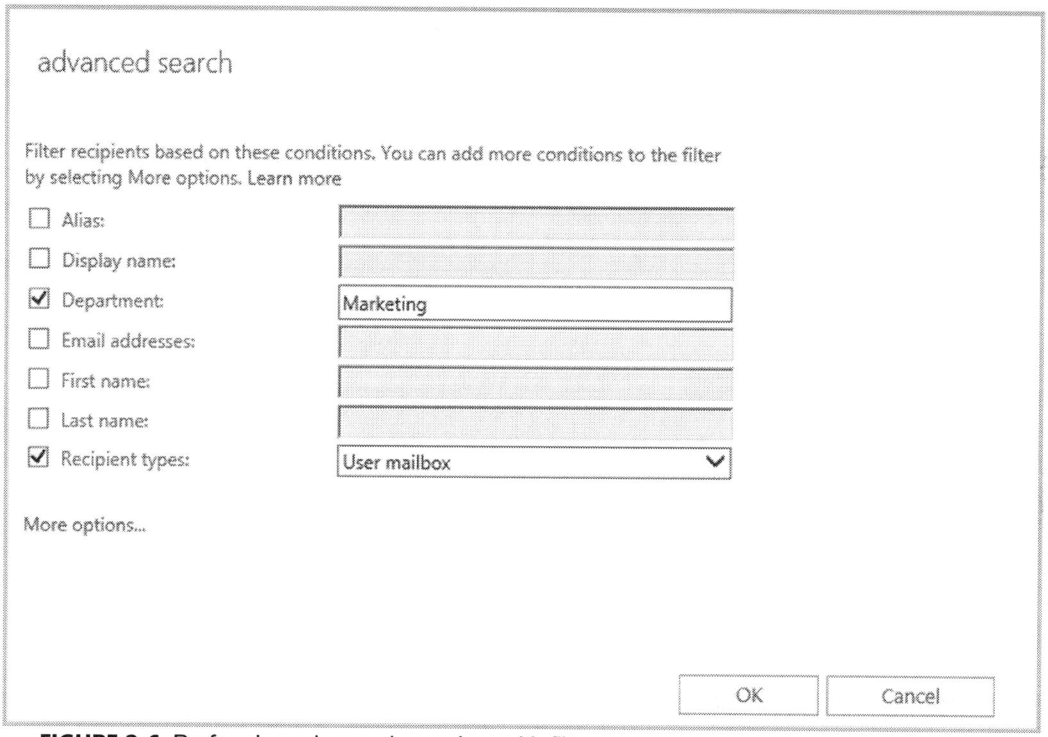

FIGURE 2-6 Performing advanced searches with filters.

In a remote session with Exchange Online, you can find mailboxes, contacts, and groups by using the following commands:

- **Get-User**   Use the Get-User cmdlet to retrieve all users in the forest that match the specified conditions.

Get-User [-Identity **UserId** | -Anr **Identifier**] [-AccountPartition **PartitionId**]
[-Arbitration <$true | $false>] [-Credential **Credential**]
[-Filter FilterString] [-IgnoreDefaultScope <$true | $false>]
[-Organization **OrgName**] [-PublicFolder <$true | $false>]
[-RecipientTypeDetails **Details**] [-ResultSize **Size**] [-SortBy **String**]

- **Get-Contact** Use the Get-Contact cmdlet to retrieve information about a specified contact or contacts.

Get-Contact [-Identity **ContactId** | -Anr **ContactID**] [-AccountPartition **PartitionId**] [-Credential **Credential**] [-Filter **FilterString**]
[-IgnoreDefaultScope <$true | $false>] [-Organization **OrgName**]
[-RecipientTypeDetails **Details**] [-ResultSize **Size**] [-SortBy **Value**]

- **Get-Group** Use the Get-Group cmdlet to query for existing groups.

Get-Group [-Identity **GroupId** | -Anr **GroupID**]
[-AccountPartition **PartitionId**] [-Credential **Credential**]
[-Filter **FilterString**] [-IgnoreDefaultScope <$true | $false>]
[-Organization **OrgName**] [-RecipientTypeDetails {"Contact" | "MailContact" | "MailUser" | "RoleGroup" | "User" | "UserMailbox" | ... }]
[-ResultSize **Size**] [-SortBy **Value**]

Finding Unlicensed, Inactive and Blocked Users

When you are working with Exchange Online, you'll often want to find:

- **Unlicensed users** These users haven't been assigned an Exchange Online license. Although there is a grace period for licensing after creating a mailbox user online, the user may lose mailbox data after the grace period expires.
- **Inactive users** These users have been deleted by an admin, which puts them in inactive status for a period of 30 days. When the recovery period expires, the account and any unprotected data is removed.
- **Sign-in Allowed users** These users can sign in and the related accounts are active.
- **Sign-in Blocked users** These users cannot sign in and the related accounts are blocked, such as may happen when a user's password expires.
- **Users with errors** These users have errors associated with their accounts.

You can find allowed users, blocked users, unlicensed users, or users with errors by completing the following steps:

1. Open Office 365 Admin Center. Select **Users** in the Navigation menu, and then click **Active Users**.
2. On the Filters drop-down list, select Sign-in Allowed Users, Sign-in Blocked Users, Unlicensed Users, or Users With Errors as appropriate.

In Office 365 Admin Center, you can find inactive users by selecting Users in the Navigation menu and then selecting the Deleted Users tab.

PART 2
Management Essentials for Users, Contacts & Mailboxes

Chapter 3. Managing Users

Exchange Admin Center and remote sessions with Exchange Online are the primary administration tools you use to manage mailboxes and mail contacts. You can use these tools to create and manage mail-enabled user accounts, mailbox-enabled user accounts, and mail-enabled contacts, as well as any other configurable aspect of Exchange Online.

Creating Mailbox-Enabled and Mail-Enabled User Accounts

Generally speaking, you need to create a user account for each user who wants to use network resources. The following sections explain how to create user accounts that are either mailbox-enabled or mail-enabled, and how to add a mailbox to an existing user account. If a user needs to send and receive email, you need to create a new mailbox-enabled account for the user or add a mailbox to the user's existing account. Otherwise, you can create a mail-enabled account.

Working with Logon Names and Passwords

Before you create a user account, you should think for a moment about the new account's logon name and password. You identify all user accounts with a logon name. This logon name can be (but doesn't have to be) the same as the user's email address. Logon names have two parts:

- **User name** The account's text label
- **User domain** The domain where the user account exists

For the user Williams whose account is created in imaginedlands.onmicrosoft.com, the full logon name for Windows is williams@imaginedlands.onmicrosoft.com.

User accounts can also have passwords and public certificates associated with them. *Passwords* are authentication strings for an account. *Public certificates* combine a public and private key to identify a user. You log on with a password by typing the password. You log on with a public certificate by using a smart card and a smart card reader.

Although Windows Azure, Office 365 and Exchange Online display user names to describe privileges and permissions, the key identifiers for accounts are security identifiers (SIDs). SIDs are unique identifiers that Windows Azure generates when you create accounts. SIDs consist of the hosted domain's security ID prefix and a unique relative ID. Windows Azure uses these identifiers to track accounts independently from user names. SIDs serve many purposes; the two most important are to allow you to easily change user names and to allow you to delete accounts without worrying that someone could gain access to resources simply by re-creating an account with the same user name.

When you change a user name, you tell Windows Azure to map a particular SID to a new name. When you delete an account, you tell Windows that a particular SID is no longer valid. Afterward, even if you create an account with the same user name, the new account won't have the same privileges and permissions as the previous one because the new account will have a new SID.

Mail-Enabling New User Accounts

Mail-enabled users are defined as custom recipients in Exchange Online. They have an Exchange alias and an external email address, but they do not have an Exchange mailbox. All email messages sent to a mail-enabled user are forwarded to the remote email address associated with the account.

In Exchange Admin Center, mail-enabled users are listed as Mail Users under Recipients > Contacts. You can manage mail-enabled users through Exchange Admin Center or a remote session with Exchange Online.

> **NOTE** When mail-enabled users and contacts are no longer needed, you'll need to delete the mail-enabled user or contact.

You can create a new mail-enabled user by completing the following steps:

1. In Exchange Admin Center, select **Recipients** in the Navigation menu and then select **Contacts**.

2. Click **New** ( ) and then select **Mail User**. This opens the New Mail User dialog box, shown in Figure 3-1.

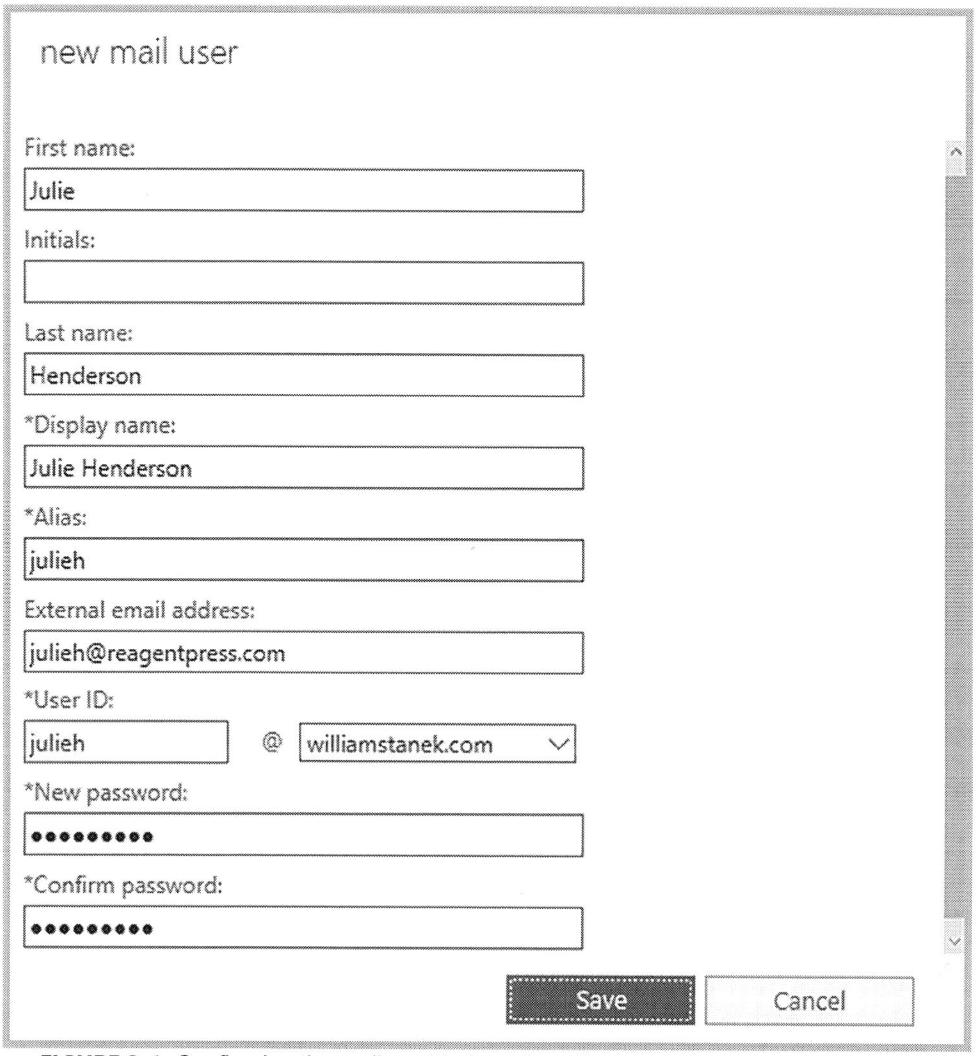

new mail user

First name:

Julie

Initials:

Last name:

Henderson

*Display name:

Julie Henderson

*Alias:

julieh

External email address:

julieh@reagentpress.com

*User ID:

julieh @ williamstanek.com

*New password:

•••••••••

*Confirm password:

•••••••••

[Save] [Cancel]

FIGURE 3-1 Configuring the mail-enabled user's settings.

3. Type the user's first name, middle initial, and last name in the text boxes provided. These values are used to create the Display Name entry.

4. The Display Name and Name properties can't exceed 64 characters. As necessary, make changes to the Display Name, Name, or both text boxes. For example, you might want to type the name in LastName FirstName MiddleInitial format or in FirstName MiddleInitial LastName format.

> **IMPORTANT** The difference between the Display Name and the Name properties is subtle but important. The Display Name property sets the name displayed in Exchange and Outlook. The Name property sets the display name in Exchange Online and is the Common Name (CN) value associated with the user.

5. In the Alias text box, type an alias for the mail-enabled user. This alias should uniquely identify the mail-enabled user in the Exchange organization. Alias names cannot contain spaces.

6. In the External Email Address text box, type the mail user's external email address. By default, the address is configured as a standard SMTP email address.

7. In the User ID text box, type the user's logon name. Use the drop-down list to select the domain with which you want to associate the account. This sets the fully qualified logon name, such as williams@imaginedlands.onmicrosoft.com.

8. Type and then confirm the password for the account. This password must follow the conventions of your organization's password policy. Typically, this means that the password must include at least eight characters and must use three of the four available character types: lowercase letters, uppercase letters, numbers, and symbols.

9. Click **Save**. Exchange Admin Center creates the new mail-enabled user.

If an error occurs, the user will not be created. You will need to click OK, correct the problem, and then click Save again. Consider the error example shown in Figure 3-2. In this instance, the user logon name/user ID was already in use so the user couldn't be created.

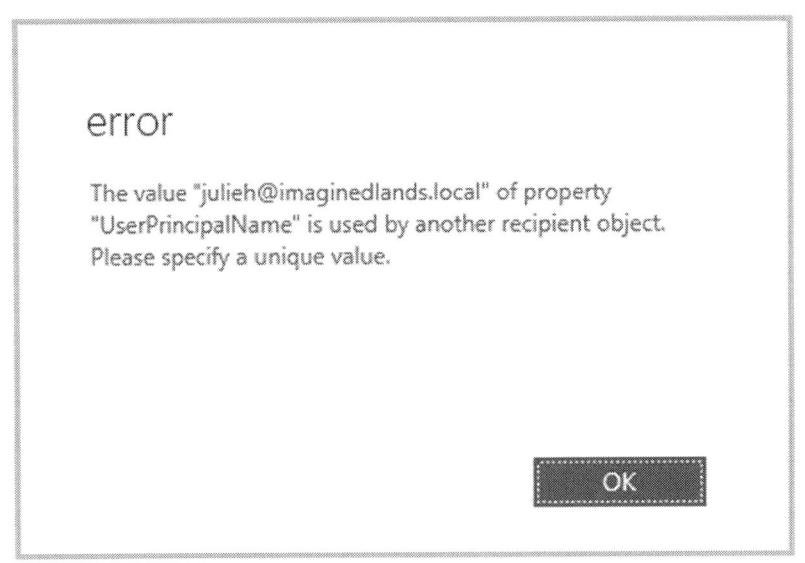

error

The value "julieh@imaginedlands.local" of property "UserPrincipalName" is used by another recipient object. Please specify a unique value.

OK

FIGURE 3-2 An error occurs when a user's principal name is already in use.

You can list all mail-enabled users by typing **get-mailuser** at the remote session prompt. Sample 3-1 provides the full syntax and usage for Get-MailUser.

SAMPLE 3-1 Get-MailUser cmdlet syntax and usage

Syntax

```
Get-MailUser [-Identity Identifier | -Anr Name] [-AccountPartition PartitionId]
[-Credential Credential] [-Filter FilterString] [-IgnoreDefaultScope {$true |
$false}] [-Organization OrgName] [-ResultSize Size] [-SortBy Value]
```

Usage

```
Get-MailUser -Identity "aaron1" | fl
```

```
Get-MailUser | fl
```

> **NOTE** By default, Get-MailUser lists the name and recipient type for matches. In the example, fl is an alias for Format-List and is used to get detailed information about matching entries.

You can create a new mail-enabled user account using the New-MailUser cmdlet. Sample 3-2 shows the syntax and usage. When prompted, provide a secure password for the user account.

> **NOTE** The syntax and usage are entered on multiple lines for ease of reference. You must enter the command-line values for a cmdlet on a single line.

SAMPLE 3-2 New-MailUser cmdlet syntax and usage

Syntax

```
New-MailUser -Name CommonName -ExternalEmailAddress EmailAddress
[-Password Password] [-UserPrincipalName LoginName] {AddtlParams1}
```

```
New-MailUser -Name CommonName -FederatedIdentity FederatedId
-WindowsLiveID WindowsLiveId [-EvictLiveId <$true | $false>]
[-ExternalEmailAddress EmailAddress] [-NetID NetID] {AddtlParams2}
```

```
New-MailUser -Name CommonName -FederatedIdentity FederatedId
-MicrosoftOnlineServicesID WindowsLiveId [-NetID NetID] {AddtlParams2}
```

```
New-MailUser -Name CommonName -ImportLiveId <$true | $false>
-WindowsLiveID WindowsLiveId [-ExternalEmailAddress EmailAddress]
[-UsageLocation CountryInfo] {AddtlParams2}

New-MailUser -Name CommonName [-MicrosoftOnlineServicesID WindowsLiveId]
{AddtlParams2}

New-MailUser -Name CommonName -MicrosoftOnlineServicesID WindowsLiveId
-Password Password [-ExternalEmailAddress EmailAddress] [-UsageLocation
CountryInfo] {AddtlParams2}

New-MailUser -Name CommonName -Password Password -WindowsLiveID
WindowsLiveId [-EvictLiveId <$true | $false>] [-ExternalEmailAddress
EmailAddress] [-UsageLocation CountryInfo] {AddtlParams2}

New-MailUser -Name CommonName -UseExistingLiveId <$true | $false>
-WindowsLiveID WindowsLiveId [-BypassLiveId <$true | $false>]
[-ExternalEmailAddress EmailAddress] [-NetID NetID]
[-UsageLocation CountryInfo] {AddtlParams2}


{AddtlParams1}
[-Alias ExchangeAlias] [-ArbitrationMailbox ModeratorMailbox]
[-DisplayName Name] [-FirstName FirstName] [-Initials Initials]
[-LastName LastName] [-MacAttachmentFormat <BinHex | UuEncode | AppleSingle |
AppleDouble>] [-MessageBodyFormat <Text | Html | TextAndHtml>]
[-MessageFormat <Text | Mime>] [-ModeratedBy Moderators] [-ModerationEnabled
 <$true | $false>] [-Organization OrgName] [-PrimarySmtpAddress
SmtpAddress] [-ResetPasswordOnNextLogon <$true | $false>]
[-SamAccountName PreWin2000Name] [-SendModerationNotifications <Never |
Internal | Always>] [-UsageLocation CountryInfo] [-UsePreferMessageFormat
<$true | $false>]


{AddtlParams2}
[-Alias ExchangeAlias] [-ArbitrationMailbox ModeratorMailbox]
[-DisplayName Name] [-FirstName FirstName] [-Initials Initials]
[-LastName LastName] [-ModeratedBy Moderators] [-ModerationEnabled <$true |
```

```
$false>] [-Organization OrgName] [-PrimarySmtpAddress SmtpAddress]
[-RemotePowerShellEnabled <$true | $false>] [-ResetPasswordOnNextLogon
<$true | $false>] [-SamAccountName PreWin2000Name]
[-SendModerationNotifications <Never | Internal | Always>]
```

Usage

```
New-MailUser -Name "Frank Miller" -Alias "Frankm"
-UserPrincipalName "Frankm@imaginedlands.onmicrosoft.com" -SamAccountName
"Frankm" -FirstName "Frank" -Initials "" -LastName "Miller"
-ResetPasswordOnNextLogon $false
-ExternalEmailAddress "SMTP:Frankm@hotmail.com"
```

Removing Mail-Enabled User Accounts

If you no longer need a mail-enabled user account, you can permanently remove it from the Exchange organization. To remove a mail-enabled user account, select the mail user in Exchange Admin Center and then select Delete (🗑). When prompted to confirm, click Yes.

At the remote session prompt, you can remove a mail-enabled user account by using the Remove-MailUser cmdlet, as shown in Sample 3-3.

SAMPLE 3-3 Remove-MailUser cmdlet syntax and usage

Syntax

```
Remove-MailUser -Identity "Identity"
[-IgnoreDefaultScope {$true | $false}]
```
[-**KeepWindowsLiveID** {$true | $false}]

Usage

```
Remove-MailUser -Identity "Frank Miller"
```

Creating Office 365 User Accounts with Mailboxes

You also can create user accounts with mailboxes in Office 365 Admin Center. These accounts are then available in the online organization.

To create an Office 365 user account, follow these steps:

1. In the dashboard for Office 365 Admin Center, select **Users** in the Navigation menu and then select **Active Users**.
2. On the Active Users page, click **Add A User**. This opens the New User window, shown in Figure 3-3.
3. Type the user's first name and last name in the text boxes provided. These values are used to create the Display Name entry.
4. The Display Name and Name properties can't exceed 64 characters. As necessary, make changes to the Display Name. For example, you might want to type the name in LastName FirstName format or in FirstName LastName format.
5. In the User Name text box, type the user's logon name. Use the drop-down list to select the domain with which you want to associate the account. This sets the fully qualified logon name, such as mikejackson@imaginedlands.onmicrosoft.com (which is referred to as the logon ID with Exchange Online).

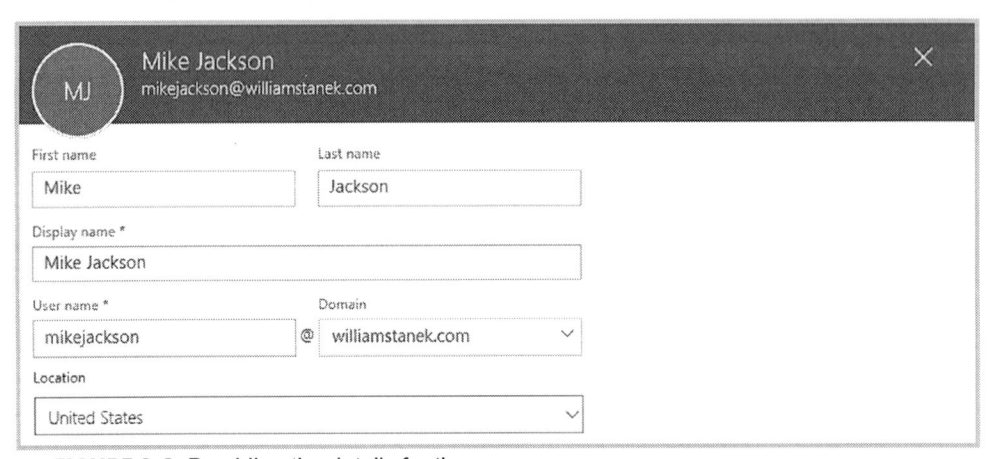

FIGURE 3-3 Providing the details for the new user.

6. Expand the Contact Information panel by clicking on it and add contact information, such as Job Title and Department, as appropriate.
7. By default, Exchange Online will generate a temporary password for the user and email the account information along with the password to the email address associated with your logon. Exchange Online will also make the user change the password when the first sign in. To change these settings, expand the Password panel by clicking on it and then specify the desired options. You can create a password for the user, specify an alternative address for emailing the account information or both.
8. By default, the user account is created with no administrator access. If you are creating an account for an administrator, expand the Roles panel by

clicking on it and then specify the desired options. You can specify that the user is a global administrator or create a custom administrator role.

9. Expand the Product Licenses panel by clicking on it and select a product plan, license or both to assign to the user. Click **Save** to create the user account and mailbox.

> **IMPORTANT** The available licenses will depend on the license types previously purchased for your organization. If you don't have available subscriptions, the appropriate subscriptions and licenses will be purchased for you automatically.

Contact information		
Password	Auto-generated	
Roles	User (no administrator access)	
Products	Exchange Online Plan 1	

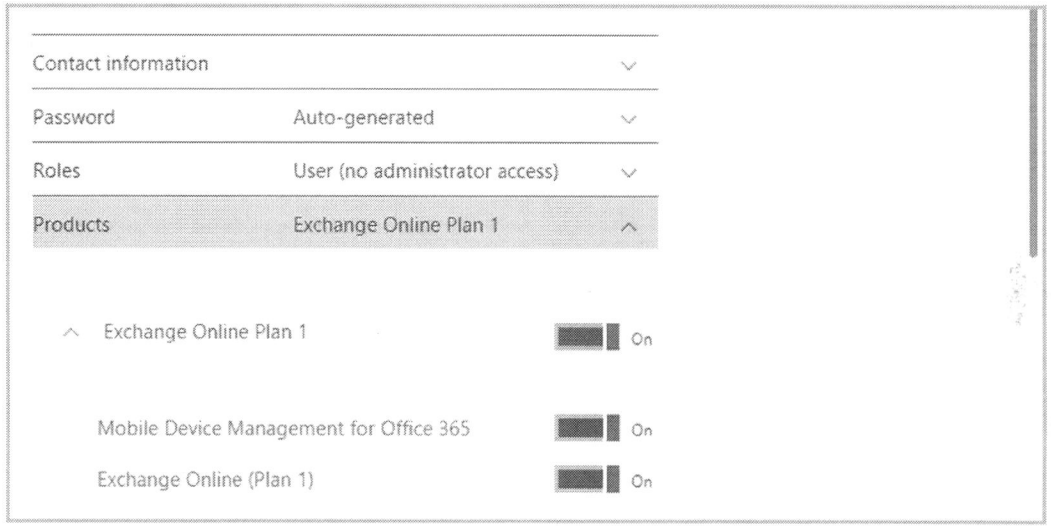

- Exchange Online Plan 1 — On
  - Mobile Device Management for Office 365 — On
  - Exchange Online (Plan 1) — On

FIGURE 3-4 Providing additional account information and selecting product plans.

Creating the online user account and mailbox isn't necessarily the final step. You might also want to do the following:

- Add the user to security and distribution groups
- Enable or disable mailbox features for the account
- Modify the user's default delivery options, storage limits, and restrictions on the account
- Associate additional email addresses with the account

In a remote session with Exchange Online, you can create an online user account using the New-Mailbox cmdlet. Keep in mind that a mailbox is created only when you use the -MailboxPlan parameter to assign a mailbox plan to the new user.

Setting or Changing Contact Information for User Accounts

You can set contact information for a user account by completing the following steps:

1. In Exchange Admin Center, select **Recipients** in the Navigation menu and then select **Mailboxes**.
2. Double-click the mailbox entry for the user with which you want to work.
3. On the Contact Information page, shown in Figure 3-5, use the text boxes provided to set the user's business address or home address. Normally, you'll want to enter the user's business address. This way, you can track the business locations and mailing addresses of users at various offices.

> **NOTE** You need to consider privacy issues before entering private information, such as home addresses and home phone numbers, for users. Discuss the matter with the appropriate groups in your organization, such as the human resources and legal departments. You might also want to get user consent before releasing home addresses.

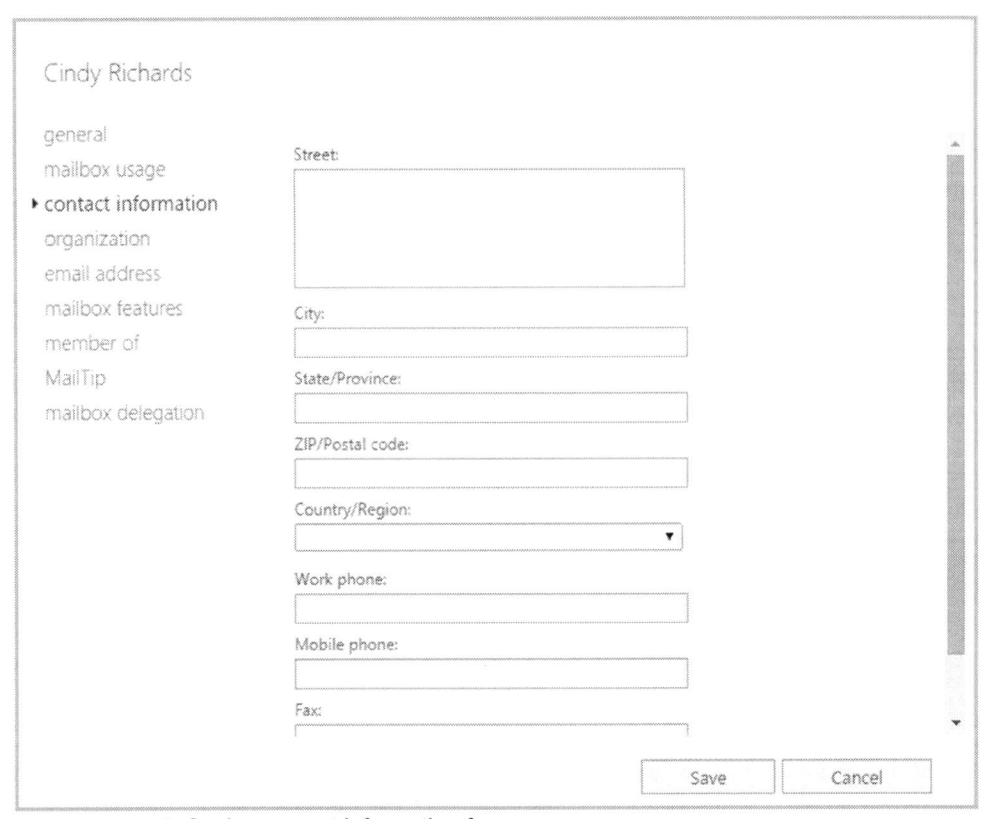

FIGURE 3-5 Setting contact information for a user.

4. Use the Work Phone, Mobile Phone, and Fax text boxes to set the user's primary business telephone, mobile phone, and fax numbers.

5. Click More Options. Use the Office text box to set the user's office and the Web Page text box to set the URL of the user's home page, which can be on the Internet or the company intranet.

6. On the Organization page, shown in Figure 3-6, as appropriate, type the user's title, department, and company.

7. To specify the user's manager, click **Browse**. In the Manager dialog box, select the user's manager and then click **OK**. When you specify a manager, the user shows up as a direct report in the manager's account. Click **Save** to apply the changes.

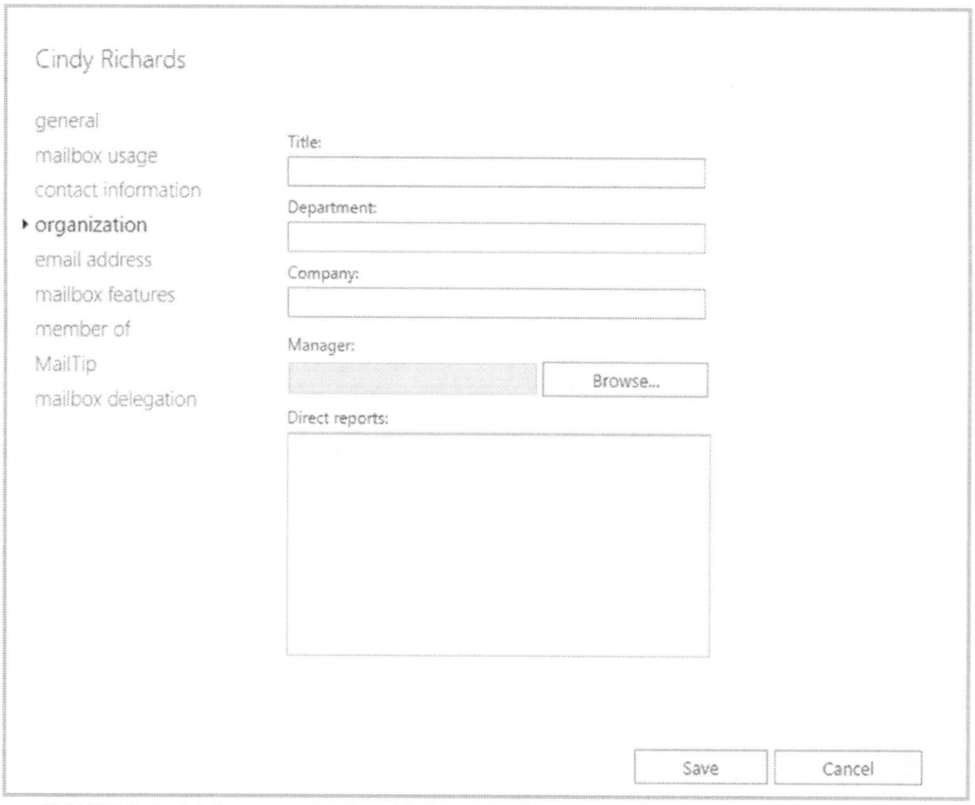

FIGURE 3-6 Adding organizational information for a user.

Changing Logon ID or Logon Domain for Online Users

For Exchange Online, the fully-qualified logon ID is the user's name followed by the @ symbol and the user's logon domain. You can modify this information for an online user account by completing the following steps:

1. In the dashboard for Office 365 Admin Center, select **Users** in the Navigation menu and then select **Active Users**.

2. Click the entry for the user with which you want to work. This opens a properties dialog box for the user.

3. Click **Edit** on the Email Addresses panel and then use the User Name and Domain text boxes to set the user's logon name and domain.

4. Click **Save** to apply your changes.

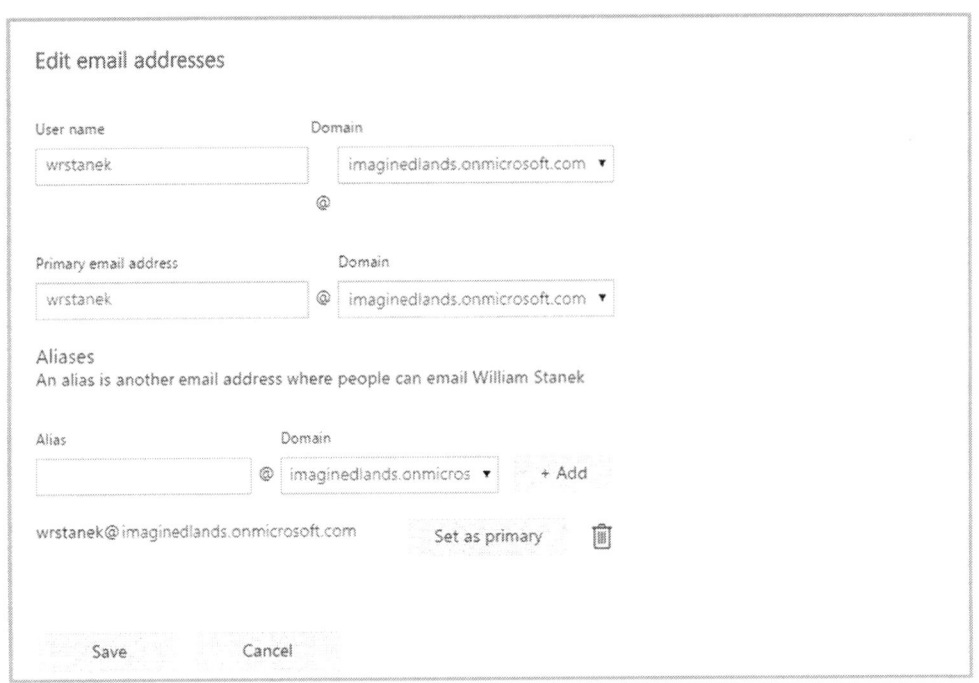

FIGURE 3-7 Updating the user name for an Exchange Online user.

Changing a User's Exchange Alias and Display Name

Each mailbox has an Exchange alias and display name associated with it. The Exchange alias is used with address lists as an alternative way of specifying the user in the To, Cc, or Bcc text boxes of an email message. The alias also sets the primary SMTP address associated with the account.

> **NOTE** Changing a user's Exchange alias doesn't normally change the primary SMTP address for the user. You can, however, modify the primary SMTP address or add additional SMTP addresses.

To change the Exchange alias and mailbox name on a user account, complete the following steps:

1. In Exchange Admin Center, select **Recipients** in the Navigation menu and then select **Mailboxes**.
2. Double-click the entry for the mailbox you want to work with.
3. On the General page, the Display Name text box sets the mailbox name. Change this text box if you'd like the mailbox to have a different display name.
4. The Alias text box sets the Exchange alias. If you'd like to assign a new alias, enter the new Exchange alias in this text box.
5. Click **Save**.

> **NOTE** Often, the user logon name and the Exchange alias are set to the same value. If you've implemented this practice in your organization, you may also want to modify the user logon name. However, this is not a best practice when security is a concern.

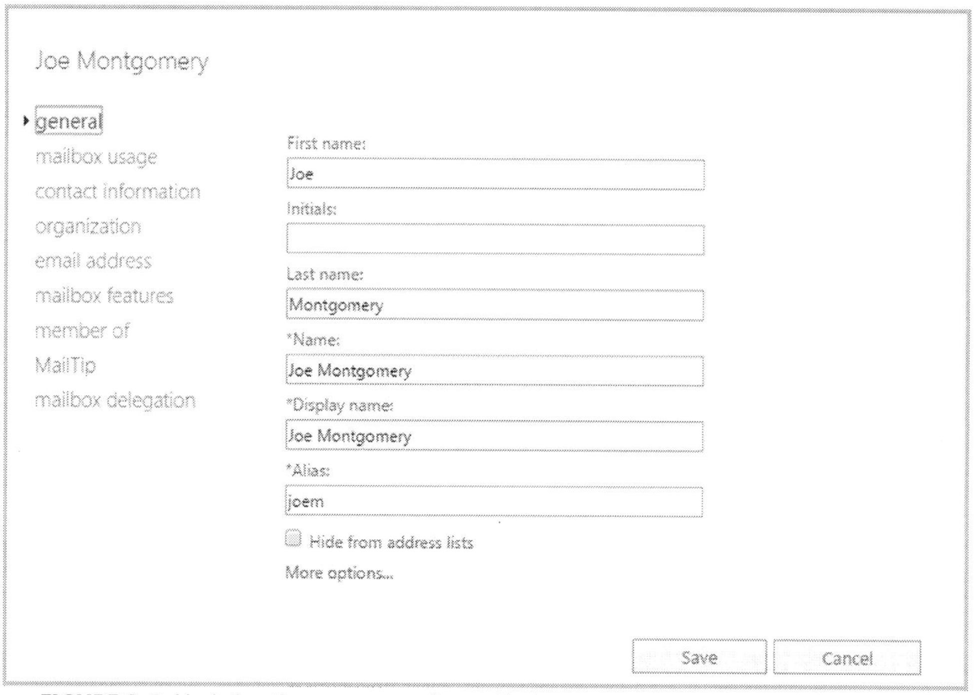

FIGURE 3-8 Updating the user name for an Exchange user.

Adding, Changing, and Removing Email and Other Addresses

When you create a mailbox-enabled user account, default email addresses are created. Changing a user's Exchange alias doesn't normally change the email address for the user. You can, however, modify the primary SMTP address or add additional SMTP addresses.

Exchange also allows you to create non-SMTP addresses for users:

- Exchange Unified Messaging (EUM) addresses used by the Unified Messaging service to locate UM-enabled users within the Exchange organization
- Custom addresses for legacy Exchange (Ex) as well as these non-Exchange mail organizations: X.400, X.500, MSMail, CcMail, Lotus Notes, and Novell GroupWise

To add, change, or remove an email or other address, follow these steps:

1. In Exchange Admin Center, select **Recipients** in the Navigation menu and then select **Mailboxes**.
2. Double-click the mailbox entry for the user you want to work with.
3. On the Email Address page, shown in Figure 3-9, you can use the following techniques to manage the user's email addresses:

- **Create a new SMTP address**   Click Add (✛). Because the address type SMTP is selected by default, enter the SMTP email address, and then click OK to save your changes.

- **Create a new EUM address**   Click Add (✛), and then select the EUM option. Enter the custom address or extension. Next, click Browse and then select a dial plan Click OK to save your changes.

- **Create a custom address**   Click Add (✛), and then select the Custom Address Type option. Enter the custom address type in the text box provided. Valid types include: X.400, X.500, EUM, MSMail, CcMail, Lotus Notes, and NovellGroupWise. Next, enter the custom address. This address must comply with the format requirements for the address type. Click OK to save your changes.

> *TIP*   Use SMTP as the address type for standard Internet email addresses. For custom address types, such as X.400, you must enter the address in the proper format.

- **Edit an existing address** Double-click the address entry, or select the entry and then select Edit on the toolbar. Modify the settings in the Address dialog box, and then click OK.
- **Delete an existing address** Select the address, and then click Remove.

> **NOTE** You can't delete the primary SMTP address without first promoting another email address to the primary position. Exchange uses the primary SMTP address to send and receive messages.

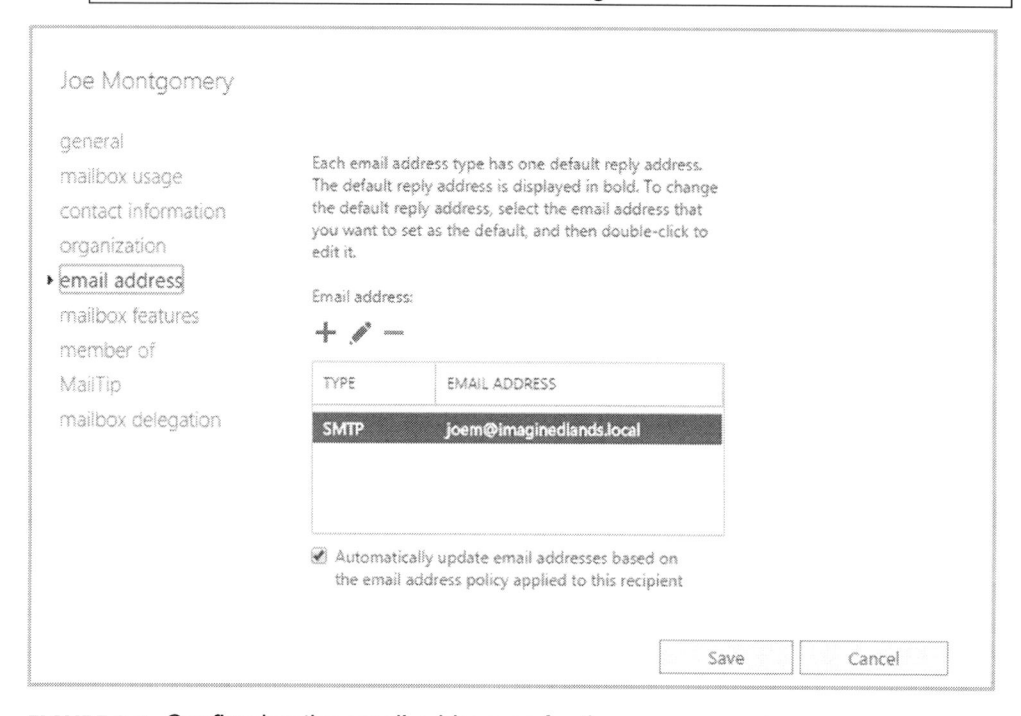

FIGURE 3-9 Configuring the email addresses for the user account.

Setting a Default Reply Address for a User Account

Each email address type has one default reply address. This email address sets the value of the Reply To text box. To change the default reply address, follow these steps:

1. In Exchange Admin Center, select **Recipients** in the Navigation menu and then select **Mailboxes**.
2. Double-click the mailbox entry for the user with which you want to work.
3. On the Email Address page, current default email addresses are highlighted with bold text. Email addresses that aren't highlighted are used only as alternative addresses for delivering messages to the current mailbox.

4. To change the current default settings, select an email address that isn't highlighted and then click **Edit** (✎).

5. In the Email Address dialog box, select the **Make This The Reply Address** checkbox. Click **OK** to save the changes.

Changing A User's Web, Wireless Service, And Protocol Options

When you create user accounts with mailboxes, global settings determine the web, wireless services, and protocols that are available. You can change these settings for individual users at any time by completing the following steps:

1. In Exchange Admin Center, select **Recipients** in the Navigation menu and then select **Mailboxes**.
2. Double-click the mailbox entry for the user with which you want to work.
3. Click the **Mailbox Features** tab. As shown in Figure 3-10, configure the following web, wireless services, and protocols for the user:

- **Exchange ActiveSync**   Allows the user to synchronize the mailbox and to browse wireless devices. Properties allow you to specify an Exchange ActiveSync policy. When you enable Exchange ActiveSync, the account users the default mobile device mailbox policy. To set an alternative policy, click the related View Details option.
- **Outlook Web App**   Permits the user to access the mailbox with a web browser. Properties allow you to specify an Outlook Web App mailbox policy.
- **Unified Messaging**   Allows the user to access unified messaging features, such as the voice browser. In a standard configuration of Exchange Online, all new mailbox users have unified messaging enabled. However, a default UM Mailbox policy is required to fully activate the feature. If one hasn't been assigned, click Enable to display a dialog box that will allow you to specify the required policy.
- **MAPI**   Permits the user to access the mailbox with a Messaging Application Programming Interface (MAPI) email client
- **POP3**   Permits the user to access the mailbox with a Post Office Protocol version 3 (POP3) email client.
- **IMAP4**   Permits the user to access the mailbox with an Internet Message Access Protocol version 4 (IMAP4) email client.

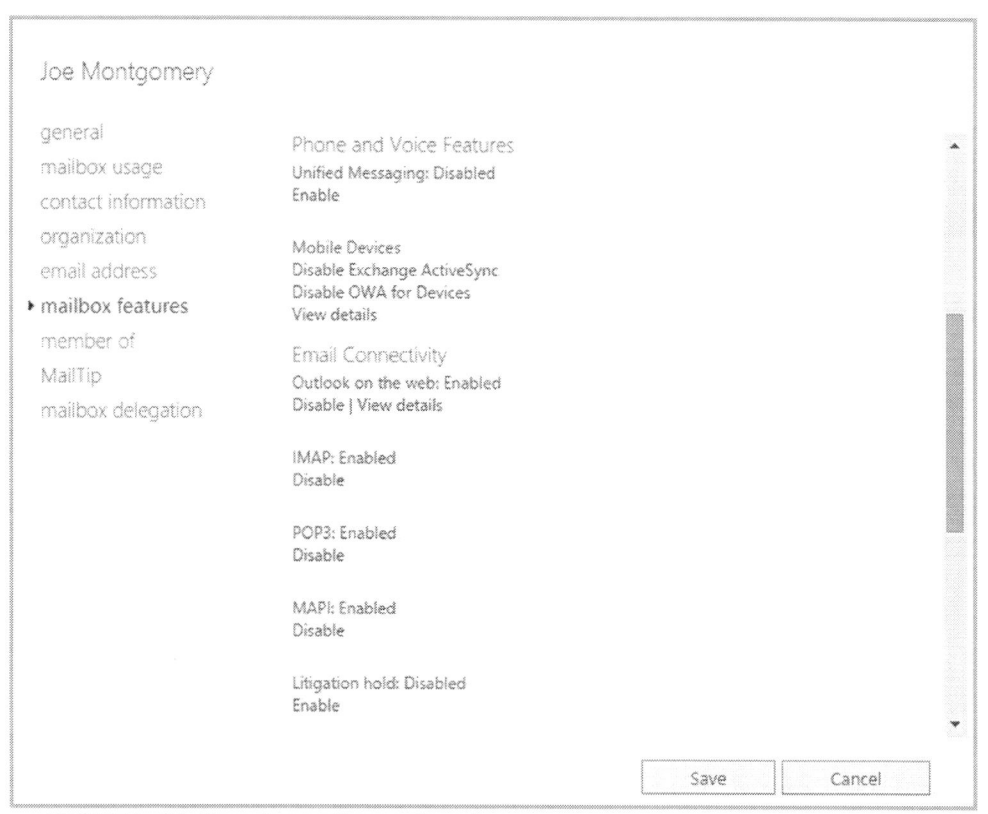

```
Joe Montgomery

general                    Phone and Voice Features
mailbox usage              Unified Messaging: Disabled
contact information        Enable
organization
                           Mobile Devices
email address              Disable Exchange ActiveSync
▸ mailbox features         Disable OWA for Devices
                           View details
member of
MailTip                    Email Connectivity
mailbox delegation         Outlook on the web: Enabled
                           Disable | View details

                           IMAP: Enabled
                           Disable

                           POP3: Enabled
                           Disable

                           MAPI: Enabled
                           Disable

                           Litigation hold: Disabled
                           Enable

                                              Save        Cancel
```

FIGURE 3-10 Changing mailbox options for users.

- **Litigation Hold** Indicates whether a mailbox is subject to litigation hold where users can delete mail items but the items are retained by Exchange. Properties allow you to provide a note to users about litigation hold and the URL of a webpage where they can learn more.
- **Archive** Indicates whether an in-place archive mailbox has been created for the user. Properties allow you to specify the name of the folder in the user's mailbox that contains the archive.

    4. Select an option and then click **Enable** or **Disable**, as appropriate, to change the status. If an option has required properties, you'll be prompted to configure these properties when you enable the option. If an option has additional configurable properties, click the related View Details option to configure them.

    5. Click **Save** to close the Properties dialog box.

Requiring Users to Change Passwords

Office 365 policy settings typically require users to periodically change their passwords. Sometimes, you might have to ensure that a user changes her password the next time she logs on. For example, if you have to reset a password and give it to the user over the phone, you might want the user to change the password the next time she logs on.

You can set a user account to require the password to be changed on next logon by completing the following steps:

1. Select **Users** on the Office 365 dashboard or click **Active Users** under the Users heading in the Navigation menu to display active users.
2. On the Users page, click a user that you want to work with
3. Click **Reset Password.**

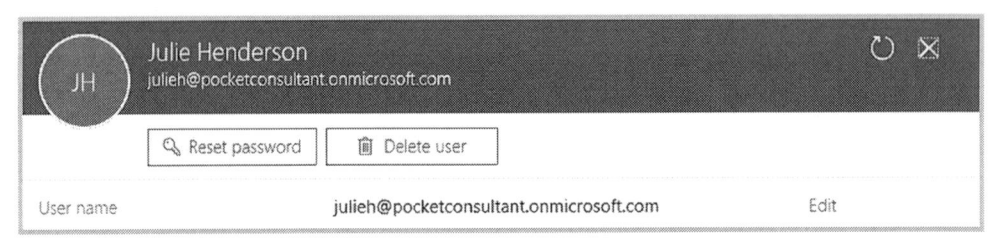

	Julie Henderson julieh@pocketconsultant.onmicrosoft.com		
	Reset password	Delete user	
User name	julieh@pocketconsultant.onmicrosoft.com		Edit

4. On the Reset Password panel, select the **Make This Person Change Their Password…** check box. Click **Reset**.
5. You can send the password in email to up to 5 recipients. By default, the new password is sent only to a designated administrator. You can change the default as necessary or add recipients. Be sure to separate each email address with a semicolon. When you are ready to continue, click **Send Email And Close**.

You can use the Set-User cmdlet to perform the same task, following the syntax shown in Sample 3-4.

SAMPLE 3-4 Requiring a user password change

Syntax

```
Set-User -Identity UserIdentity
-ResetPasswordOnNextLogon <$false|$true>
```

Usage

```
Set-User -Identity "Oliver Lee" -ResetPasswordOnNextLogon $true
```

Deleting Mailboxes from User Accounts

If you remove the Exchange Online license for an online user account, the user's account is marked as an unlicensed account. Exchange Online deletes mailboxes from unlicensed accounts automatically after the grace period expires. By default, this grace period is 30 days. Keep in mind that retention hold, archiving and litigation hold settings also determine whether some or any mailbox data is held.

You can remove a license from an online user account by completing the following steps:

1. In the dashboard for Office 365 Admin Center, select **Users** in the Navigation menu and then select **Active Users**.
2. Next, click the user whose license you want to remove.
3. Click **Edit** on the Product Licenses panel and then click the toggle to Off for the plan or license you want to remove.
4. Click **Save**. The license that was previously assigned to this user will become available to be assigned to another user.

You can use the Disable-Mailbox cmdlet to delete mailboxes while retaining the user accounts as well. Sample 3-5 shows the syntax and usage.

SAMPLE 3-5 Disable-Mailbox cmdlet syntax and usage

Syntax

```
Disable-Mailbox -Identity Identifier
```

Usage

```
Disable-Mailbox -Identity "Oliver Lee"
```

Deleting User Accounts and Their Mailboxes

If you delete the corresponding Office 365 user account for a mailbox, the online user's mailbox is marked for deletion and the account is marked as a deleted account.

Deleted online users aren't removed immediately. Instead, the accounts are inactivated and marked for deletion. By default, the retention period is 30 days. When the retention period expires, a user and all related data is permanently deleted and is not recoverable. Keep in mind that retention hold, archiving, and litigation hold settings also determine whether some or any mailbox data is held.

You can delete an online user account by completing the following steps:

1. In the dashboard for Office 365 Admin Center, select **Users** in the Navigation menu and then select **Active Users**.

2. Click the user whose license you want to remove and then click **Delete User**.
3. When prompted to confirm this action, select **Delete**. The license that was previously assigned to this user will become available to be assigned to another user.

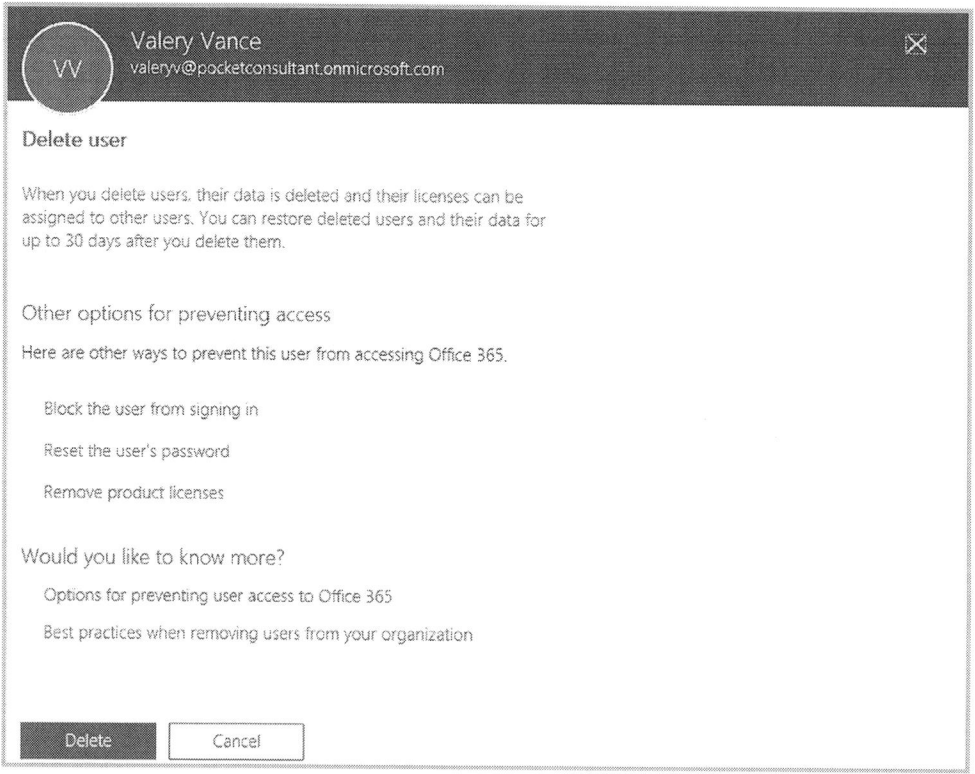

FIGURE 3-11 Confirming the deletion.

You also can use the Remove-Mailbox cmdlet to delete user accounts. Sample 3-6 shows the standard syntax. By default, the –Permanent flag is set to $false and mailboxes are retained in a disconnected state according to the mailbox retention policy. Otherwise, set the –Permanent flag to $true to remove the mailbox from Exchange.

SAMPLE 3-6 Remove-Mailbox cmdlet syntax and usage

Syntax

```
Remove-Mailbox -Identity UserIdentity {AddtlParams}
{AddtlParams}
```

{AddtlParams}

```
[-Arbitration <$false|$true>] [-IgnoreDefaultScope {$true | $false}]
[-KeepWindowsLiveID {$true | $false}] [-Permanent <$false | $true>]
[-RemoveLastArbitrationMailboxAllowed {$true | $false}]
```

Usage

```
Remove-Mailbox -Identity "Oliver Lee"

Remove-Mailbox -Identity "Oliver Lee" -Permanent $true
```

Chapter 4. Managing Contacts

Contacts represent people with whom you or others in your organization want to get in touch. Contacts can have directory information associated with them, but they don't have network logon privileges.

The only difference between a standard contact and a mail-enabled contact is the presence of email addresses. A mail-enabled contact has one or more email addresses associated with it; a standard contact doesn't. When a contact has an email address, you can list the contact in the global address list or other address lists. This allows users to send messages to the contact.

In Exchange Admin Center, mail-enabled contacts and mail-enabled users are both listed in the Mail Contact node. Mail-enabled contacts are listed with the recipient type Mail Contact, and mail-enabled users are listed with the recipient type Mail User.

Creating Mail-Enabled Contacts

You can create and mail-enable a new contact by completing the following steps:

1. In Exchange Admin Center, select **Recipients** in the Navigation menu and then select **Contacts**.

2. Click **New** ( ) and then select **Mail Contact**. This opens the New Mail Contact dialog box, shown in Figure 4-1.

3. Type the contact's first name, middle initial, and last name in the text boxes provided. These values are used to automatically create the display name, which is the name displayed in the global address list and other address lists created for the organization. It is also used when addressing email messages to the contact.

4. Enter the Exchange alias for the contact. Aliases provide an alternative way of addressing users and contacts in To, Cc, and Bcc text boxes of email messages.

5. In the External Email Address text box, enter the address to associate with the contact. Only standard SMTP addresses are accepted.

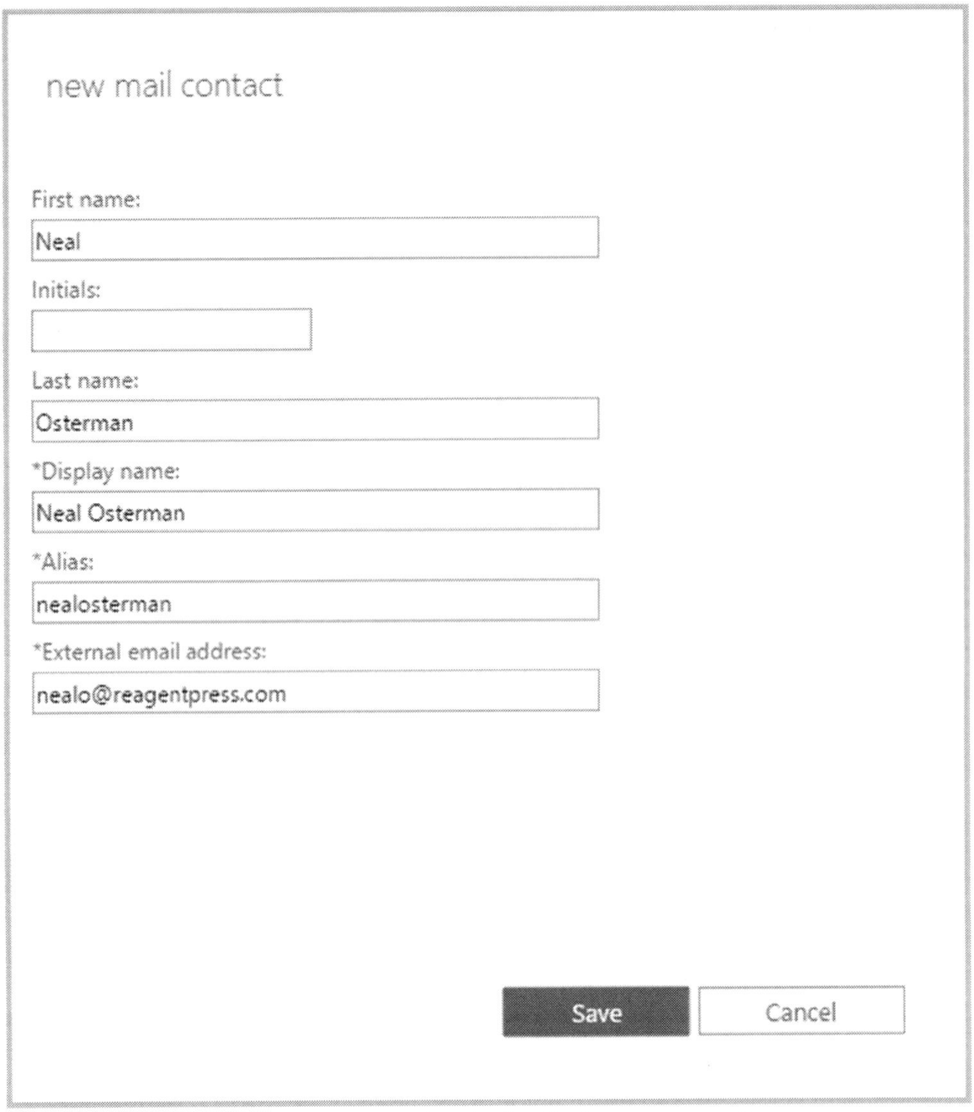

> **new mail contact**
>
> First name:
> [Neal]
>
> Initials:
> [   ]
>
> Last name:
> [Osterman]
>
> *Display name:
> [Neal Osterman]
>
> *Alias:
> [nealosterman]
>
> *External email address:
> [nealo@reagentpress.com]
>
> [**Save**]   [Cancel]

FIGURE 4-1 Creating a new mail contact for the Exchange organization

    6. Click **Save**. Exchange Admin Center creates the new contact and mail-enables it. If an error occurs, the contact will not be created. You will need to correct the problem and repeat this procedure.

In a remote session with Exchange Online, you can create a new mail-enabled contact using the New-MailContact cmdlet. Sample 4-1 provides the syntax and usage.

SAMPLE 4-1 New-MailContact cmdlet syntax and usage

Syntax

```
New-MailContact -Name Name -ExternalEmailAddress TYPE:EmailAddress
[-ArbitrationMailbox ModeratorMailbox] [-Alias ExchangeAlias]
[-DisplayName Name] [-FirstName FirstName] [-Initials Initials]
[-LastName LastName] [-MacAttachmentFormat <BinHex | UuEncode | AppleSingle |
 AppleDouble>] [-MessageBodyFormat <Text | Html |
TextAndHtml>] [-MessageFormat <Text | Mime>] [-ModeratedBy Moderators]
[-ModerationEnabled <$true | $false>] [-Organization OrgName]
[-PrimarySmtpAddress SmtpAddress] [-SendModerationNotifications <Never |
Internal | Always>]
[-UsePreferMessageFormat <$true | $false>]
```

Usage

```
New-MailContact -ExternalEmailAddress "SMTP:wendywheeler@msn.com"
 -Name "Wendy Wheeler" -Alias "WendyWheeler"
 -FirstName "Wendy" -Initials "" -LastName "Wheeler"
```

In a remote session with Exchange Online, you can mail-enable an existing contact using the Enable-MailContact cmdlet. Sample 4-2 provides the syntax and usage.

SAMPLE 4-2 Enable-MailContact cmdlet syntax and usage

Syntax

```
Enable-MailContact -Identity ContactId -ExternalEmailAddress EmailAddress
[-Alias ExchangeAlias] [-DisplayName Name]
[-MacAttachmentFormat <BinHex | UuEncode | AppleSingle | AppleDouble>]
[-MessageBodyFormat <Text | Html | TextAndHtml>] [-MessageFormat <Text |
Mime>] [-PrimarySmtpAddress SmtpAddress] [-UsePreferMessageFormat <$true |
$false>]
```

Usage

```
Enable-MailContact -Identity "imaginedlands.onmicrosoft.com/John Smith"
 -ExternalEmailAddress "SMTP:johnsmith@reagentpress.com"
 -Alias "JohnSmith" -DisplayName "John Smith"
```

Setting or Changing a Contact's Name and Alias

Mail-enabled contacts can have the following name components:

- **First Name, Initials, Last Name** The first name, initials, and last name of the contact
- **Display Name** The name displayed in the global address list
- **Alias** The Exchange alias for the contact

You can set or change name and alias information for a mail-enabled contact or user by completing the following steps:

1. In Exchange Admin Center, select **Recipients** in the Navigation menu and then select **Contacts**.
2. Double-click the name of the mail-enabled contact or user you want to work with. The Properties dialog box appears.

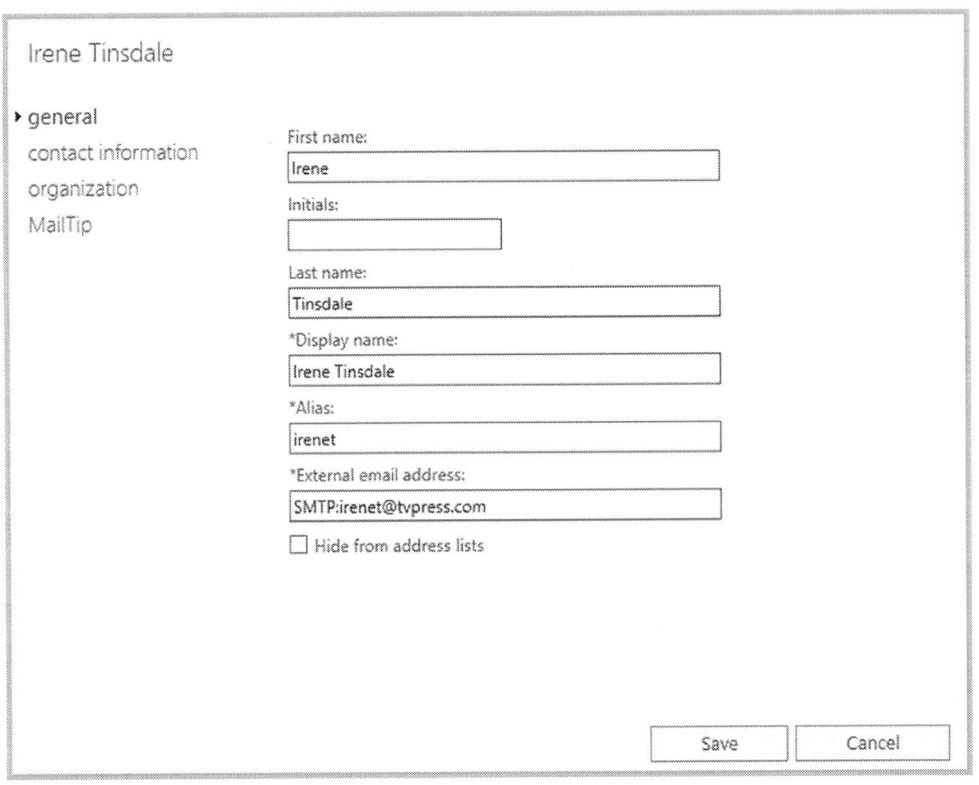

FIGURE 4-2 Updating a contact.

3. On the General tab, use the textboxes provided to update the first name, middle initial, and last name as necessary. Changes you make will update the

display name but not the common name. Therefore, as necessary, use the Name text box to update the common name.

4. With mail-enabled contacts, the Alias text box sets the Exchange alias. If you'd like to assign a new alias, enter the new Exchange alias in this text box.

5. With mail-enabled users, the User Logon Name text box sets the name used to log on to the hosted domain as well as the domain suffix.

6. Click **Save** to apply your changes.

Setting Additional Directory Information for Contacts

You can set additional directory information for a mail-enabled contact or user by completing the following steps:

1. In Exchange Admin Center, select **Recipients** in the Navigation menu and then select **Contacts**.

2. Double-click the name of the mail-enabled contact or user you want to work with. The Properties dialog box appears.

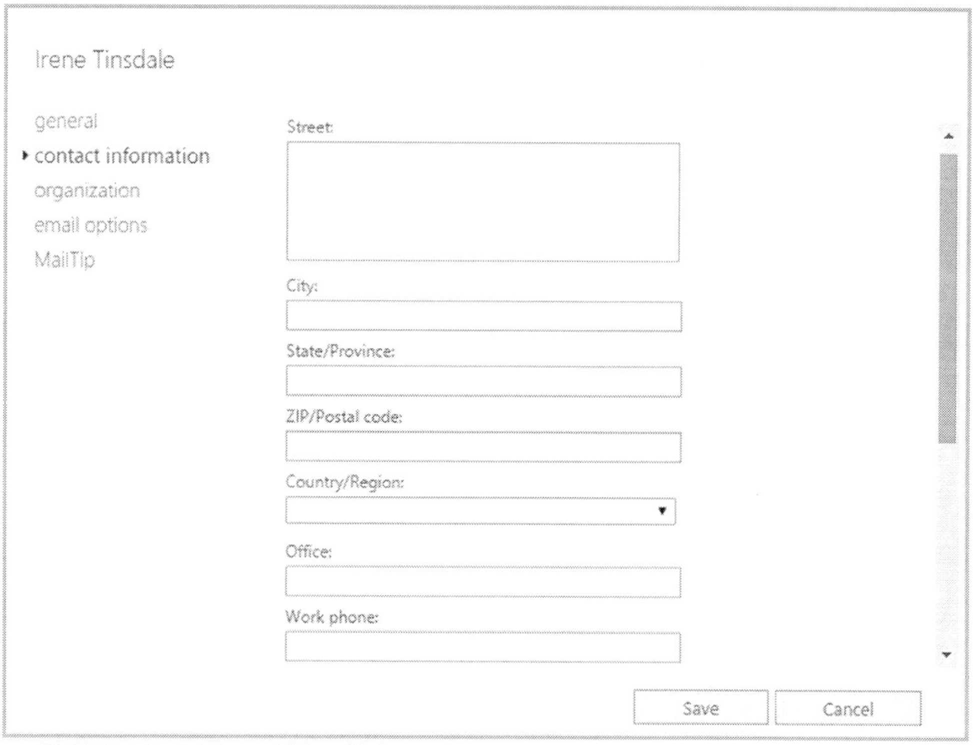

FIGURE 4-3 Adding additional information to a contact.

3. On the Contact Information page, use the text boxes provided to set the contact's business address or home address. Normally, you'll want to enter the contact's business address. This way, you can track the business locations and mailing addresses of contacts at various offices.

4. Use the Work Phone, Mobile Phone, and Fax text boxes to set the contact or user's primary business telephone, mobile phone, and fax numbers.

5. Use the Office text box to set the user's Office and the Notes text box to add any important notes about the contact.

6. On the Organization page, as appropriate, type the contact or user's title, department, and company.

7. To specify the contact or user's manager, click **Browse**. In the Manager dialog box, select the manager and then click **OK**. When you specify a manager, the contact or user shows up as a direct report in the manager's account. Click **Save** to apply the changes.

> **NOTE** You need to consider privacy issues before entering private information, such as home addresses and home phone numbers, for users. Discuss the matter with the appropriate groups in your organization, such as the human resources and legal departments. You might also want to get user consent before releasing home addresses.

Changing Email Addresses Associated with Contacts

Mail-enabled contacts and users have several types of email addresses associated with them:

- An internal, automatically generated email address used for routing within the organization
- An external email address to which mail routed internally is forwarded for delivery

With mail-enabled contacts, you can only use SMTP email addresses. You can change the SMTP email addresses associated with a mail-enabled contact by completing the following steps:

1. In Exchange Admin Center, select **Recipients** in the Navigation menu and then select **Contacts**.

2. Double-click the name of the mail-enabled contact you want to work with. The Properties dialog box appears.

3. On the General page, the external SMTP email address of the mail-enabled contact is listed. This is the primary SMTP email address for the mail-enabled contact. As necessary, enter a new email address.

> **NOTE** The primary email address is listed with the prefix SMTP:. When you enter a new email address, you aren't required to enter this prefix. Thus, you could enter SMTP:williams@treyresearch.net or williams@treyresearch.net.

4. Click **Save** to apply your changes.

With mail-enabled users, you can use SMTP and non-SMTP email addresses. You can change the email addresses associated with a mail-enabled user by completing the following steps:

1. In Exchange Admin Center, select **Recipients** in the Navigation menu and then select **Contacts**.
2. Double-click the name of the mail-enabled user you want to work with. The Properties dialog box appears.

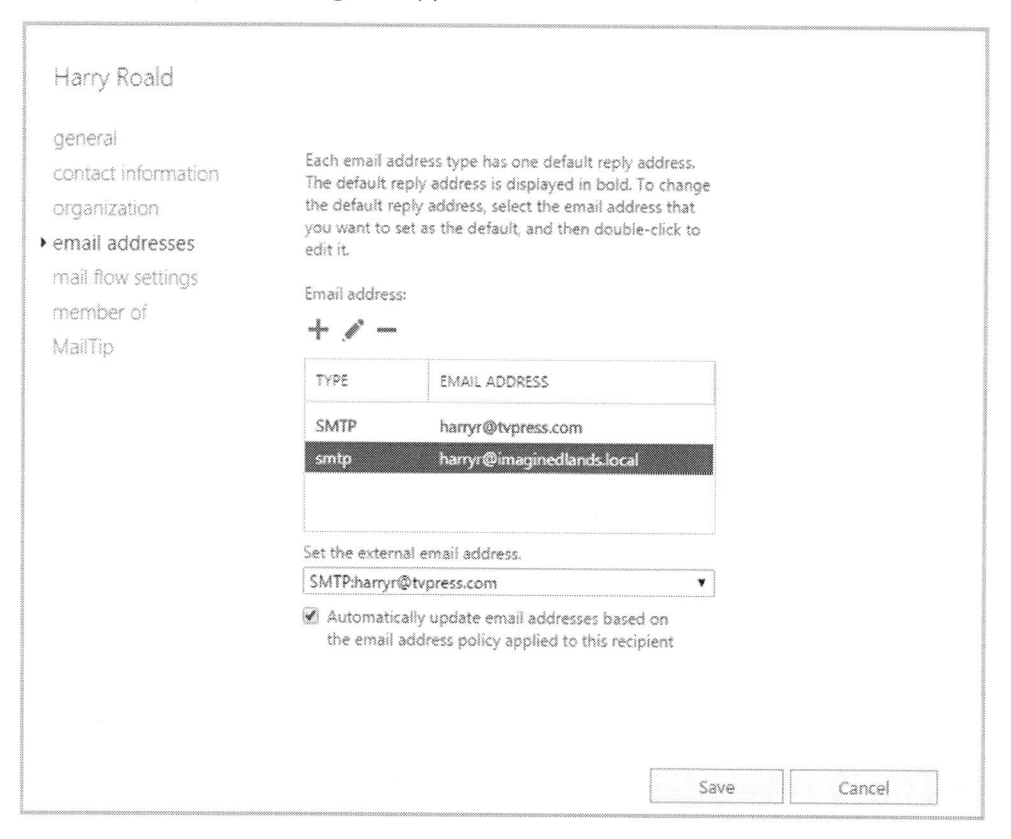

FIGURE 4-4 Modifying the email addresses for a mail-enabled user.

3. On the Email Addresses page, you can use the following techniques to manage the mail-enabled user's email addresses:

- **Create a new SMTP address**   Click Add (✚). Because the address type SMTP is selected by default, enter the SMTP email address, and then click OK to save your changes.

- **Create a custom address**   Click Add (✚), and then select the Custom Address Type option. Enter the custom address type in the text box provided. Valid types include: X.400, X.500, EUM, MSMail, CcMail, Lotus Notes, and NovellGroupWise. Next, enter the custom address. This address must comply with the format requirements for the address type. Click OK to save your changes.
- **Edit an existing address**   Double-click the address entry, or select the entry and then select Edit on the toolbar. Modify the settings in the Address dialog box, and then click OK.
- **Delete an existing address**   Select the address, and then click Remove.

> **NOTE**   You can't delete the primary SMTP address without first promoting another email address to the primary position. Exchange uses the primary SMTP address to send and receive messages.

4. The external email address of the mail-enabled user is also listed on the Email Addresses page. This is the primary email address for the mail user or contact. As necessary, select an alternative email address to be the primary.

5. Click **Save** to apply your changes.

Deleting Contacts

When you delete a mail-enabled user or contact from Exchange Online, the mail-enabled user or contact is permanently removed from Exchange Online. You can delete contacts by following these steps:

1. In Exchange Admin Center, select **Recipients** in the Navigation menu and then select **Contacts**.
2. Select the contact that you want to delete and then click **Delete**.
3. When prompted to confirm this action, select **Yes**.

> **warning**
>
> Are you sure you want to delete contact "Irene Tinsdale"?
>
> [Yes] [No]

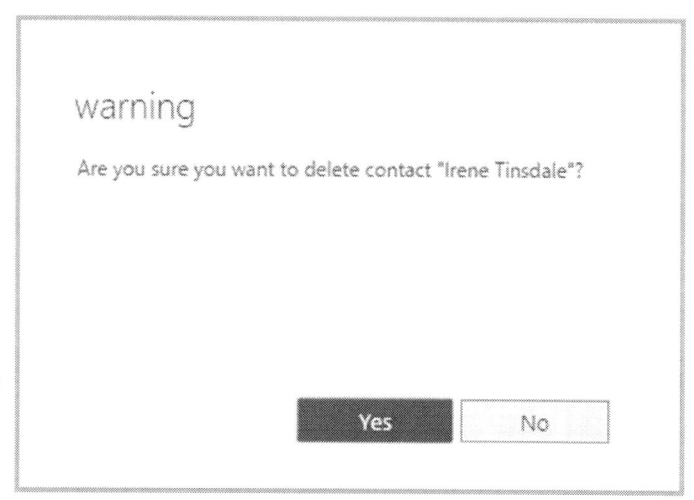

FIGURE 4-5 Deleting a contact.

You can use the Remove-MailContact cmdlet to delete contacts as well. Sample 4-3 shows the syntax and usage.

SAMPLE 4-3 Remove-MailContact cmdlet syntax and usage

Syntax

```
Remove-MailContact -Identity ContactIdentity
```

Usage

```
Remove-MailContact -Identity "Henrik Larsen"
```

Chapter 5. Adding Special-Purpose Mailboxes

Exchange Online makes it easy to create several special-purpose mailbox types, including:

- **Room mailbox**   A room mailbox is a mailbox for room scheduling.
- **Equipment mailbox**   An equipment mailbox is a mailbox for equipment scheduling.
- **Archive mailbox**   An archive mailbox is used to store a user's messages, such as might be required for executives and needed by some managers.
- **Arbitration mailbox**   An arbitration mailbox is used to manage approval requests, such as may be required for handling moderated recipients and distribution group membership approval.
- **Discovery mailbox**   A Discovery mailbox is the target for Discovery searches and can't be converted to another mailbox type after it's created. In-Place eDiscovery is a feature of Exchange Online that allows authorized users to search mailboxes for specific types of content as might be required to meet legal discovery requirements.
- **Shared mailbox**   A shared mailbox is a mailbox that is shared by multiple users, such as a general mailbox for customer inquiries.
- **Public folder mailbox**   A public folder mailbox is a shared mailbox for storing public folder data.

The sections that follow discuss techniques for working with these special-purpose mailboxes.

Using Room and Equipment Mailboxes

You use room and equipment mailboxes for scheduling purposes only. You'll find that

- Room mailboxes are useful when you have conference rooms, training rooms, and other rooms for which you need to coordinate the use.
- Equipment mailboxes are useful when you have projectors, media carts, or other items of equipment for which you need to coordinate the use. Every room and equipment mailbox must have a separate user account associated with it. Although these accounts are required so that the mailboxes can be used for scheduling, the accounts are disabled by default so that they cannot be used for logon. To ensure that the resource accounts do not get enabled accidentally, you need to coordinate closely with other administrators in your organization.

> **IMPORTANT** Each room or piece of equipment must have a separate user account. This is necessary to track the unique free/busy data for each resource.

Because the number of scheduled rooms and amount of equipment grows as your organization grows, you'll want to carefully consider the naming conventions you use with rooms and equipment:

- With rooms, you may want to use display names that clearly identify the rooms' physical locations. For example, you might have rooms named "Conference Room B on Fifth Floor" or "Building 83 Room 15."
- With equipment, you may want the display name to identify the type of equipment, the equipment's characteristics, and the equipment's relative location. For example, you might have equipment named "Dell LED Projector at Seattle Office" or "Fifth Floor Media Cart."

As with standard user mailboxes, room and equipment mailboxes have contact information associated with them (see Figure 5-1). To make it easier to find rooms and equipment, you should provide as much information as possible. If a room has a conference or call-in phone, be sure to provide this phone number. Also, provide location details that help people find the conference room and specify the room capacity. The phone, location, and capacity are displayed in Office Outlook.

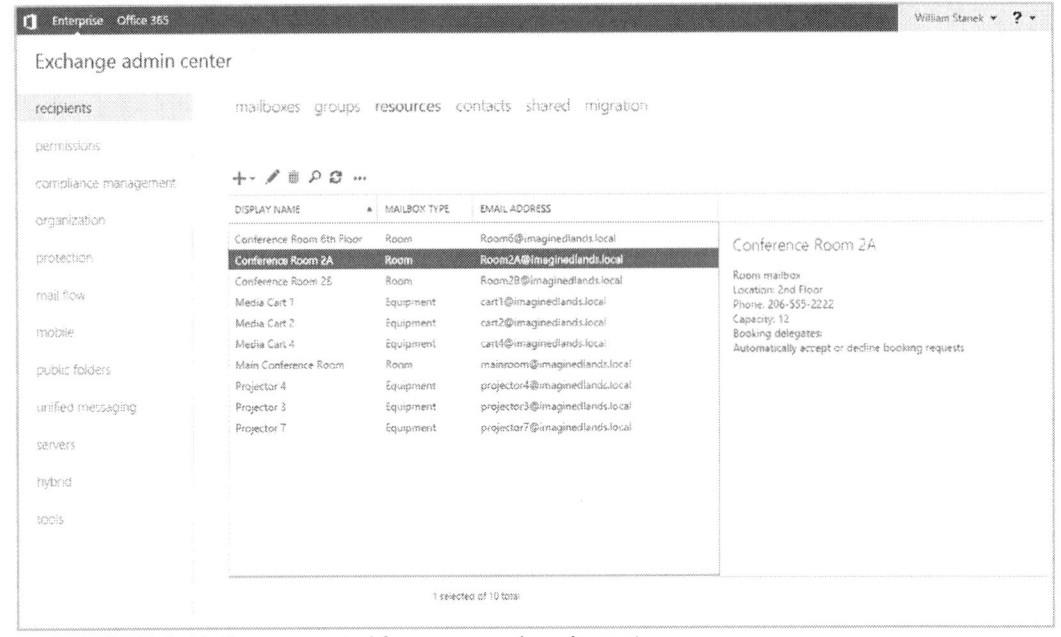

FIGURE 5-1 Mailboxes created for rooms and equipment.

After you've set up mailboxes for your rooms and equipment, scheduling the rooms and equipment is straightforward. In Exchange, room and equipment availability is tracked using free/busy data. In Outlook, a user who wants to reserve rooms, equipment, or both simply makes a meeting request that includes the rooms and equipment that are required for the meeting.

The steps to schedule a meeting and reserve equipment are as follows:

1. Create a meeting request. In Outlook 2010 or later, click **New Items**, and then select **Meeting**. Or press Ctrl+Shift+Q.

2. In the To text box, invite the individuals who should attend the meeting by typing their display names, Exchange aliases, or email addresses, as appropriate (see Figure 5-2).

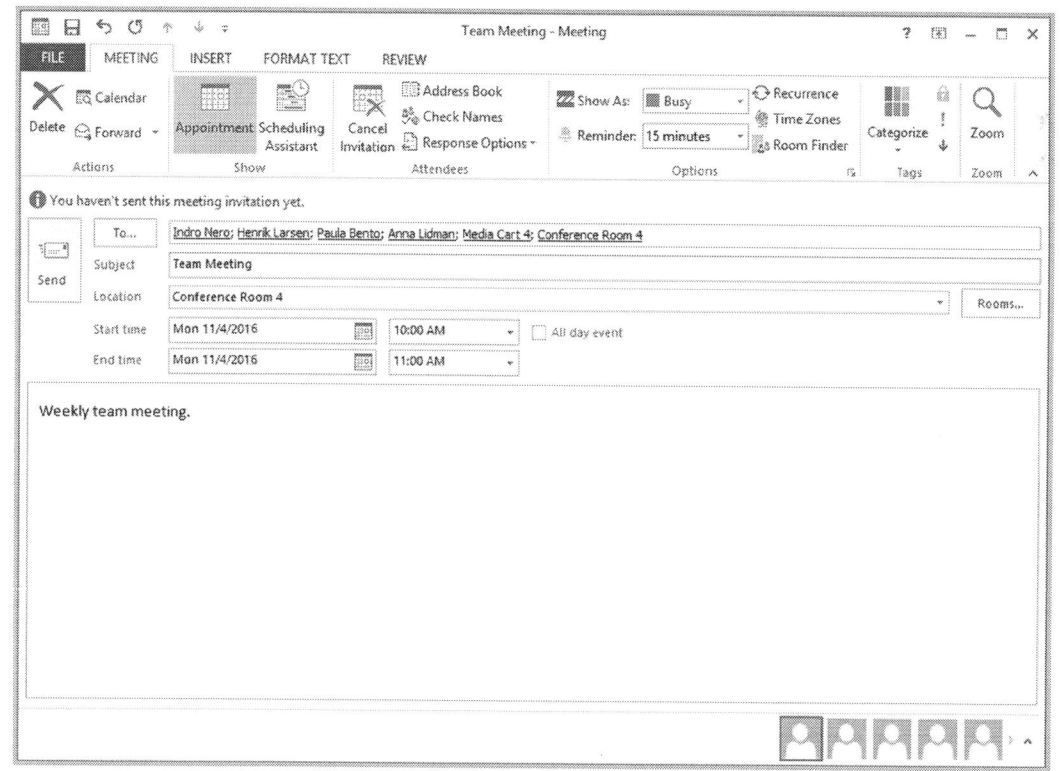

FIGURE 5-2 You can schedule a meeting that includes a reserved room and reserved equipment.

3. Type the display name, Exchange alias, or email address for any equipment you need to reserve.

4. Click Rooms to the right of the Location text box. The Select Rooms dialog box appears, as shown in Figure 5-3. By default, the Select Rooms dialog box

uses the All Rooms address book. Rooms are added to this address book automatically when you create them.

5. Double-click the room you'd like to use. This adds the room to the Rooms list. Click OK to close the Select Rooms dialog box.

6. In the Subject text box, type the meeting subject.

7. Use the Start Time and End Time options to schedule the start and end times for the meeting.

8. Click Scheduling Assistant to view the free/busy data for the invited users and the selected resources. Use the free/busy data to make changes if necessary.

9. After you type a message to accompany the meeting request, click Send.

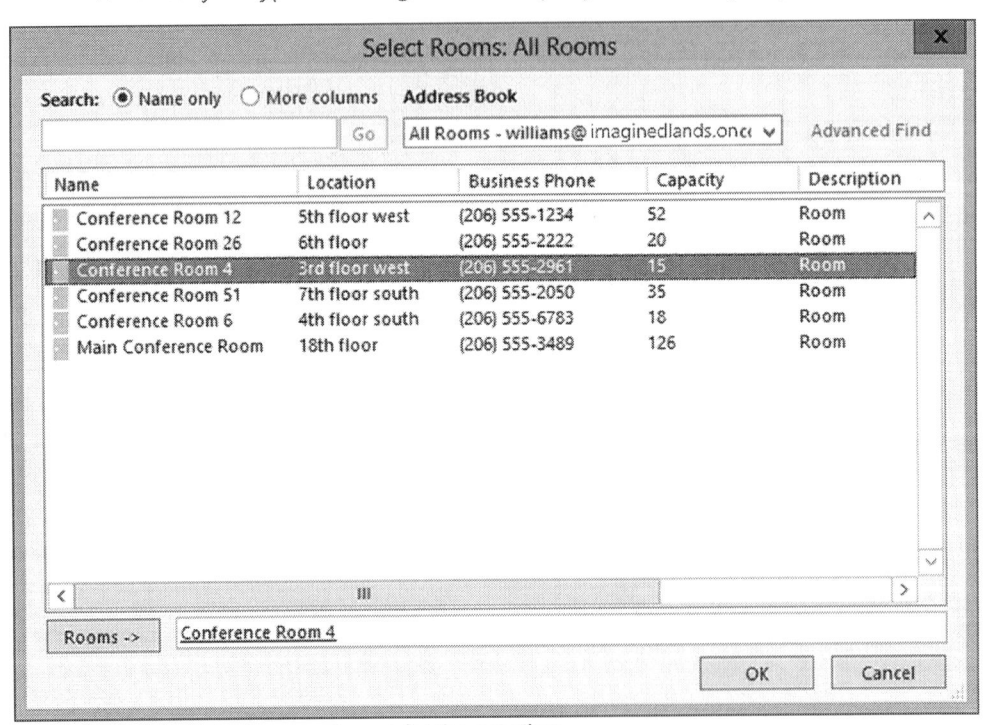

FIGURE 5-3 Select a room to use for the meeting.

Exchange can be configured to accept booking requests automatically, based on availability, or to route requests through delegates, such as office administrators, who review requests. Although small organizations might not need coordinators for rooms and equipment, most large organizations will need coordinators to prevent conflicts. However, Exchange Online does provide additional options that can help to reduce conflicts (see Figure 5-4).

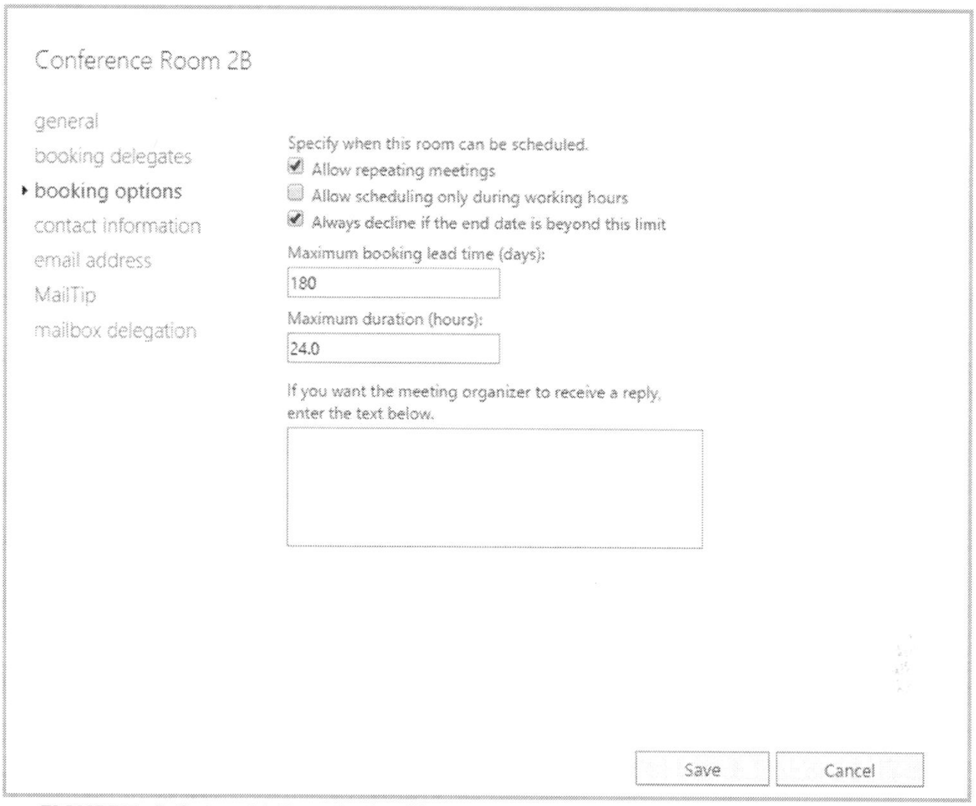

FIGURE 5-4 Set restrictions for booking rooms.

The booking options are the same for both rooms and equipment. The options allow you to:

- Specify whether repeat bookings are allowed. By default, repeat bookings are allowed. If you disable the related settings, users won't be able to schedule repeating meetings.
- Specify whether the room or equipment can be scheduled only during working hours. By default, this option is disabled, which allows rooms and equipment to be scheduled for use at any time. The standard working hours are defined as 8:00 AM to 5:00 PM Monday through Friday but can be changed using the Calendaring options in Outlook.
- Specify the maximum number of days in advance the room or equipment can be booked. By default, rooms and equipment can be booked up to 180 days in advance. You can change the default to any value from 0 to 1080. A value of 0 removes the lead time restriction completely.
- Specify the maximum duration that the room or equipment can be reserved. By default, rooms and equipment can be reserved for up to 24 hours, which allows for preparation and maintenance that may be required. You can change the

default to any value from 0 to 35791394.1. A value of 0 removes the duration restriction completely.

You can configure booking options after you create the room or equipment mailbox. In Exchange Admin Center, navigate to Recipients > Resources and then double-click the resource you want to configure. Next, in the properties dialog box for the resource, select Booking Options. After you change the booking options, click Save to apply the changes.

Adding Room Mailboxes

In Exchange Admin Center, room mailboxes are displayed under Recipients > Resources. In a remote session with Exchange Online, you can find all room mailboxes in the organization by entering:

```
Get-Mailbox -ResultSize unlimited -Filter {(RecipientTypeDetails
-eq 'RoomMailbox')}
```

You can create room mailboxes by completing the following steps:

1. In Exchange Admin Center, select **Recipients** in the Navigation menu and then select **Resources**.

2. Click **New** ( ), and then select **Room Mailbox**. This opens the New Room Mailbox dialog box, shown in Figure 5-5.

3. Type a descriptive display name in the Room Name text box.

4. Enter the Exchange alias in the Email Address text box and then use the drop-down list to select the domain with which the room is to be associated. The Exchange Alias and the domain name are combined to set the fully qualified name, such as room4@imaginedlands.onmicrosoft.com.

5. Specify the room location, phone number and capacity using the text boxes provided.

6. Click Save to create the room mailbox. If an error occurs during account or mailbox creation, neither the account nor the related mailbox will be created. You need to correct the problem before you can complete this procedure.

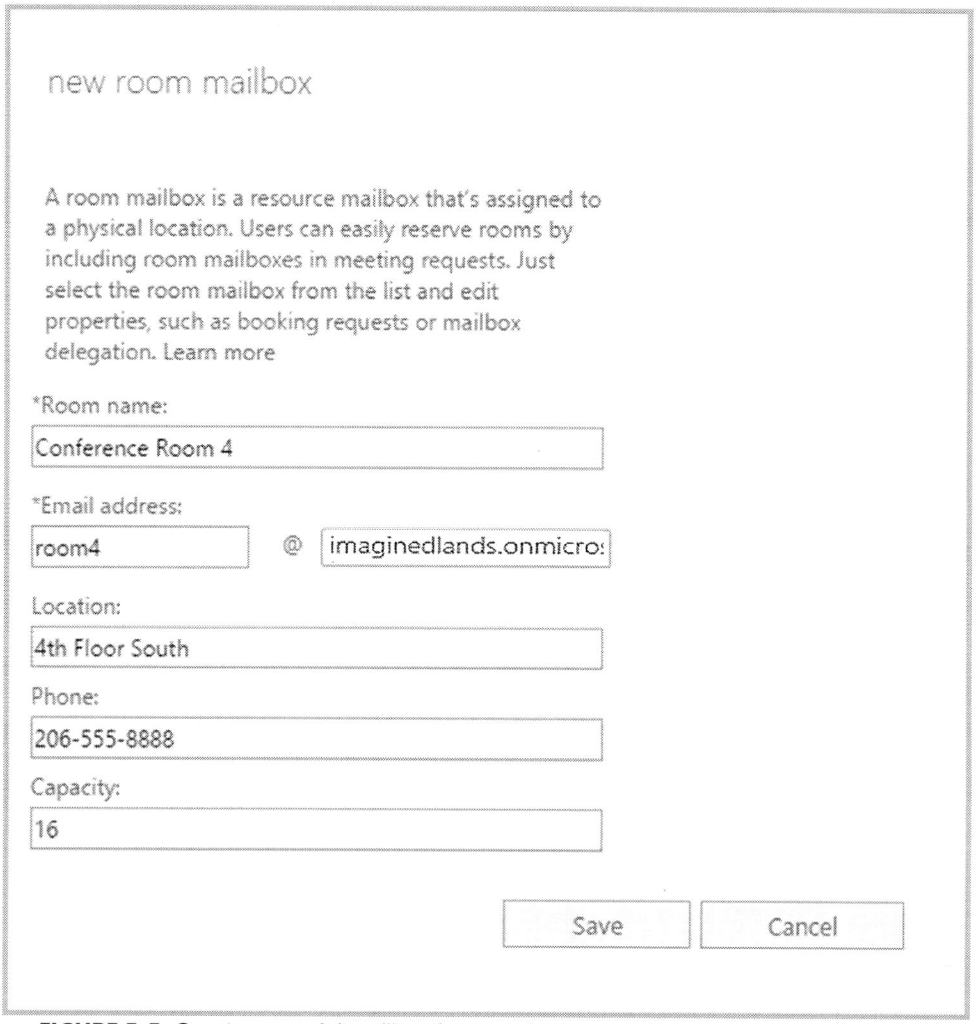

new room mailbox

A room mailbox is a resource mailbox that's assigned to a physical location. Users can easily reserve rooms by including room mailboxes in meeting requests. Just select the room mailbox from the list and edit properties, such as booking requests or mailbox delegation. Learn more

*Room name:

    Conference Room 4

*Email address:

    room4   @   imaginedlands.onmicros

Location:

    4th Floor South

Phone:

    206-555-8888

Capacity:

    16

[Save]   [Cancel]

FIGURE 5-5 Create a special mailbox for a conference room.

By default, booking requests are accepted or declined automatically based on availability. Here, the first person to reserve the room gets the reservation. If your organization has resource coordinators, you can change the booking options by completing the following steps:

1. Double-click the room mailbox with which you want to work.
2. On the Booking Delegates page, choose the Select Delegates option.
3. Next, use the options under Delegates to specify the coordinator. Click the Add button, use the Select Delegates dialog box to select coordinators for the room. Simply double-click to add a name to the list of delegates.

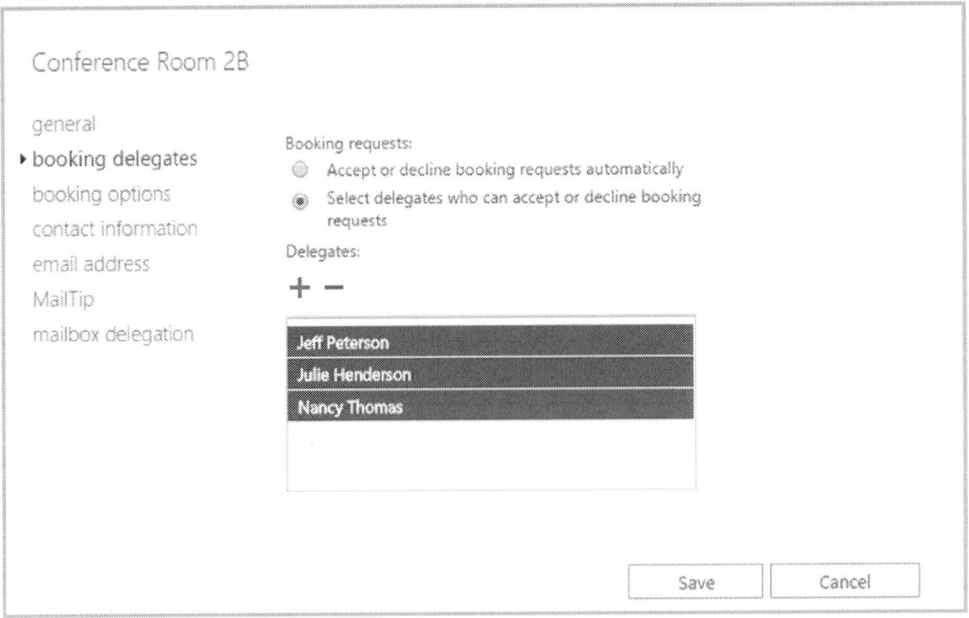

FIGURE 5-6 Add delegates if you don't want booking requests to be handled automatically.

In a remote session with Exchange Online, you can create a user account with a mailbox for rooms by using the New-Mailbox cmdlet. Sample 5-1 provides the syntax and usage.

> **NOTE** For rooms, you must use the –Room parameter. For equipment, you must use the –Equipment parameter. By default, when you use either parameter, the related value is set as $true. Additionally, although with earlier releases of Exchange you needed to set a password for the related user account, this is no longer required.

SAMPLE 5-1 Creating room mailboxes

Syntax

```
New-Mailbox -Name 'DisplayName' -Alias 'ExchangeAlias'
  -UserPrincipalName 'LogonName' -SamAccountName 'prewin2000logon'
  -FirstName '' -Initials '' -LastName ''
  -Room
```

Usage

```
New-Mailbox -Name 'Conference Room 27' -Alias 'room27'
  -UserPrincipalName 'room27@imaginedlands.onmicrosoft.com'
  -SamAccountName 'room27'  -FirstName '' -Initials '' -LastName ''
  -Room
```

Adding Equipment Mailboxes

In Exchange Admin Center, equipment mailboxes are displayed under Recipients > Resources. In a remote session with Exchange Online, you can find all equipment mailboxes in the organization by entering:

```
Get-Mailbox -ResultSize unlimited -Filter {(RecipientTypeDetails -eq 'EquipmentMailbox')}
```

You can create equipment mailboxes by completing the following steps:

1. In Exchange Admin Center, select **Recipients** in the Navigation menu and then select **Resources**.

2. Click **New** (![+]), and then select **Equipment Mailbox**. This opens the New Equipment Mailbox dialog box, shown in Figure 5-7.

new equipment mailbox

An equipment mailbox is a resource mailbox assigned to a resource such as a laptop, projector or company car. Users can easily reserve the equipment by including equipment mailboxes in meeting requests. Just select the equipment mailbox from the list and edit properties, such as booking requests or mailbox delegation. Learn more

*Equipment name:
Projector 5

*Email address:
projector5 @ imaginedlands.onmicro

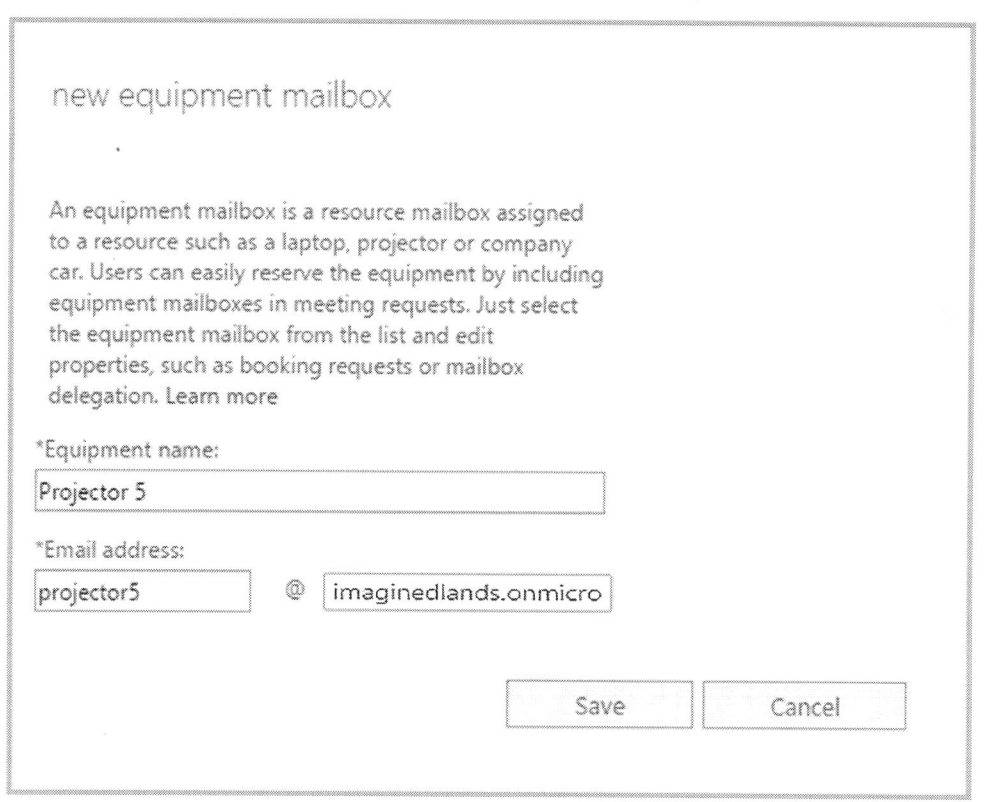

Save   Cancel

FIGURE 5-7 Create a special mailbox for equipment.

3. Type a descriptive display name in the Equipment Name text box.

4. Enter the Exchange alias in the Email Address text box and then use the drop-down list to select the domain with which the room is to be associated. The Exchange Alias and the domain name are combined to set the fully qualified name, such as projector5@imaginedlands.onmicrosoft.com.

5. Click **Save** to create the equipment mailbox. If an error occurs during account or mailbox creation, neither the account nor the related mailbox will be created. You need to correct the problem before you can complete this procedure.

By default, booking requests are accepted or declined automatically based on availability. Here, the first person to reserve the equipment gets the reservation. If your organization has resource coordinators, you can change the booking options by completing the following steps:

1. Double-click the room mailbox with which you want to work.
2. On the Booking Delegates page, choose the Select Delegates option.
3. Next, use the options under Delegates to specify the coordinator. Click the Add button, use the Select Delegates dialog box to select coordinators for the room. Simply double-click to add a name to the list of delegates.

In a remote session with Exchange Online, you can create a user account with a mailbox for equipment by using the New-Mailbox cmdlet. Sample 5-2 provides the syntax and usage. Although with earlier releases of Exchange you needed to set a password for the related user account, this is no longer required.

SAMPLE 5-2 Creating equipment mailboxes

Syntax

```
New-Mailbox -Name 'DisplayName' -Alias 'ExchangeAlias'
 -UserPrincipalName 'LogonName' -SamAccountName 'prewin2000logon'
 -FirstName '' -Initials '' -LastName '' -Equipment
```

Usage

```
New-Mailbox -Name 'Media Cart 3' -Alias 'cart3'
 -UserPrincipalName 'cart3@imaginedlands.onmicrosoft.com'
 -SamAccountName 'cart3' -FirstName '' -Initials '' -LastName ''
 -Equipment
```

Working with Archive Mailboxes

Each user can have an alternate mailbox for archives. An archive mailbox is used to store a user's old messages, such as might be required for executives and needed by some managers and users. In Outlook and Outlook Web App, users can access archive mailboxes in much the same way as they access a regular mailbox.

Adding Archive Mailboxes

Archive mailboxes are created in several ways. The standard approach is to create an in-place archive. You can create an in-place archive mailbox at the same time you create the user's standard mailbox or afterward.

To create an in-place archive mailbox, complete the following steps:

1. In Exchange Admin Center, select Recipients in the Navigation menu and then select Mailboxes. Double-click the entry for the user's standard mailbox. Any user that already has an archive mailbox has "User (Archive)" as the mailbox type.

2. On the Mailbox Features page, the status of archiving is listed under the Archiving heading. If archiving is disabled, select **Enable** under the Archiving heading and continue with this procedure.

3. Click **Save**. If an error occurs during mailbox creation, the archive mailbox will not be created. You need to correct the problem before you can complete this procedure and create the archive mailbox.

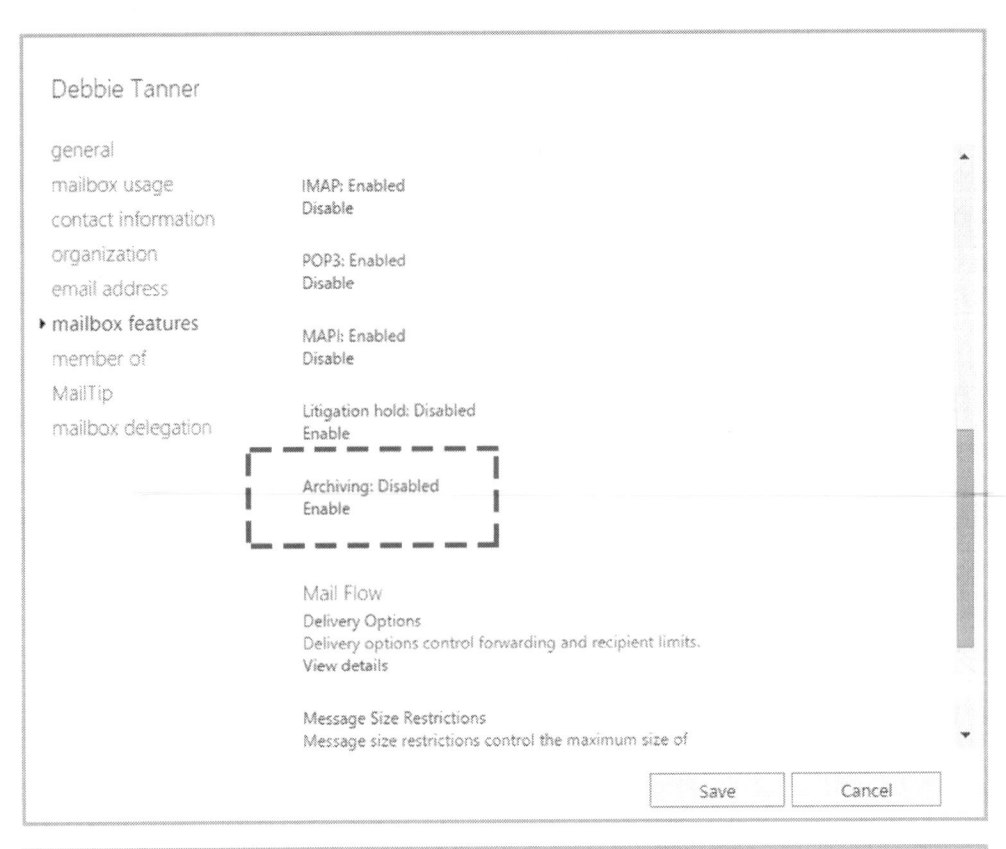

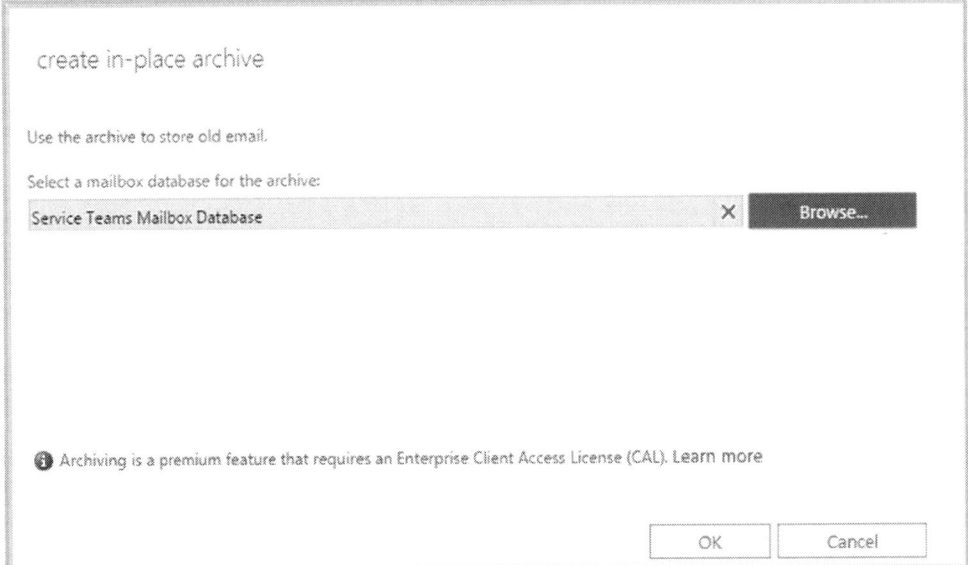

When you are working with Exchange Admin Center, you can enable in-place archiving for multiple mailboxes as well. When you select multiple mailboxes using the Shift or Ctrl keys, the Details pane displays bulk editing options. Scroll down the list of available options and then click **More Options**. Next, under Archive, click **Enable**.

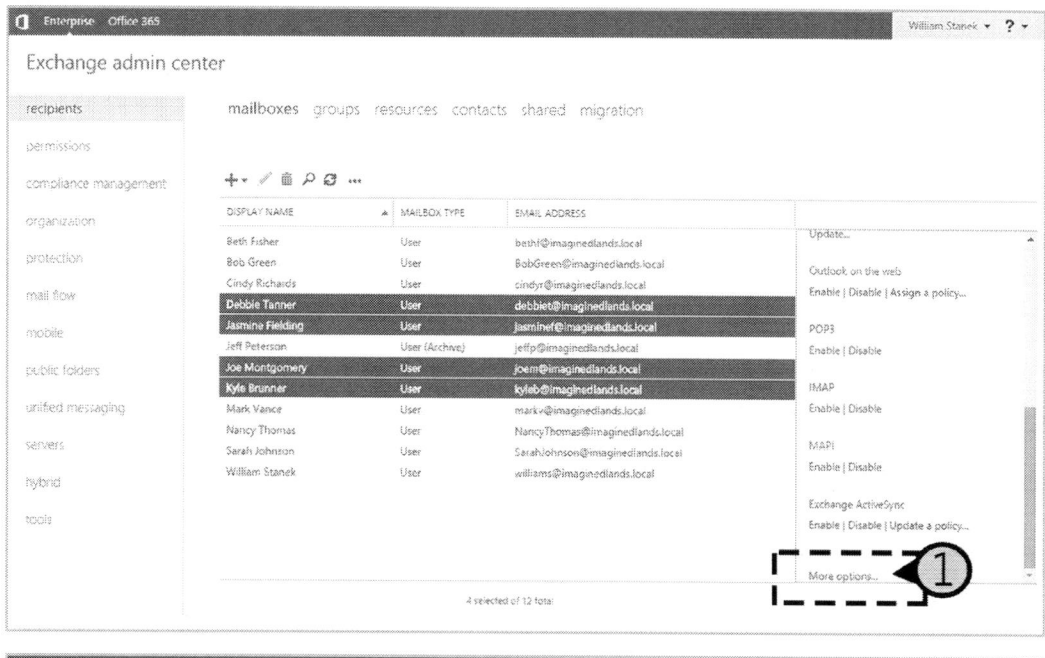

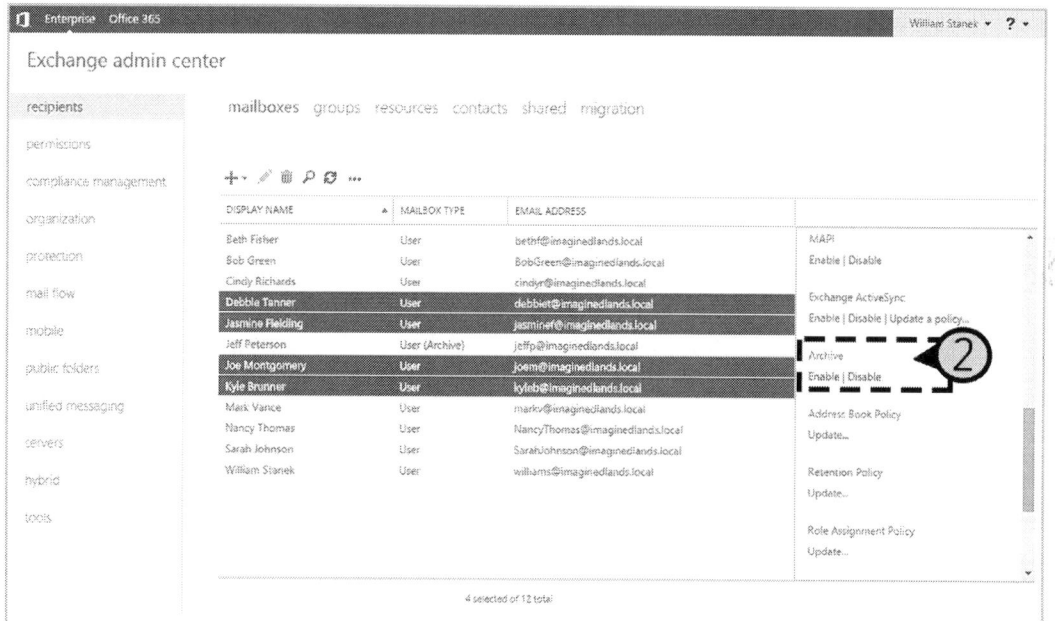

Using a remote session with Exchange Online, you can create an archive mailbox using the Enable-Mailbox cmdlet. The basic syntax is as follows:

```
Enable-Mailbox [-Identity] Identity –Archive
```

such as:

```
Enable-Mailbox imaginedlands.onmicrosoft.com/tonyg –archive
```

Because each user can have only one archive mailbox, you get an error if the user already has an archive mailbox. Items in the user's mailbox will be moved automatically to the archive mailbox based on the archive and retention policy. When you set up the Exchange organization, a default archive and retention policy is created for all archive mailboxes. This policy is named Default MRM Policy. Because of this policy, email messages from the entire mailbox are moved to the archive after two years by default.

For bulk editing, you can use various techniques. Generally, you'll want to:

- Ensure you are working with mailboxes for regular users and not mailboxes for rooms, equipment, and so on. To do this, filter the results based on the RecipientTypeDetails.
- Ensure the mailbox doesn't already have an archive. To do this, filter the results based on whether the mailbox has an associated ArchiveGuid.
- Ensure you don't enable archives on mailboxes that shouldn't have them, such as the Discovery Search Mailbox. To do this, filter based on the name or partial name of mailboxes to exclude.

Consider the following example:

```
Get-Mailbox –Filter {RecipientTypeDetails –eq 'UserMailbox'
–AND ArchiveGuid –eq $null –AND Name –NotLike
"DiscoverySearchMailbox*"} | Enable-Mailbox –Archive
```

In this example, Get-Mailbox retrieves all mailboxes for regular users that don't have in-place or online archiving enabled and that also don't have a name starting with: DiscoverySearchMailbox. The results are then piped through Enable-Mailbox to add an archive mailbox to these mailboxes.

Managing Archive Settings

Whether you use Exchange Admin Center or a remote session with Exchange Online, several other parameters are set for archive mailboxes. The default name for the archive mailbox is set as In-Place Archive – *UserDisplayName,* such as In-Place Archive – Henrik Larsen. With Exchange Online, the default quota and warning quota are set as 25 GB and 22.5 GB, respectively.

You can confirm the details for a user's archive mailbox by entering the following command:

Get-Mailbox "**Name**" | fl name, alias, servername, *archive*

where *name* is the display name or alias of the user you want to work with, such as:

Get-Mailbox "Henrik Larsen" | fl name, alias, servername, *archive*

You can change the archive name and set quotas by using Set-Mailbox. The basic syntax is as follows:

Set-Mailbox [-Identity] **Identity**
-ArchiveName **Name** -ArchiveQuota **Quota** -ArchiveWarningQuota **Quota**

When you set a quota, specify the value with MB (for megabytes), GB (for gigabytes), or TB (for terabytes), or enter 'Unlimited' to remove the quota. Here is an example:

set-mailbox imaginedlands.onmicrosoft.com/tonyg
-ArchiveQuota '28GB' -ArchiveWarningQuota '27GB'

For bulk editing, you can use Get-Mailbox to retrieve the user mailboxes you want to work with and then apply the changes by piping the results to Set-Mailbox. If you do so, ensure that you filter the results appropriately. Consider the following example:

Get-Mailbox -ResultSize unlimited -Filter {RecipientTypeDetails -eq 'UserMailbox' -AND ArchiveGuid -ne $null} | Set-Mailbox -ArchiveQuota '20GB' -ArchiveWarningQuota '18GB'

In this example, Get-Mailbox retrieves all mailboxes for regular users in the entire organization that have archiving enabled. The results are then piped through Set-Mailbox to modify the quota and quota warning values.

In Exchange Admin Center, you manage archive settings by completing these steps:

1. In Exchange Admin Center, select Recipients in the Navigation menu and then select Mailboxes. Double-click the entry for the user's standard mailbox. Any user that already has an archive mailbox has "User (Archive)" as the mailbox type.

2. On the Mailbox Features page, click View Details under the Archiving heading.

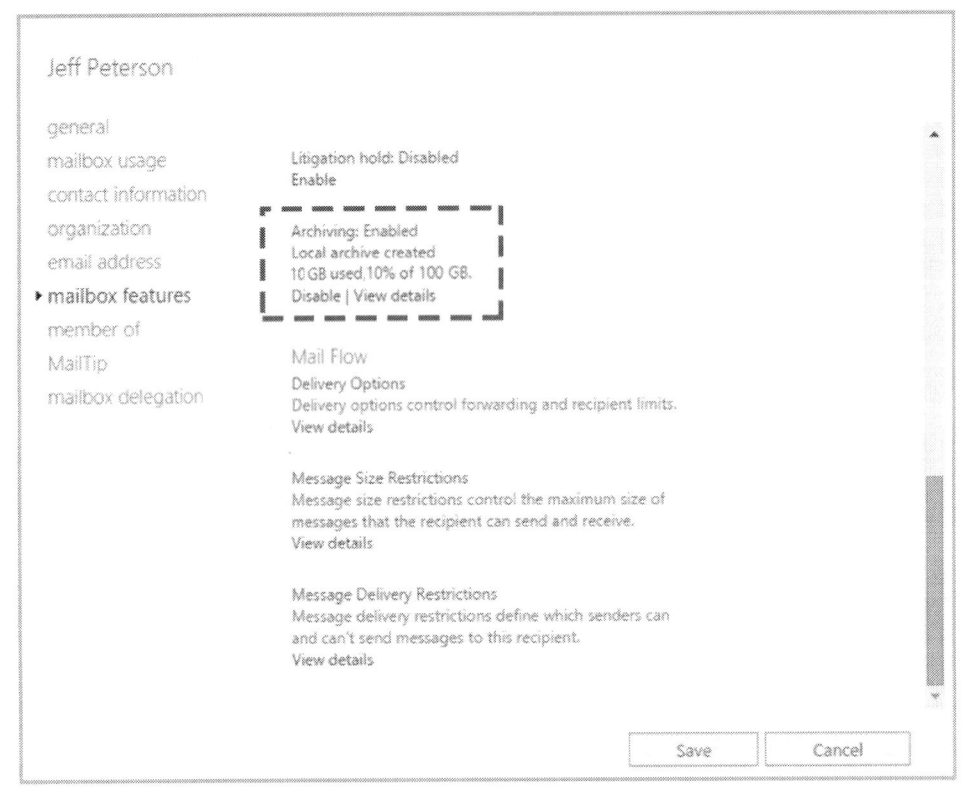

3. To change the name of the archive mailbox, enter the new name in the Name text box.

4. To set a quota, enter the desired value in gigabytes in the Archive Quota combo box.

5. To set a quota warning, enter a quota warning in gigabytes in the Issue Warning At combo box.

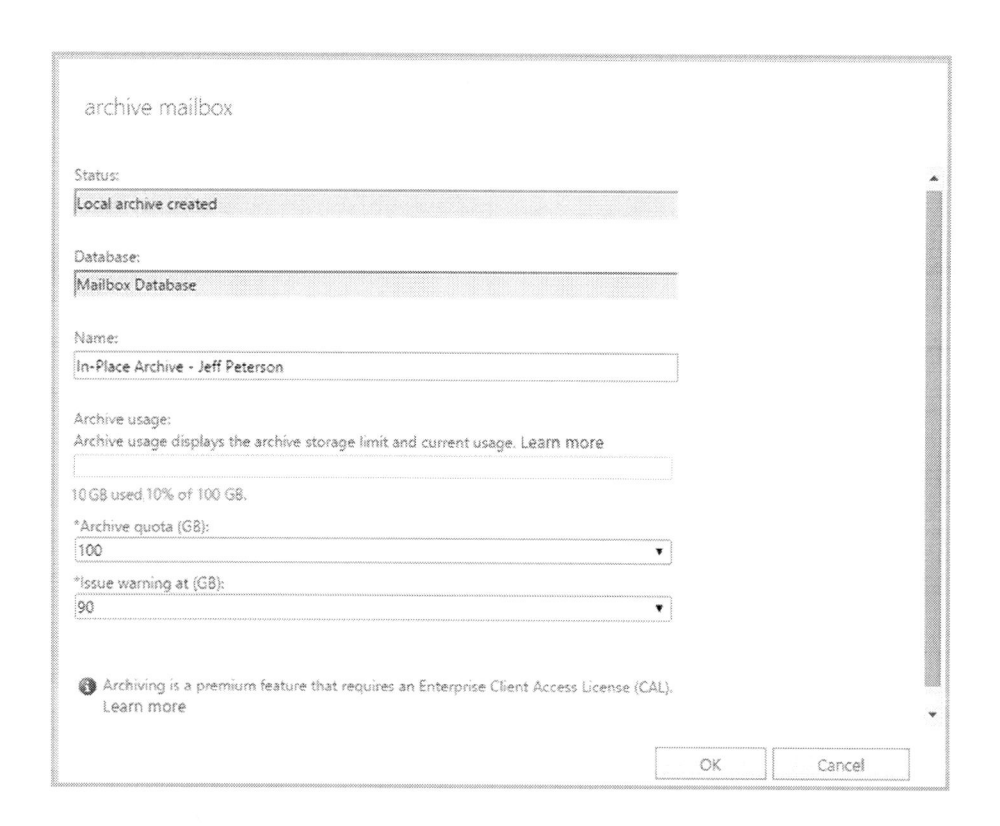

```
archive mailbox

Status:
Local archive created

Database:
Mailbox Database

Name:
In-Place Archive - Jeff Peterson

Archive usage:
Archive usage displays the archive storage limit and current usage. Learn more

10 GB used 10% of 100 GB.
*Archive quota (GB):
100
*Issue warning at (GB):
90

  Archiving is a premium feature that requires an Enterprise Client Access License (CAL).
  Learn more

                                                OK       Cancel
```

To disable an archive mailbox, open the properties dialog box for the user to the Mailbox Features page and then select **Disable** under the Archiving heading. Click **Yes** when prompted to confirm.

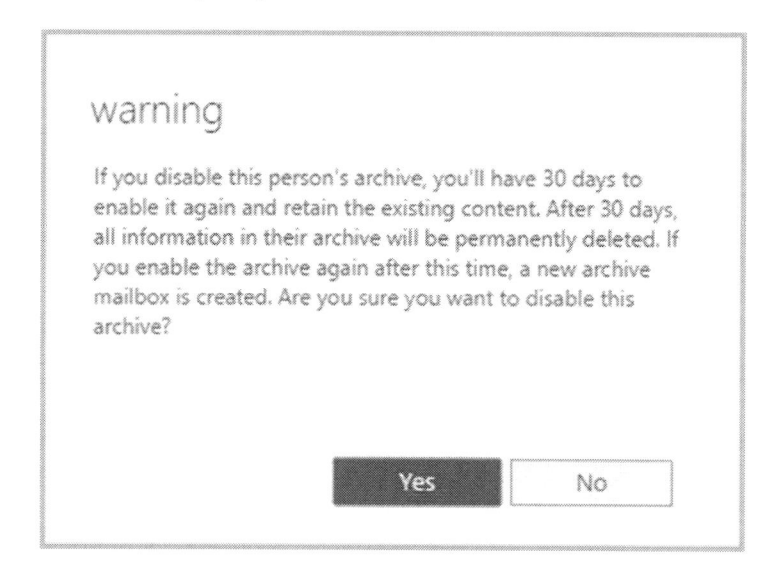

```
warning

If you disable this person's archive, you'll have 30 days to
enable it again and retain the existing content. After 30 days,
all information in their archive will be permanently deleted. If
you enable the archive again after this time, a new archive
mailbox is created. Are you sure you want to disable this
archive?

                            Yes          No
```

REAL WORLD When you disable an archive mailbox for a user, the archive mailbox is marked for deletion and disconnected from the user account. The archive mailbox is retained according to the mailbox retention policy. To connect the disabled archive mailbox to the existing mailbox, you must use the Connect-Mailbox cmdlet with the -Archive parameter. Otherwise, if you disable an archive mailbox for a user mailbox and then enable an archive mailbox for that same user, a new archive mailbox is created for the user.

When you are working with Exchange Admin Center, you can disable in-place archiving for multiple mailboxes as well. When you select multiple mailboxes using the Shift or Ctrl keys, the Details pane displays bulk editing options. Scroll down the list of available options and then click **More Options**. Next, under Archive, click **Disable**. When the Bulk Disable Archive dialog box is displayed, click **OK**.

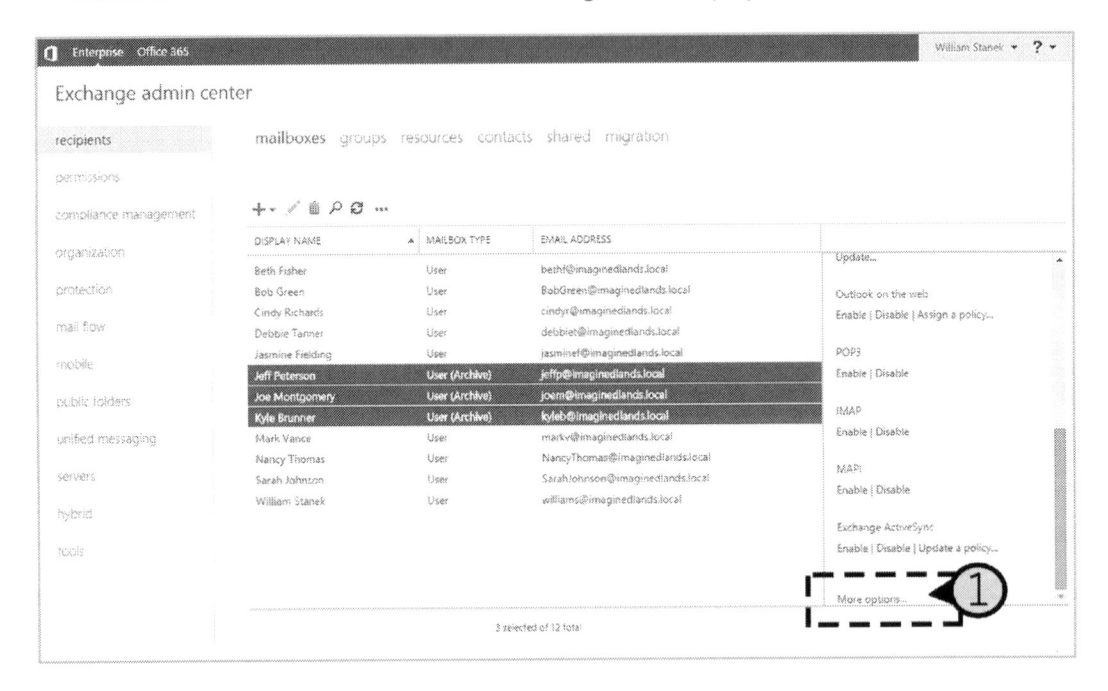

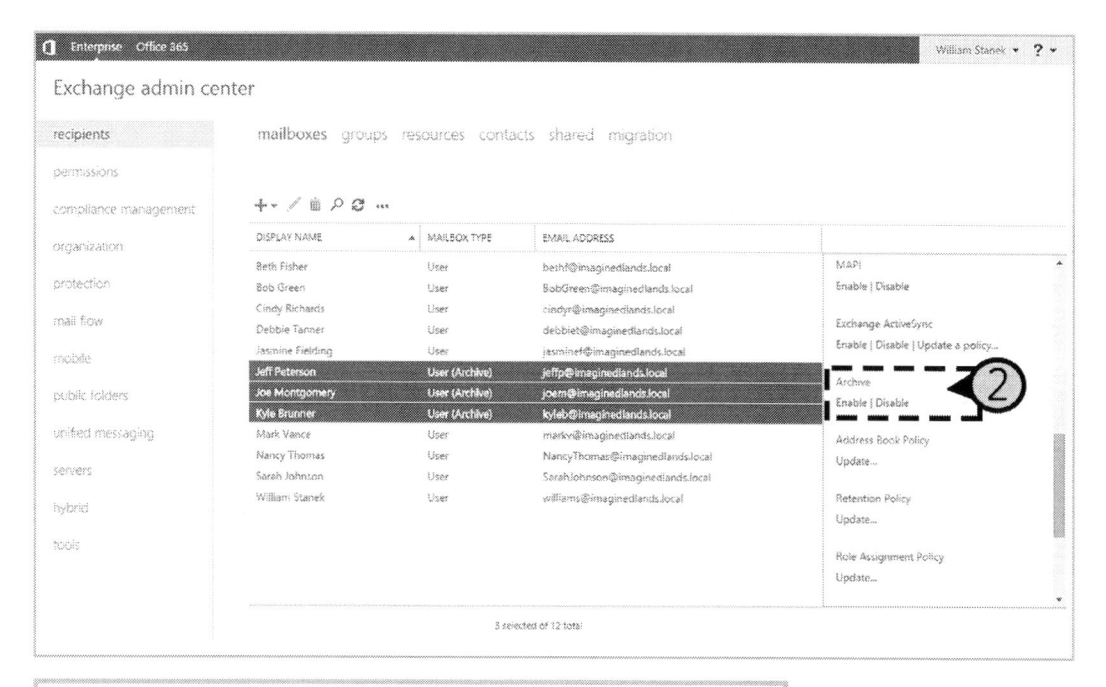

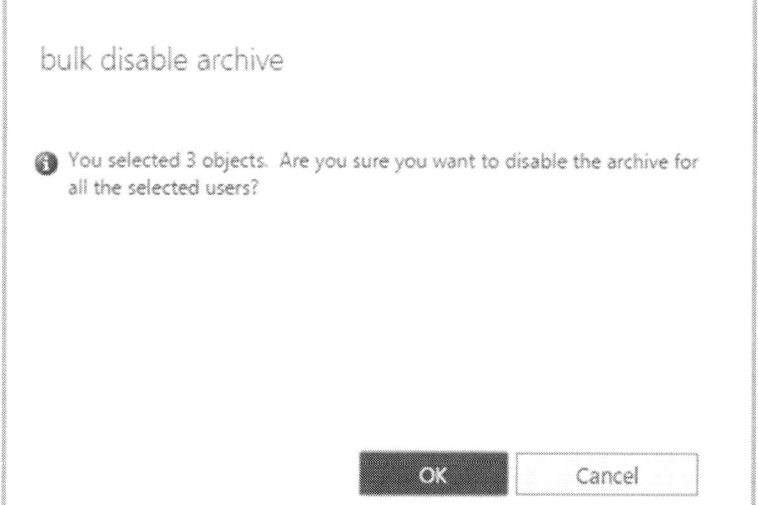

In a remote session with Exchange Online, you can disable an archive mailbox by using Disable-Mailbox. The basic syntax is as follows:

Disable-Mailbox [-Identity] **Identity** -Archive

such as:

disable-mailbox imaginedlands.onmicrosoft.com/tonyg -archive

For bulk editing, you can use a technique similar to the one discussed for enabling archives. Consider the following example:

```
Get-Mailbox -Filter {RecipientTypeDetails -eq 'UserMailbox'
-AND ArchiveGuid -ne $null} | Disable-Mailbox -Archive
```

In this example, Get-Mailbox retrieves all mailboxes for regular users that have archiving enabled. The results are then piped through Disable-Mailbox to remove the archive mailbox from these mailboxes.

Adding Arbitration Mailboxes

Exchange moderated transport requires all email messages sent to specific recipients to be approved by moderators. You can configure any type of recipient as a moderated recipient, and Exchange will ensure that all messages sent to those recipients go through an approval process.

Distribution groups are the only types of recipients that use moderation by default. Membership in distribution groups can be closed, owner approved, or open. While any Exchange recipient can join or leave an open distribution group, joining or leaving a closed group requires approval. Group owners receive join and remove requests and can either approve or deny those requests.

Distribution groups can also be unmoderated or moderated. With unmoderated groups, any approved sender (which is all senders by default) can send messages to the group. With moderated groups, messages are sent to moderators for approval before being distributed to members of the group. The only exception is for a message sent by a moderator. A message from a moderator is delivered immediately because a moderator has the authority to determine what is and isn't an appropriate message.

> **NOTE** The default moderator for a distribution group is the group's owner.

Arbitration mailboxes are used to store messages that are awaiting approval. A default arbitration mailbox is created automatically. For the purposes of load balancing or for other reasons, you can convert other mailboxes to the arbitration mailbox type by using the Enable-Mailbox cmdlet. The basic syntax is as follows:

```
Enable-Mailbox [-Identity] Identity -Arbitration
```

such as:

```
enable-mailbox imaginedlands.onmicrosoft.com/moderatedmail -Arbitration
```

You can create an arbitration mailbox by using New-Mailbox as shown in this example:

```
New-Mailbox ModeratedMail -Arbitration -UserPrincipalName
ModeratedMail@imaginedlands.onmicrosoft.com
```

Adding Discovery Mailboxes

Exchange Discovery helps organizations comply with legal discovery requirements and can also be used as an aid in internal investigations or as part of regular monitoring of email content. Exchange Discovery uses content indexes created by Exchange Search to speed up the search process.

> **NOTE** By default, Exchange administrators do not have sufficient rights to perform Discovery searches. Only users with the Discovery Management role can perform Discovery searches. If a user is not a member of the role, she doesn't have access to the related options. This means she can't access the In-Place eDiscovery & Hold interface in Exchange Admin Center or the In-Place eDiscovery & Hold cmdlets in PowerShell.

When you are working in an online organization, you use Exchange Admin Center to perform searches. Discovery searches are performed against designated mailboxes or all mailboxes in the Exchange organization. Items in mailboxes that match the Discovery search are copied to a target mailbox.

> **TIP** By default, Discovery search does not include items that cannot be indexed by Exchange Search. To include such items in the search results, select the Include Items That Can't Be Searched check box in Exchange Admin Center.

Only mailboxes specifically designated as Discovery mailboxes can be used as targets. In Exchange Admin Center, you can access the discovery and hold settings by selecting Compliance Management in the Navigation menu and then selecting In-Place eDiscovery & Hold. While working with In-Place eDiscovery & Hold, you can create searches across mailboxes by specifying filters and hold options for search results.

A default Discovery mailbox is created automatically. You can convert other mailboxes to the Discovery mailbox type by using the Enable-Mailbox cmdlet. The basic syntax is as follows:

Enable-Mailbox [-Identity] **Identity** -Discovery

such as:

enable-mailbox imaginedlands.onmicrosoft.com/legalsearch -discovery

You can create a Discovery mailbox by using New-Mailbox as shown in this example:

New-Mailbox LegalSearch -Discovery -UserPrincipalName LegalSearch@imaginedlands.onmicrosoft.com

Once a Discovery mailbox is established, you can't convert it to another mailbox type. You can't use Exchange Admin Center to create Discovery mailboxes.

Adding Shared Mailboxes

Shared mailboxes are mailboxes that are shared by multiple users. Although shared mailboxes must have an associated user account, this account is not used for logon and is disabled by default. Users who access the shared mailbox do so using access permissions.

You can create a shared mailbox by using New-Mailbox, as shown in this example:

New-Mailbox -Shared -Name "Customer Service" -DisplayName "Customer Service" -Alias Service -UserPrincipalName customerservice@imaginedlands.onmicrosoft.com

In this example, a user account named CustomerService is created for this mailbox. This user account is disabled by default to prevent logon using this account. After creating the mailbox, you need to grant Send On Behalf Of permission to the appropriate users or security groups by using Set-Mailbox and the -GrantSendOnBehalfTo parameter. Finally, you need to add access rights that allow these users or security groups to log on to the mailbox by using Add-MailboxPermission and the -AccessRights parameter. Ensure these rights are inherited at all levels of the mailbox using -InheritanceType All as well. One way this would all come together is shown in the following example:

```
New-Mailbox -Shared -Name "Customer Service" -DisplayName
"Customer Service" -Alias Service -UserPrincipalName
customerservice@imaginedlands.onmicrosoft.com | Set-Mailbox -
GrantSendOnBehalfTo
CustomerServiceGroup | Add-MailboxPermission -User CustomerServiceGroup
-AccessRights FullAccess -InheritanceType All
```

In Exchange Admin Center, you can create a shared mailbox by following these steps:

1. Select **Recipients** in the Navigation menu and then select **Shared**.
2. Click **New** (＋). This opens the New Shared Mailbox dialog box, shown in Figure 5-8.
3. In the Display Name text box, type a descriptive name for the shared mailbox.
4. Enter the Exchange alias in the Email Address text box and then use the drop-down list to select the domain with which the room is to be associated. The Exchange Alias and the domain name are combined to set the fully qualified name, such as service@imaginedlands.onmicrosoft.com.

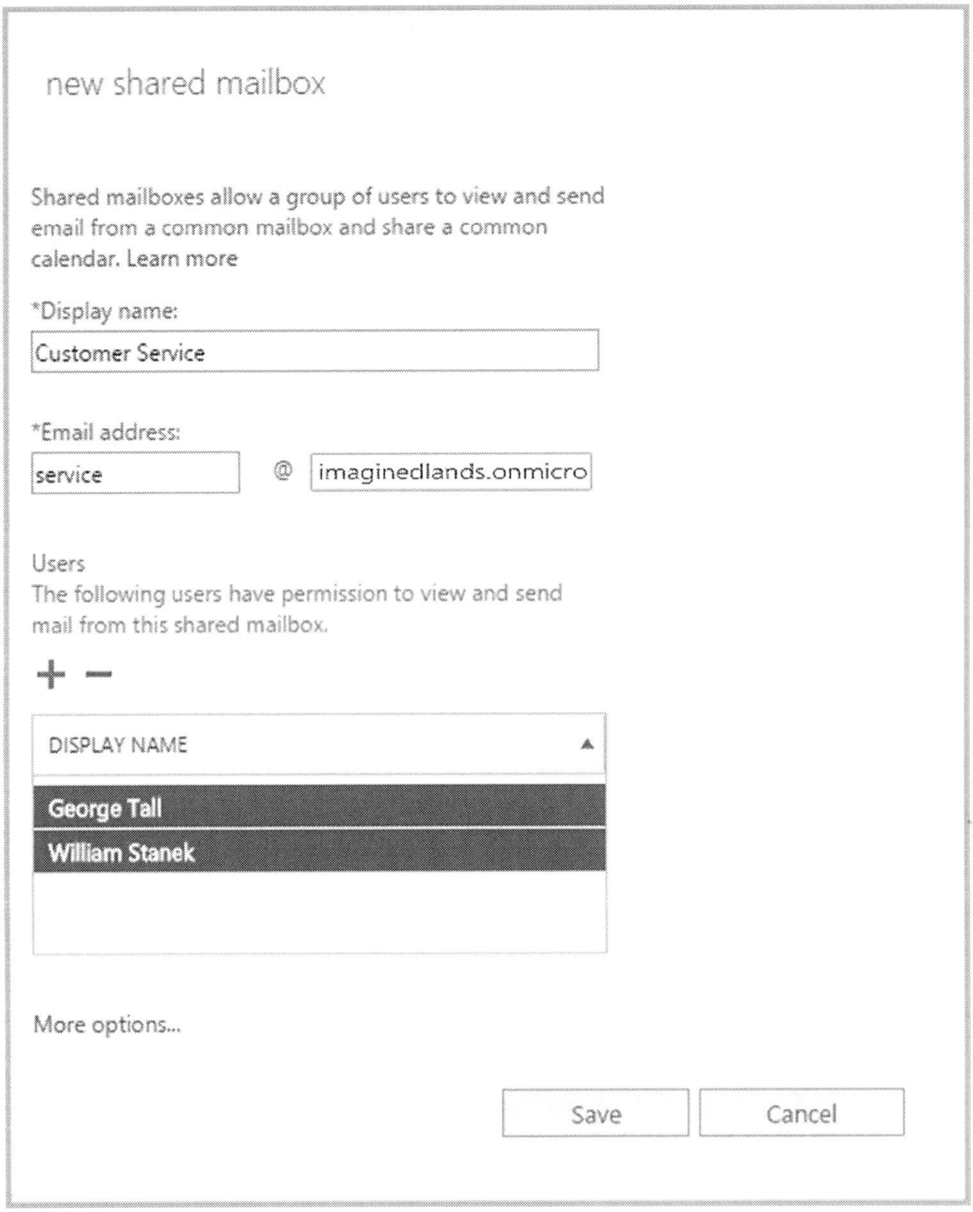

>
> ### new shared mailbox
>
> Shared mailboxes allow a group of users to view and send email from a common mailbox and share a common calendar. Learn more
>
> *Display name:
>
> [Customer Service]
>
> *Email address:
>
> [service] @ [imaginedlands.onmicro]
>
> Users
> The following users have permission to view and send mail from this shared mailbox.
>
> ➕ ➖
>
> | DISPLAY NAME ▲ |
> |---|
> | **George Tall** |
> | **William Stanek** |
>
> More options...
>
> [Save] [Cancel]

FIGURE 5-8 Create a mailbox to share with multiple users.

5. Under Users, click Add (➕). In the Select Full Access dialog box, select users, security groups, or both that should be able to view and send email from the shared mailbox. Select multiple users and groups using the Shift or Ctrl keys.

6. Click **More Options.** As appropriate use the Alias text box to set the Exchange alias and override the default value you set previously using the

Email Address text box. This allows a resource to have an alias that is different from the name portion of its email address.

7. Click **Save** to create the shared mailbox. If an error occurs during account or mailbox creation, neither the account nor the related mailbox will be created. You need to correct the problem before you can complete this procedure.

Adding Public Folder Mailboxes

Public folders are used to share messages and files in an organization. Public folder trees define the structure of an organization's public folders. You can make the default public folder tree accessible to users based on criteria you set, and then users can create folders and manage their content.

Each public folder in the default public folder tree can have specific access permissions. For example, you can create public folders called CompanyWide, Marketing, and Engineering. Whereas you would typically make the CompanyWide folder accessible to all users, you would make the Marketing folder accessible only to users in the marketing department and the Engineering folder accessible only to users in the engineering department.

Users access public folders from Outlook clients, including Outlook Web App and Outlook 2010 or later. With Outlook Web App and Outlook 2010 or later, users can add and remove favorite public folders and perform item-level operations, such as creating and managing posts. However, users can create or delete public folders only from Outlook 2010 or later.

Exchange Online stores public folder data in mailboxes. In Exchange Admin Center, you work with public folders by selecting Public Folders in the Navigation menu and then selecting either Public Folder Mailboxes or Public Folders as appropriate. You use the options under Public Folder Mailboxes to create and manage the mailboxes that store public folder data. You use the options under Public Folders to view and manage the public folder hierarchy.

An Exchange organization can have one or more public folder mailboxes and those mailboxes can be created on one or more Mailbox servers throughout the organization. While each public folder mailbox can contain public folder content, only the first public folder mailbox created in an Exchange organization contains the writable copy of the public folder hierarchy. This mailbox is referred to as the hierarchy mailbox. Any additional public folder mailboxes contain read-only copies of the public-folder hierarchy.

Because there's only one writeable copy of the public folder hierarchy, proxying is used to relay folder changes to the hierarchy mailbox. This means that any time users working with folders in an additional mailbox create new subfolders, the folder creation, modification, or removal is proxied to the hierarchy mailbox by the content mailbox users are connected to.

In Exchange Admin Center, you can create a public folder mailbox by following these steps:

1. Select **Public Folders** in the Navigation menu and then select **Public Folder Mailboxes**.

2. Click **New** (✚). This opens the New Public Folder Mailbox dialog box, shown in Figure 5-9.

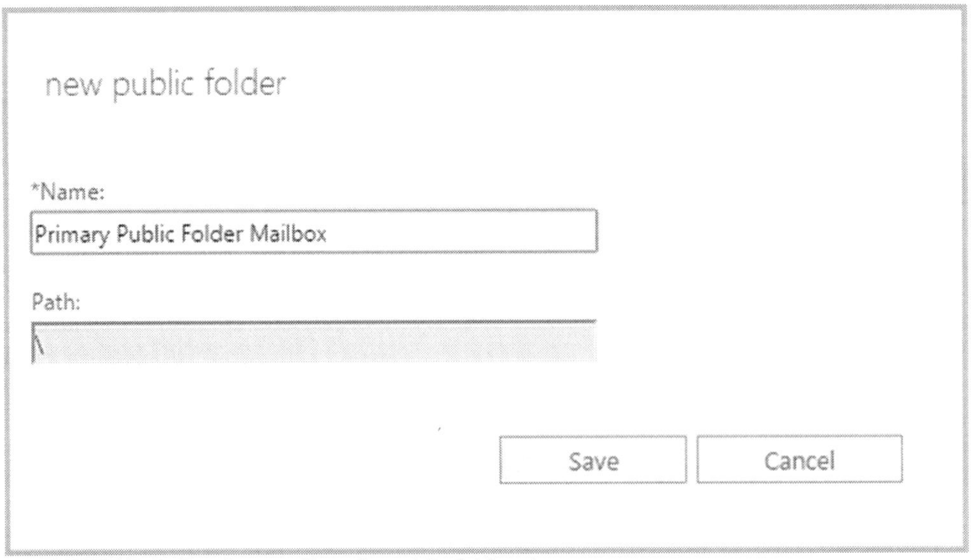

FIGURE 5-9 Create a mailbox for public folder storage.

3. Type a descriptive name for the mailbox.
4. Click **Save** to create the public folder mailbox. If an error occurs during account or mailbox creation, neither the account nor the related mailbox will be created. You need to correct the problem before you can complete this procedure.

Public folder content can include email messages, documents, and more. The content is stored in the public folder mailbox but isn't replicated across multiple public folder mailboxes. Instead, all users access the same public folder mailbox for the same set of content.

When you create the first public folder in the organization, you establish the root of the public folder hierarchy. You can then create subfolders and assign access permissions on folders. In Exchange Admin Center, select Public Folders > Public Folders and then use the available options to create subfolders and set permissions on those folders.

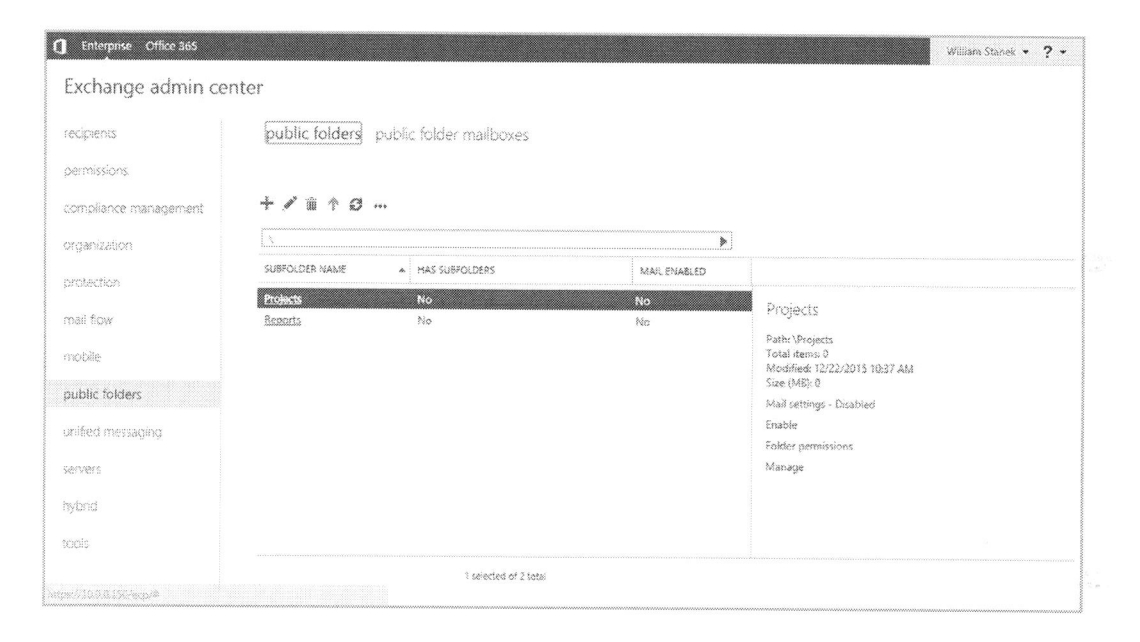

When you create public folder mailboxes, they inherit the default quota limits of Exchange Online. You can modify the quota limits using the properties dialog for the mailbox. Double-click the mailbox entry. In the Public Folder Mailbox dialog box, on the Mailbox Usage page, click More Options and then select Customize The Settings For This Mailbox. Next, use the selection lists provided to specify when warnings are issued, what posts are prohibited, and the maximum size of items. Apply the changes by clicking Save.

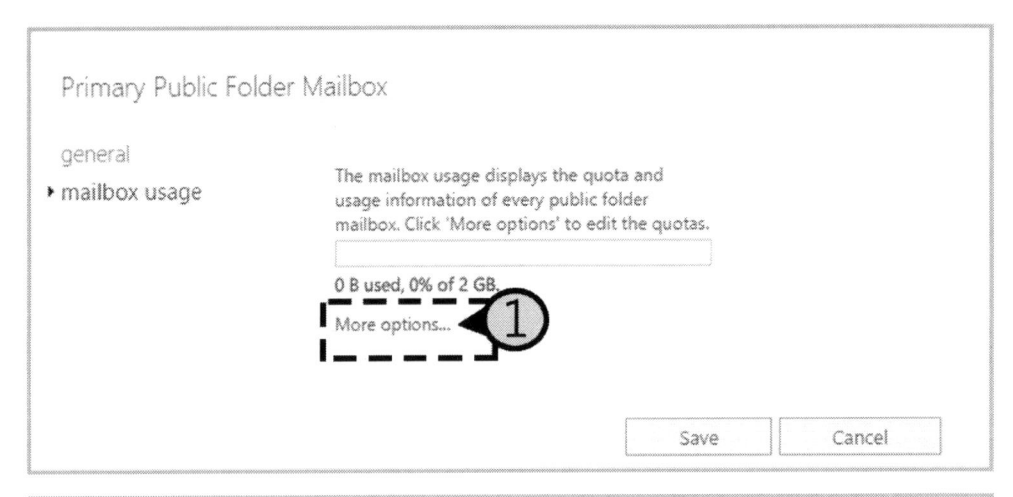

Primary Public Folder Mailbox

general

▸ mailbox usage

The mailbox usage displays the quota and usage information of every public folder mailbox. Click 'More options' to edit the quotas.

0 B used, 0% of 2 GB.

More options... ①

Save   Cancel

Primary Public Folder Mailbox

general

▸ mailbox usage

○ Use the default quota settings from the mailbox database

◉ Customize the quota settings for this mailbox ②

*Issue a warning at (GB):
210

*Prohibit post at (GB):
250

*Maximum item size (GB):
unlimited

Save   Cancel

When users are connected to public folder mailboxes and make routine changes to an Exchange store hierarchy or content, the changes are synchronized every 15 minutes using Incremental Change Synchronization (ICS). Immediate syncing is used for non-routine changes, such as folder creation. If no users are connected to public folder mailboxes, synchronization occurs once every 24 hours by default.

Chapter 6. Managing Mailboxes

The difference between a good Exchange administrator and a great one is the attention he or she pays to mailbox administration. Mailboxes are private storage places for messages you've sent and received, and they are created as part of private storage in Exchange Online. Mailbox settings control mail delivery, permissions, and storage limits. Although you can configure some mailbox settings on a per-mailbox basis, most settings are configured for all users of the service while other settings are fixed as part of the service and cannot be changed.

Managing Mailboxes: The Essentials

You often need to manage user mailboxes the way you do user accounts. Some of the management tasks are intuitive and others aren't. If you have questions, be sure to read the sections that follow.

You can use bulk editing techniques to work with multiple user mailboxes at the same time. To select multiple user mailboxes not in sequence, hold down the Ctrl key and then click the left mouse button on each user mailbox you want to select. To select a series of user mailboxes, select the first mailbox, hold down the Shift key, and then click the last mailbox.

The actions you can perform on multiple resources depend on the types of recipients you've selected. The actions you can perform on multiple user mailboxes include:

- Updating contact information, organization information, or custom attributes
- Viewing mailbox quotas or deleted item retention settings
- Enabling or disabling Outlook Web App, POP3, IMAP, MAPI, or ActiveSync
- Managing policy for Outlook Web App, ActiveSync, Address Books, Retention, Role Assignment, or Sharing
- Enabling or disabling mailbox archives

Although you cannot bulk edit room or equipment mailboxes, you can perform these actions on shared mailboxes.

Viewing Current Mailbox Size, Message Count, and Last Logon

You can use Exchange Admin Center to view the last logon date and time, the mailbox size, and how much of the total mailbox quota has been used by completing these steps:

1. Select **Recipients** in the Navigation menu and then select **Mailboxes**.
2. Double-click the mailbox with which you want to work.
3. On the Mailbox Usage page, review the Last Logon text box to see the last logon date and time (see Figure 6-1). If a user hasn't logged on to her mailbox, you can't get mailbox statistics and will get an error when you view this page.
4. Under the last logon time, notice the mailbox usage statistics, depicted in a bar graph and numerically as a percentage of the total mailbox quota that has been used.

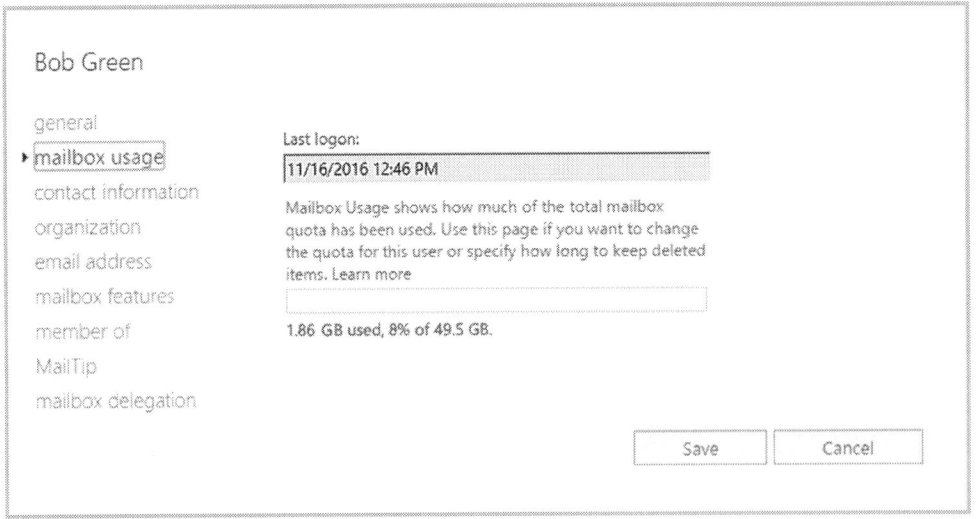

FIGURE 6-1 View mailbox statistics.

Configuring Apps for Mailboxes

Exchange Online allows you to add apps to the Outlook Web App interface to add functionality. Several apps are installed and made available to users by default, including the following apps created by Microsoft:

- **Action Items**   Makes action item suggestions based on message content
- **Bing Maps**   Allows users to map addresses found in their messages

- **My Templates** Allows users to save text and images to insert into messages.
- **Suggested Meetings** Shows meeting suggestions found in messages and allows users to add the meetings to their calendars.
- **Unsubscribe** Allows users to easily block or unsubscribe from email subscription feeds.

Other apps can be added from the Office Store, from a URL, or from a file. All of these apps have various levels of read, read/write, or other permissions on user mailboxes. Because apps also may send data to a third-party service, you may want to consider carefully whether apps should be enabled in your organization. Where strict, high security is a requirement, my recommendation is to disable all apps.

In Exchange Admin Center, you manage apps as part of the organization configuration. Select Organization in the Navigation menu and then select Apps. As shown in Figure 6-2, you'll then see the installed apps and their status. To work with Apps for Outlook, you must have View-Only Organization Management, Help Desk or Organization Management permissions.

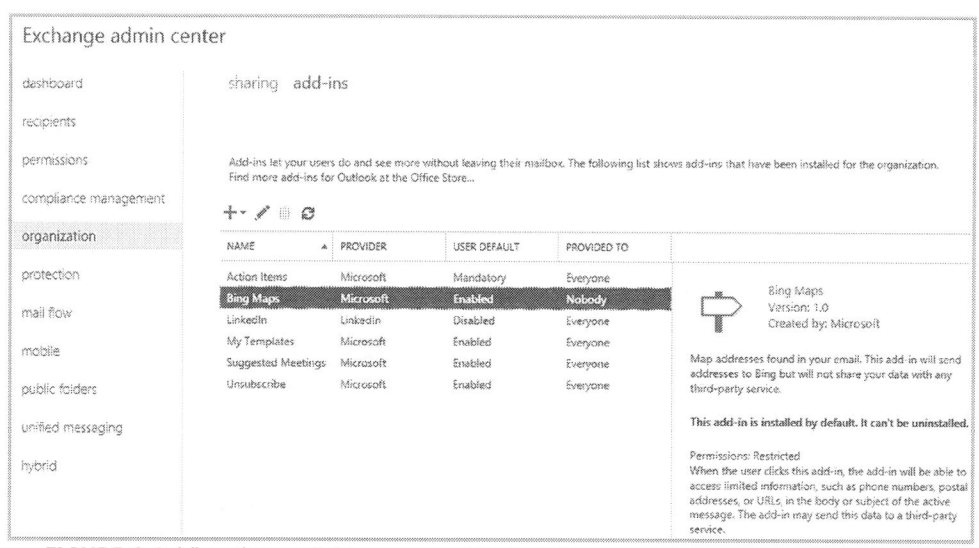

FIGURE 6-2 View the available apps and their status.

To add an app, do one of the following:

- To add an app from the Office store, click New ( ), select **Add From The Office Store** to open a new browser window to the Office store, and then select an app to add. When you select the app's Add option, review the app details and then click Add. When prompted to confirm, select Yes.

- If you know the URL of the manifest file for the app you want to add, click New and then select Add From URL. In the Add From URL dialog box, enter the URL and then click Install. Be sure to use the full path.
- If you've copied the manifest file to a local server, click New and then select Add From File. In the Add From File dialog box, select Browse. In the Choose File To Upload dialog box, locate and select the manifest file and then select Open. Manifest files end with the .xml extension.

All apps have two status values:

- **User Default**   Reflects whether the app is disabled by default, enabled by default, or enabled and mandatory.
- **Provided To**   Reflects whether the app is available to all users in the organization (everyone) or to no users in the organization (nobody).

The default apps are made available to all users and enabled by default. This is reflected in the status of Enabled for User Default and Everyone for Provided To by default.

When you install a new app, the app is made available to all users but disabled by default. This is reflected in the status of Disabled for User Default and Everyone for Provided To.

If you have appropriate permissions, you can manage app status by clicking the app and then clicking Edit. In the Action Items dialog box, shown in Figure 6-3, do one of the following:

- If you don't want the app to be available to users, clear the Make This App Available checkbox and then click Save.
- If you want the app to be available to users, select the Make This App Available checkbox and then specify the app status as optional and enabled by default, optional and disabled by default, or mandatory and always enabled. Finally, click Save.

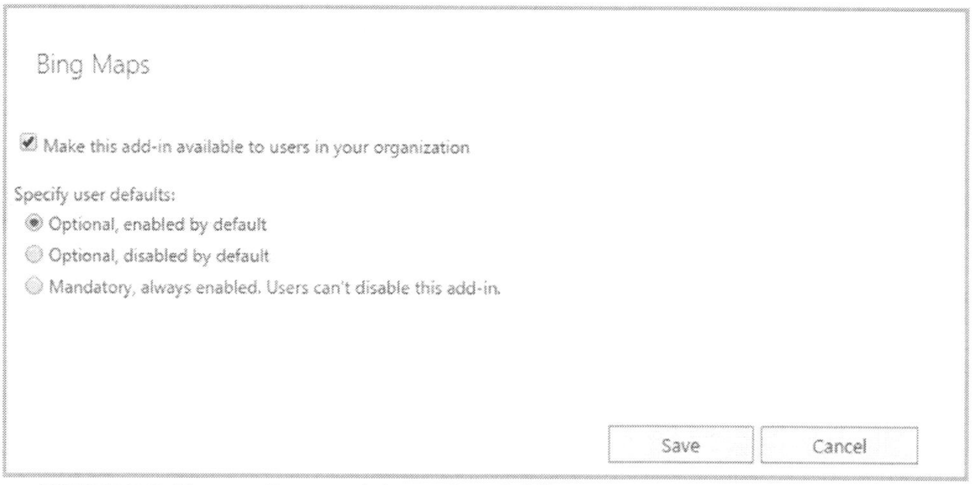

FIGURE 6-3 Manage the app status and availability.

Any app you install can be removed by selecting it and then selecting the Delete option. Although you can't uninstall the defaults apps, you can make any or all of the default apps unavailable to users.

Hiding Mailboxes from Address Lists

Occasionally, you might want to hide a mailbox so that it doesn't appear in the global address list or other address lists. One reason for doing this is if you have administrative mailboxes that you use only for special purposes. To hide a mailbox from the address lists, follow these steps:

1. Open the Properties dialog box for the mailbox-enabled user account by double-clicking the user name in Exchange Admin Center.
2. On the General page, select **Hide From Address Lists**.
3. Click **Save**.

Defining Custom Mailbox Attributes for Address Lists

Address lists, such as the global address list, make it easier for users and administrators to find available Exchange resources, including users, contacts, distribution groups, and public folders. The fields available for Exchange resources are based on the type of resource. If you want to add more values that should be displayed or searchable in address lists, such as an employee identification number, you can assign these values as custom attributes.

Exchange provides 15 custom attributes—labeled Customer Attribute 1, Custom Attribute 2, and so on through Custom Attribute 15. You can assign a value to a custom attribute by completing the following steps:

1. Open the Properties dialog box for the mailbox-enabled user account by double-clicking the user name in Exchange Admin Center.

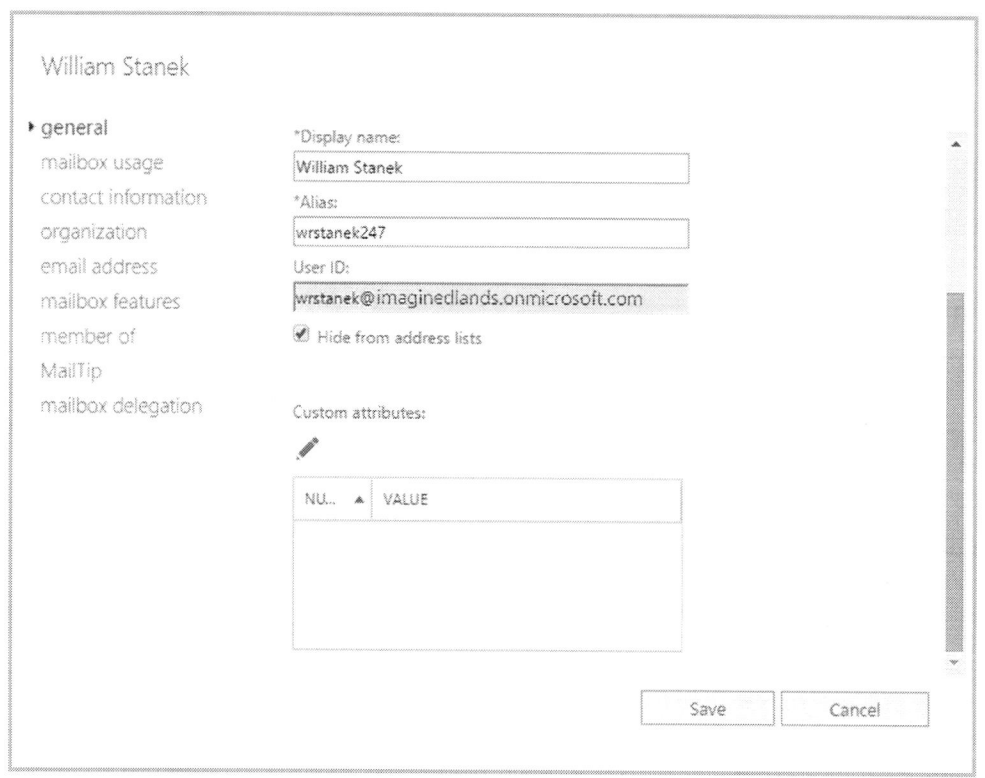

2. On the General page, click **More Options**. Under the Custom Attributes heading, you'll see any currently defined custom attributes. Click **Edit** (![pencil icon]) to display the Custom Attributes dialog box.

3. Enter attribute values in the text boxes provided. Click **OK** and then click **Save**.

Restoring Online Users and Mailboxes

If you remove the Exchange Online license for an online user account, the user's account is marked as an unlicensed account. Exchange Online deletes mailboxes from unlicensed accounts automatically after the grace period expires. By default, this grace period is 30 days. If you delete a user account in the online organization, the user account is marked as deleted but retained until the retention period expires, which is 30 days by default.

In Office 365 Admin Center, you can find deleted users and restore them by completing these steps:

1. Select Deleted Users under the Users heading in the Navigation menu to view deleted users, as shown in Figure 6-4. If the online organization has available licenses, you can restore the deleted users.

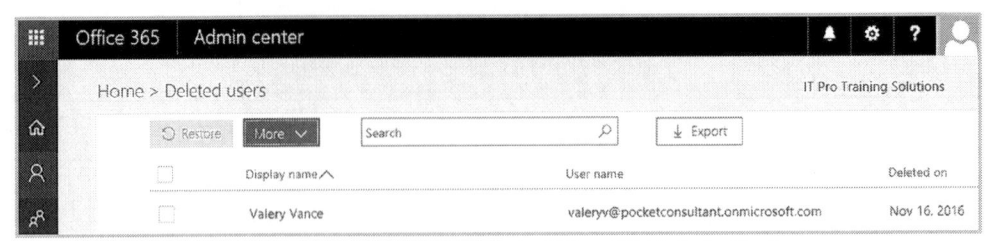

FIGURE 6-4 View deleted but retained users in Office 365 Admin Center.

2. Select the account to restore and then click **Restore**.

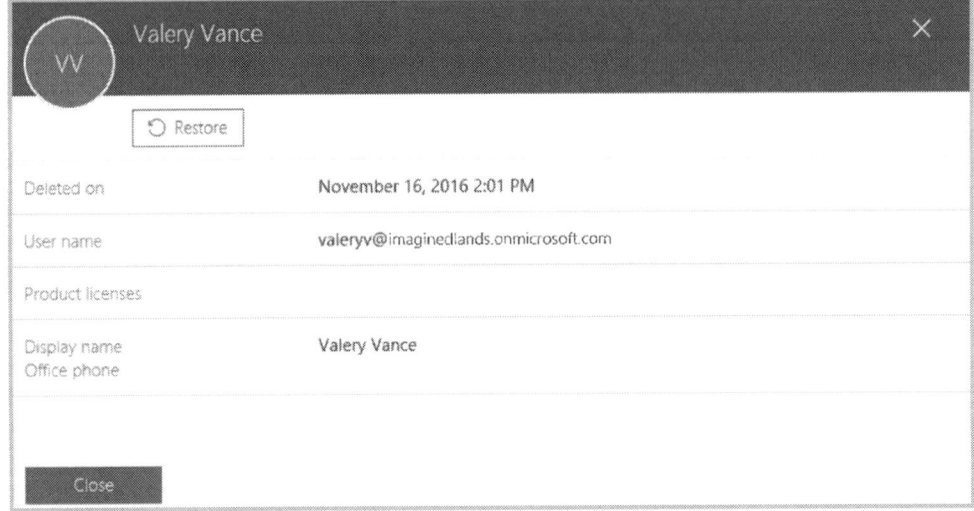

FIGURE 6-5 Restore online users in Office 365 Admin Center.

3. Before you confirm the action by clicking Restore again when prompted. Consider whether you want to assign the user an automatically generated password or one you designate. You also can specify whether the user must change their password when they first sign on.

Restore

Valery Vance
valeryv@pocketconsultant.onmicrosoft.com

Before you restore Valery Vance you need to make sure you have a product license available. Restoring Valery Vance will restore all associated data, assign product licenses, and give access to all services they could access before they were deleted.

- ● Auto-generate password
- ○ Let me create the password
- ☑ Make this user change their password when they first sign in

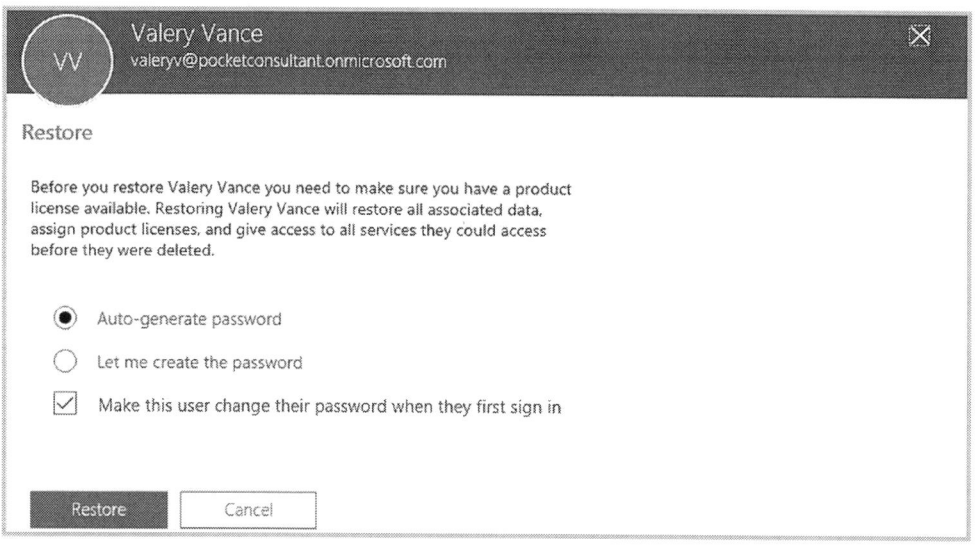

[Restore] [Cancel]

4. Whether you assign a password or generate one, the new password is sent in email to a designated administrator. You can change the default as necessary or add recipients. Be sure to separate each email address with a semicolon. When you are ready to continue, click **Send Email And Close**.

> **NOTE** Keep in mind that account restoration will fail if there are any naming or other conflicts. The User Principal Name must be unique within the organization. If another user account has the same the User Principal Name, you'll see a warning about a user name conflict. You'll then be able to edit the user name or replace the active user with the deleted user.

When you connect to Microsoft Online Services as discussed in "Connecting to Exchange Online Using PowerShell" in Chapter 1, you can get information about accounts in Windows PowerShell. Enter **Get-MsolUser** to get a list of active user accounts. As shown in the following example the default output shows the User Principal Name, display name, and licensing status of user accounts:

```
UserPrincipalName                        DisplayName          isLicensed
-----------------                        -----------          ----------
cart3@imaginedlands.onmicrosoft.com      Media Cart 3         False
wrstanek@imaginedlands.onmicrosoft.com   William Stanek       True
room3@imaginedlands.onmicrosoft.com      Conference Room 3    False
georges@imaginedlands.onmicrosoft.com    George Schaller      False
room42@imaginedlands.onmicrosoft.com     Conference Room 42   False
```

The output shows the user accounts associated with all types of users, including the user accounts associated with room and equipment mailboxes. Although room and equipment mailboxes don't need to be licensed, standard user accounts require licenses.

You can get a list of users whose accounts have been marked for deletion by entering **Get-MsolUser –ReturnDeletedUsers**. Accounts marked for deletion are listed by User Principal Name, display name, and licensing status. To restore a deleted account, use Restore-MsolUser. The basic syntax for this command is:

```
Restore-MsolUser -UserPrincipalName OnlineId
```

where OnlineId is the User Principal Name of the account to restore:

```
Restore-MsolUser -UserPrincipalName valv@imaginedlands.onmicrosoft.com
```

The account restore will fail if there are any naming or other conflicts. To resolve a name conflict, use the -NewUserPrincipalName parameter to set a new User Principal Name for the user.

Repairing Mailboxes

You can use New-MailboxRepairRequest to detect and repair mailbox corruption. By default, the command attempts to repair all types of mailbox corruption issues, including issues associated with search folders, aggregate counts, provisioned folders, and folder views.

The basic syntax for New-MailboxRepairRequest is:

```
New-MailboxRepairRequest -Mailbox ExchangeID
```

where ExchangeID identifies the mailbox to repair, such as:

```
New-MailboxRepairRequest -Mailbox TonyS
```

```
New-MailboxRepairRequest -Mailbox tonys@imaginedlands.onmicrosoft.com
```

```
New-MailboxRepairRequest -Mailbox "Tony Smith"
```

During the repair process, the mailbox cannot be accessed. Once started, the detect and repair process cannot be stopped. Add the -Archive parameter to repair the archive mailbox associated with an Exchange identifier rather than the primary mailbox.

Managing Delivery Restrictions, Permissions, and Storage Limits

You use mailbox properties to set delivery restrictions, permissions, and storage limits. To change these configuration settings for mailboxes, follow the techniques discussed in this section.

Setting Message Size Restrictions for Contacts

You set message size restrictions for contacts in much the same way that you set size restrictions for users. Follow the steps listed in the next section.

Setting Message Size Restrictions on Delivery to and from Individual Mailboxes

Message size restrictions control the maximum size of messages that can be sent or received in the Exchange organization. With Exchange Online, the maximum size of messages that users can send is 35,840 KB and the maximum size of messages that users can receive is 36,864 KB by default. You can override these defaults by setting different maximum send and receive sizes, up to 153600 KB.

You set individual delivery restrictions by completing the following steps:

1. Open the Properties dialog box for the mailbox-enabled user account by double-clicking the user name in Exchange Admin Center under Recipients > Mailboxes.

2. On the Mailbox Features page, scroll down and then click **View Details** under Message Size Restrictions.

3. As shown in Figure 6-6, you can set the following send and receive restrictions:

- **Sent Messages > Maximum Message Size**   Sets a limit on the size of messages the user can send. The value is set in kilobytes (KBs). If an outgoing message exceeds the limit, the message isn't sent and the user receives a non-delivery report (NDR).

- **Received Messages > Maximum Message Size**   Sets a limit on the size of messages the user can receive. The value is set in KBs. If an incoming message exceeds the limit, the message isn't delivered and the sender receives an NDR.

FIGURE 6-6 You can apply individual delivery restrictions on a per-user basis.

4. Click **OK** and then click **Save**. The restrictions that you set override the global default settings.

Setting Send and Receive Restrictions for Contacts

You set message send and receive restrictions for contacts in the same way that you set these restrictions for users. Follow the steps listed in the next section.

Setting Message Send and Receive Restrictions on Individual Mailboxes

By default, user mailboxes are configured to accept messages from anyone. To override this behavior, you can do the following:

- Specify that only messages from the listed users, contacts, or groups be accepted.
- Specify that messages from specific users, contacts, or groups be rejected.
- Specify that only messages from authenticated users—meaning users who have logged on to the Exchange system or Office 365—be accepted.

You set message send and receive restrictions by completing the following steps:

1. Open the Properties dialog box for the mailbox-enabled user account by double-clicking the user name in Exchange Admin Center under Recipients > Mailboxes.

2. On the Mailbox Features page, scroll down and then click **View Details** under Message Delivery Restrictions. As shown in Figure 6-7, you can then set message acceptance restrictions.

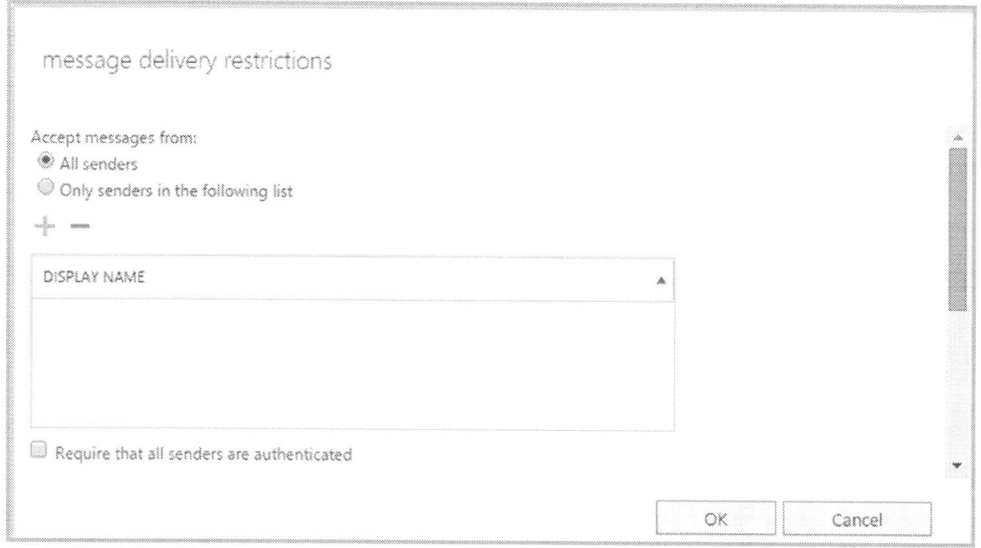

FIGURE 6-7 You can apply send and receive restrictions on messages on a per-user basis.

3. To accept messages from all email addresses except those on the reject list, under Accept Messages From, select **All Senders**.

4. To specify that only messages from the listed users, contacts, or groups be accepted, select the **Only Senders In The Following List** option and then add acceptable recipients by following these steps:

- Click Add ( ) to display the Select Members dialog box.
- Select a recipient, and then click OK. Repeat as necessary.

> **TIP** You can select multiple recipients at the same time. To select multiple recipients individually, hold down the Ctrl key and then click each recipient that you want to select. To select a sequence of recipients, select the first recipient, hold down the Shift key, and then click the last recipient.

5. If you want to ensure that messages are accepted only from authenticated users, select the **Require That All Senders Are Authenticated** check box.

6. To specify that no recipients should be rejected, under Reject Messages From, select **No Senders**.

7. To reject messages from specific recipients, under Reject Messages From, select **Senders In The Following List** and then add unacceptable recipients by following these steps:

- Click Add (➕) to display the Select Members dialog box.
- Select a recipient, and then click OK. Repeat as necessary

8. Click **OK**.

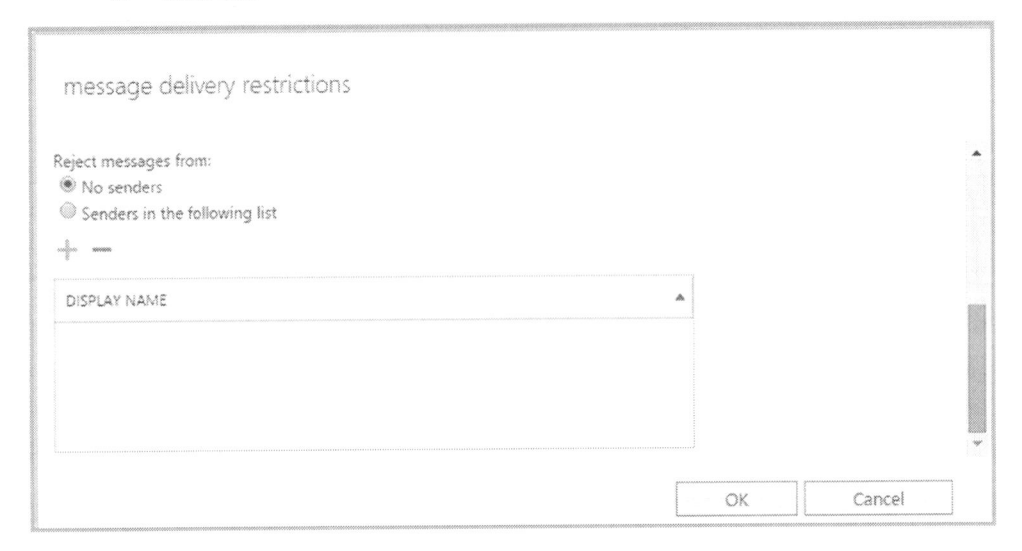

Permitting Others to Access a Mailbox

Occasionally, users need to access someone else's mailbox, and in certain situations, you should allow this. For example, if John is Susan's manager and Susan is going on vacation, John might need access to her mailbox while she's away. Another situation in which someone might need access to another mailbox is when you've set up special-purpose mailboxes, such as a mailbox for Webmaster@domain.com or a mailbox for Info@domain.com.

You can grant permissions for a mailbox in three ways:

- You can grant access to a mailbox and its content. If you want to grant access to a mailbox and its contents but not grant Send As permissions, use the Full Access settings. In Exchange Admin Center, open the Properties dialog box for the mailbox you want to work with and then select Mailbox Delegation. On the Mailbox Delegation page, under Full Access, click Add (➕), and then use the

Select Full Access dialog box to choose the recipients who should have access to the mailbox. To revoke the authority to access the mailbox, select an existing user name in the Display Name list box and then click Remove.

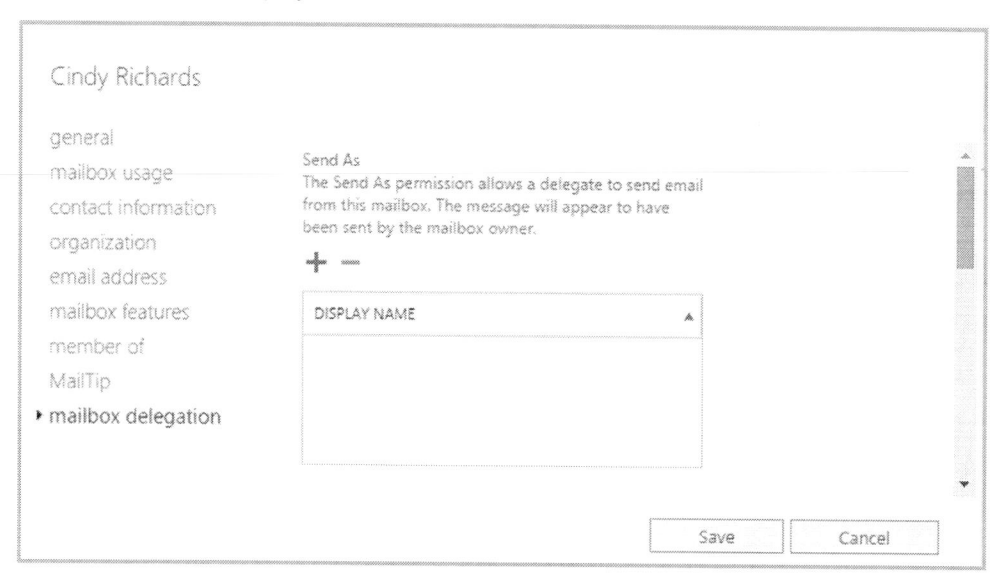

- You can grant the right to send messages as the mailbox owner. If you want to grant Send As permissions, use the Send As settings. In Exchange Admin Center, open the Properties dialog box for the mailbox you want to work with and then select Mailbox Delegation. On the Mailbox Delegation page, under Send As, click Add ( ), and then use the Select Send As dialog box to choose the recipients who should have this permission. To revoke this permission, select an existing user name in the Display Name list box and then click Remove.

- You can grant the right to send messages on behalf of the mailbox owner. If you want to allow a user to send messages from a user's mailbox but want recipients to know a message was sent on behalf of the mailbox owner (rather than by the mailbox owner), grant Send On Behalf Of permissions. In Exchange Admin Center, open the Properties dialog box for the mailbox, and then select Mailbox Delegation. On the Mailbox Delegation page, under Send On Behalf Of, click the Add button, and then use the Select Send On Behalf Of dialog box to choose the recipients who should have this permission. To revoke this permission, select an existing user name in the Display Name list box and then click Remove.

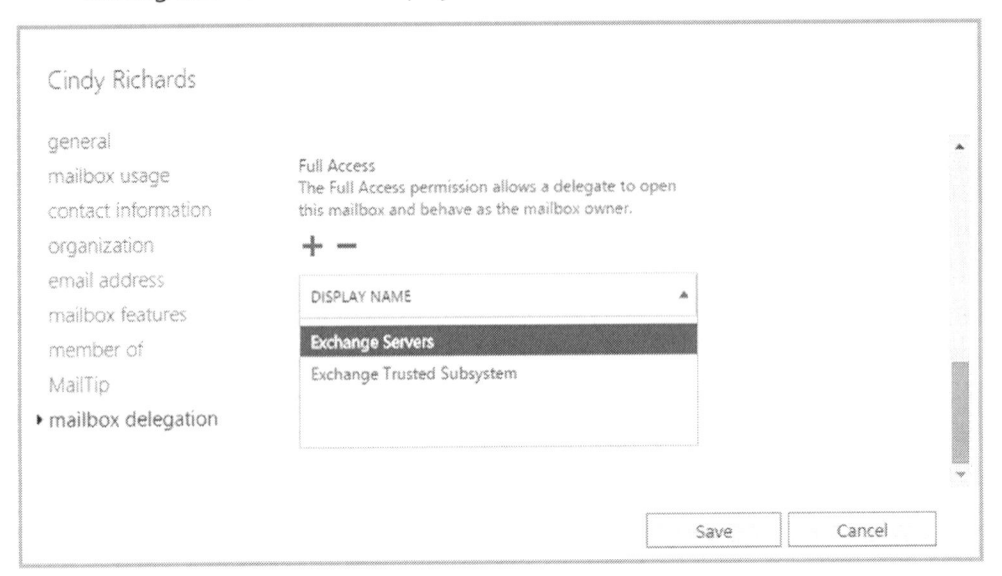

In a remote session with Exchange Online, you can use the Add-MailboxPermission and Remove-MailboxPermission cmdlets to manage full access permissions. Samples 6-1 and 6-2 show examples of using these cmdlets. In these examples, the AccessRights parameter is set to FullAccess to indicate full access permissions on the mailbox.

SAMPLE 6-1 Adding full access permissions

Syntax

```
Add-MailboxPermission -Identity UserBeingGrantedPermission
 -User UserWhoseMailboxIsBeingConfigured -AccessRights 'FullAccess'
```

Usage

Add-MailboxPermission -Identity
'CN=Mike Lam,OU=Engineering,DC=pocket-consultant,DC=com'
-User '**IMAGINEDLANDS\boba**' -AccessRights 'FullAccess'

SAMPLE 6-2 Removing full access permissions

Syntax

Remove-MailboxPermission -Identity 'UserBeingGrantedPermission'
 -User '**UserWhose**MailboxIsBeingConfigured' -AccessRights 'FullAccess'
-InheritanceType 'All'

Usage

Remove-MailboxPermission -Identity 'CN=Jerry Orman,
OU=Engineering,DC=pocket-consultant,DC=com'
 -User '**IMAGINEDLANDS\boba**' -AccessRights 'FullAccess' **-InheritanceType 'All'**

In a remote session with Exchange Online, you can use the Add-ADPermission and Remove-ADPermission cmdlets to manage Send As permissions. Samples 6-3 and 6-4 show examples using these cmdlets. In these examples, the -ExtendedRights parameter is set to Send-As to indicate you are setting Send As permissions on the mailbox.

SAMPLE 6-3 Adding send as permissions

Syntax

Add-ADPermission -Identity **UserBeingGrantedPermission**
-User **UserWhoseMailboxIsBeingConfigured** -ExtendedRights 'Send-As'

Usage

Add-ADPermission -Identity 'CN=Jerry
Orman,OU=Engineering,DC=cpandl,DC=com'
-User '**IMAGINEDLANDS\boba**' -ExtendedRights 'Send-As'

SAMPLE 6-4 Removing send as permissions

Syntax

Remove-ADPermission -Identity **UserBeingRevokedPermission**
-User **UserWhoseMailboxIsBeingConfigured** -ExtendedRights 'Send-As'

```
-InheritanceType 'All' -ChildObjectTypes $null
-InheritedObjectType $null -Properties $null
```

Usage

```
Remove-ADPermission -Identity 'CN=Jerry
Orman,OU=Engineering, DC=pocket-consultant,DC=com'
 -User 'IMAGINEDLANDS\boba' -ExtendedRights 'Send-As'
-InheritanceType 'All' -ChildObjectTypes $null -InheritedObjectTypes $null
-Properties $null
```

> **NOTE** Another way to grant access permissions to mailboxes is to do so through Outlook. Using Outlook, you have more granular control over permissions. You can allow a user to log on as the mailbox owner, delegate mailbox access, and grant various levels of access. For more information on this issue, see the "Accessing Multiple Exchange Mailboxes" and "Granting Permission to Access Folders Without Delegating Access" sections in Chapter 9 "Working with Exchange Clients."

Forwarding Email to a New Address

Except when rights management prevents it, any messages sent to a user's mailbox can be forwarded to another recipient. This recipient can be another user or a mail-enabled contact. To configure mail forwarding, follow these steps:

1. Open the Properties dialog box for the mailbox-enabled user account by double-clicking the user name in Exchange Admin Center.
2. On the Mailbox Features page, scroll down and then click **View Details** under Mail Flow.

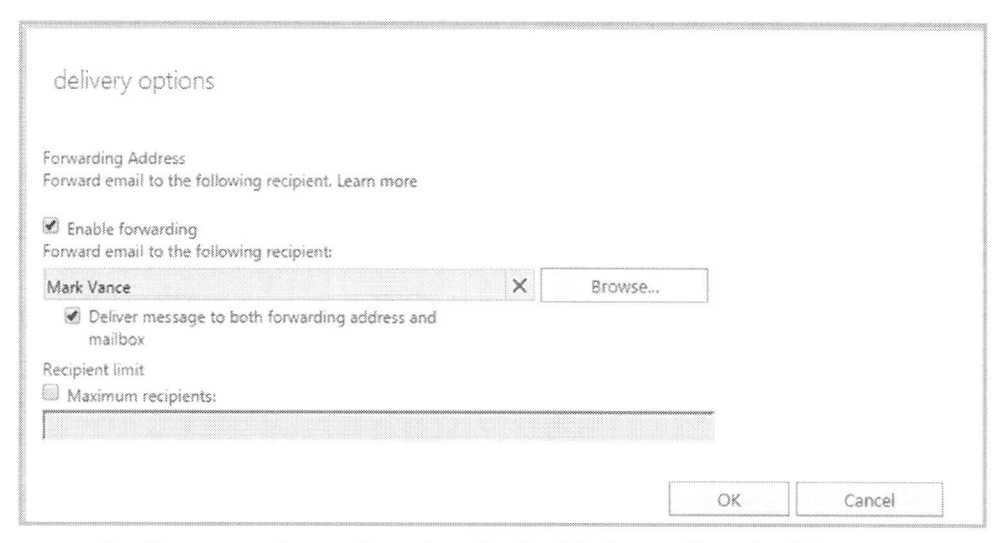

```
delivery options

Forwarding Address
Forward email to the following recipient. Learn more

☑ Enable forwarding
Forward email to the following recipient:

Mark Vance                              ✕    Browse...

    ☑ Deliver message to both forwarding address and
      mailbox
Recipient limit
    ☐ Maximum recipients:


                                       OK         Cancel
```

3. To remove forwarding, clear the Enable Forwarding check box.

4. To add forwarding, select the Enable Forwarding check box and then click **Browse**. Use the Select Mailbox User And Mailbox dialog box to choose the alternate recipient.

5. If you enabled forward, you can optionally specify that copies of forwarded messages should be retained in the original mailbox by selecting the **Deliver Message To Both Forwarding Address And Mailbox** checkbox.

If you use a remote session with Exchange Online to configure forwarding, you can specify that messages should be delivered to both the forwarding address and the current mailbox by setting the -DeliverToMailboxAndForward parameter to $true when using Set-Mailbox.

Understanding Storage Restrictions on Mailbox and Archives

In a standard configuration of Exchange Online, each licensed user gets 50 GB of mailbox storage and a storage warning is issued when the mailbox reaches 42.5 GB. If a user has a licensed in-place archive, the archive can have up to 25 GB of storage; a storage warning is issued when the archive mailbox reaches 22.5 GB. Other licensing options are available that may grant additional storage rights.

You can view the current storage size for a user by completing the following steps:

1. Open the Properties dialog box for the mailbox-enabled user account by double-clicking the user name in Exchange Admin Center.

2. Select the Mailbox Usage page. You'll then see the current storage size of the mailbox.

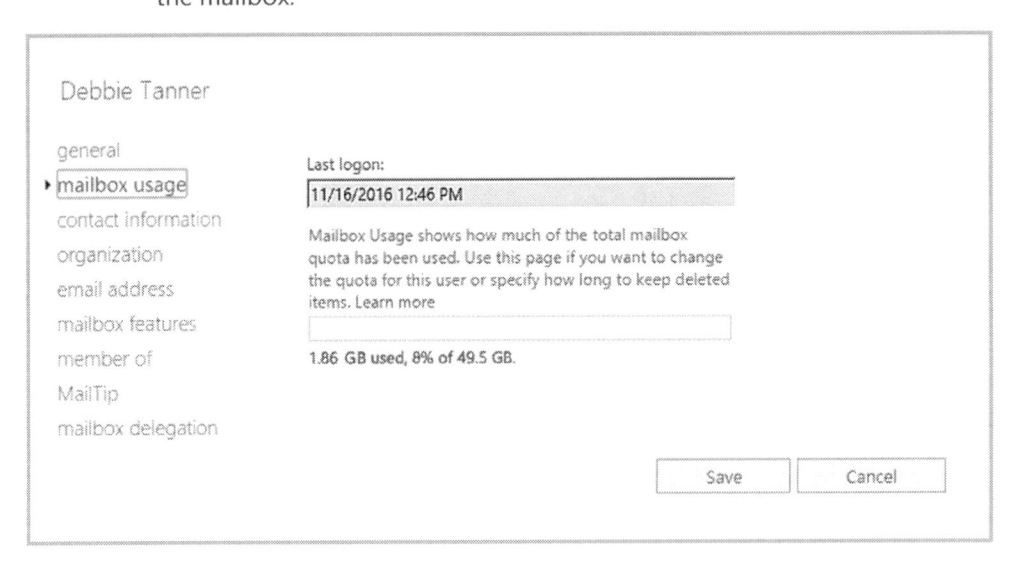

Debbie Tanner

general
▸ mailbox usage
contact information
organization
email address
mailbox features
member of
MailTip
mailbox delegation

Last logon:
11/16/2016 12:46 PM

Mailbox Usage shows how much of the total mailbox quota has been used. Use this page if you want to change the quota for this user or specify how long to keep deleted items. Learn more

1.86 GB used, 8% of 49.5 GB.

Save   Cancel

Users who have an archive mailbox have the mailbox type User (Archive). You view individual storage for archive mailboxes by completing the following steps:

1. Select the user name in Exchange Admin Center.
2. In the Details pane, scroll down until you see the In-Place Archive heading and the related options. Click **View Details**.

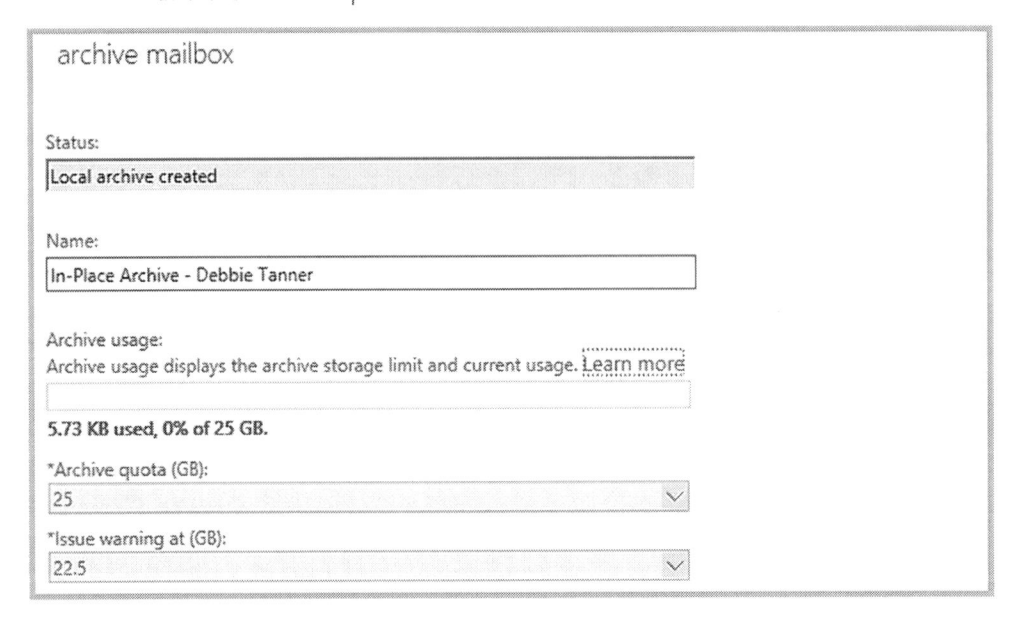

archive mailbox

Status:
Local archive created

Name:
In-Place Archive - Debbie Tanner

Archive usage:
Archive usage displays the archive storage limit and current usage. Learn more

5.73 KB used, 0% of 25 GB.

*Archive quota (GB):
25

*Issue warning at (GB):
22.5

Understanding Deleted Item Retention

Normally, when a user deletes a message in Outlook, the message is placed in the Deleted Items folder. The message remains in the Deleted Items folder until the user deletes it manually or allows Outlook to clear out the Deleted Items folder. With personal folders, the message is then permanently deleted and you can't restore it. With server-based mailboxes, the message isn't actually deleted from Exchange Online. Instead, the message is marked as hidden and kept for a specified period of time called the *deleted item retention period*.

> **NOTE** The standard processes can be modified in several different ways. A user could press Shift+Delete to bypass Deleted Items. As an administrator, you can create and apply policies that prevent users from deleting items (even if they try to use Shift+Delete). You can also configure policy to retain items indefinitely.

With Exchange Online, the default retention settings are as follows:

- Deleted items are retained for a maximum of 30 days.
- Items removed from the Deleted Items folder are retained for a maximum of 14 days.
- Items in the Junk Folder are retained for a maximum of 30 days before they are removed.

If you want to modify these settings, you can create a retention policy that specifies the delete and move-to-archive rules that are used. In Exchange Admin Center, you create and manage retention policies using the options found under Compliance Management > Retention Policies. After you create a retention policy, you can apply it by completing these steps:

1. Open the Properties dialog box for the mailbox-enabled user account by double-clicking the user name in Exchange Admin Center.
2. On the Mailbox Features page, use the Retention Policy list to specify the retention policy that should be applied to the selected user.
3. Click **Save**.

Debbie Tanner

general
mailbox usage
contact information
organization
email address
▸ mailbox features
member of
MailTip
mailbox delegation

Select the mailbox settings, phone and voice features, and email connectivity options for this mailbox. Learn more

Sharing policy:
[Default Sharing Policy ▼]

Role assignment policy:
[Default Role Assignment Policy ▼]

Retention policy:
[Default MRM Policy ▼]

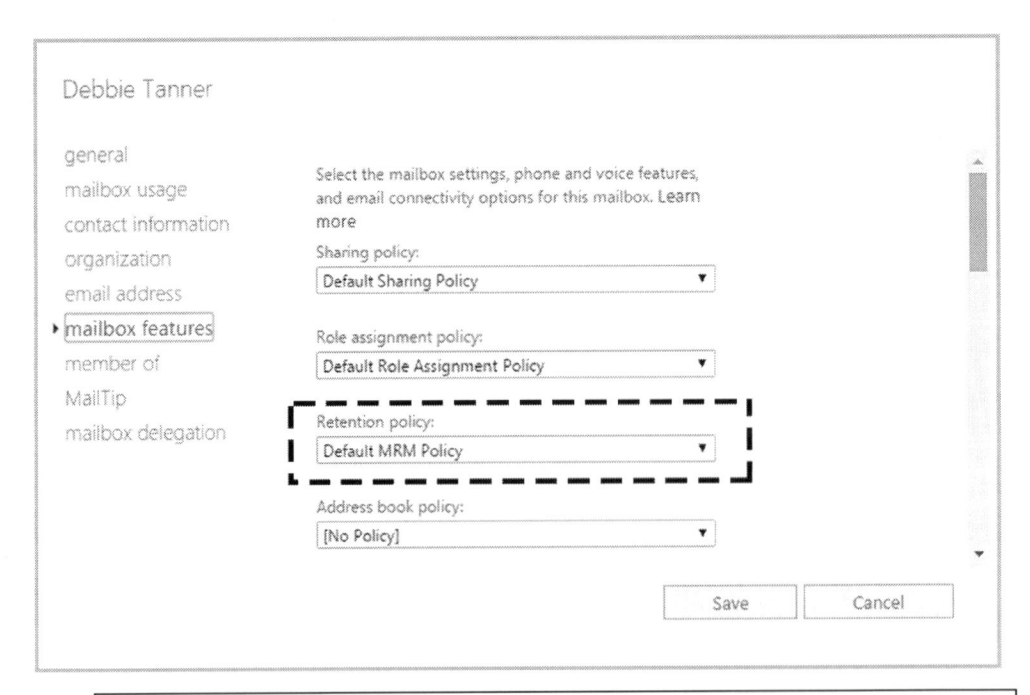

Address book policy:
[No Policy] ▼

[Save] [Cancel]

> **REAL WORLD** Deleted item retention is convenient because it allows the administrator the chance to salvage accidentally deleted email without restoring a user's mailbox from backup. I strongly recommend that you create retention policies and apply them accordingly.

PART 3
Managing Groups, Clients & Security

Chapter 7. Configuring Groups for Exchange Online

Learning the ins and outs of groups and distribution lists will greatly facilitate the efficiency and effectiveness of Office 365 and Exchange Online administration. Careful planning of your organization's groups and distribution lists can save you time and help your organization run more efficiently. Study the concepts discussed in this chapter which focuses on Exchange Online groups and the next which focuses on Office 365 groups then use the step-by-step procedures to implement the groups and distribution lists for your organization.

Using Exchange Groups

You use groups to grant permissions to similar types of users, to simplify account administration, and to make it easier to contact multiple users. For example, you can send a message addressed to a group, and the message will go to all the users in that group. Thus, instead of having to enter 20 different email addresses in the message header, you enter one email address for all of the group members.

Group Types, Scope, And Identifiers

Windows Azure defines several different types of groups, and each of these groups has a unique purpose when used with Exchange Online. The three primary group types you can use are:

- **Security**   You use security groups to control access to resources and manage permissions. You can also use user-defined security groups to distribute email, such groups are also referred to as security-enabled distribution groups.
- **Standard distribution**   Standard distribution groups have fixed membership, and you use them only as email distribution lists. You can't use these groups to assign permissions or control access to resources.
- **Dynamic distribution**   Membership for dynamic distribution groups is determined based on a dynamic query; you use these groups only as email distribution lists. The query is used to build the list of members whenever messages are sent to the group.

> **NOTE**   As with user accounts, Windows Azure uses unique security identifiers (SIDs) to track groups. This means that you can't delete a group, re-create it with the same name, and then expect all the permissions and privileges to remain the same. The new group will have a new SID, and all the permissions and privileges of the old group will be lost.

> **REAL WORLD** In Windows Azure, security groups can have different scopes—*domain local, global,* and *universal*—so that they are valid in different areas of your organizational hierarchy. Exchange Online only supports groups with universal scope. You can mail-enable security groups with universal scope, and you can create new distribution groups with universal scope.

Office 365 adds a fourth group type, called Office 365 groups, which you can use to enable collaboration and sharing within the organization. You'll learn more about Office 365 groups in Chapter 8, "Configuring Groups for Office 365."

All security groups created in Exchange Online are mail-enabled. When you work with these groups in Office 365, they are listed as security-enabled distribution groups to distinguish them from security groups created in Office 365, which are not mail-enabled by default and cannot be mail-enabled. Why? Security groups in Office 365 are used to control access to OneDrive and SharePoint as well as Mobile Device Management.

In Exchange Admin Center, you select Recipients in the Navigation menu and then select Groups to work with groups (see Figure 7-1). You'll then see any security or distribution groups created in the Exchange organization. Keep in mind that only mail-enabled groups with universal scope are displayed and that you can only view Office 365 groups using Office 365 Admin Center. This includes any security groups you create in Office 365 as they are not mail-enabled.

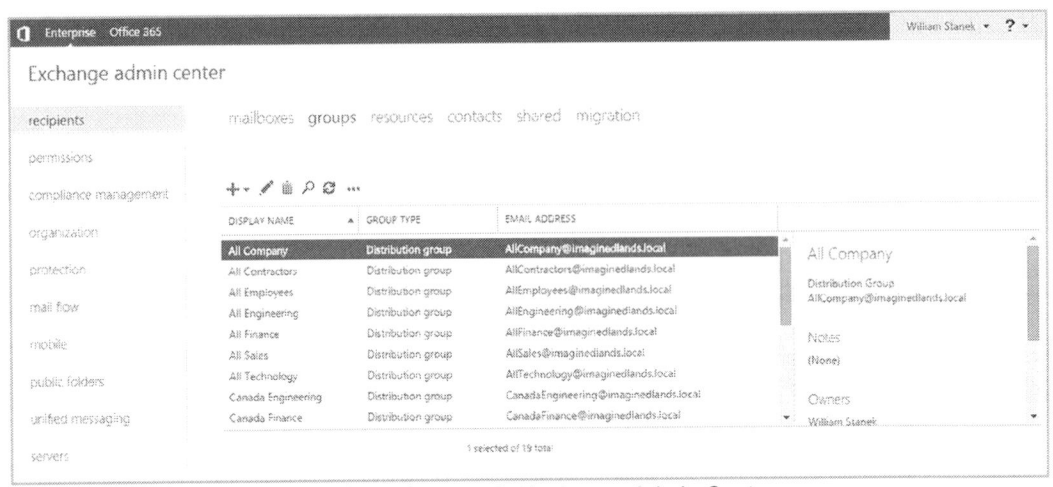

FIGURE 7-1 Viewing the configured groups in Exchange Admin Center.

When you work with dynamic distribution groups, keep in mind that the membership can include only members of the hosted domain. For example, of you are working with the imaginedlands.onmicrosoft.com domain, this hosted domain determines the scope of the group. You can then apply filters to ensure the group only contains specific recipients, such as only members of the Engineering department.

To reduce the time administrators spend managing groups, Exchange defines several additional control settings, including

- **Group ownership**   Mail-enabled security groups, standard distribution groups, and dynamic distribution groups can have one or more owners. A group's owners are the users assigned as its managers, and they can control membership in the group. A group's managers are listed when users view the properties of the group in Microsoft Office Outlook. Additionally, managers can receive delivery reports for groups if you select the Send Delivery Reports To Group Manager option when configuring group settings.
- **Membership approval**   Mail-enabled security groups and standard distribution groups can have open or closed membership. There are separate settings for joining and leaving a group. For joining, the group can be open to allow users to join without requiring permission, be closed to allow only group owners and administrators to add members, or require owner approval to allow users to request membership in a group. Membership requests must be approved by a group owner. For leaving, a group can either be open to allow users to leave a group without requiring owner approval or closed to allow only group owners and administrators to remove members.

Your management tool of choice will determine your options for configuring group ownership and membership approval. When you create groups in Exchange Admin Center, you can specify ownership, membership, and approval settings when you create the group and can edit these settings at any time by editing the group's properties. When you create groups in a remote session with Exchange Online, you can configure additional advanced options that you'd otherwise have to manage after creating the group in Exchange Admin Center.

When to Use Dynamic Distribution Groups

It's a fact of life that over time users will move to different departments, leave the company, or accept different responsibilities. With standard distribution groups, you'll spend a lot of time managing group membership when these types of changes occur—and that's where dynamic distribution groups come into the picture. With dynamic distribution groups, there isn't a fixed group membership and you don't have to add or remove users from groups. Instead, group membership is determined by the results of a dynamic query.

One other thing to note about dynamic distribution is that you can associate only one specific query with each distribution group. For example, you could create separate groups for each department in the organization. You could have groups called QD-Accounting, QD-BizDev, QD-Engineering, QD-Marketing, QD-Operations, QD-Sales, and QD-Support. You could, in turn, create a standard distribution group or a dynamic distribution group called AllEmployees that contains these groups as members—thereby establishing a distribution group hierarchy.

When using multiple parameters with dynamic distribution, keep in mind that multiple parameters typically work as logical AND operations. For example, if you create a query with a parameter that matches all employees in the state of Washington with all employees in the Marketing department, the query results do not contain a list of all employees in Washington or all Marketing employees. Rather, the results contain a list of recipients who are in Washington and are members of the Marketing group. In this case, you get the expected results by creating a dynamic distribution group for all Washington State employees, another dynamic distribution group for all Marketing employees, and a final group that has as members the other two distribution groups.

Working with Exchange Groups

As you set out to work with groups, you'll find that some tasks are specific to each type of group and some tasks can be performed with any type of group. Because of this, I've divided the group management discussion into three sections. In this section, you'll learn about the typical tasks you perform with security and standard distribution groups. The next section discusses tasks you'll perform only with dynamic distribution groups. The third section discusses general management tasks.

You can use Exchange Admin Center or a remote session with Exchange Online to work with groups.

Group Naming Policy

Whether you work at a small company with 50 employees or a large enterprise with 5,000 employees, you should consider establishing a group naming policy that ensures a consistent naming strategy is used for group names. For administrators, your naming policy should be implemented through written policies within your IT department and could be applied to both security groups and distribution groups.

Exchange Online also allows you to establish official naming policy for standard distribution groups. Group naming policy is:

- Applied to non-administrators whenever they create or rename distribution groups.
- Applied to administrators only when they create or rename distribution groups using the shell (and omit the -IgnoreNamingPolicy parameter).

> **IMPORTANT** Group naming policy doesn't apply to security groups or dynamic distribution groups. Each Exchange organization can have one and only one naming policy. Any naming policy you define is applied throughout the Exchange organization.

Understanding Group Naming Policy

You use group naming policy to format group names according to a defined standard. The rules for naming policy allow for one or more prefixes, a group name, and one or more suffixes, giving an expanded syntax of:

`<Prefix1><Prefix2>...<PrefixN><GroupName><Suffix1><Suffix2>...<SuffixN>`

You can use any Exchange attribute as the prefix or suffix. You also can use a text string as a prefix or suffix. The prefix, group name and suffix are combined without spacing. To improve readability, you can separate the prefix, name and suffix with a placeholder character, such as a space ( ), a period (.) or a dash (-).

Group naming policy works like this:

- A user creates a standard distribution group and specifies a display name for the group. After creating the group, Exchange applies the group naming policy by adding any prefixes or suffixes defined in the group naming policy to the display name.

- The display name is displayed in the distribution groups list in Exchange Admin Center, the shared address book, and the To:, Cc:, and From: fields in email messages.

You can create a naming policy with only a prefix and group name or with only a suffix and a group name. Common attributes that you might want to use as prefixes or suffixes include city, country code, department, office, and state. For example, you might want all distribution groups to have the following syntax:

`State_ GroupName`

To do this, you would create a naming policy with two prefixes. As shown in Figure 7-2, the first prefix would have the <State> attribute. The second prefix would have the _ text value. Thus, if a user in the state of New York (NY) creates a standard distribution group called Sales, Exchange adds the defined prefixes according to the naming policy and the display name becomes NY_Sales.

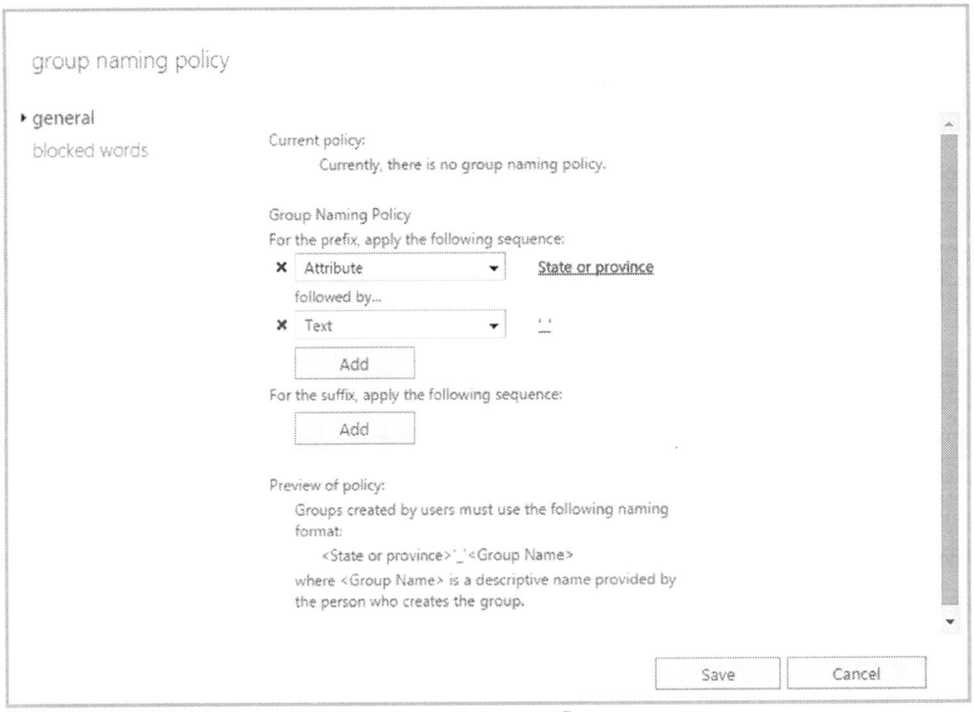

FIGURE 7-2 Creating a naming policy with two prefixes.

Group naming policy also allows you to specify blocked words. Users who try to use a word that you've blocked see an error message when they try to create the new group and are asked to remove the blocked word and create the group again.

Defining Group Naming Policy for Your Organization

Group naming policy formats display names so that they follow a defined standard. When setting the naming format, keep in mind that users enter the desired display name when they create the group and Exchange transforms the format according to the defined policy. Because the display name is limited to 64 characters, you must consider this limit when defining the prefixes and suffixes in your naming policy.

You can create the group naming policy for the Exchange organization by completing the following steps:

1. In Exchange Admin Center, select **Recipients** in the Navigation menu and then select **Groups**.

2. Click the **More** button (•••) and then select **Configure Group Naming Policy**. This displays the Group Naming Policy dialog box.

3. If you want the naming policy to have a prefix, do one of the following and then optionally click **Add** to add additional prefixes using the same technique:

- Use the selection list to choose Attribute as the prefix. In the Select The Attribute dialog box, select the attribute to use and then click OK.
- Use the selection list to choose Text as the prefix. In the Enter Text dialog box, select the text string to use and then click OK.

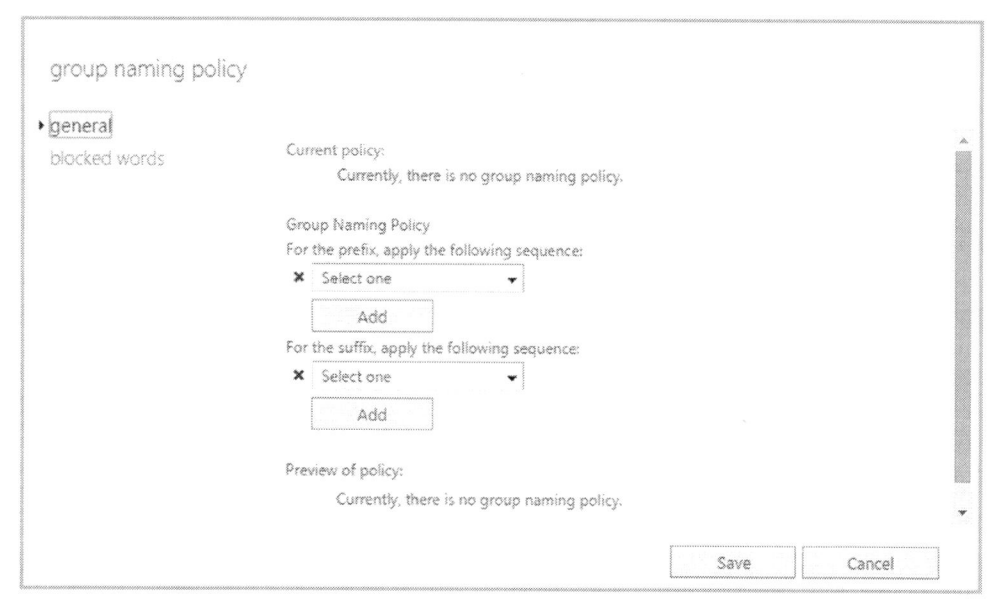

4. If you want the naming policy to have a suffix do one of the following and then optionally click **Add** to add additional suffixes using the same technique:

- Use the selection list to choose Attribute as the suffix. In the Select The Attribute dialog box, select the attribute to use and then click OK.
- Use the selection list to choose Text as the suffix. In the Enter Text dialog box, select the text string to use and then click OK.

5. As you define the naming policy, the Preview Of Policy area shows the naming format. When you are satisfied with the naming format, click **Save**.

Defining Blocked Words in Group Naming Policy

Blocked words allow you to specify words that users can't use in the names of standard distribution groups they create. You can define or manage the blocked words list by completing the following steps:

1. In Exchange Admin Center, select **Recipients** in the Navigation menu and then select **Groups**.

2. Click the More button (•••) and then select Configure Group Naming Policy. This displays the Group Naming Policy dialog box.

3. On the Blocked Words page, any currently blocked words are displayed. Use the following techniques to manage the blocked word list:

- To add a blocked word, type the word in the text box provided and then click Add (＋). Alternatively, type the word to block in the text box provided and then press Enter.
- To modify a blocked word, select the word in the blocked word list and then click **Edit** (✎). Modify the word and then click outside the text box provided for editing. Alternatively, press Enter to apply the edits.
- To remove a blocked word, click the word to remove and then click Remove.

4. Click **Save**.

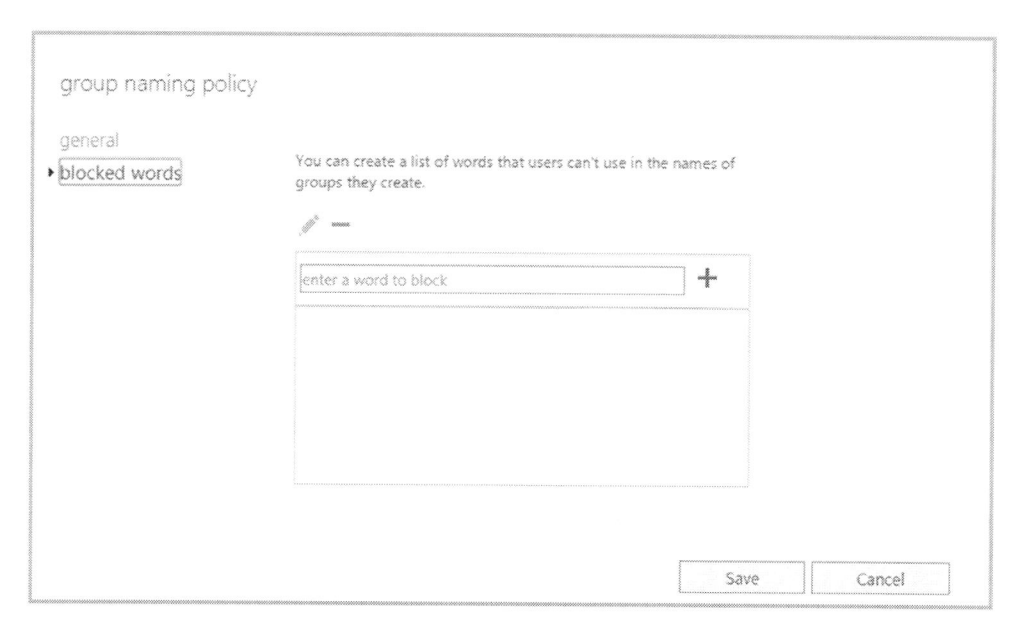

Creating Security and Standard Distribution Groups

Security groups and distribution groups are available to help you manage permissions and to distribute email. As you set out to create groups, remember that you create groups for similar types of users. Consequently, you might want to create the following types of groups:

- **Groups for departments within the organization**   Generally, users who work in the same department need access to similar resources and should be a part of the same email distribution lists.
- **Groups for roles within the organization**   You can also organize groups according to the users' roles within the organization. For example, you could use a group called Executives to send email to all the members of the executive team and a group called Managers to send email to all managers and executives in the organization.
- **Groups for users of specific projects**   Often, users working on a major project need a way to send email to all the members of the team. To address this need, you can create a group specifically for the project.

You can create groups in several ways. You can create a new distribution group, you can create a mail-enabled universal security group, or you can mail-enable an existing universal security group.

Creating a New Group

You can create a new distribution group or a new mail-enabled security group by completing the following steps:

1. In Exchange Admin Center, select **Recipients** in the Navigation menu and then select **Groups**.

2. Click **New** (   ) and then do one of the following:

- Select Distribution Group to create a new Distribution Group. This opens the New Distribution Group dialog box, shown in Figure 7-3.
- Select Security Group to create a new mail-enabled Security Group. This opens the New Security Group dialog box, and the options are the same as those for new distribution groups.

new distribution group

*Display name:
US Tech Services Team

*Alias:
ustech

*Email address:
ustech @ imaginedlands.onmi ▼

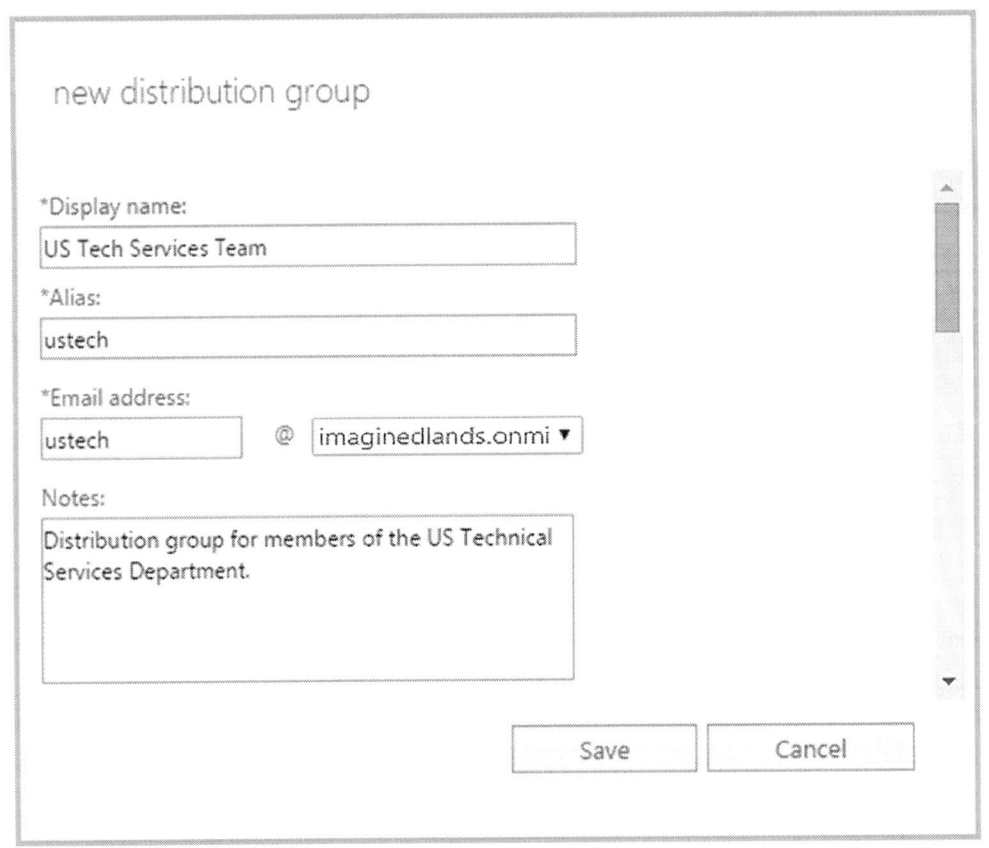

Notes:
Distribution group for members of the US Technical Services Department.

Save   Cancel

FIGURE 7-3 Configuring the group's settings.

3. In the Display Name text box, type a display name for the group. Group names aren't case-sensitive and can be up to 64 characters long. Keep in

mind that group naming policy doesn't apply to administrators creating distribution groups in Exchange Admin Center (or to mail-enabled security groups in any way).

4. Like users, groups have Exchange aliases. Enter an alias. The Exchange alias is used to set the group's SMTP email address. Exchange uses the SMTP address for receiving messages.

5. The name and domain components of the default email address are displayed in the Email Address text boxes. As appropriate, change the default name and use the drop-down list to select the domain with which you want to associate the group. This sets the fully qualified email address, such as ustech@imaginedlands.onmicrosoft.com.

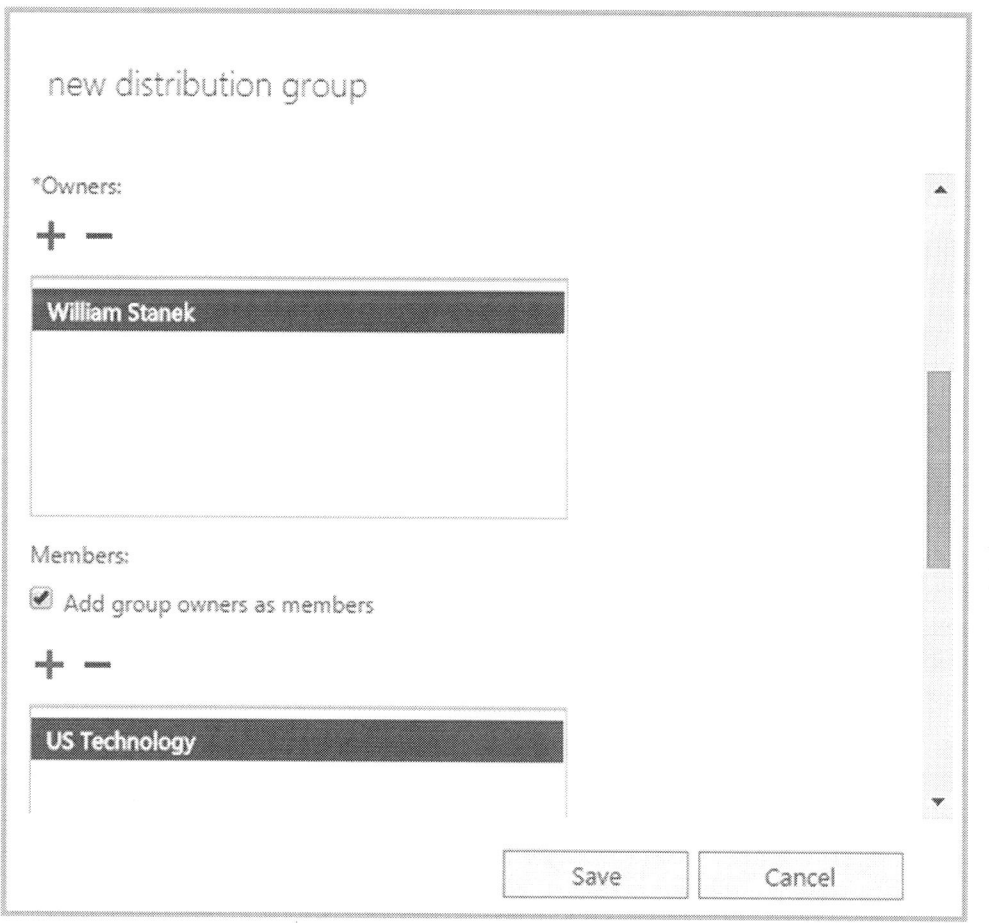

new distribution group

*Owners:

＋ －

William Stanek

Members:

☑ Add group owners as members

＋ －

US Technology

[Save]   [Cancel]

6. Group owners are responsible for managing a group. To add owners, under Owners, click Add (＋). In the Select Owner dialog box, select users,

groups, or both that should have management responsibility for the group. Select multiple users and groups using the Shift or Ctrl keys.

> **IMPORTANT** While dynamic distribution groups don't have to have owners, every mail-enabled security group and standard distribution group must have at least one owner. By default, the account you are using is set as the group owner.

7. Members of a group receive messages sent to the group. By default, the group owners are set as members of the group. If you don't want the currently listed owners to be members of the group, clear the **Add Group Owners As Members** checkbox.

8. To add members, under Members, click Add (✚). In the Select Members dialog box, select users, groups, or both that should be members of the group. Select multiple users and groups using the Shift or Ctrl keys.

9. Choose settings for joining the group. The options are:

- **Open** Anyone can join this group without being approved by the group owners.
- **Closed** Members can be added only by the group owners. All requests to join will be rejected automatically.
- **Owner Approval** All requests are approved or rejected by the group owners.

10. Choose settings for leaving the group. The options are:

- **Open** Anyone can leave this group without being approved by the group owners.
- **Closed** Members can be removed only by the group owners. All requests to leave will be rejected automatically.

11. Click **Save** to create the group. If an error occurs during group creation, the related group will not be created. You need to correct the problem before you can complete this procedure. After creating a group, you might want to do the following:

- Set message size restrictions for messages mailed to the group.
- Limit users who can send to the group.
- Change or remove default email addresses.
- Add more email addresses.

> **NOTE** By default, the new distribution group is open for joining and open for leaving.

new distribution group

Choose whether owner approval is required to join the group.
- ⦿ Open: Anyone can join this group without being approved by the group owners.
- ◯ Closed: Members can be added only by the group owners. All requests to join will be rejected automatically.
- ◯ Owner approval: All requests are approved or rejected by the group owners.

Choose whether the group is open to leave.
- ⦿ Open: Anyone can leave this group without being approved by the group owners.
- ◯ Closed: Members can be removed only by the group owners. All requests to leave will be rejected automatically.

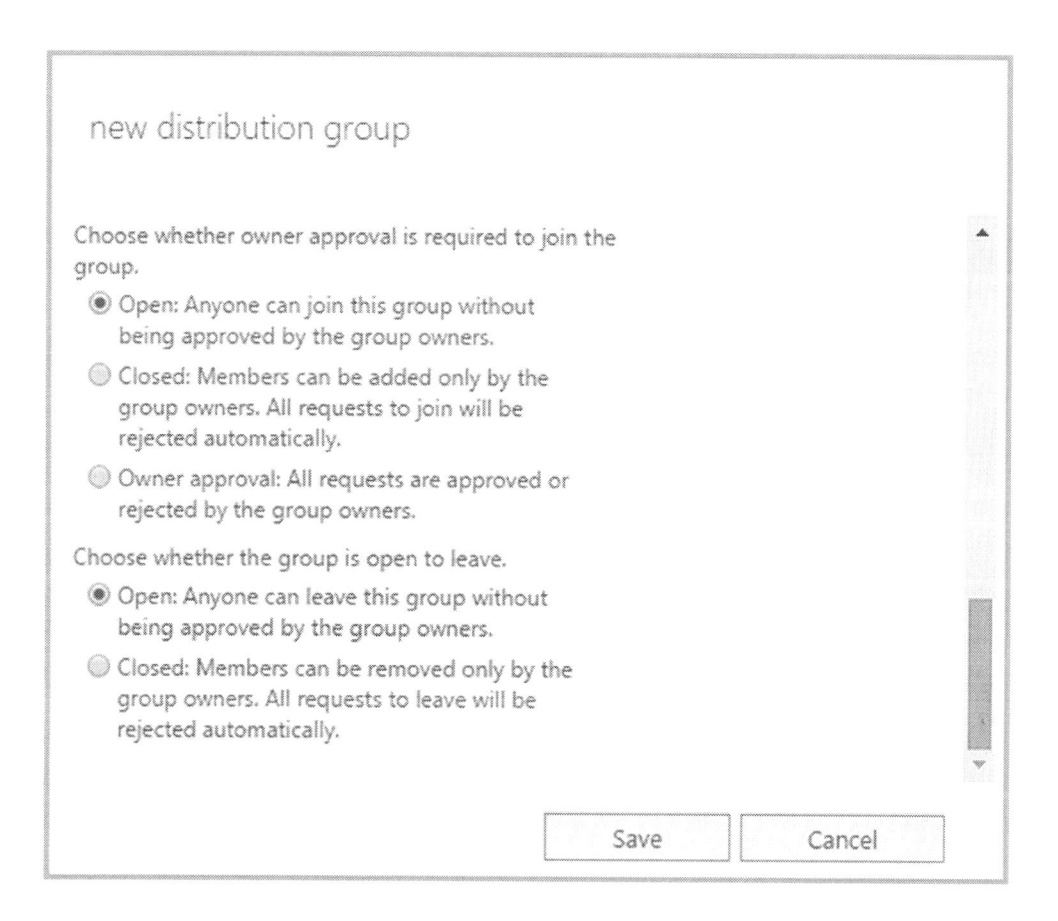

[Save]   [Cancel]

In a remote session with Exchange Online, you can create a new distribution group using the New-DistributionGroup cmdlet. Sample 7-1 provides the syntax and usage. You can set the -Type parameter to Distribution for a distribution group or to Security for a mail-enabled security group.

SAMPLE 7-1 New-DistributionGroup cmdlet syntax and usage

Syntax

```
New-DistributionGroup -Name ExchangeName [-Alias ExchangeAlias]
[-DisplayName DisplayName] [-PrimarySmtpAddress SmtpAddress]
[-SamAccountName PreWin2000Name] [-Type <Distribution | Security>]
{AddtlParams}
```

```
{AddtlParams}
[-ArbitrationMailbox ModeratorMailbox] [-BypassNestedModerationEnabled
<$true | $false>] [-CopyOwnerToMember {$true | $false}]
[-IgnoreNamingPolicy {$true | $false}] [-ManagedBy
```

RecipientIdentities] [-MemberDepartRestriction <Closed | Open | ApprovalRequired>] [-MemberJoinRestriction <Closed | Open | ApprovalRequired>] [-Members **RecipientIdentities**] [-ModeratedBy **Moderators**] [-ModerationEnabled <$true | $false>] [-Notes **String**] [-Organization **OrgName**] [-RoomList {$true | $false}] [-SendModerationNotifications <Never | Internal | Always>]

Usage

```
New-DistributionGroup -Name 'CorporateSales' -Type 'Distribution'
 -SamAccountName 'CorporateSales'
 -DisplayName 'Corporate Sales'
 -Alias 'CorporateSales'
```

Mail-Enabling Universal Security Groups

You can't use Exchange Admin Center to mail-enable a security group. In a remote session with Exchange Online, you can mail-enable a universal security group using the Enable-DistributionGroup cmdlet. Sample 7-2 provides the syntax and usage.

SAMPLE 7-2 Enable-DistributionGroup cmdlet syntax and usage

Syntax

Enable-DistributionGroup -Identity **GroupIdentity** [-Alias **ExchangeAlias**] [-DisplayName **DisplayName**] [-OverrideRecipientQuotas {$true | $false}] [-PrimarySmtpAddress **SmtpAddress**]

Usage

```
Enable-DistributionGroup -Identity 'AllSales'
-DisplayName 'All Sales' -Alias 'AllSales'
```

> **NOTE** Group naming policy applies only to distribution groups.

You can manage mail-enabled security groups in several ways. You can add or remove group members as discussed in the "Assigning and Removing Membership for Individual Users, Groups, and Contacts" section of this chapter. If a group should no longer be mail-enabled, you can use Disable-DistributionGroup to remove the Exchange settings from the group. If you no longer need a mail-enabled security group and it is not a built-in group, you can permanently remove it from Windows

Azure Active Directory by selecting it in Exchange Admin Center and clicking Delete. Alternatively, you can delete a group using Delete-DistributionGroup.

Using a remote session with Exchange Online, you can disable a group's Exchange features using the Disable-DistributionGroup cmdlet, as shown in Sample 7-3.

SAMPLE 7-3 Disable-DistributionGroup cmdlet syntax and usage

Syntax

```
Disable-DistributionGroup -Identity GroupIdentity
[-IgnoreDefaultScope {$true | $false}]
```

Usage

```
Disable-DistributionGroup -Identity 'AllSales'
```

Assigning and Removing Membership for Individual Users, Groups, and Contacts

All users, groups, and contacts can be members of other groups. To configure a group's membership, follow these steps:

1. In Exchange Admin Center, double-click the group entry. This opens the group's Properties dialog box.

2. On the Membership page, you'll see a list of current members. Click Add (✚) to add recipients to the group. In the Select Members dialog box, select users, groups, or both that should be members of the group. Select multiple users and groups using the Shift or Ctrl keys.

3. You can remove members on the Membership page as well. To remove a member from a group, select a recipient, and then click Remove (▬). When you're finished, click **Save**.

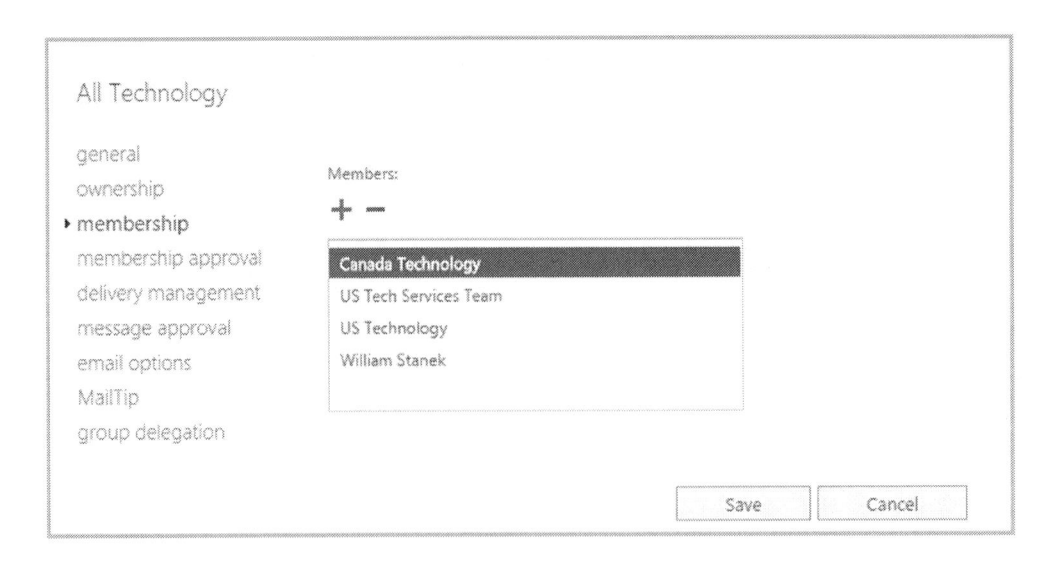

In a remote session with Exchange Online, you can view group members using the Get-DistributionGroupMember cmdlet. Sample 7-4 provides the syntax and usage.

SAMPLE 7-4 Get-DistributionGroupMember cmdlet syntax and usage

Syntax

```
Get-DistributionGroupMember -Identity GroupIdentity [-Credential
Credential] [-IgnoreDefaultScope {$true | $false}] [-ResultSize Size]
```

Usage

```
Get-DistributionGroupMember -Identity 'CorpSales'
```

You add members to a group using the Add-DistributionGroupMember cmdlet. Sample 7-5 provides the syntax and usage.

SAMPLE 7-5 Add-DistributionGroupMember cmdlet syntax and usage

Syntax

```
Add-DistributionGroupMember -Identity GroupIdentity [-Member
RecipientIdentity] [-BypassSecurityGroupManagerCheck {$true | $false}]
```

Usage

```
Add-DistributionGroupMember -Identity 'CorpSales'
  -Member 'imaginedlands.onmicrosoft.com/April Stewart'
```

You remove members from a group using the Remove-DistributionGroupMember cmdlet. Sample 7-6 provides the syntax and usage.

SAMPLE 7-6 Remove-DistributionGroupMember cmdlet syntax and usage

Syntax

```
Remove-DistributionGroupMember -Identity GroupIdentity [-Member
RecipientIdentity] [-BypassSecurityGroupManagerCheck {$true | $false}]
```

Usage

```
Remove-DistributionGroupMember -Identity 'CorpSales'
 -Member 'imaginedlands.onmicrosoft.com/April Stewart'
```

Adding and Removing Managers

Group owners are responsible for managing a group. Every group must have at least one owner. To configure a group's managers, follow these steps:

4. In Exchange Admin Center, double-click the group entry. This opens the group's Properties dialog box.

5. On the Ownership page, lists current owners. Click Add (+) to add recipients to the group. In the Select Owners dialog box, select users, groups, or both that should be owners of the group. Select multiple users and groups using the Shift or Ctrl keys.

6. You can remove owners on the Ownership page as well. To remove an owner from a group, select a recipient, then click Remove (—). When you're finished, click **Save**.

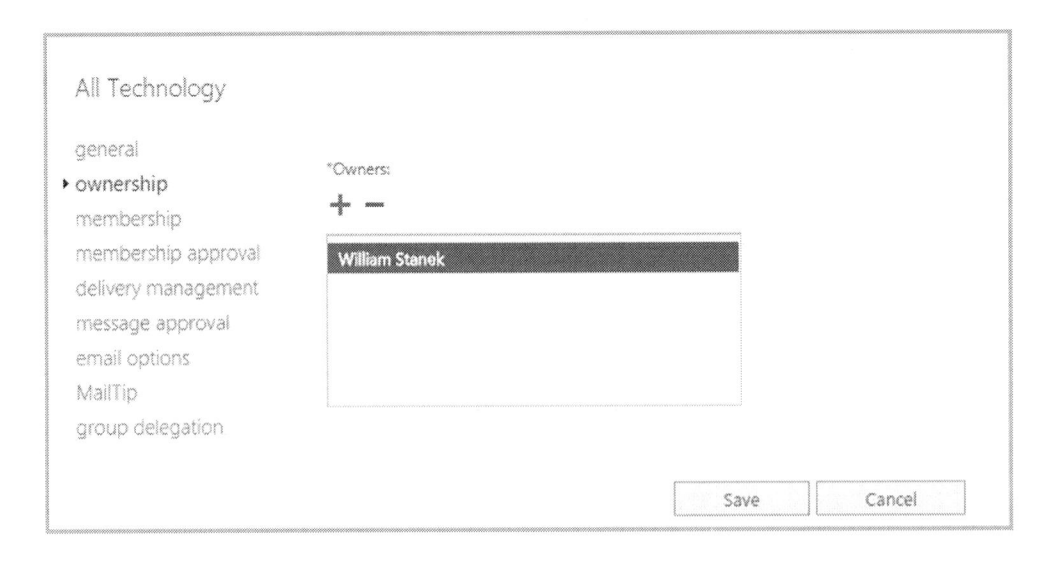

```
All Technology

general
▶ ownership                *Owners:
  membership               + −
  membership approval      ┌─────────────────────────────┐
  delivery management      │ William Stanek              │
  message approval         │                             │
  email options            │                             │
  MailTip                  │                             │
  group delegation         └─────────────────────────────┘

                                        [ Save ]  [ Cancel ]
```

In a remote session with Exchange Online, you can add or remove group managers using the -ManagedBy parameter of the Set-DistributionGroup cmdlet. To set this parameter, you must specify the full list of managers for the group by doing the following:

- Add managers by including existing managers and specifying the additional managers when you set the parameter.
- Remove managers by specifying only those who should be managers and excluding those who should not be managers.

If you don't know the current managers of a group, you can list the managers using Get-DistributionGroup. You'll need to format the output and examine the value of the -ManagedBy property.

Sample 7-7 provides syntax and usage examples for adding and removing group managers.

SAMPLE 7-7 Adding and removing group managers

Syntax

```
Get-DistributionGroup -Identity GroupIdentity | format-table
-property ManagedBy

Set-DistributionGroup -Identity GroupIdentity -ManagedBy GroupManagers
```

Usage

```
Get-DistributionGroup -Identity 'CorpSales' |
format-table -property ManagedBy
```

```
Set-DistributionGroup -Identity 'CorpSales'
-ManagedBy 'imaginedlands.onmicrosoft.com/Oliver Lee',
'imaginedlands.onmicrosoft.com/Jamie Stark'
```

Usage

```
$g = Get-DistributionGroup -Identity 'CorpSales'
$h = $g.managedby + 'imaginedlands.onmicrosoft.com/William Stanek'
```

```
Set-DistributionGroup -Identity 'CorpSales'
-ManagedBy $h
```

Configuring Member Restrictions and Moderation

Membership in distribution groups can be restricted in several ways. Groups can be open or closed for joining or require group owner approval for joining. Groups can be open or closed for leaving. Groups also can be moderated. With moderated groups, messages are sent to designated moderators for approval before being distributed to members of the group. The only exception is for a message sent by a designated moderator. A message from a moderator is delivered immediately because a moderator has the authority to determine what is and isn't an appropriate message.

To configure member restrictions and moderation, follow these steps:

1. In Exchange Admin Center, double-click the group entry. This opens the group's Properties dialog box.
2. On the Membership Approval page, choose settings for joining the group. The options are:

- **Open** Anyone can join this group without being approved by the group owners.
- **Closed** Members can be added only by the group owners. All requests to join will be rejected automatically.
- **Owner Approval** All requests are approved or rejected by the group owner.

3. Choose settings for leaving the group. The options are:

- **Open** Anyone can leave this group without being approved by the group owners.
- **Closed** Members can be removed only by the group owners. All requests to leave will be rejected automatically.

    4. The Message Approval page displays the moderation options. To disable moderation, clear the **Messages Sent To This Group Have To Be Approved By A Moderator** check box. To enable moderation, select the **Messages Sent To This Group Have To Be Approved By A Moderator** check box, and then use the options provided to specify group moderators, specify senders who don't require message approval, and configure moderation notifications.
    5. Click **Save** to apply your changes.

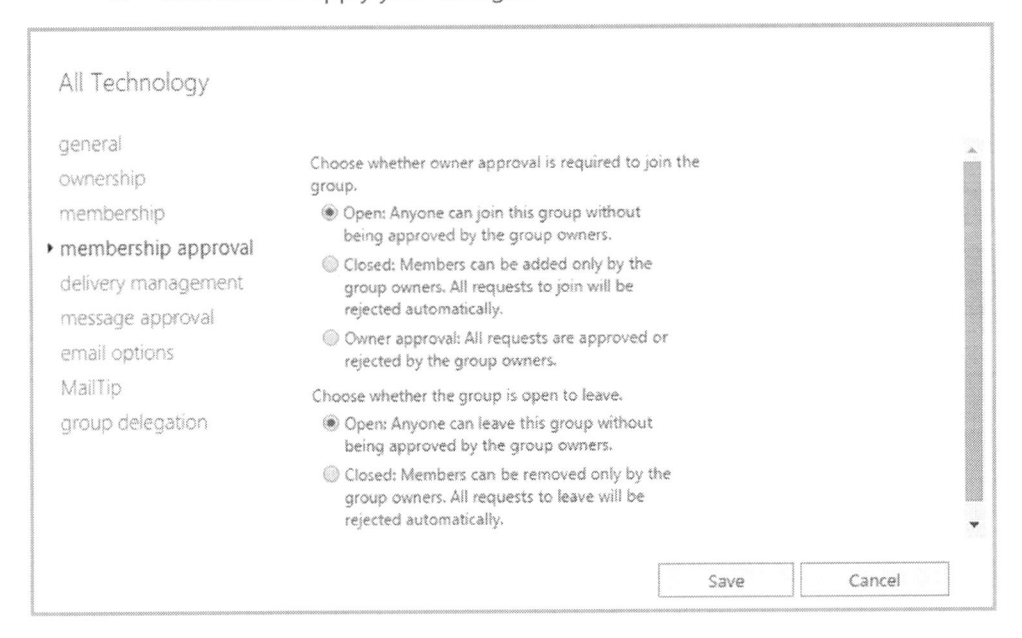

In a remote session with Exchange Online, you manage distribution group settings using Set-DistributionGroup. You configure member restrictions for joining a group using the -MemberJoinRestriction parameter and configure member restrictions for leaving a group using the -MemberDepartRestriction parameter. If you want to check the current restrictions, you can do this using Get-DistributionGroup. You'll need to format the output and examine the values of the -MemberJoinRestriction property, the -MemberDepartRestriction property, or both.

Sample 7-8 provides syntax and usage examples for configuring member restrictions.

SAMPLE 7-8 Configuring member restrictions for groups

Syntax

```
Get-DistributionGroup -Identity GroupIdentity | format-table –property
Name, MemberJoinRestriction, MemberDepartRestriction

Set-DistributionGroup -Identity GroupIdentity
[-MemberJoinRestriction <Closed | Open | ApprovalRequired>]
[-MemberDepartRestriction <Closed | Open | ApprovalRequired>]
```

Usage

```
Get-DistributionGroup -Identity 'AllMarketing' |
format-table –property Name, MemberJoinRestriction,
MemberDepartRestriction

Set-DistributionGroup -Identity 'AllMarketing'
-MemberJoinRestriction 'Closed' -MemberDepartRestriction 'Closed'
```

Set-DistributionGroup parameters for configuring moderation include -ModerationEnabled, -ModeratedBy, -BypassModerationFromSendersOrMembers, and -SendModerationNotifications. You enable or disable moderation by using -ModerationEnabled. If moderation is enabled, you can do the following:

- Designate moderators using -ModeratedBy.
- Specify senders who don't require message approval by using -BypassModerationFromSendersOrMembers.
- Configure moderation notifications using -SendModerationNotifications.

Sample 7-9 provides syntax and usage examples for configuring moderation.

SAMPLE 7-9 Configuring moderation for groups

Syntax

```
Get-DistributionGroup -Identity GroupIdentity | format-table –property
Name, ModeratedBy, BypassModerationFromSendersOrMembers,
SendModerationNotifications

Set-DistributionGroup -Identity GroupIdentity
```

```
[-ModeratedBy Moderators] [-ModerationEnabled <$true | $false>]
[-BypassModerationFromSendersOrMembers Recipients]
[-SendModerationNotifications <Never | Internal | Always>]
```

Usage

```
Get-DistributionGroup -Identity 'AllMarketing' |
format-table -property Name, ModeratedBy,
BypassModerationFromSendersOrMembers, SendModerationNotifications
```

```
Set-DistributionGroup -Identity 'AllMarketing'
-ModerationEnabled $true -Moderators 'AprilC'
-SendModerationNotifications 'Internal'
```

Working with Dynamic Distribution Groups

Just as there are tasks that apply only to security and standard distribution groups, there are also tasks that apply only to dynamic distribution groups. These tasks are discussed in this section.

Creating Dynamic Distribution Groups

With dynamic distribution groups, group membership is determined by the results of an LDAP query. You can create a dynamic distribution group and define the query parameters by completing the following steps:

1. In Exchange Admin Center, select **Recipients** in the Navigation menu and then select **Groups**.

2. Click **New** (✚▾) and then select **Dynamic Distribution Group**. This opens the New Dynamic Distribution Group dialog box.

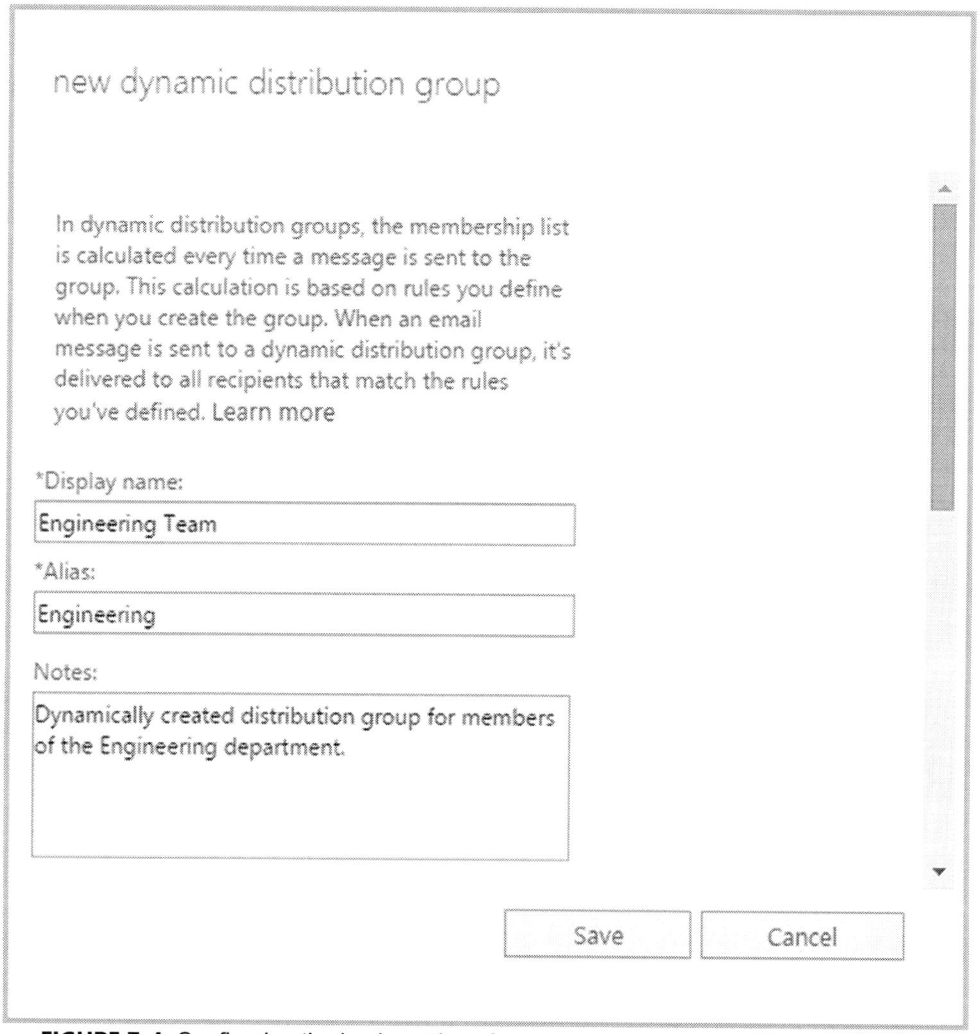

new dynamic distribution group

In dynamic distribution groups, the membership list is calculated every time a message is sent to the group. This calculation is based on rules you define when you create the group. When an email message is sent to a dynamic distribution group, it's delivered to all recipients that match the rules you've defined. Learn more

*Display name:

[Engineering Team]

*Alias:

[Engineering]

Notes:

[Dynamically created distribution group for members of the Engineering department.]

[Save]   [Cancel]

FIGURE 7-4 Configuring the basic settings for the dynamic distribution group.

3. In the Display Name text box, type a display name for the group. Group names aren't case-sensitive and can be up to 64 characters long. Keep in mind that group naming policy doesn't apply to administrators creating distribution groups in Exchange Admin Center.

4. Like users, groups have Exchange aliases. Enter an alias. The Exchange alias is used to set the group's SMTP e-mail address. Exchange uses the SMTP address for receiving messages.

5. Group owners are responsible for managing groups. Unlike standard distribution groups, dynamic distribution groups don't need to be assigned an owner. If you want to specify an owner, under Owner, click Add (✚).

In the Select Owner dialog box, select the user or group that should have management responsibility for the group.

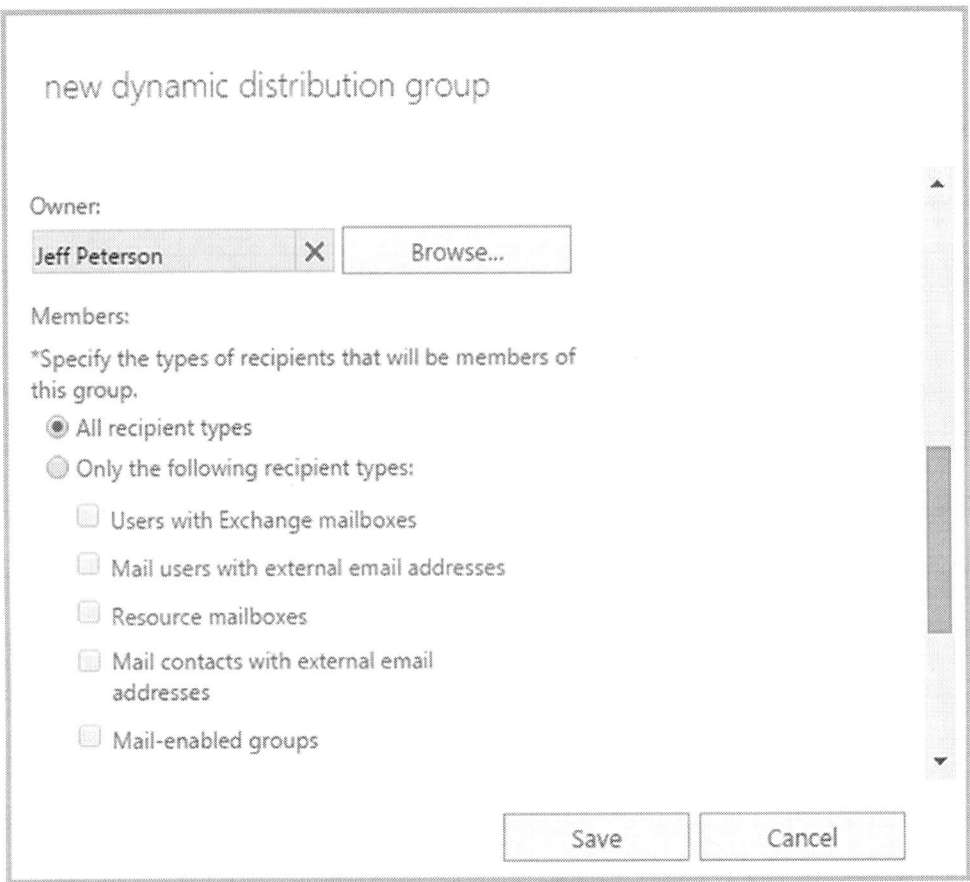

FIGURE 7-5 Configuring ownership and membership settings for the dynamic distribution group.

6. Specify the recipients to include in the group. To allow any recipient type to be a member of the group, select **All Recipient Types**. Otherwise, choose **Only The Following Recipient Types** and then choose the types of recipients to include in the dynamic distribution group.

7. Membership in the group is determined by the rules you define. To define a rule, click **Add A Rule** and set the filter conditions. The following types of conditions as well as conditions for custom attributes are available:

- **State Or Province** Filters recipients based on the value of the State/Province text box on the Contact Information page in the related Properties dialog box. Selecting this option displays the Specify Words Or Phrases dialog box. Type a state or province identifier to use as a filter condition and then press Enter or click Add. Repeat as necessary, and then click OK.

- **Department** Filters recipients based on the value of the Department text box on the Organization page in the related Properties dialog box. Selecting this option displays the Specify Words Or Phrases dialog box. Type a department name to use as a filter condition and then press Enter or click Add. Repeat as necessary, and then click OK.
- **Company** Filters recipients based on the value of the Company text box on the Organization page in the related Properties dialog box. Selecting this option displays the Specify Words Or Phrases dialog box. Type a company name to use as a filter condition and then press Enter or click Add. Repeat as necessary, and then click OK.

> **IMPORTANT** Although each rule acts as an OR condition for matches on specified values, the rules are aggregated as AND conditions. This means that a user that matches one of the values in a rule passes that filter but must be a match for all the rules to be included in the group. For example, if you were to define a state rule for Oregon, California, or Washington and a department rule for Technology, only users who are in Oregon, California, or Washington *and* in the Technology department match the filter and are included as members of the group.

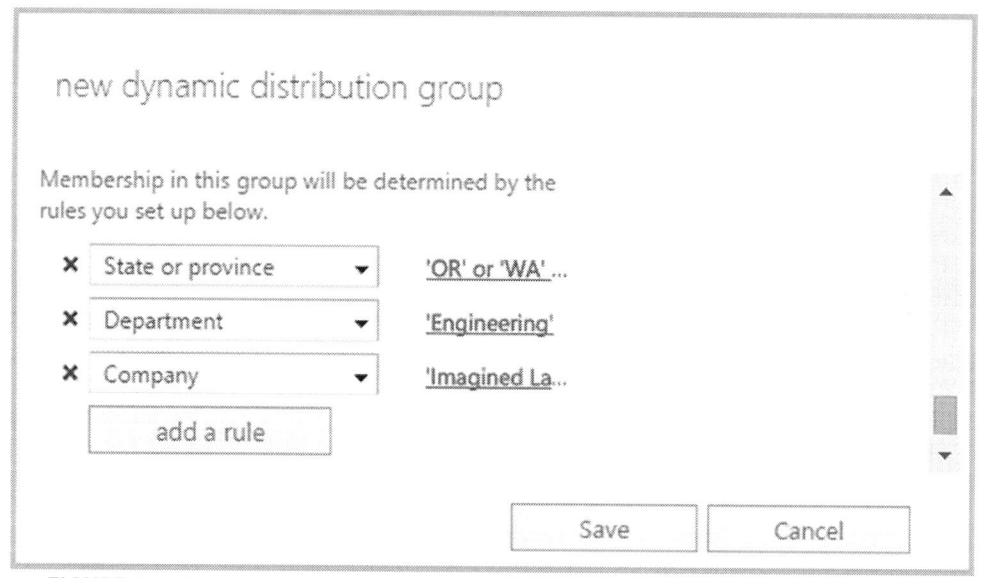

FIGURE 7-6 Setting the filter conditions.

8. Click **Save** to create the group. If an error occurs during group creation, the related group will not be created. You need to correct the problem before you can complete this procedure.

9. Creating the group isn't the final step. Afterward, you might want to do the following:

- Set message size restrictions for messages mailed to the group.

- Limit users who can send to the group.
- Change or remove default email addresses.
- Add more email addresses.

In a remote session with Exchange Online, you can create a dynamic distribution group using the New-DynamicDistributionGroup cmdlet. Sample 7-10 provides the syntax and usage.

SAMPLE 7-10 New-DynamicDistributionGroup cmdlet syntax and usage

Syntax

```
New-DynamicDistributionGroup -Name ExchangeName
-IncludedRecipients <None, MailboxUsers, MailContacts, MailGroups,
Resources, AllRecipients> [-Alias ExchangeAlias] [-DisplayName DisplayName]
[-ConditionalCompany CompanyNameFilter1, CompanyNameFilter2,...]
[-ConditionalCustomAttributeX Value1, Value2,...]
[-ConditionalDepartment DeptNameFilter1, DeptNameFilter2, ... ]
[-ConditionalStateOrProvince StateNameFilter1, StateNameFilter2, ...]
[-RecipientContainer ApplyFilterContainer] {AddtlParams}


New-DynamicDistributionGroup -Name ExchangeName -RecipientFilter Filter
[-Alias ExchangeAlias] [-DisplayName DisplayName]
[-RecipientContainer ApplyFilterContainer] {AddtlParams}
```

{AddtlParams}

```
[-ArbitrationMailbox ModeratorMailbox] [-ExternalDirectoryObjectId ObjectId]
[-ModeratedBy Moderators] [-ModerationEnabled <$true | $false>]
[-Organization OrgName] [-PrimarySmtpAddress SmtpAddress]
[-SendModerationNotifications <Never | Internal | Always>]
```

Usage

```
New-DynamicDistributionGroup -Name 'CrossSales'
  -DisplayName 'CrossSales' -Alias 'CrossSales'
  -IncludedRecipients 'MailboxUsers, MailContacts, MailGroups'
  -ConditionalCompany 'Imagined Lands'
  -ConditionalDepartment 'Sales','Marketing'
  -ConditionalStateOrProvince 'Washington','Oregon','California'
  -RecipientContainer 'imaginedlands.onmicrosoft.com'
```

Changing Query Filters and Filter Conditions

With dynamic distribution groups, the filter conditions determine the exact criteria that must be met for a recipient to be included in the dynamic distribution group. You can modify the filter conditions by completing the following steps:

1. In Exchange Admin Center, double-click the dynamic distribution group entry. This opens the group's Properties dialog box.
2. On the Membership page, use the Specify The Types Of Recipients options to specify the types of recipients to include in the query. Select either **All Recipient Types** or select **Only The Following Recipient Types**, and then select the types of recipients.
3. The Membership page lists the current conditions. The following types of conditions as well as conditions for custom attributes are available:

- **State Or Province** Filters recipients based on the value of the State/Province text box on the Contact Information page in the related Properties dialog box. Click the related Enter Words link. In the Specify Words Or Phrases dialog box, type a state or province identifier to use as a filter condition and then press Enter or click Add. Repeat as necessary, and then click OK.
- **Department** Filters recipients based on the value of the Department text box on the Organization page in the related Properties dialog box. Click the related Enter Words link. In the Specify Words Or Phrases dialog box, type a department name to use as a filter condition and then press Enter or click Add. Repeat as necessary, and then click OK.
- **Company** Filters recipients based on the value of the Company text box on the Organization page in the related Properties dialog box. Click the related Enter Words link. In the Specify Words Or Phrases dialog box, type a company name to use as a filter condition and then press Enter or click Add. Repeat as necessary, and then click OK.

4. Click **Save** to apply the changes.

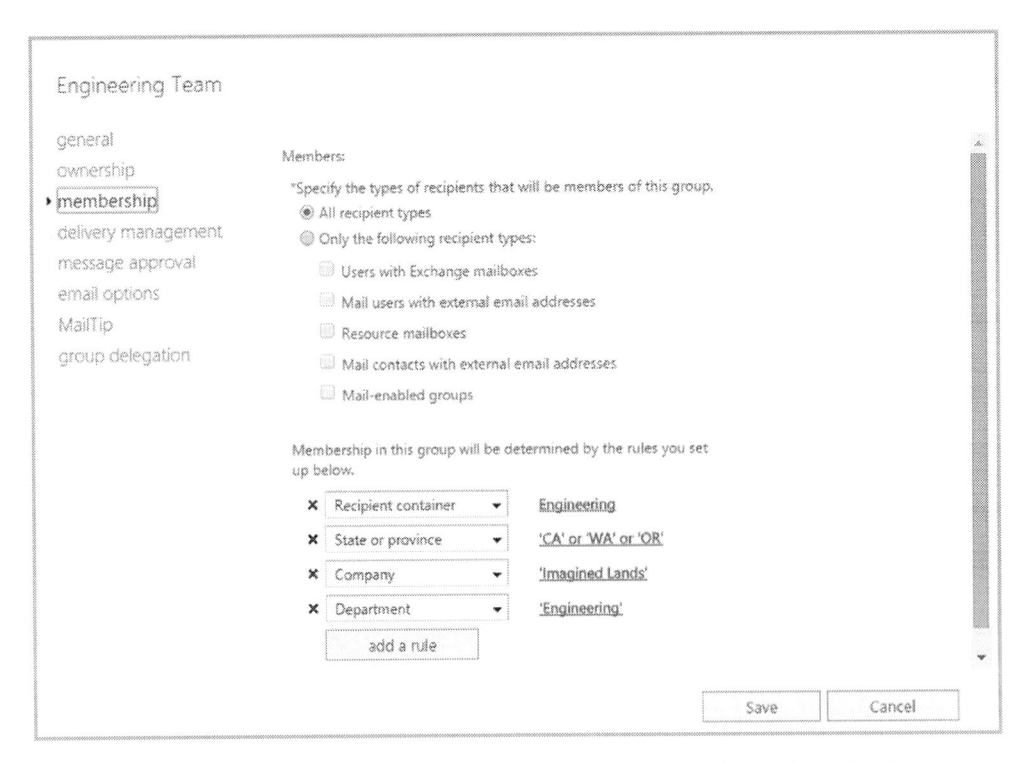

Modifying Dynamic Distribution Groups Using Cmdlets

In a remote session with Exchange Online, you can use the Get-DynamicDistributionGroup cmdlet to get information about dynamic distribution groups and modify their associated filters and conditions using the Set-DynamicDistributionGroup cmdlet.

Sample 7-11 provides the syntax and usage for the Get-DynamicDistributionGroup cmdlet.

SAMPLE 7-11 Get-DynamicDistributionGroup cmdlet syntax and usage

Syntax

Get-DynamicDistributionGroup [-Identity **GroupIdentify** | -Anr **Name**
 | -ManagedBy **Managers**]
[-AccountPartition **PartitionID**] [-Credential **Credential**]
[-Filter **FilterString**] [-IgnoreDefaultScope {$true | $false}]
[-Organization **OrgName**] [-ResultSize **Size**] [-SortBy **Value**]

Usage

```
Get-DynamicDistributionGroup -Identity 'CrossSales'
```

Sample 7-12 provides the syntax and usage for the Set-DynamicDistributionGroup cmdlet.

SAMPLE 7-12 Set-DynamicDistributionGroup cmdlet syntax and usage

Syntax

```
Set-DynamicDistributionGroup -Identity GroupIdentity
[-Alias NewAlias] [-AcceptMessagesOnlyFrom Recipients]
[-AcceptMessagesOnlyFromDLMembers Recipients]
[-AcceptMessagesOnlyFromSendersOrMembers Recipients]
[-ArbitrationMailbox ModeratorMailbox]
[-BypassModerationFromSendersOrMembers Recipients]
[-ConditionalCompany Values] [-ConditionalDepartment Values]
[-ConditionalCustomAttributeX Values]
[-ConditionalStateOrProvince Values] [-CreateDTMFMap <$true | $false>]
[-DisplayName Name] [-EmailAddresses ProxyAddress]
[-EmailAddressPolicyEnabled <$false|$true>] [-ForceUpgrade <$false|$true>]
[-ExtensionCustomAttributeX Value1, Value2,...] [-GrantSendOnBehalfTo Mailbox]
[-HiddenFromAddressListsEnabled <$false|$true>]
[-IgnoreDefaultScope {$true | $false}] [-IncludedRecipients <None,
MailboxUsers, MailContacts, MailGroups, Resources, AllRecipients>]
[-MailTip String] [-MailTipTranslations Locale:TipString, Locale:TipString, ...]
[-ManagedBy Managers] [-MaxReceiveSize Size] [-MaxSendSize Size]
[-ModeratedBy Moderators] [-ModerationEnabled <$true | $false>]
[-Name Name] [-Notes Value] [-PhoneticDisplayName PhName]
[-PrimarySmtpAddress SmtpAddress]    [-RecipientContainer OUName]
[-RecipientFilter String] [-RejectMessagesFrom Recipients]
[-RejectMessagesFromDLMembers Recipients]
[-RejectMessagesFromSendersOrMembers Recipients]
[-ReportToManagerEnabled <$false|$true>]
[-ReportToOriginatorEnabled <$false|$true>]
[-RequireSenderAuthenticationEnabled <$false|$true>]
[-SendModerationNotifications <Never | Internal | Always>]
```

```
[-SendOofMessageToOriginatorEnabled <$false|$true>]
[-SimpleDisplayName Name] [-UMDtmfMap Values]
[-WindowsEmailAddress SmtpAddress]
```

Usage

```
Set-DynamicDistributionGroup -Identity 'CrossSales'
 -IncludedRecipients 'AllRecipients'
 -ConditionalCompany 'Imagined Lands'
 -ConditionalDepartment 'Sales','Accounting'
 -ConditionalStateOrProvince 'Washington','Idaho','Oregon'
 -RecipientContainer 'imaginedlands.onmicrosoft.com'
```

Usage

```
Set-DynamicDistributionGroup -Identity 'CrossSales'
 -ForceUpgrade $true
```

Usage

```
Set-DynamicDistributionGroup -Identity 'CrossSales'
```

Previewing Dynamic Distribution Group Membership

You can preview a dynamic distribution group to confirm its membership and determine how long it takes to return the query results. The specific actions you take depend on the following factors:

- In some cases, membership isn't what you expected. If this happens, you need to change the query filters, as discussed earlier.
- In other cases, it takes too long to execute the query and return the results. If this happens, you might want to rethink the query parameters and create several query groups.

You can quickly determine how many recipients are in the group by checking how many recipients received the last message sent to the group. One way to do this is to follow these steps:

1. In Exchange Admin Center, select the dynamic distribution group entry.
2. In the details pane, look under Membership to see the number of recipients who received the last message sent to the group.

In a remote session with Exchange Online, you can determine the exact membership of a dynamic distribution group by getting the dynamic group and then using the associated recipient filter to list the members. Consider the following example:

```
$Members = Get-DynamicDistributionGroup "TechTeam"
Get-Recipient -RecipientPreviewFilter $Members.RecipientFilter
```

In this example, Get-DynamicDistributionGroup stores the object for the TechTeam group in the $Members variable. Then Get-Recipient lists the recipients that match the recipient filter on this object. Note that the Exchange identifier can be the display name or alias for the group.

Other Essential Tasks for Managing Groups

Previous sections covered tasks that were specific to a type of group. As an Exchange administrator, you'll need to perform many additional group management tasks. These essential tasks are discussed in this section.

Changing a Group's Name Information

Each mail-enabled group has a display name, an Exchange alias, and one or more email addresses associated with it. The display name is the name that appears in address lists. The Exchange alias is used to set the email addresses associated with the group.

Whenever you change a group's naming information, new email addresses can be generated and set as the default addresses for SMTP. These email addresses are used as alternatives to email addresses previously assigned to the group. To learn how to change or delete these additional email addresses, see the "Changing, Adding, or Deleting a Group's Email Addresses" section later in this chapter.

To change the group's Exchange name details, complete the following steps:

1. In Exchange Admin Center, double-click the group entry. This opens the group's Properties dialog box.
2. On the General page, the first text box shows the display name of the group. If necessary, type a new display name.

3. The Alias text box shows the Exchange alias. If necessary, type a new alias. Click **Save**.

> **NOTE** When you change a group's display name, you give the group a new label. Changing the display name doesn't affect the SID, which is used to identify, track, and handle permissions independently from group names.

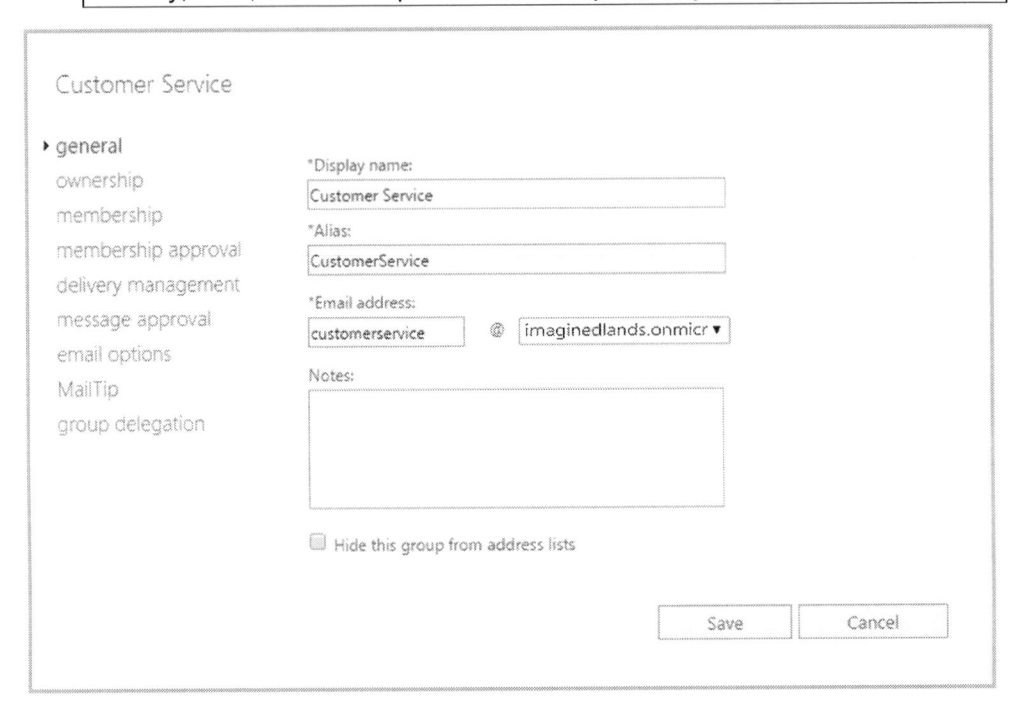

Customer Service

- ▸ general
- ownership
- membership
- membership approval
- delivery management
- message approval
- email options
- MailTip
- group delegation

*Display name:
Customer Service

*Alias:
CustomerService

*Email address:
customerservice @ imaginedlands.onmicr ▼

Notes:

☐ Hide this group from address lists

Save   Cancel

Changing, Adding, or Deleting a Group's Email Addresses

When you create a mail-enabled group, default email addresses are created for SMTP. Any time you update the group's Exchange alias, new default email addresses can be created. The old addresses aren't deleted, however; they remain as alternative email addresses for the group.

To change, add, or delete a group's email addresses, follow these steps:

1. In Exchange Admin Center, double-click the group entry. This opens the group's Properties dialog box.
2. On the Email Options page, use the following techniques to manage the group's email addresses:

- **Create a new SMTP address**   Click Add (+). In the New Email Address dialog box, SMTP is selected as the address type by default. Enter the email address, and then click OK.

- **Create a custom address**   Click Add (+). In the New Email Address dialog box, select Custom Address Type. Enter a prefix that identifies the type of email address, and then enter the associated address. Click OK.

> **TIP**   Use SMTP as the address type for standard Internet email addresses. For custom address types, such as X.400, you must manually enter the address in the proper format.

- **Set a new Reply To Address**   Double-click the address that you want to use as the primary SMTP address. Select Make This The Reply Address, and then click OK. (Exchange Online Only)
- **Edit an existing address**   Double-click the address entry. Modify the settings in the Address dialog box, and then click OK.
- **Delete an existing address**   Select the address, and then click Remove.

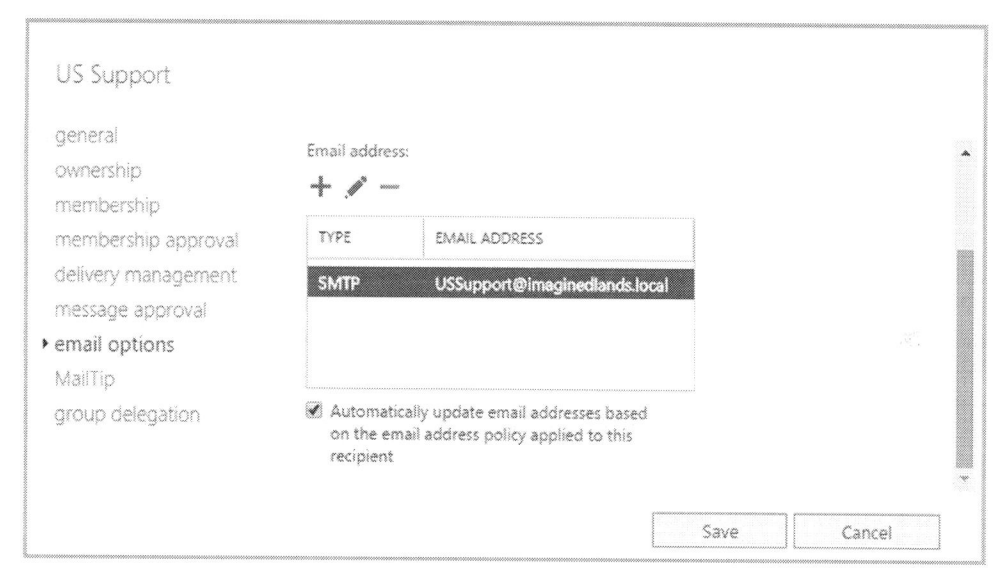

Sample 7-13 provides syntax and usage examples for configuring a group's primary SMTP email address. If email address policy is enabled, you won't be able to update the email address unless you set -EmailAddressPolicyEnabled to $false.

SAMPLE 7-13 Configuring a group's primary SMTP email address

Syntax

```
Get-DistributionGroup -Identity GroupIdentity | format-list -property
Name, EmailAddresses, PrimarySmtpAddress

Set-DistributionGroup -Identity GroupIdentity
-PrimarySmtpAddress SmtpAddress -EmailAddressPolicyEnabled $false
```

Usage

```
Get-DistributionGroup -Identity 'AllSales' | format-list -property
Name, EmailAddresses, PrimarySmtpAddress

Set-DistributionGroup -Identity 'AllSales'
-PrimarySmtpAddress allsales@imaginedlands.onmicrosoft.com
-EmailAddressPolicyEnabled $false
```

Hiding Groups from Exchange Address Lists

By default, any mail-enabled security group or other distribution group that you create is shown in Exchange address lists, such as the global address list. If you want to hide a group from the address lists, follow these steps:

1. In Exchange Admin Center, double-click the group entry. This opens the group's Properties dialog box.
2. On the General page, select the **Hide This Group From Address Lists** check box. Click **OK**.

> **NOTE** When you hide a group, it isn't listed in Exchange address lists. However, if a user knows the name of a group, he or she can still use it in the mail client. To prevent users from sending to a group, you must set message restrictions, as discussed in the next section, "Setting Usage Restrictions on Groups."
>
> **TIP** Hiding group membership is different from hiding the group itself. In Outlook, users can view the membership of groups. In Exchange Online, you cannot prevent viewing the group membership. In addition, membership of dynamic distribution groups is not displayed in global address lists because it is generated only when mail is sent to the group.

In a remote session with Exchange Online, you can return a list of groups hidden from address lists using either of the following commands:

```
Get-DistributionGroup -filter {HiddenFromAddressListsEnabled -eq $true}
```

```
Get-DistributionGroup | where {$_.HiddenFromAddressListsEnabled -eq $true}
```

Setting Usage Restrictions on Groups

Groups are great resources for users in an organization. They let users send mail quickly and easily to other users in their department, business unit, or office. However, if you aren't careful, people outside the organization could use groups as well. Would your boss like it if spammers sent unsolicited email messages to company employees through your distribution lists? Probably not—and you'd probably be sitting in the hot seat, which would be uncomfortable, to say the least.

To prevent unauthorized use of mail-enabled groups, groups are configured by default to accept mail only from authenticated users so that only senders inside an organization can send messages to groups. An authenticated user is any user accessing the system through a logon process. It does not include anonymous users or guests. If you use the default configuration, any message from a sender outside the organization is rejected. Off-site users will need to log on to Exchange before they can send mail to groups, which might present a problem for users who are at home or travelling.

> **REAL WORLD** If you have users who telecommute or send email from home using a personal account, you might be wondering how these users can send mail with a restriction that allows only senders inside the organization to send messages to the group. What I've done in the past is create a group called OffsiteEmailUsers and then added this as a group that can send mail to my mail-enabled groups. The OffsiteEmailUsers group contains separate mail-enabled contacts for each authorized off-site email address.
> Alternatively, users could simply log on using MAPI over HTTP, Outlook Anywhere (RPC over HTTP), Outlook Web App, or Exchange ActiveSync and send mail to the group; this is an approach that doesn't require any special groups with permissions to be created or maintained.

Alternatively, you can allow senders inside and outside the organization to send email to a group. This setting allows unrestricted access to the group, so anyone can send messages to the group. However, this exposes the group to spam from external mail accounts.

Another way to prevent unauthorized use of mail-enabled groups is to specify that only certain users or members of a particular group can send messages to the group. For example, if you create a group called AllEmployees, of which all company employees are members, you can specify that only the members of AllEmployees can send messages to the group. You do this by specifying that only messages from members of AllEmployees are acceptable.

To prevent mass spamming of other groups, you can set the same restriction. For example, if you have a group called Technology, you could specify that only members of AllEmployees can send messages to that group.

You can set or remove usage restrictions by completing the following steps:

1. In Exchange Admin Center, double-click the group entry. In the Properties dialog box for the group, select the **Delivery Management** page.

2. To ensure that messages are accepted only from authenticated users, select **Only Senders Inside My Organization**.

3. To accept messages from all email addresses, select **Senders Inside And Outside Of My Organization**.

4. To restrict senders, specify that messages only from the listed users, contacts, or groups be accepted. To do this, click Add (✚) to display the Select Allowed Senders dialog box. Select a recipient, and then click **OK**. Repeat as necessary.

> **TIP** You can select multiple recipients at the same time. To select multiple recipients individually, hold down the Ctrl key and then click each recipient that you want to select. To select a continuous sequence of recipients, select the first recipient, hold down the Shift key, and then click the last recipient.

5. Click **Save**.

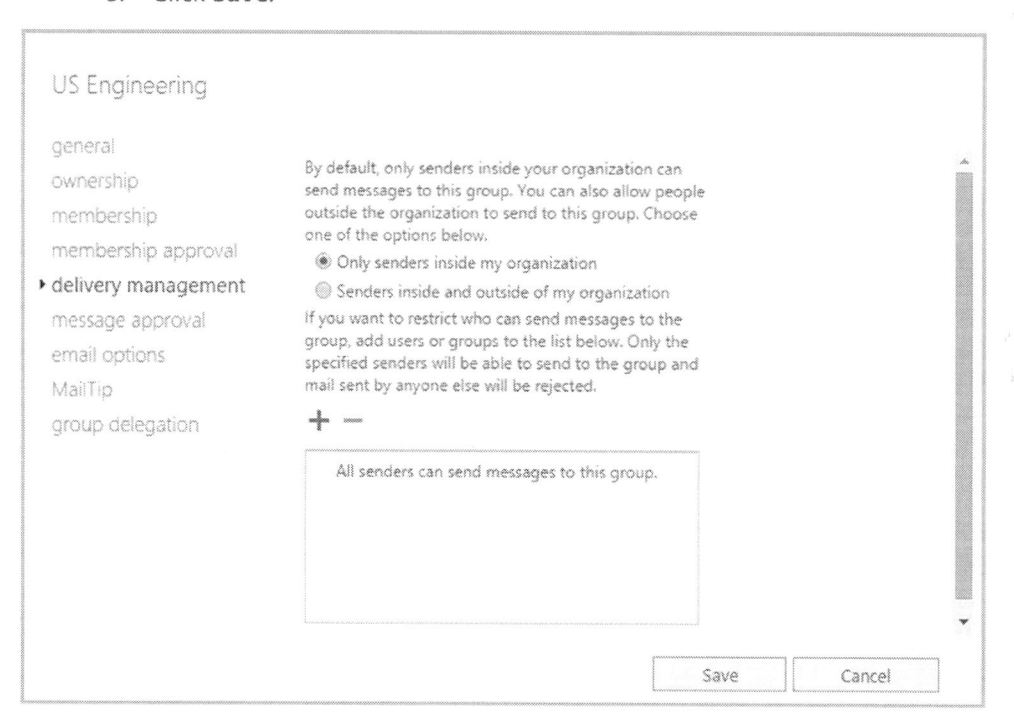

Creating Moderated Groups

By default, senders don't require approval for their messages to be sent to all members of a group. Sometimes though you'll want to appoint moderators who must approve messages before they are sent to all members of the group. If you enable moderation but don't specify a moderator or moderators, the group owner is responsible for reviewing and approving messages. When moderation is enabled, you also can specify users who don't require approval for their messages to be sent to all members of the group.

To see how moderation could be used, consider the following example. A project team is set up to work on a restricted project. The team leader wants a moderated group for the project team so that she must review and approve all messages sent to the group before they are sent to members of the team. As the moderator, the team leader's messages don't require approval and are sent directly to all members of the group.

To configure moderation for a group, complete the following steps:

1. In Exchange Admin Center, double-click the group name to open the Properties dialog box for the group.

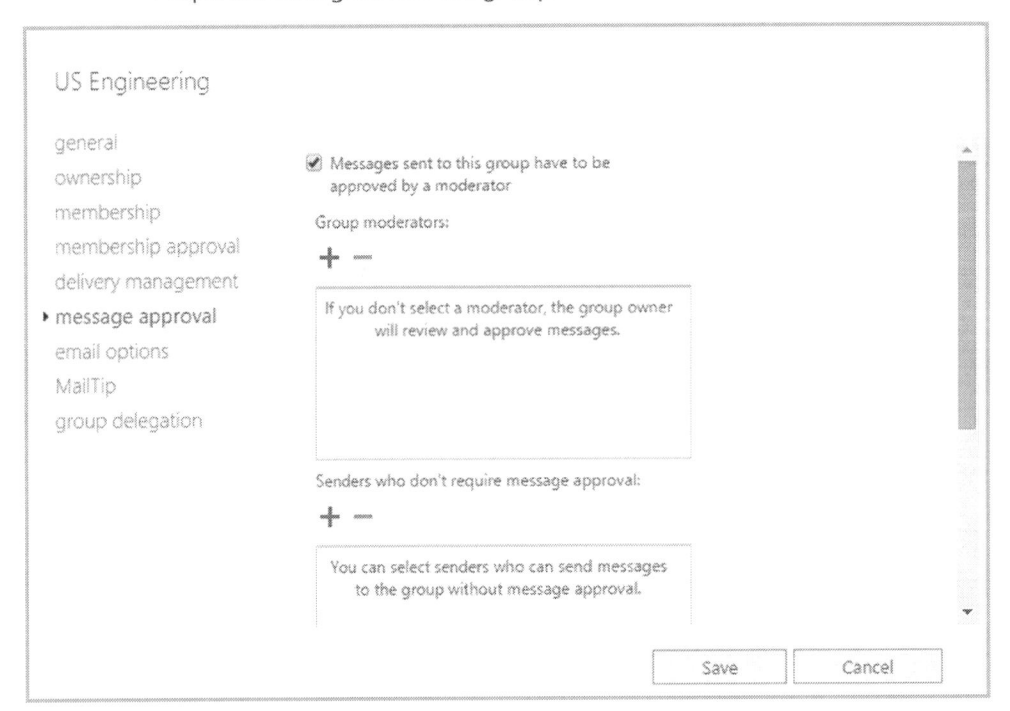

2. On the Message Approval page, do one of the following:

- To enable moderation, select Messages Sent To This Group Have To Be Approved By A Moderator. Next, use the options provided to specify moderators and senders who don't required message approval.

- To disable moderation, clear Messages Sent To This Group Have To Be Approved By A Moderator. Click Save and then skip the rest of the steps.

    3. Use the Group Moderators options to add moderators. If there are any senders who don't require message approval, add these as well using the options provided.

    4. If a message addressed to the group isn't approved, the message isn't distributed to members of the group, and all users receive a nondelivery report (NDR) by default whether they are inside or outside the organization. Alternatively, you can notify only senders in your organization when their messages aren't approved or you can disable notification completely.

    5. Click **Save**.

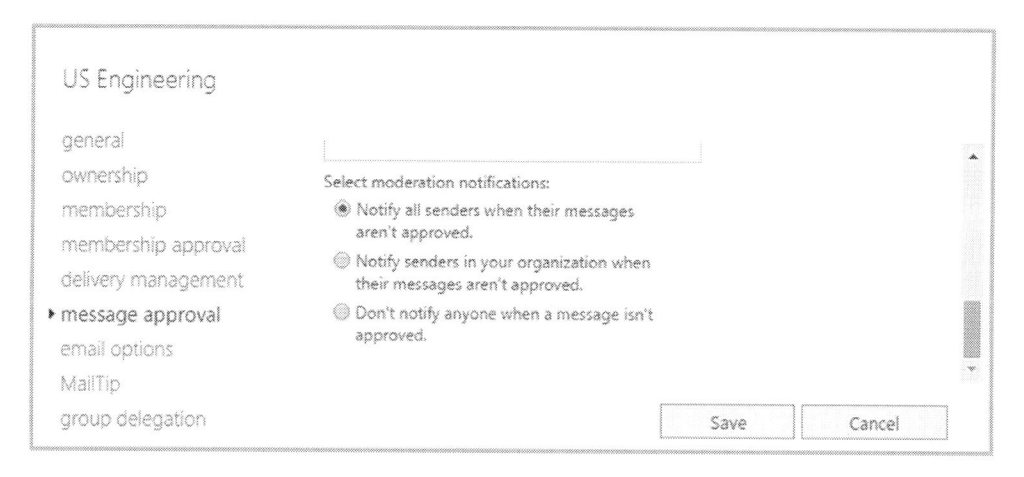

Deleting Exchange Groups

If you are an owner of a group, you can delete it. Deleting a group removes it permanently. After you delete a security group, you can't create a security group with the same name and automatically restore the permissions that the original group was assigned because the SID for the new group won't match the SID for the old group. You can reuse group names, but remember that you'll have to re-create all permissions settings.

You cannot delete built-in groups in Windows. In Exchange Admin Center, you can remove other types of groups by selecting them and clicking Delete. When prompted, click Yes to delete the group. If you click No, Exchange Admin Center will not delete the group.

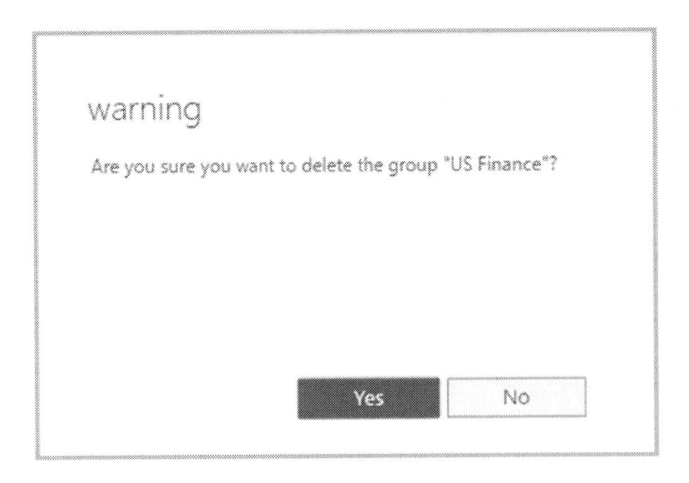

> **warning**
>
> Are you sure you want to delete the group "US Finance"?
>
> [Yes] [No]

In a remote session with Exchange Online, only a group's manager or other authorized user can remove a group. Use the Remove-DistributionGroup cmdlet to remove distribution groups, as shown in Sample 7-14.

SAMPLE 7-14 Remove-DistributionGroup cmdlet syntax and usage

Syntax

```
Remove-DistributionGroup -Identity GroupIdentity
[-BypassSecurityGroupManagerCheck {$true | $false}]
[-IgnoreDefaultScope {$true | $false}]
```

Usage

```
Remove-DistributionGroup -Identity 'imaginedlands.onmicrosoft.com/AllSales'
```

To remove dynamic distribution groups, you can use the Remove-DynamicDistributionGroup cmdlet. Sample 7-15 shows the syntax and usage.

SAMPLE 7-15 Remove-DynamicDistributionGroup cmdlet syntax and usage

Syntax

```
Remove-DynamicDistributionGroup -Identity GroupIdentity
[-IgnoreDefaultScope {$true | $false}]
```

Usage

```
Remove-DynamicDistributionGroup -Identity 'CrossSales'
```

Chapter 8. Configuring Groups for Office 365

When you are working with Office 365, you have access to:

- Exchange Online groups
- Office 365 groups

Exchange Online groups are primarily used for e-mail distribution while Office 365 groups , enable collaboration and sharing within the organization. Chapter 7, "Configuring Groups for Exchange Online," provides a complete discussion of groups used with Exchange Online; this chapter focuses on Office 365 groups.

Getting Started with Groups in Office 365

Office 365 supports three group types:

- **Office 365**   The standard group type, used to enable collaboration and sharing within the organization.
- **Security**   Used to control access to One Drive and SharePoint and for mobile device management.
- **Distribution list**   Used to distribute email to multiple users.

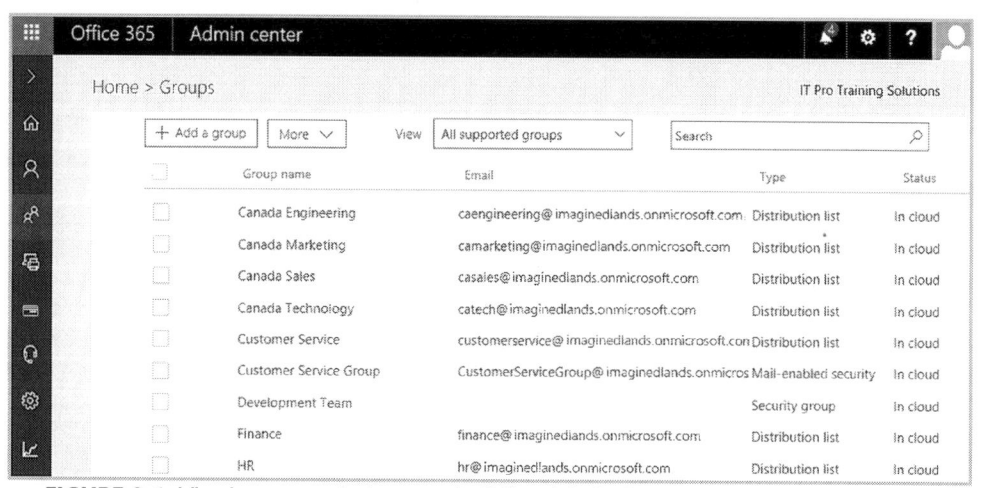

FIGURE 8-1 Viewing supported groups in Office Admin Center

You use Office Admin Center, shown in Figure 8-1, to manage these group types. When you are managing the Office 365 service, select **Groups** in the Navigation menu and then select **Groups** to view a list of all supported groups in the organization.

When working with groups, it's important to keep the following in mind:

- In Exchange Admin Center distribution lists are shown as distribution groups. Distribution lists and standard distribution groups are the same thing.
- Office 365 does not support dynamic distribution groups and these groups are not displayed in Office 365 Admin Center.
- Exchange Admin Center does not support the Office 365 group type and these groups are not displayed in Exchange Admin Center.
- When you create a security group in Exchange Admin Center, the group is mail-enabled automatically (and you can't change this). Such groups are listed as security-enabled distribution lists in Office Admin Center.
- When you create a security group in Office Admin Center, there is no option to mail-enable the group using the graphical interface. Further, security groups without email functionality are listed only in Office Admin Center.
- When you are working with Office Admin Center, only users can be members and you cannot manage other types of members even if they were added in Exchange Admin Center.

The Groups page has a number of management options, including:

[+ Add a group] **Add a Group** – Displays the New Group dialog box which you can use to add supported group types.

[More ∨] **More** – Displays additional options. Click **More** and then click **Refresh** to update the group list. It can take up to 5 minutes or longer for changes made in Exchange Admin Center to be available in Office Admin Center and vice versa.

[Search] **Search** – Performs a search. Find groups by typing their name in full or part and then clicking the Search button ( ). Alternatively, type the search string and then press Enter. After you perform a search, click the Close button (✕) to see the full list of groups again.

View — Controls the type of groups displayed. By default, all supported groups are displayed. Click in the list and then select a group type to filter the view so that only the selected group type is shown.

Creating Security Groups in Office 365

In Office 365, you use security groups to control, access, and manage mobile devices. As security groups created in Office 365 are not mail-enabled, you must use Exchange Admin Center to create mail-enabled security groups. Whether a security group is mail-enabled or not, the group provides the same access and management controls for One Drive, SharePoint and mobile devices.

To create a new security group, complete the following steps:

1. In Office Admin Center, select **Groups** in the Navigation menu and then select **Groups**.
2. Click **Add A Group** to display the New Group dialog box, as shown in Figure 8-2.
3. On the Type drop-down list, select **Security Group**.
4. In the Name text box, type a unique display name for the group. Group names aren't case-sensitive and can be up to 64 characters long.
5. Click **Add** and then click **Close**. If an error occurs, it is most likely because the group name already exists. As the group name must be unique, you'll need to change the name to continue.

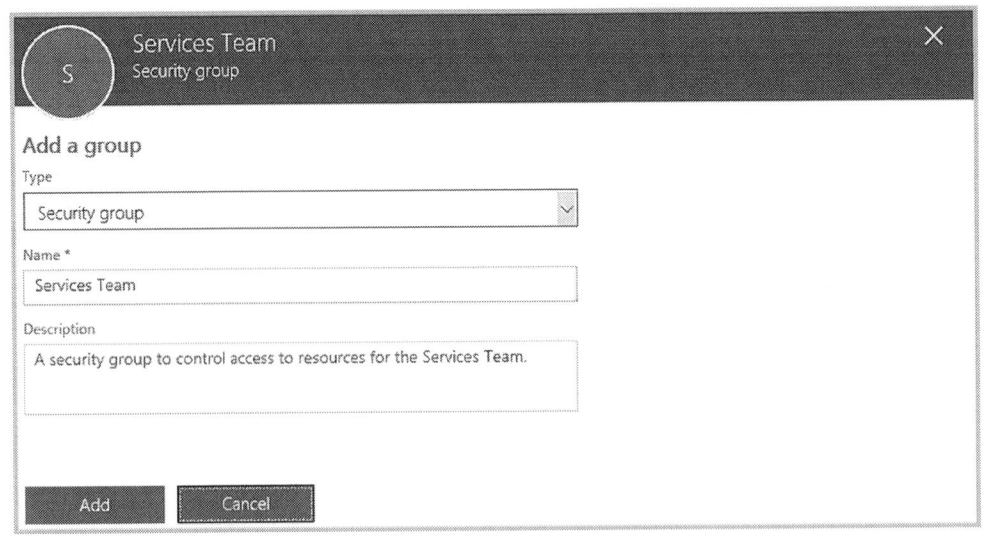

FIGURE 8-2 Creating security groups in Office Admin Center.

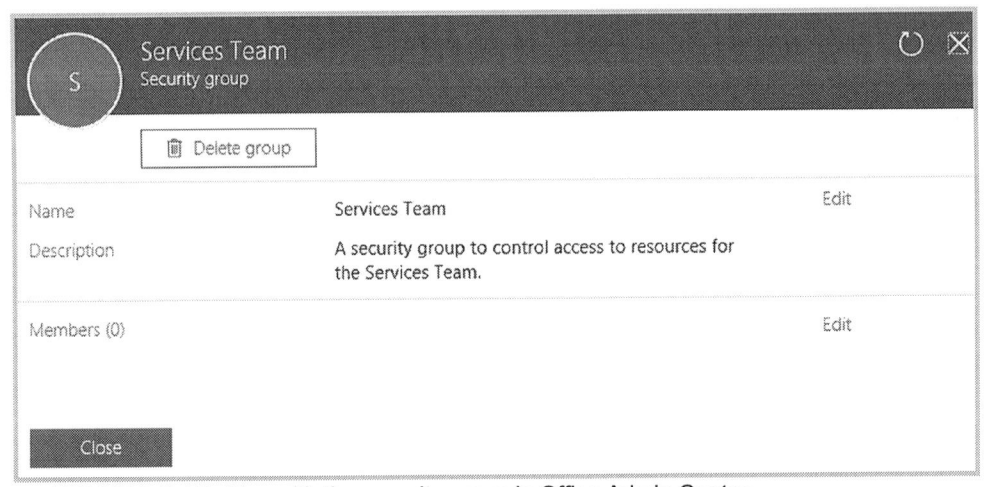

FIGURE 8-3 Working with the security group in Office Admin Center.

6. In Office 365 Admin Center, click the group in the Groups list to display the properties dialog box for the group, shown in Figure 8-3.

7. On the Members panel, click **Edit** and then click **Add Members**.

8. In the Add Members dialog box, shown in Figure 8-4, type a full or partial name entry for a user that you want to add to the group.

9. When a user is listed in the search results, select the related check box to add the user to the Members list. If you make a mistake, clear the related checkbox to remove the user from the Members list.

10. Scroll down and then click **Save** and then click **Close**.

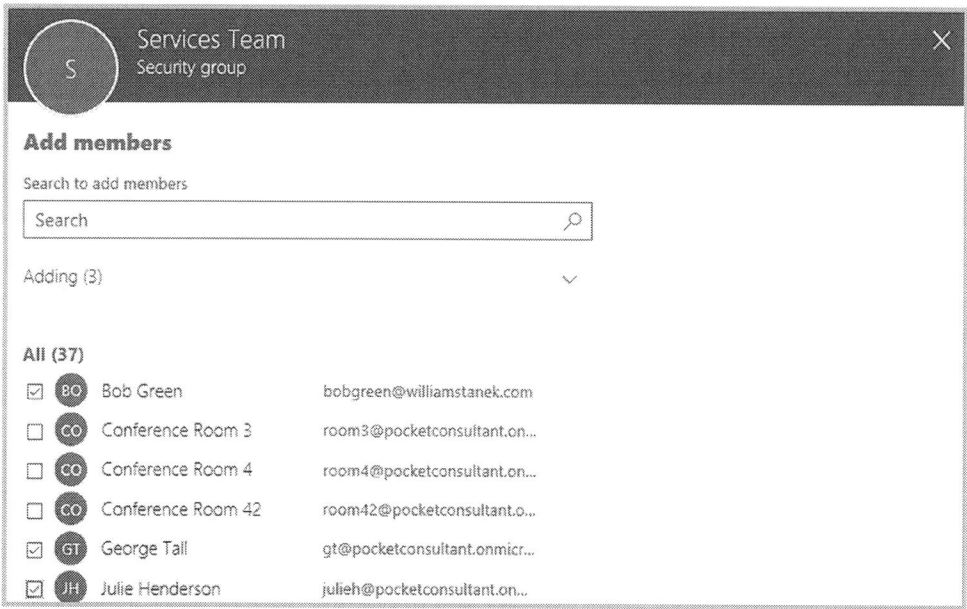

[Screenshot: Services Team Security group dialog showing Add members interface with search box, "Adding (3)" section, and "All (37)" list containing Bob Green, Conference Room 3, Conference Room 4, Conference Room 42, George Tall, and Julie Henderson with checkboxes.]

FIGURE 8-4 Adding members to the security group.

Working with Security Groups in Office 365

After you create a security group, you can manage it in a variety of ways. If you later decide that you want to mail-enable a security group, you'll need to use a PowerShell to do so. In a remote session, use the Enable-DistributionGroup cmdlet to mail-enable the group. The group will then be listed as a security-enabled distribution list in Office Admin Center.

An example showing how to mail-enable a group follows:

```
Enable-DistributionGroup -Identity 'Sales Services Team'
```

You can add or remove group members as discussed in the "Managing Security Group Membership in Office 365" section of this chapter. If a group should no longer be mail-enabled, you can use Disable-DistributionGroup to remove the Exchange settings from the group. If you no longer need a security group, you can permanently remove it by selecting the checkbox for the group in Office Admin Center, clicking the group to open its properties dialog box and then clicking **Delete Group**. When prompted to confirm, click **Delete**.

You also can delete a group using Delete-DistributionGroup. Using a remote session, you can disable a group's Exchange features using the Disable-DistributionGroup cmdlet. An example follows:

```
Disable-DistributionGroup -Identity 'Sales Services Team'
```

Managing Security Group Membership in Office 365

When you are working with Office 365, you can view and manage membership of groups on the Groups page. Although users can be added as members, you cannot manage other member types as these options are only configurable when working with mail-enabled security groups in Exchange Admin Center.

To add members to a security group, follow these steps:

1. In Office Admin Center, select **Groups** in the Navigation menu and then select **Groups**.
2. Click the security group you want to configure. This opens the group's Properties dialog box.
3. On the Members panel, click **Edit** and then click **Add Members**.
4. In the Add Members dialog box, type a full or partial name entry for a user that you want to add to the group.
5. When a user is listed in the search results, select the related check box to add the user to the Members list. If you make a mistake, clear the related checkbox to remove the user from the Members list.
6. Scroll down if necessary. Click **Save** and then click **Close**.

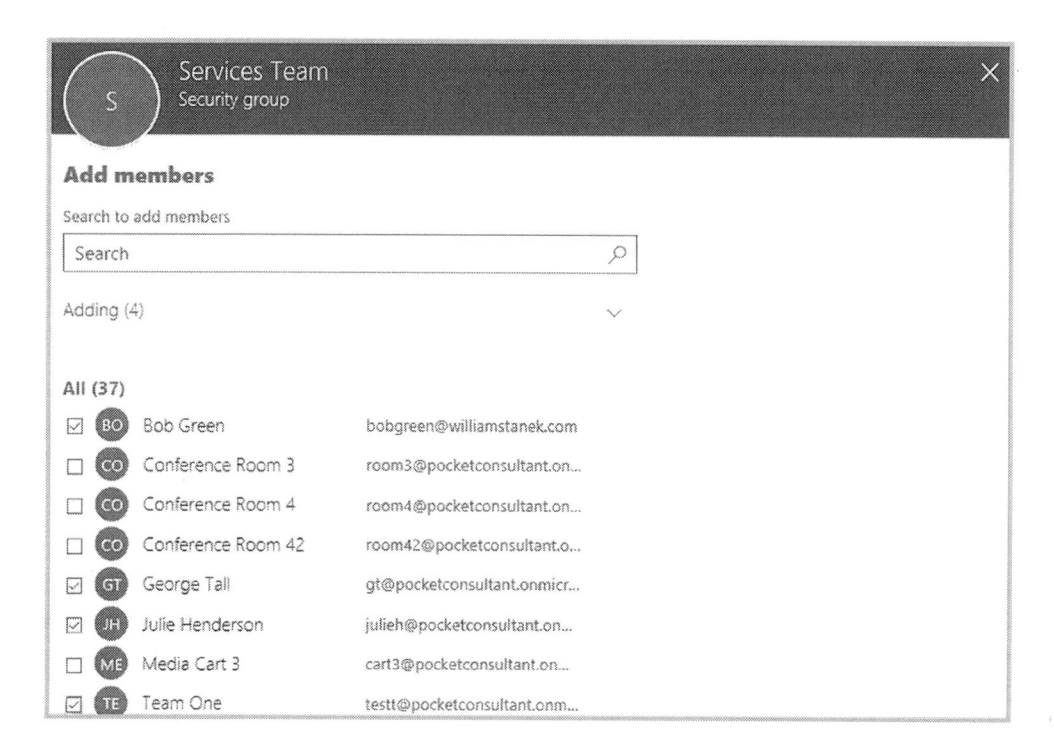

To remove members from a security group, follow these steps:

1. In Office Admin Center, select **Groups** in the Navigation menu and then select **Groups**.
2. Click the security group you want to configure. This opens the group's Properties dialog box.
3. On the Members panel, click **Edit** and then click **Remove Members**.
4. In the Remove Members dialog box, each member is listed by name, followed by an X. To delete a member, click the X that follows the member's name.
5. Scroll down if necessary. Click **Save** and then click **Close**.

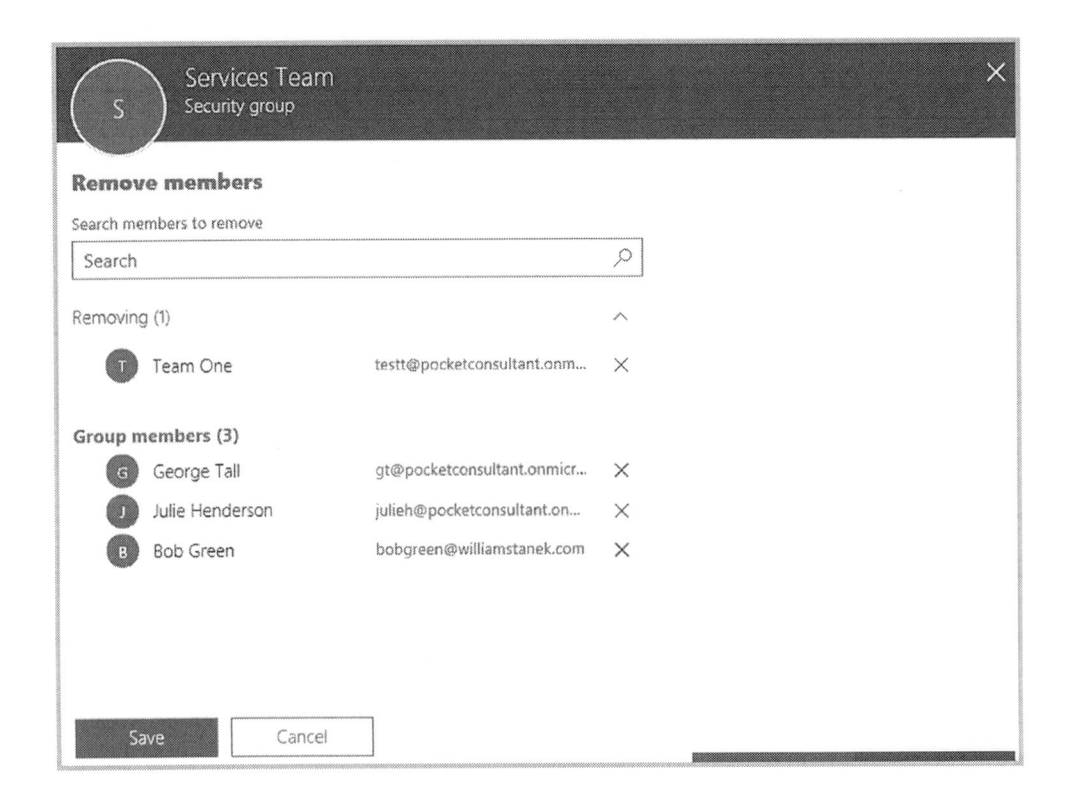

Creating Distribution Lists in Office 365

In Office 365, you use distribution lists to distribute email to multiple users. When you create distribution lists in Office 365, you assign an email address and ownership, much as you do in Exchange Admin Center. However, only users can be added as members. Further, as Office 365 does not support dynamic distribution groups, these groups are not displayed or supported in Office 365 Admin Center.

To create a new distribution list, complete the following steps:

1. In Office Admin Center, select **Groups** in the Navigation menu and then select **Groups**.
2. Click **Add A Group** to display the New Group dialog box, as shown in Figure 8-5.

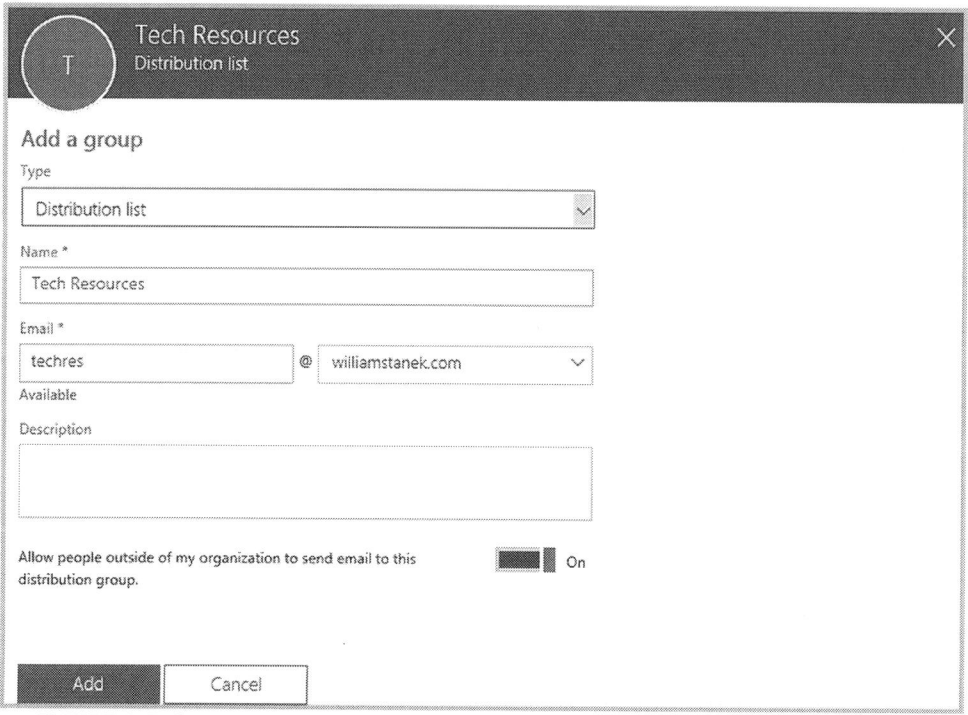

FIGURE 8-5 Creating distribution lists in Office Admin Center.

3. On the Type drop-down list, select **Distribution List**.

4. In the Name text box, type a unique display name for the group. Group names aren't case-sensitive and can be up to 64 characters long.

> **NOTE** Like users, distribution lists have Exchange aliases. The Exchange alias is set automatically based on the group name and used to set the group's SMTP email address. Exchange uses the SMTP address for receiving messages.

5. The name and domain components of the default email address are displayed in the Email Address text boxes. As appropriate, change the default name and use the drop-down list to select the domain with which you want to associate the group. This sets the fully qualified email address, such as ustech@imaginedlands.onmicrosoft.com. Keep in mind that the alias portion of the name must be unique in the organization.

6. By default, people outside the organization can send email to the group. If you want to prevent this, which is a good best practice in most instances, click the related toggle to Off.

7. Click **Add** to create the group and then click **Close**. If an error occurs, it is most likely because the group name or alias already exists. As the group

name and alias must be unique, you'll need to change the name components as appropriate to continue.

8. In Office 365 Admin Center, click the group on the Groups page. Next, on the Members panel, click **Edit** and then click **Add Members**.

```
Tech Resources
Distribution list

Add members
Search to add members
[Search]

Adding (1)

All (31)
☑ BO  Bob Green           bobgreen@williamstanek.com
☐ CA  Canada Engineering  caengineering@pocketconsu...
☐ CA  Canada Marketing    camarketing@pocketconsult...
```

9. In the Add Members dialog box, type a full or partial name entry for a user that you want to add to the group.

10. When a user is listed in the search results, select the related check box to add the user to the Members list. If you make a mistake, clear the related checkbox to remove the user from the Members list.

11. Click **Save** and then click **Close**. The properties dialog box for the group should still be open.

12. Next, add group owners. Group owners are responsible for managing a group. Every distribution list should have at least one group owner. On the Owners panel, click **Edit** and then click **Add Owners**.

13. In the Add Owners dialog box, select the related check box to add a user to the Owners list. If you make a mistake, clear the related checkbox to remove the user from the Owners list. Click **Save** and then click **Close**.

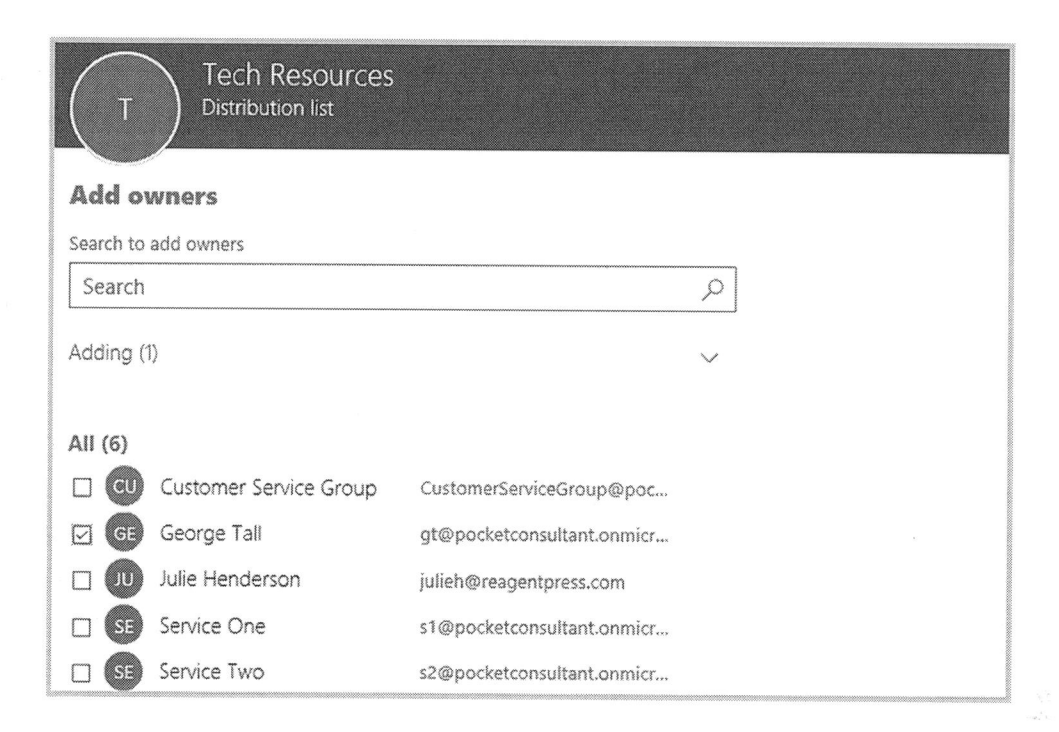

After you create a distribution list, you can manage it in a variety of ways by managing membership, ownership and naming components. All of which are discussed in the sections that follow. If you no longer need a distribution list, you can permanently remove it by selecting the checkbox for the group in Office Admin Center, clicking the group to open its properties dialog box and then clicking **Delete Group**. When prompted to confirm, click **Delete**. Alternatively, you can delete a group using Delete-DistributionGroup.

Managing Distribution List Membership in Office 365

When you are working with Office 365, you can view and manage membership of distribution lists on the Groups page. Although users can be added as members, you cannot manage other member types as these options are only configurable when working with distribution groups in Exchange Admin Center.

To add a member to a distribution list, follow these steps:

1. In Office Admin Center, select **Groups** in the Navigation menu and then select **Groups**.
2. Click the distribution list you want to configure. This opens the group's Properties dialog box.

3. On the Members panel, click **Edit** and then click **Add Members**.

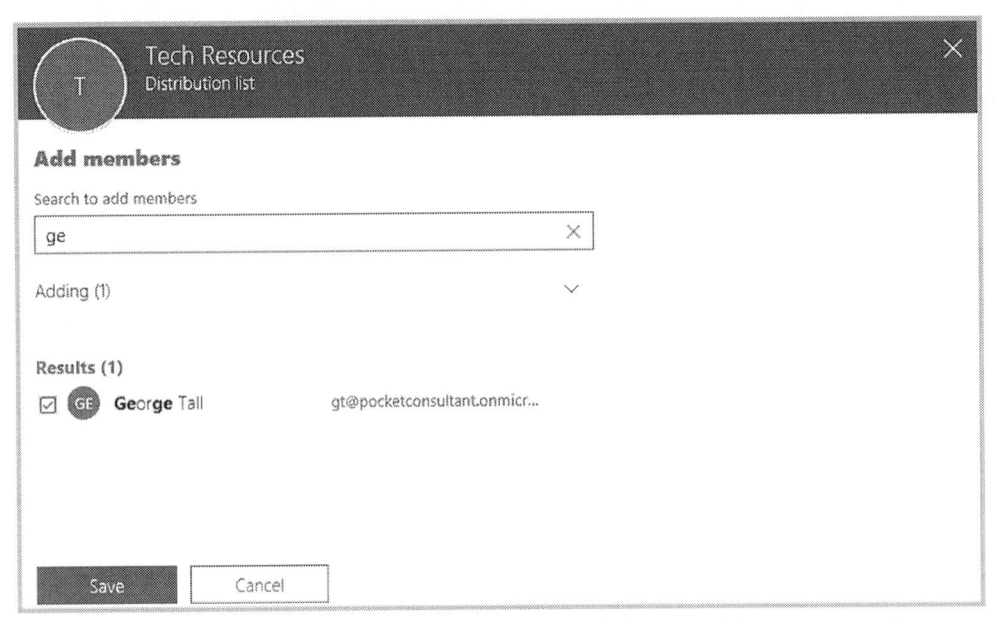

Tech Resources
Distribution list

Add members

Search to add members

ge

Adding (1)

Results (1)

☑ GE George Tall   gt@pocketconsultant.onmicr...

Save   Cancel

4. In the Add Members dialog box, type a full or partial name entry for a user that you want to add to the group.

5. When a user is listed in the search results, select the related check box to add the user to the Members list. If you make a mistake, clear the related checkbox to remove the user from the Members list.

6. Scroll down if necessary. Click **Save** and then click **Close**.

To remove members from a distribution list, follow these steps:

1. In Office Admin Center, select **Groups** in the Navigation menu and then select **Groups**.

2. Click the distribution list you want to configure. This opens the group's Properties dialog box.

3. On the Members panel, click **Edit** and then click **Remove Members**.

4. In the Remove Members dialog box, each member is listed by name, followed by an X. To delete a member, click the X that follows the member's name.

5. Scroll down if necessary. Click **Save** and then click **Close**.

Tech Resources
Distribution list

Remove members

Search members to remove

[Search]

Group members (4)

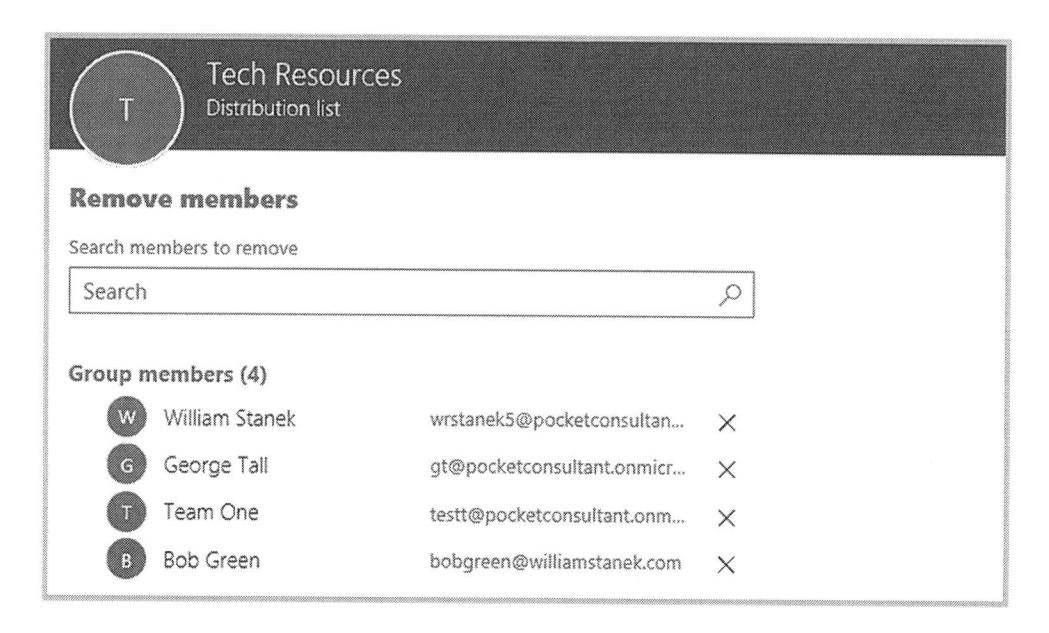

W William Stanek	wrstanek5@pocketconsultan...	×
G George Tall	gt@pocketconsultant.onmicr...	×
T Team One	testt@pocketconsultant.onm...	×
B Bob Green	bobgreen@williamstanek.com	×

In a remote session, you can view group members using the Get-DistributionGroupMember cmdlet. An example follows:

```
Get-DistributionGroupMember -Identity 'Tech Resources'
```

As shown in the following examples, you can add members to a group using the Add-DistributionGroupMember cmdlet and remove members using the Remove-DistributionGroupMember cmdlet:

```
Add-DistributionGroupMember -Identity 'Tech Resources'
 -Member 'imaginedlands.onmicrosoft.com/Mike Caulfield'

Remove-DistributionGroupMember -Identity 'Tech Resources'
 -Member 'imaginedlands.onmicrosoft.com/Sam Fields'
```

Adding and Removing Distribution List Owners

List owners are responsible for managing the properties of distribution lists. Every list must have at least one owner. To add owners to a list, follow these steps:

1. In Office Admin Center, select **Groups** in the Navigation menu and then select **Groups**.
2. Click the distribution list you want to configure. This opens the list's Properties dialog box.

3. On the Owners panel, click **Edit** and then click **Add Owners**.
4. In the Add Owners dialog box, type a full or partial name entry for a user that you want to add as an owner. When a user is listed in the search results, select the related check box to add the user to the Owners list.
5. Click **Save** and then click **Close**.

To remove owners from a list, follow these steps:

1. In Office Admin Center, select **Groups** in the Navigation menu and then select **Groups**.
2. Click the distribution list you want to configure. This opens the list's Properties dialog box.
3. On the Owners panel, click **Edit** and then click **Remove Owners**.
4. In the Remove Owners dialog box, each owner is listed by name, followed by an X. To delete an owner, click the X that follows the owner's name.
5. Click **Save** and then click **Close**.

In a remote session, use the -ManagedBy parameter of the Set-DistributionGroup cmdlet to add or remove members. To set this parameter, you must specify the full list of managers for the group by doing the following:

- Add managers by including existing managers and specifying the additional managers when you set the parameter.
- Remove managers by specifying only those who should be managers and excluding those who should not be managers.

If you don't know the current managers of a group, you can list the managers using Get-DistributionGroup. You'll need to format the output and examine the value of the -ManagedBy property. See Sample 7-7 in Chapter 7 for an example.

Creating Office 365 Groups

You use Office 365 Groups to enable collaboration and sharing within the organization. Members of an Office 365 group have access to a group mailbox and its features, which include:

- Group mail for sending and receiving e-mail to members
- Group conversations for posting and replying to short messages
- A group calendar for viewing and adding meeting invitations and events

- Shared files and folders, typically via the One Drive for Business page used by the group

By default, Office 365 groups can be created and managed by users themselves, who use Outlook or Outlook Web App to do so. As these sharing and collaboration groups are public and open to everyone in the organization by default, users can search for and join available groups. To secure a group and protect its content, a group administrator can make it private . Although any user can search for and see the name of a private group, joining a private group requires the approval of a group administrator. Further, while any user can send email to a private group and receive replies, only the members of a private group can view group conversations, group calendars and shared content.

The privacy of a group cannot be changed once set. Therefore, if you specify a group is public the group cannot be changed to private, and vice versa. It's also important to note that the group alias and email address cannot be changed once set.

You can create an Office 365 group by completing the following steps:

1. In Office Admin Center, select **Groups** in the Navigation menu and then select **Groups**.
2. Click **Add A Group** to display the New Group dialog box.
3. As shown in Figure 8-6, select **Office 365 Group** on the Type drop-down list.

FIGURE 8-6 Creating Office 365 groups.

4. In the Name text box, type a name for the group. Group names aren't case-sensitive and can be up to 64 characters long. The name sets the default Exchange alias for the group, which must be unique in the organization.

5. The name and domain components of the default email address are displayed in the Email Address text boxes. As appropriate, change the default name and use the drop-down list to select the domain with which you want to associate the group. This sets the fully qualified email address, such as testteam@imaginedlands.onmicrosoft.com.

6. By default, Office 365 groups are public and open. To create a private, closed group instead, select **Private** on the Privacy drop-down list.

7. Use the Language selection list to specify the language for group notifications, which include instructions regarding how to work with the group shown in group footers.

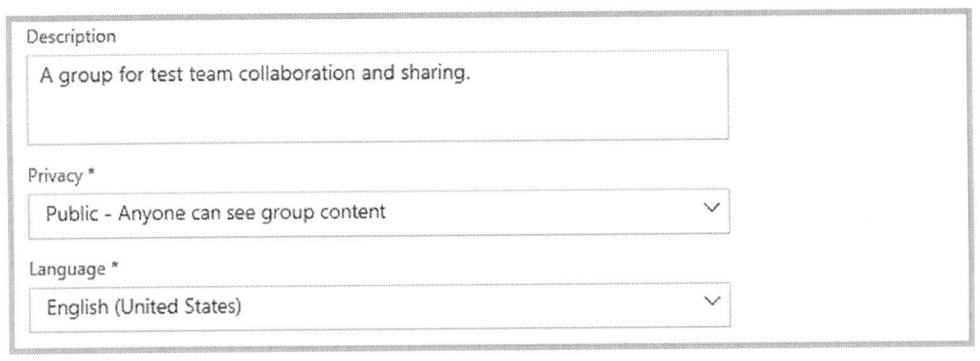

```
Description
A group for test team collaboration and sharing.

Privacy *
Public - Anyone can see group content          ∨

Language *
English (United States)                         ∨
```

8. By default, members are subscribed to group emails, which ensures they see group email, conversations and notifications in their inbox. If members shouldn't receive these emails and instead should only have access to the group inbox, set the Send Copies of Group Conversations switch to Off.

9. Group owners are responsible for managing a group. Every Office 365 group must have an owner. To add designate the group owner, click Select Owner. Next, in the Users list, click the user that should be responsible for the group and then click **Add**.

10. In the Add A Group dialog box, click **Add** to create the group. When the group is ready to use, click **Close**. If an error occurs, it is most likely because the group name or alias already exists. As the group name and alias must be unique, you'll need to change the name components as appropriate to continue.

11. Click the group on the Groups page. Next, on the Members panel, click **Edit** and then click **Add Members**.

12. In the Add Members dialog box, type a full or partial name entry for a user that you want to add to the group.

13. When a user is listed in the search results, select the related check box to add the user to the Members list. If you make a mistake, clear the related checkbox to remove the user from the Members list.

14. Scroll down if necessary. Click **Save** and then click **Close**.

Managing the Properties of Office 365 Groups

You can manage the privacy, subscription, membership and ownership properties of Office 365 groups by completing the following steps:

1. In Office Admin Center, select **Groups** in the Navigation menu and then select **Groups**.

2. Click the Office 365 group you want to configure. This opens the group's Properties dialog box.

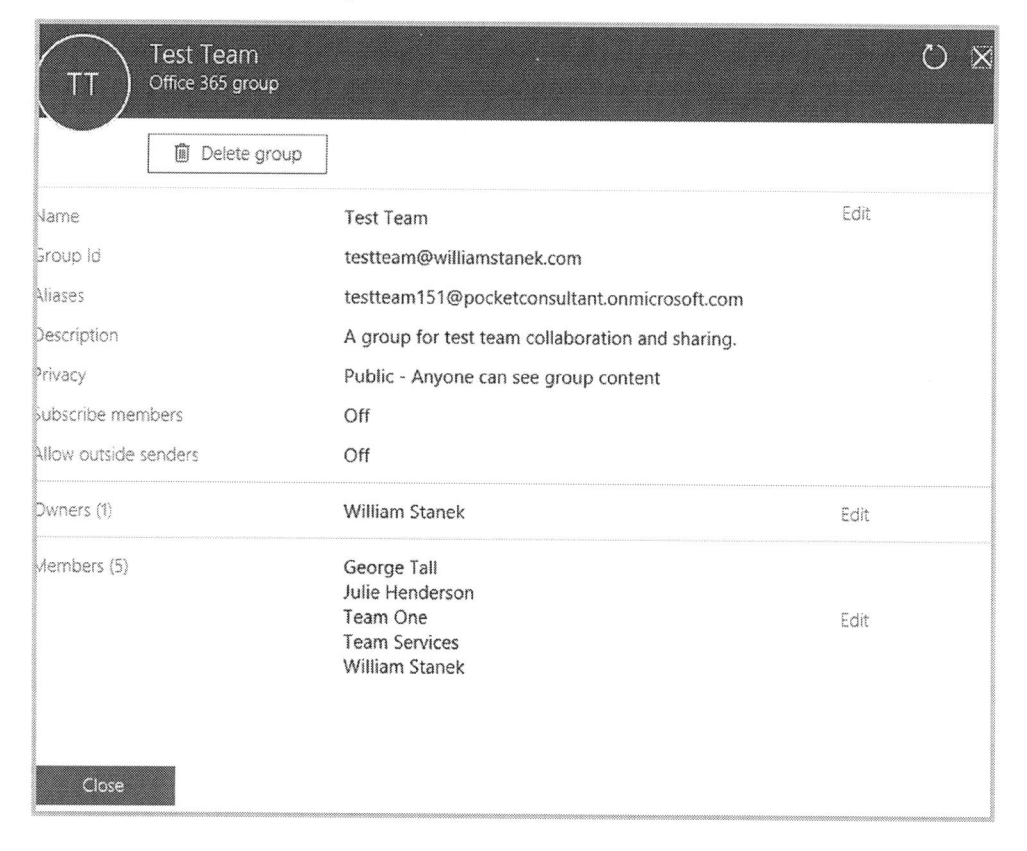

Test Team Office 365 group		
Delete group		
Name	Test Team	Edit
Group Id	testteam@williamstanek.com	
Aliases	testteam151@pocketconsultant.onmicrosoft.com	
Description	A group for test team collaboration and sharing.	
Privacy	Public - Anyone can see group content	
Subscribe members	Off	
Allow outside senders	Off	
Owners (1)	William Stanek	Edit
Members (5)	George Tall Julie Henderson Team One Team Services William Stanek	Edit
Close		

While you are working with the group's properties, you can click **Edit** on the Details panel to edit the display name and description of the group. You can also modify the subscription settings. If members shouldn't receive group emails and notifications in their inbox, set Send Copies Of Group Conversations to Off. Otherwise, set this option to On.

By default, people outside the organization cannot email the group—a setting designed to protect the integrity of the group. To allow people outside the organization to email the group, switch the Let People Outside The Organization Email The Group option to the On position by clicking it. When you are finished changing the basic options for the group, click **Save** to ensure any changes you made are applied.

Modifying the Membership and Ownership of Office 365 Groups

Membership and ownership are the two most common properties of an Office 365 group you'll need to modify. To add owners to an Office 365 grou7p, follow these steps:

1. In Office Admin Center, select **Groups** in the Navigation menu and then select **Groups**.
2. Click the Office 365 you want to configure. This opens the list's Properties dialog box.
3. On the Owners panel, click **Edit** and then click **Add Owners**.
4. In the Add Owners dialog box, type a full or partial name entry for a user that you want to add as an owner. When a user is listed in the search results, select the related check box to add the user to the Owners list.
5. Click **Save** and then click **Close**.

To remove owners from an Office 365 group, follow these steps:

1. In Office Admin Center, select **Groups** in the Navigation menu and then select **Groups**.
2. Click the distribution list you want to configure. This opens the list's Properties dialog box.
3. On the Owners panel, click **Edit** and then click **Remove Owners**.
4. In the Remove Owners dialog box, each owner is listed by name, followed by an X. To delete an owner, click the X that follows the owner's name.
5. Click **Save** and then click **Close**.

Office 365 groups can only have users as members. To add members to an Office 365 group, follow these steps:

1. In Office Admin Center, select **Groups** in the Navigation menu and then select **Groups**.
2. Click the Office 365 group you want to configure. This opens the group's Properties dialog box.
3. On the Members panel, click **Edit** and then click **Add Members**.
4. In the Add Members dialog box, type a full or partial name entry for a user that you want to add to the group.
5. When a user is listed in the search results, select the related check box to add the user to the Members list. If you make a mistake, clear the related checkbox to remove the user from the Members list.
6. Scroll down if necessary. Click **Save** and then click **Close**.

To remove members from an Office 365 group, follow these steps:

1. In Office Admin Center, select **Groups** in the Navigation menu and then select **Groups**.
2. Click the Office 365 you want to configure. This opens the group's Properties dialog box.
3. On the Members panel, click **Edit** and then click **Remove Members**.
4. In the Remove Members dialog box, each member is listed by name, followed by an X. To delete a member, click the X that follows the member's name.
5. Scroll down if necessary. Click **Save** and then click **Close**.

Changing the Naming Information for Groups and Lists

Each group and list that you create in Office 365 has a display name, an Exchange alias, and an email address associated with it. The display name is the name that appears in address lists. The Exchange alias is used to set the email addresses associated with the group.

When you are working with security groups and distribution lists, you can change any of these naming components at any time. However, when you are working with Office 365 groups, the Exchange alias and email address are fixed once set and only the display name can be changed. The reason for this is that Office 365 groups have mailboxes and associated mail data that needs to be fixed so that all members of the group can access the group's shared content.

To change the naming details for a group, complete the following steps:

1. In Office Admin Center, select **Groups** in the Navigation menu and then select **Groups**.
2. Click the group you want to configure. This opens the group's properties dialog box.
3. On the Details panel, click **Edit**.
4. As appropriate, type a new display name for the group in the Name text box. Keep in mind the display name must be unique.
5. As appropriate, change the Exchange alias portion of the email address and use the drop-down list to select the domain with which you want to associate the group. This sets the fully qualified email address, such as testteam@imaginedlands.onmicrosoft.com.
6. Click **Save** and then click **Close**.

Controlling Group Creation

Although any user can create Office 365 groups by default, you can use Outlook Web App (OWA) mailbox policy to control whether users can create groups. The default OWA policy is applied automatically to all users and can be used to control group creation permissions.

In a remote session, you can work with OWA mailbox policies using Get-OwaMailboxPolicy and Set-OwaMailboxPolicy. View available OWA mailbox policies using the Get-OwaMailboxPolicy cmdlet. Sample 8-1 provides the syntax and usage.

SAMPLE 8-1 Get-OwaMailboxPolicy cmdlet syntax and usage

Syntax

```
Get-OwaMailboxPolicy -Identity OrganizationIdentity
```

Usage

```
Get-OwaMailboxPolicy -Identity 'imaginedlands.onmicrosoft.com'
```

The output of Get-OwaMailboxPolicy lists the name of the default policy and any other OWA mailbox policies available. Once you know the policy name, you can use Set-OwaMailboxPolicy to control group creation. If users shouldn't be able to create groups, set the policy's -GroupCreationEnabled parameter to $false. Otherwise, set this option to $true.

Sample 8-2 provides the syntax and a usage example for disabling group creation for all users who have a specified policy applied to their mailbox.

SAMPLE 8-2 Set-OwaMailboxPolicy cmdlet syntax and usage

Syntax

```
Set-OwaMailboxPolicy -Identity PolicyIdentity
-GroupCreationEnabled [<$true | $false>]
```

Usage

```
Set-OwaMailboxPolicy -Identity
'imaginedlands.onmicrosoft.com\OwaMailboxPolicy-Default'
-GroupCreationEnabled $false

Set-OwaMailboxPolicy -Identity
'imaginedlands.onmicrosoft.com\ContractorsOwaMPolicy'
-GroupCreationEnabled $false
```

You can apply a specific OWA mailbox policy to users in several different ways. One way is to use the Set-CASMailbox cmdlet as shown in Sample 8-3. Here the -Identity parameter sets the name of the user you want to work with and the -OwaMailboxPolicy option specifies the policy that should be applied to this user.

SAMPLE 8-3 Set-CASMailbox cmdlet syntax and usage

Syntax

```
Set-OwaMailboxPolicy -Identity "UserMailboxId"
-OwaMailboxPolicy 'PolicyIdentity'
```

Usage

```
Set-OwaMailboxPolicy -Identity "Frank Miller" -OwaMailboxPolicy
'imaginedlands.onmicrosoft.com\ContractorsOwaMPolicy'
```

You also can use Exchange Admin Center to assign an OWA mailbox policy to a user:

1. In Exchange Admin Center under Recipients > Mailboxes, double-click the name of the mailbox user.

2. On the Mailbox Features page, scroll down and then click **View Details** under Email Connectivity.

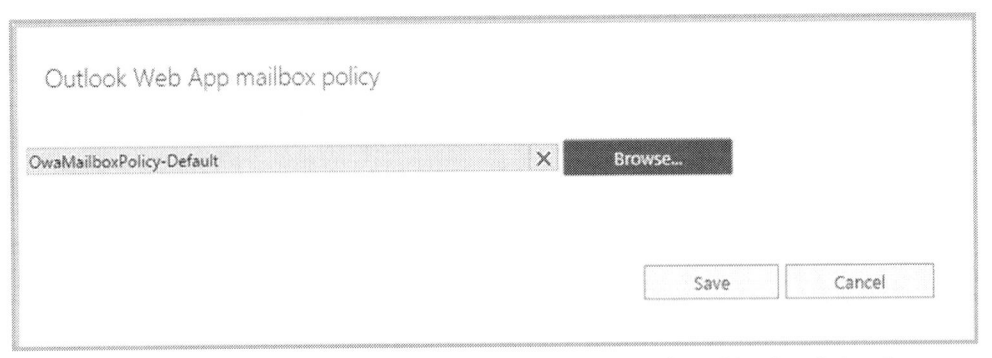

```
Outlook Web App mailbox policy

OwaMailboxPolicy-Default                    X    Browse...

                                            Save        Cancel
```

3. The currently assigned OWA mailbox policy is listed in the dialog box provided. Click **Browse**.

4. When you click a policy in the left pane to select it, the enabled features are listed in the right pane. After you select the policy that you want to assign, click **OK** and then click **Save**.

Deleting Groups in Office 365 Admin Center

If you are an owner of an Office 365 group or have appropriate administrator permissions, you can delete it. Deleting a group removes it permanently. After you delete a group, you can't create a group with the same name and automatically restore the contents associated with the group. With Office 365 groups, the mailbox associated with the group is removed and the associated data is removed as well.

Test Team
Office 365 group

Delete group

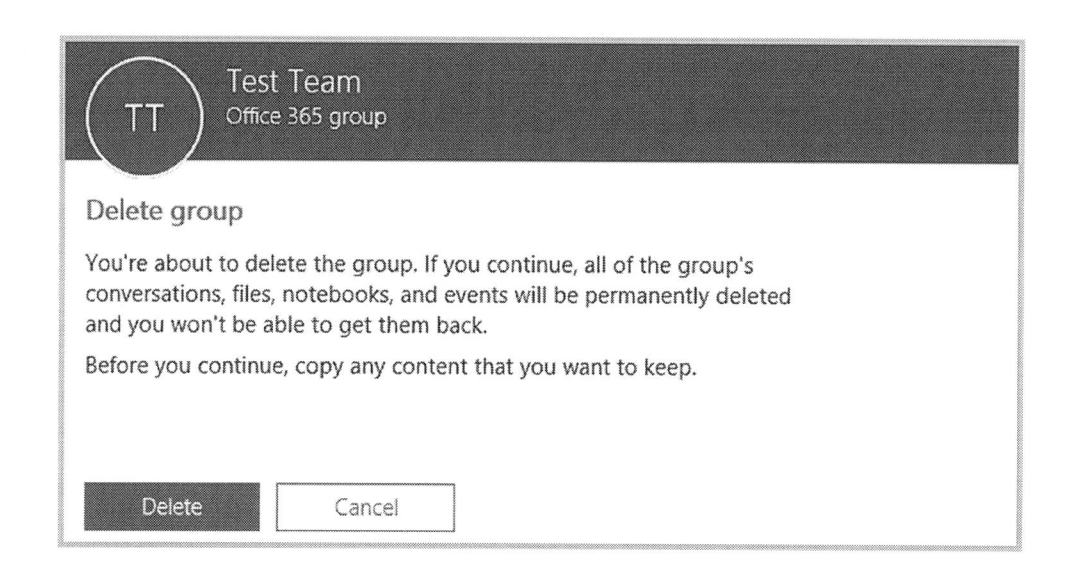

You're about to delete the group. If you continue, all of the group's conversations, files, notebooks, and events will be permanently deleted and you won't be able to get them back.

Before you continue, copy any content that you want to keep.

[Delete] [Cancel]

To delete a group, complete the following steps:

1. In Office Admin Center, select **Groups** in the Navigation menu and then select **Groups**.
2. Click the group you want to remove. This opens the group's properties dialog box.
3. Click **Delete Group**.
4. When prompted, confirm that you want to delete the group by clicking **Delete** and then click **Close**.

Chapter 9. Working with Exchange Clients

Knowing how to configure and maintain Exchange clients is essential for administrators. With Exchange Online, you can use any mail client that supports standard mail protocols. For ease of administration, however, you'll want to choose specific clients for users. I recommend focusing on Microsoft Office Outlook 2010 and later and Outlook Web App as your clients of choice. Each client supports a slightly different set of features and messaging protocols, and each client has its advantages and disadvantages, including the following:

- With Outlook 2010 or later, you get a full-featured client that on-site, off-site, and mobile users can use. Outlook 2010 or later is part of the Microsoft Office system of applications. They are the only mail clients that support the latest messaging features in Exchange. Corporate and workgroup users often need their rich support for calendars, scheduling, voice mail, and email management.
- With Outlook Web App, you get a mail client that you can access securely through a standard web browser whether you are using Windows desktop, Windows Server, iOS or Android. With Microsoft Edge, Internet Explorer 11.0 or later, and current versions of Firefox, Chrome and Safari, Outlook Web App supports many of the features found in Outlook 2010 and later, including calendars, scheduling, and voice mail. With other browsers, the client functionality remains the same, but some features might not be supported. You don't need to configure Outlook Web App on the client, and it's ideal for users who want to access email while away from the office.

Outlook 2010 and later versions are the most common Exchange clients for corporate and workgroup environments. With the MAPI over HTTP feature of Exchange, which uses the Messaging Application Programming Interface (MAPI) over Secure Hypertext Transfer Protocol (HTTPS), Outlook 2010 and later versions might also be your clients of choice for off-site and mobile users.

This chapter shows you how to manage Outlook 2010 and later. For ease of reference, I will refer to Outlook 2010 and later simply as Outlook, unless I need to differentiate between them.

Mastering Outlook Web App essentials

Outlook Web App is a standard Microsoft Exchange technology that allows users to access their mailboxes using a web browser. If public folders are hosted by Exchange

Online, users will be able to access public folder data as well. The technology works with standard Internet protocols, including HTTP and Secure HTTP (HTTPS).

When users access mailboxes and public folder data over the web, Client Access and Mailbox servers are working behind the scenes to grant access and transfer files to the browser. Because you don't need to configure Outlook Web App on the client, it's ideally suited for users who want to access email while away from the office and may also be a good choice for users on the internal network who don't need the full version of Microsoft Outlook. Outlook Web App is automatically configured for use when you set up the Exchange Online organization. This makes Outlook Web App easy to manage. That said, there are some essential concepts you should know to manage Outlook Web App more effectively, and the following section explains these concepts.

Getting started with Outlook Web App

Outlook Web App is configured automatically when you set up the Exchange Online organization. As users will be accessing Outlook Web App over the Internet, the internal firewall must be configured to allow HTTPS connections.

In most cases, you need to open only TCP port 443 on your organization's firewall to allow users to access mailboxes and public folder data over the web. After that, you simply tell users the URL path that they need to type into their browser's Address text box in order to access Outlook Web App.

Outlook Web App has a streamlined interface that is optimized for PCs, tablets, and mobile devices. The browser used to access Outlook Web App determines the experience and supported features. The following two versions are available:

- **Standard**   Provides a rich experience with performance that closely approximates Microsoft Office Outlook, including a folder hierarchy that you can expand or collapse, drag-and-drop functionality, move and copy functionality, and shortcut menus that you can access by right-clicking. In addition, you can use all of the following features: appearance color schemes, calendar views, file share integration, notifications, personal distribution lists, public folder access, recover deleted items, reminders, search, server-side rules, voice mail options, and WebReady Document Viewing.
- **Light**   Provides a basic experience with a simplified user interface when the user's browser cannot support the standard version. This version can also be useful when working over low-bandwidth connections or when there are accessibility needs.

No Standard-only features are available. In addition, calendar options are limited and messages can be composed only as plain text. Outlook Web App shortcut menus are not displayed when you right-click. The Outlook Web App toolbar has slightly different options, and the Options page itself is simplified as well.

> **IMPORTANT** By default, all users see the standard version when their browser supports it. Additionally, Outlook Web App doesn't include a spellchecker as this functionality is now being built into web browsers. Microsoft Internet Explorer 10 and later as well as some other web browsers have built-in spell checkers.

Outlook Web App uses HTML 4.0 and JavaScript [European Computer Manufacturers Association (ECMA)] script. The standard version of Outlook Web App is available for PCs, servers, tablets and smart phones running current versions of Windows, Android and iOS.

Outlook Web App has many features, including:

- **Apps** Users and administrators can add apps to the interface to add functionality. Several apps are installed and made available to users by default, including the following apps created by Microsoft: Action Items, Bing Maps, Suggested Meetings and Unsubscribe. Other apps can be added from the Office Store, from a URL, or from a file.
- **Inbox rules** Users can create Inbox rules to automatically sort incoming email into folders. Users create rules on the Inbox Rules tab or by right-clicking a message on which they want to base a rule, and then selecting Create Rule.
- **Text Messaging Notifications** Users can set up text messaging notifications to be sent to their mobile devices. Notifications are triggered by calendar events, such as meetings and Inbox rules.
- **Message attachments** Users can attach files, meeting requests, and other messages to messages by clicking the attach file icon on the toolbar.
- **Delivery reports** Users can generate delivery reports to search for delivery information about message they've sent or received during the previous two weeks.
- **Personal groups** Users can create personal groups that will appear in their address book.
- **Public groups** Users can create distribution groups that will appear in the global address book for everyone to use.

Using message options, you can specify message sensitivity as Normal, Personal, Private or Confidential. You also can request delivery receipt, read receipt or both.

Accessing Mailboxes and Public Folders

With Outlook Web App, you can easily access mailboxes and public folder data over the web. To access a user's mailbox, type the Outlook Web App URL into your browser's Address text box, and then enter the user name and password for the mailbox you want to access. The complete step-by-step procedure is as follows:

1. In a web browser, enter the secure URL for Outlook Web App, such as https://outlook.office365.com/owa/.

> NOTE   By default, you must use HTTPS to connect. If you don't, the browser is redirected to the appropriate HTTPS URL. Using HTTPS ensures data transmitted between the client browser and the online environment is encrypted and in this way secured.

2. You'll see the logon page for Outlook Web App. Enter the Office 365 email address and password, and then click Sign In.

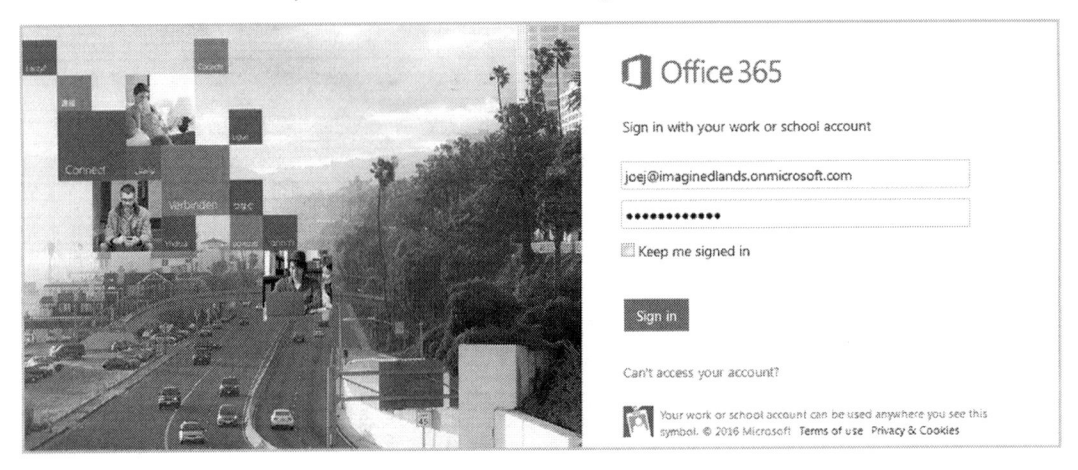

After a user has accessed his mailbox in Outlook Web App, he can access public folders data that is available as well as long as the public folders are hosted on Exchange Online. To access public folders, follow these steps:

1. In the left pane of the Outlook Web App window, right-click More.
2. Select Add Public Folder To Favorites. In the Add Public Folder dialog box, you'll see a list of the available top levels to which you have access.
3. Select a public folder and then click Add To Favorites.
4. Repeat Steps 1 through 3 to add other public folders.

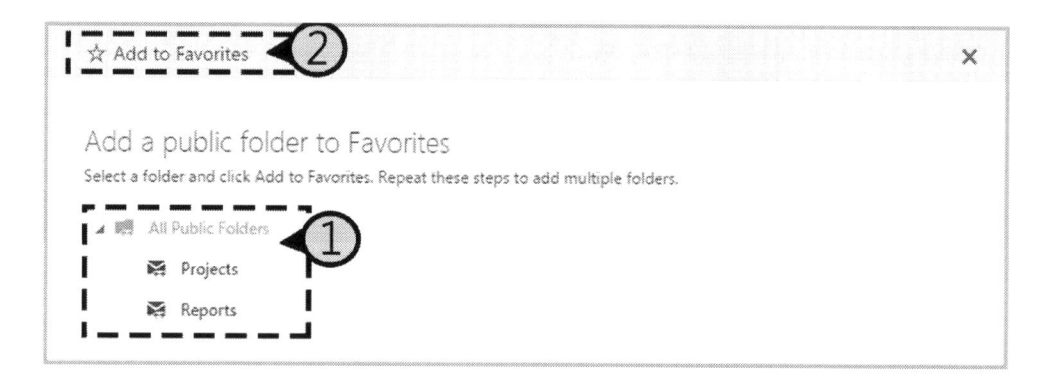

The public folders you've added are listed under the Favorites heading in the left pane. To access a folder and display its contents in the main pane, simply select it in the left pane.

Working with Outlook Web App

After you enter the Outlook Web App URL into a browser's Address text box and log in, you'll see the view of Outlook Web App compatible with your browser. Figure 9-1 shows the full-featured view of Outlook Web App. Most users see this view of Outlook Web App automatically. If their browsers don't support a necessary technology for the full-featured view, some features or options won't be available, or they might see the Light view instead. If they can right-click and see a shortcut menu, they have the full-featured view.

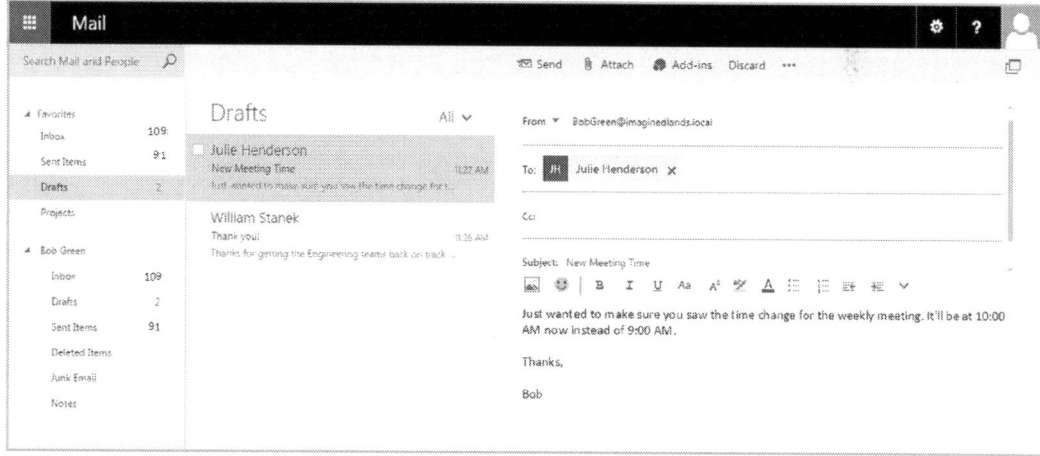

FIGURE 9-1 Outlook Web App has nearly all of the features of Microsoft Office Outlook.

As shown in Figure 9-1, the latest version of Outlook Web App has a toolbar that provides quick access to the following key features:

Apps – Displays a list of the available apps you can switch to, including Mail, Calendar, People and Tasks.

Help – Use this option to access online help for Outlook Web App. You can search for topics, print help text and more.

Settings – Provides quick access to settings for managing automatic replies, display settings, Outlook apps, offline settings, themes, and the user's password. Also allows the user to access the Options page to configure Outlook Web App properties or view current configuration details.

Account – Displays the user's name. Provides options for opening another mailbox and signing out. Also allows you to set the mailbox picture.

Open Window– Opens the message or other item you are working with in a separate window.

Outlook Web App can be configured to allow users to connect their account other email accounts. This allows users to keep send, receive, and read email from other email services. Users also can forward email from their Outlook Web App to another account. If users want to add their contacts from Facebook and LinkedIn to Outlook Web App contacts, Outlook Web App can be configured to do this, too.

Outlook Web App can be configured to allow users to work offline. Users can continue to work when they are disconnected from the Internet when Outlook Web App is configured to cache mail items and other information on the users' computers. When Offline mode is allowed in the Outlook Web App configuration, users can enable offline settings by completing the following steps:

1. In Outlook Web App, select Settings (⚙), Offline Settings, choose Turn On Offline Access. This starts the Offline Settings Wizard.

✓ OK   ✗ Cancel

Offline settings

After you turn on offline access, you can use this computer when it's not connected to a network.

☐ Turn on offline access

---

2. As the cached mail and other information stored on a user's computer could be accessed by other users of a computer, the wizard prompts to ensure the current user is the only person who uses the computer. Click **Yes** to confirm.

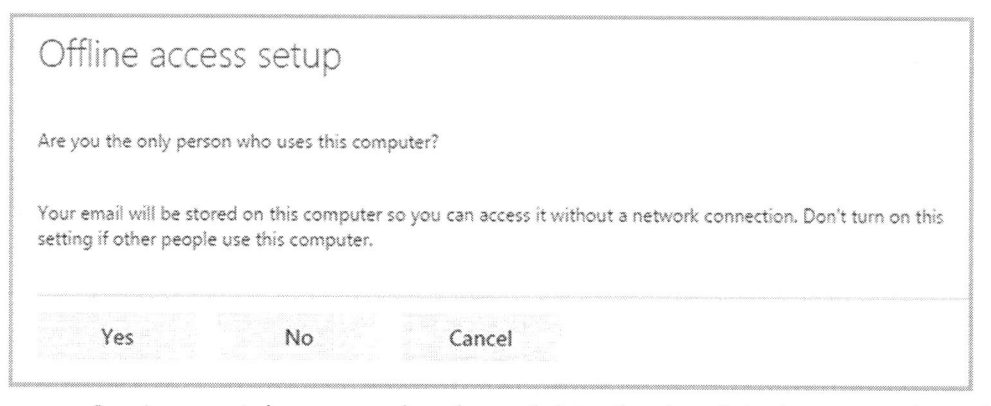

Offline access setup

Are you the only person who uses this computer?

Your email will be stored on this computer so you can access it without a network connection. Don't turn on this setting if other people use this computer.

Yes   No   Cancel

---

3. As a user's browser caches the mail data, the size of the browser cache and other related settings might need to be changed. If prompted to grant more storage to the browser, click **Yes**.
4. Click **Next** to continue. When prompted, press Ctrl+D to create a bookmark for quickly accessing Outlook Web App.
5. Click **Next** and then click **OK**.

By default, the Inbox and Drafts folder, as well as recently used folders are synced for offline use. To designate folders that should always be synced:

1. In Outlook Web App, select Settings (⚙), Offline Settings.
2. Up to five folders can be selected for syncing. Any currently selected folder is listed by name in one of the five designated slots.

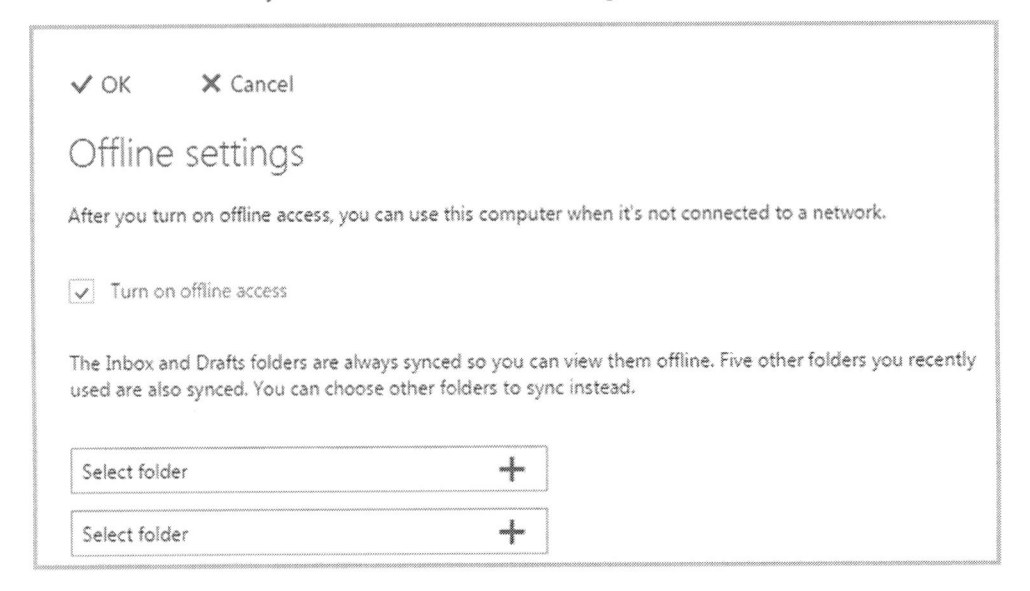

✓ OK   ✗ Cancel

Offline settings

After you turn on offline access, you can use this computer when it's not connected to a network.

☑ Turn on offline access

The Inbox and Drafts folders are always synced so you can view them offline. Five other folders you recently used are also synced. You can choose other folders to sync instead.

| Select folder | + |
| Select folder | + |

You can now add or remove synced folders:

- To add a folder, click **Select Folder**. In the Select Folder dialog box, click the folder to sync, such as Sent Items, and then click **OK**.

- To remove a folder, click the Remove button (✗) to the right of the folder name.

The primary offline data for Outlook Web App and the user's mailbox is cached under %LocalAppData%\Microsoft\Windows\WebCache on the computer. After offline access is enabled, the browser reads data from this cache, allowing users to continue to work with Outlook Web App and access mail, contacts, and other mail data when their computers aren't connected to the Internet.

If offline mode has been enabled, you can turn this feature off by:

1. In Outlook Web App, select Settings (⚙), Offline Settings.
2. Clear the Turn On Offline Access checkbox and then click **OK**.

Disabling offline access doesn't remove the cached data, nor does clearing the browser cache. Because the cached mail data is persistent across browser sessions and independent of the browser's local cache, you must manually remove this data if you want to be certain the data can no longer be accessed.

Enabling and Disabling Web Access for Users

Exchange Online enables Outlook Web App for each user by default and applies the Default Outlook Web App Mailbox policy to each user. Outlook Web App Mailbox policy controls the features that are enabled for each user and allows users to:

- Use Instant Messaging, text messaging, unified messaging, and Exchange Active Sync
- Create and manage personal contacts, and access all internal address lists
- Use Journaling, notes, Inbox rules, and recover deleted items
- Change their password and configure junk email filters
- Use themes, the premium client, and email signatures
- Manage calendars, tasks, reminders, and notifications

If necessary, you can enable or disable Outlook Web App or set a new default policy for specific users by completing the following steps:

1. In Exchange Admin Center, select Recipients in the Feature pane, and then select Mailboxes. You should now see a list of users with Exchange mailboxes in the organization.
2. Select the user you want to work with in the main pane.
3. In the details pane, the current status of Outlook Web App is listed under the Email Connectivity heading, as shown in Figure 9-2.

![Exchange admin center screenshot showing mailboxes list with Email Connectivity options highlighted]

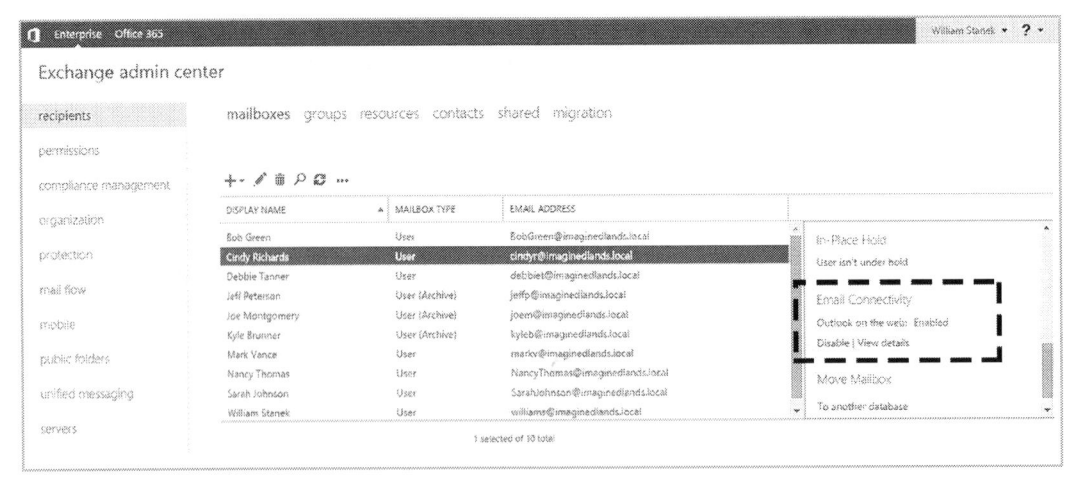

FIGURE 9-2 Use the options under Email Connectivity to manage a user's web access settings.

- To disable Outlook Web App for the user you selected, click Disable. When prompted to confirm, click Yes.

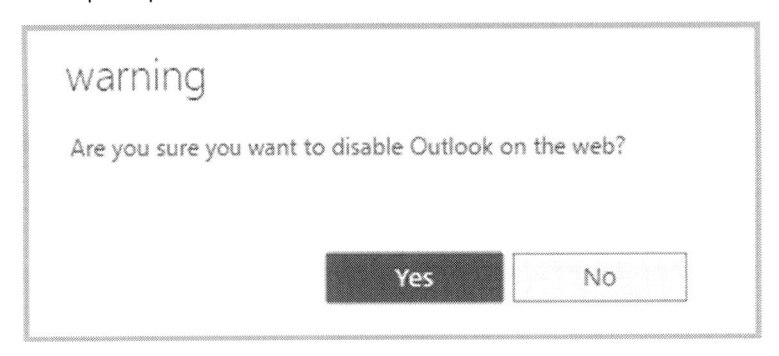

![Warning dialog: Are you sure you want to disable Outlook on the web? Yes/No]

- To enable Outlook Web App for the user you selected, click Enable. When prompted to confirm, click Yes.

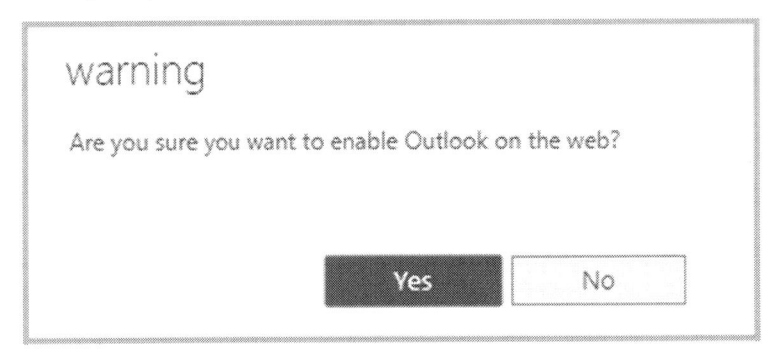

![Warning dialog: Are you sure you want to enable Outlook on the web? Yes/No]

While you are working with Outlook Web App, you may want to determine the mailbox policy currently being applied. To view or change a user's Outlook Web App mailbox policy, do the following:

- Click **View Details**. In the Outlook Web App Mailbox Policy dialog box, the currently assigned policy is listed or the policy entry is blank, which means the default policy is currently applied.
- To assign a different policy, click **Browse**. Select a policy to view its enabled features. When you've selected the policy you want to use, click **OK**, and then click **Save**.

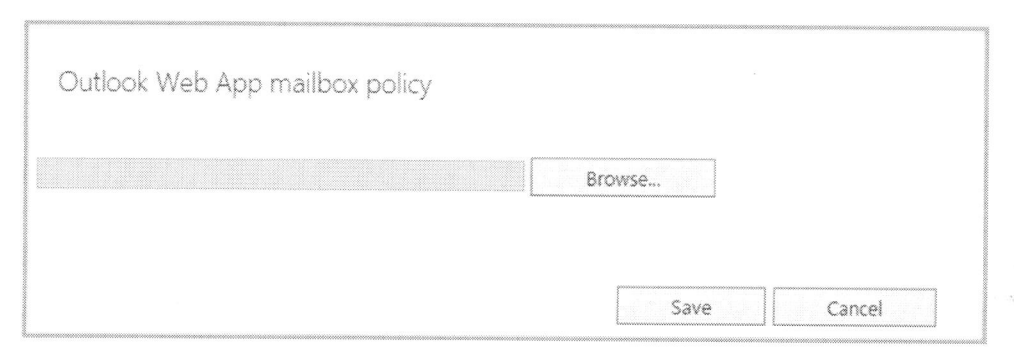

Configuring Mail Support for Outlook

You can install Outlook as a client on a user's computer. This section looks at the following topics:

- Understanding address lists, offline address books, and autodiscover
- Configuring Outlook for the first time
- Adding Internet mail accounts to Outlook
- Reconfiguring Outlook mail support

Unless specified otherwise, the procedures in this section work with desktop computers running current versions of Windows and Windows Server. Additionally, unless noted otherwise, the procedures work with Outlook 2010, Outlook 2013 and Outlook 2016.

Understanding Address Lists, Offline Address Books, and Autodiscover

Address lists are collections of recipients in an Exchange organization. Offline address books (OABs) are copies of address lists that are downloaded and cached on a computer so an Outlook user can access the address book while disconnected from the Exchange organization.

Every Exchange organization has a global address list and a default OAB. In the Exchange organization, address lists reside in Windows Azure Active Directory. If mobile users are disconnected from the Internet, they are unable to access the address lists stored on Exchange Online. If mobile users are disconnected from the corporate network, they are unable to access the address lists stored on Exchange Online. To allow users to continue working when disconnected from the network, Exchange Online generates offline address books and makes them accessible to Outlook clients so that they can be downloaded and cached for use while working offline.

Exchange Online provides these features through a web-based distribution point. Outlook clients use the web-based distribution point to obtain the global address list and the OAB automatically. Exchange Online largely manages the default address lists and OABs automatically.

Outlook 2010 and later as well as some mobile devices use the Autodiscover service to automatically configure themselves for access to Exchange. Outlook relies on DNS lookups to locate a host service (SRV) resource record for the Autodiscover service, then uses the user's credentials to authenticate and search for the Autodiscover connection points. After retrieving the connection points, the client connects to Exchange Online and obtains the profile information. The profile information includes the user's display name, the location of the user's mailbox server, connection settings and more.

Configuring Outlook for the First Time

You can install Outlook as a standalone product or as part of Microsoft Office. Outlook can be used to connect to the following types of email servers:

- **Microsoft Exchange** Connects directly to Exchange Online; best for users who are connected to the organization's network. Users will have full access to Exchange. Users can check mail and access any private or public folders to which they have been granted permissions. If you define a personal folder and specify that new email messages should be delivered to it, messages can be delivered to a personal folder on a user's computer.

- **POP3** Connects to Exchange Online or another POP3 email server through the Internet; best for users who are connecting from a remote location, such as a home or a remote office, using dial-up or broadband Internet access. With POP3, users can check mail on an email server and download it to their inboxes. Users can't, however, synchronize mailbox folders or access private or public folders on the server. By using advanced configuration settings, the user can elect to download the mail and leave it on the server for future use. By leaving the mail on the server, the user can check mail in Outlook Web App or on a home computer and then still download it to an office computer later.
- **IMAP4** Connects to Exchange Online or another IMAP4 email server through the Internet; best for users who are connecting from a remote location, such as a home or a remote office, using dial-up or broadband Internet access. Also well suited for users who have a single computer, such as a laptop, that they use to check mail both at the office and away from it. With IMAP4, users can check mail on an email server and synchronize mailbox folders. Users can also download only message headers and then access each message individually to download it. Unlike POP3, IMAP4 has no option to leave mail on the server. IMAP4 also lets users access public and private folders.
- **ActiveSync** Connects to an Exchange ActiveSync compatible service, such as Outlook.com, through the Internet; best as an additional email configuration option. Users can have an external email account with a web-based email service that they can check in addition to corporate email.
- **Additional server types** Connects to a third-party mail server or other services, such as Outlook Mobile Text Messaging.

To begin, log on to the computer as the user whose email you are configuring or have the user log on. If you are configuring email for use with a direct Exchange Online connection rather than a POP3, IMAP4, or ActiveSync connection, ensure that the user's mailbox has been created. If the user's mailbox has not been created, auto-setup will fail, as will the rest of the account configuration.

The first time you start Outlook, the application runs the Welcome Wizard. You can use the Welcome Wizard to configure email for Exchange, POP3, IMAP4, and ActiveSync mail servers, as discussed in the sections that follow.

First-Time Configuration: Connecting to Exchange Online

With Outlook 2010 or later, you can use the Welcome Wizard to configure email for Exchange Online in Outlook by completing the following steps:

1. Start Outlook and click **Next** on the Welcome page. The procedure is nearly identical whether you are working with Outlook 2010, Outlook 2013 or Outlook 2016.

2. When prompted to indicate whether you would like to configure an email account, verify that Yes is selected and then click **Next**.

3. Enter the user's account name and email address. Then type and confirm the user's password (see Figure 9-3).

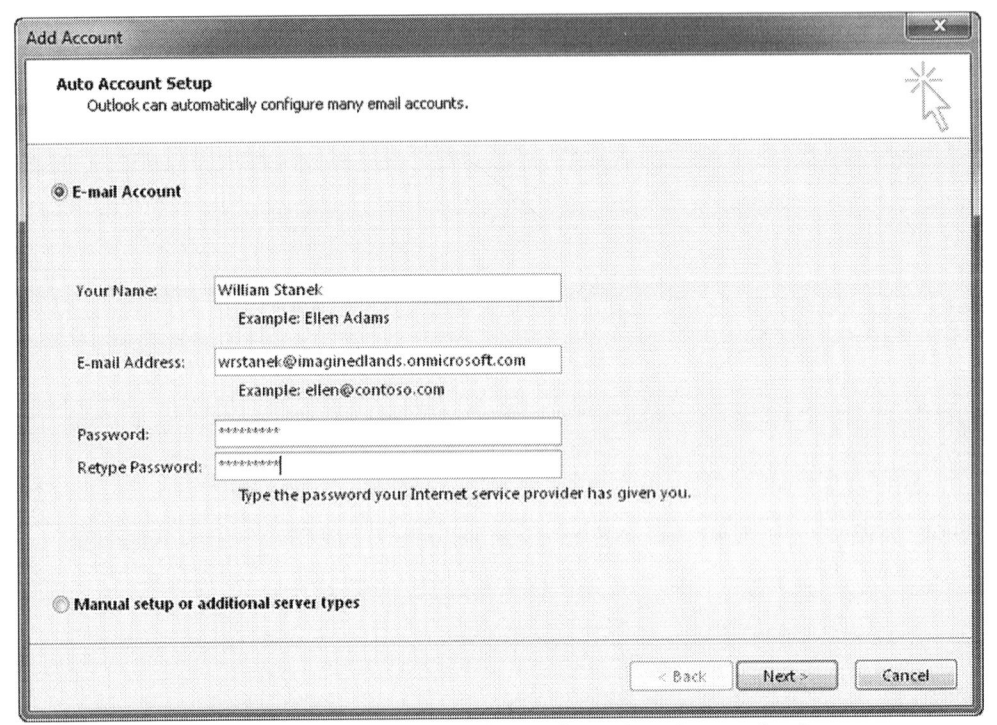

FIGURE 9-3 Provide the required information so that auto setup can begin.

4. After you click Next, the wizard uses the new Auto Account Setup feature to automatically discover the rest of the information needed to configure the account and then uses the settings to log on to the server. If the auto-configuration and server logon are successful, click **Finish** and skip the

remaining steps in this procedure. The wizard then sets up the user's Exchange mailbox on the computer as appropriate.

5. If auto-configuration is not successful, click **Next** so that the wizard can attempt to establish an unencrypted connection to the server. If the auto-configuration and server logon are successful this time, click **Finish** and then skip the remaining steps in this procedure.

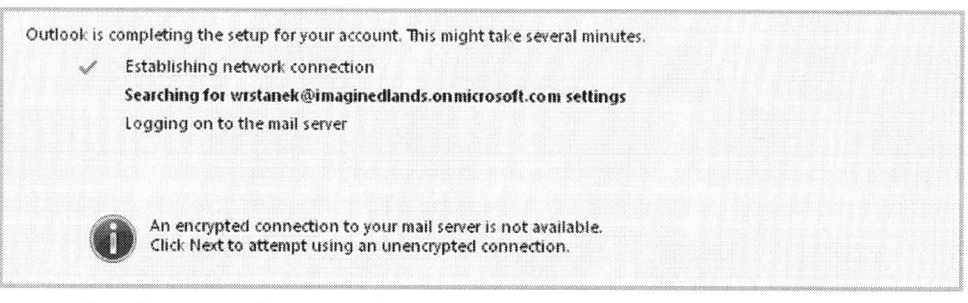

```
Outlook is completing the setup for your account. This might take several minutes.
    ✓  Establishing network connection
       Searching for wrstanek@imaginedlands.onmicrosoft.com settings
       Logging on to the mail server


    ⓘ  An encrypted connection to your mail server is not available.
       Click Next to attempt using an unencrypted connection.
```

6. If auto-configuration fails twice, you'll see a prompt to confirm the user's email address. If the email address is incorrect, correct it, and then click **Retry**. If the auto-configuration and server logon are successful this time, click **Finish** and then skip the remaining steps in this procedure.

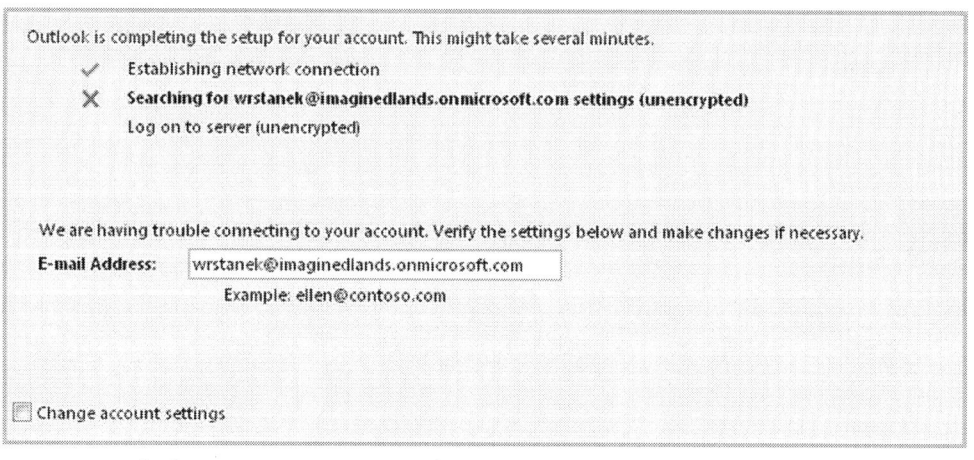

```
Outlook is completing the setup for your account. This might take several minutes.
    ✓  Establishing network connection
    ✗  Searching for wrstanek@imaginedlands.onmicrosoft.com settings (unencrypted)
       Log on to server (unencrypted)


    We are having trouble connecting to your account. Verify the settings below and make changes if necessary.
    E-mail Address:  wrstanek@imaginedlands.onmicrosoft.com
                     Example: ellen@contoso.com



    ☐ Change account settings
```

7. If all attempts at auto-configuration fail, you can try to configure settings manually (and might also want to confirm that the Autodiscover service is working properly). Click **Next**. On the Choose Service page, select a service. Click **Next**. On the next wizard page, complete the necessary information for the type of email service you selected. If necessary, click More Settings. Use the Properties dialog box to configure the additional required settings and then click **OK**. Click **Next** and then click **Finish** to complete the mail configuration.

First-Time Configuration: Connecting to Internet Email Servers

Users who need or prefer to access Exchange using POP3 or IMAP4 (rather than the default option of MAPI over HTTP) can use an alternate configuration to use email. For these users, you can complete the first-time configuration of Outlook by following these steps:

1. In the Welcome Wizard, prompted to indicate whether you would like to configure an email account, verify that Yes is selected and then click **Next**.
2. Select the manual setup option. In Outlook 2010, this checkbox is labeled as Manually Configure Server Settings Or Additional Server Types. In Outlook 2013 and Outlook 2016, this checkbox is labeled as Manual Setup Or Additional Server Types. Click **Next**.

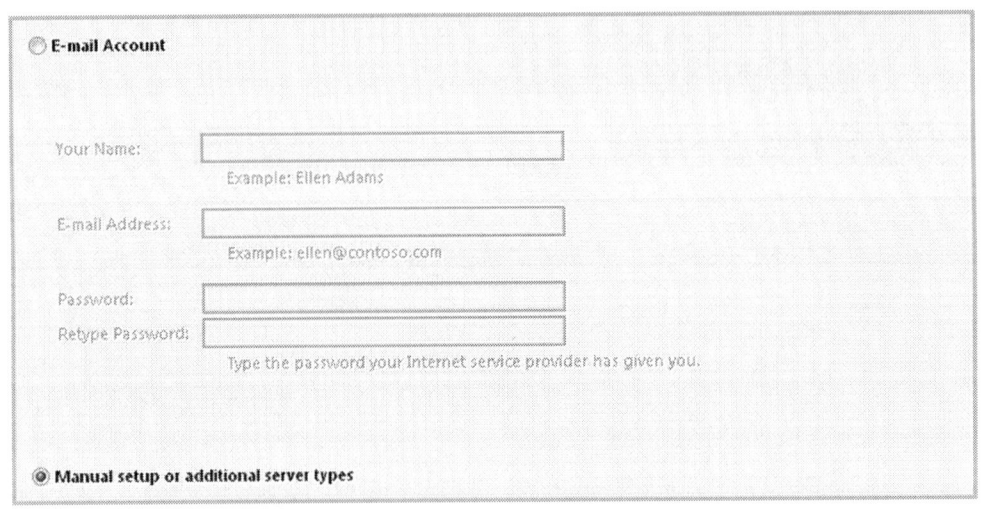

3. On the Choose Service page, choose the service to use. In Outlook 2010, choose Internet E-Mail as the service. In Outlook 2013 and Outlook 2016, choose POP Or IMAP as the service. Click **Next**.

4. In the Your Name text box, type the name to appear in the From field of outgoing messages for this user, such as **William Stanek**.

5. In the E-Mail Address text box, type the email address of the user. Be sure to type the email user name as well as the domain name, such as **williams@imaginedlands.onmicrosoft.com**.

6. From the Account Type list, select POP3 or IMAP4 as the type of protocol to use for the incoming mail server. The advantages and disadvantages of these protocols are as follows:

- POP3 is used to check mail on an email server and download it to the user's inbox. The user can't access private or public folders on the server. By using advanced configuration settings, the user can elect to download email and leave it on the server for future use. By leaving the email on the server, the user can check a message on a home computer and still download it to an office computer later.

- IMAP4 is used to check mail on an email server and download message headers. The user can then access each email individually and download it. Unlike POP3, IMAP4 has no option to leave mail on the server. IMAP4 also lets users access public and private folders. It is best suited for users who have a single computer, such as a laptop, that they use to check mail both at the office and away from it.

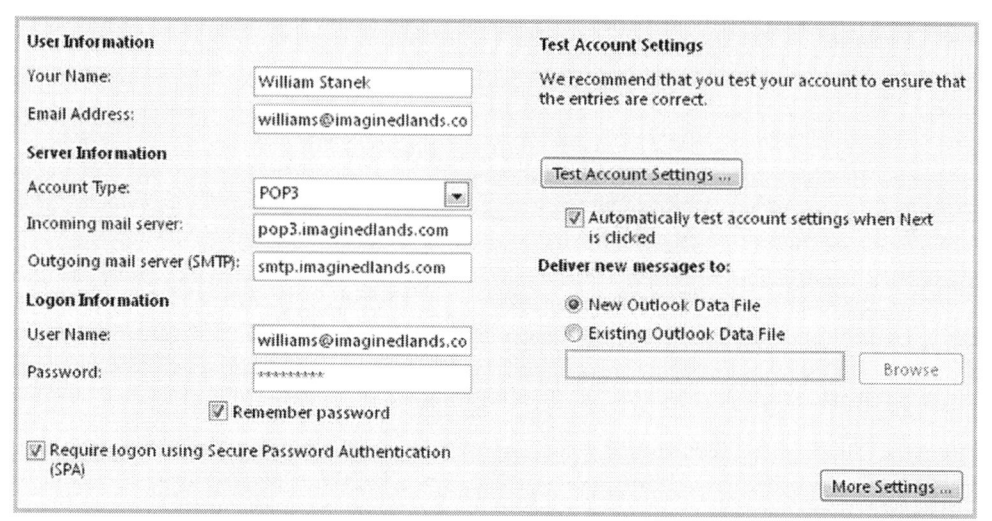

User Information		Test Account Settings
Your Name:	William Stanek	We recommend that you test your account to ensure that the entries are correct.
Email Address:	williams@imaginedlands.co	
Server Information		Test Account Settings ...
Account Type:	POP3	☑ Automatically test account settings when Next is clicked
Incoming mail server:	pop3.imaginedlands.com	
Outgoing mail server (SMTP):	smtp.imaginedlands.com	**Deliver new messages to:**
Logon Information		⦿ New Outlook Data File
User Name:	williams@imaginedlands.co	○ Existing Outlook Data File
Password:	*********	[Browse]
	☑ Remember password	
☑ Require logon using Secure Password Authentication (SPA)		[More Settings ...]

7. Enter the FQDN for the incoming and outgoing mail servers. Although these entries are often the same, some organizations have different incoming and outgoing mail servers. If you are not certain of your mail servers' FQDN, contact your network administrator.

> **NOTE** If you're connecting to Exchange with POP3 or IMAP4, you should enter the FQDN for the Exchange Online rather than just the host name. For example, you would use mail.imaginedlands.onmicrosoft.com instead of

> MailServer. This ensures Outlook will be able to find the Exchange Online organization.

8. Under Logon Information, type the user's logon name and password. If the mail server requires secure logon, select the Require Logon Using Security Password Authentication check box.

9. To verify the settings, click **Test Account Settings**. Outlook verifies connectivity to the Internet and then logs on to the Mail server. Next, Outlook sends a test message to the specified mail server. If the test fails, note the errors and make corrections as necessary.

10. If necessary, click More Settings. Use the Properties dialog box to configure the additional required settings and then click **OK**. When you are ready to continue, click **Next**, and then click **Finish** to complete the configuration.

Configuring Outlook for Exchange

If you didn't configure Outlook to use Exchange the first time it was started and elected to use Outlook without an email account, don't worry: You can change the Outlook configuration to use Exchange. It does take a bit of extra work, however.

Follow these steps to configure Outlook to use Exchange:

1. In Outlook 2013 or Outlook 2016, click **File** and then select **Add Account**. If you are using Outlook 2010, you must select Tools, Account Settings, New and then select Microsoft Exchange as the e-mail service.

2. Outlook assumes you want to configure an Internet email account for the user. You will, however, provide the information needed for Exchange. Enter the user's account name and email address for Exchange. Then type and confirm the user's password.

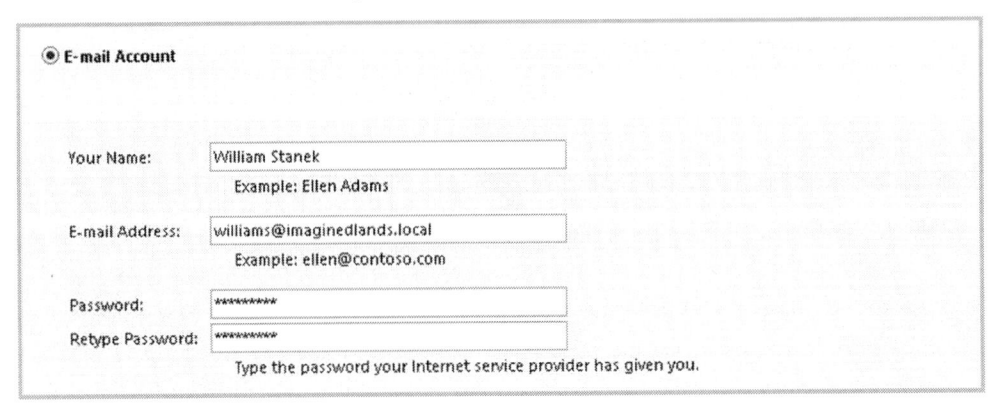

⦿ E-mail Account	
Your Name:	William Stanek
	Example: Ellen Adams
E-mail Address:	williams@imaginedlands.local
	Example: ellen@contoso.com
Password:	**********
Retype Password:	**********
	Type the password your Internet service provider has given you.

3. Click **Next**. The wizard uses the new Auto Account Setup feature to automatically discover the rest of the information needed to configure the account and then uses the settings to log on to the server. If the auto-configuration and server logon are successful, click **Finish**.

> Configuring
>
> Outlook is completing the setup for your account. This might take several minutes.
>
> ✓ Establishing network connection
> ✓ Searching for williams@imaginedlands.local settings
> ✓ Logging on to the mail server
>
> Congratulations! Your email account was successfully configured and is ready to use.

Adding Internet Mail Accounts to Outlook

Through email account configuration, each mail profile for Outlook supports only one Exchange account at a time. If you need access to multiple Exchange mailboxes in the same mail profile, you must configure access to these mailboxes as discussed in the section "Accessing Multiple Exchange Mailboxes" later in the chapter.

You can add Internet mail accounts to Outlook. In Outlook, complete the following steps:

1. In Outlook 2013 or Outlook 2016, click **File** and then select **Add Account**. If you are using Outlook 2010, you must select Tools, Account Settings, New and then select POP3, IMAP, Or HTTP as the e-mail service.
2. Click **Next**. The wizard tries to use the new Auto Account Setup feature to automatically discover the rest of the information needed to configure the account and then uses the settings to log on to the server.
3. If the auto-configuration and server logon are successful, click **Finish**. Otherwise, follow steps 2–10 outlined previously in the "First-time Configuration: Connecting to Internet Email Servers" section.

Repairing and Changing Outlook Mail Accounts

When you first configure Outlook on a computer, you can configure it to connect to Exchange Online, to Internet email, or to another email server. With Exchange Online, Outlook can use MAPI over HTTP or RPC over HTTP to connect to the appropriate Mailbox server and access the appropriate mailbox. If a user's mailbox is moved by Microsoft to a different server within the Exchange organization, the user is connected to this server automatically the next time he or she starts Outlook. If, for some reason, a user has a problem connecting to Exchange or needs to update configuration settings, you can use a repair operation. Repairing the user's account restarts the Auto Account Setup feature.

With non-Exchange servers, access to email very much depends on the account and server configuration remaining the same. If the account or server configuration changes, the account configuration in Outlook must be updated. The easiest way to do this is with a repair operation.

To start a repair, follow these steps:

1. Log on as the account of the user for whom you are repairing email.
2. In Outlook 2010, click the Office button, click **Account Settings**, and then select the **Account Settings** option. In Outlook 2013 or Outlook 2016, on the File pane, click **Account Settings**, and then select the **Account Settings** option.
3. In the Account Settings dialog box, the E-Mail tab lists all currently configured email accounts by name. Select the account to repair and then click **Repair**.
4. On the Auto Account Setup page, check the account settings. With Exchange Online, you cannot change the displayed information. With other accounts, you can modify the user's email address and password, as necessary.
5. When you click **Next**, the Repair E-Mail Account Wizard contacts the mail server and tries to determine the correct account settings. If the auto-configuration and server logon are successful, click **Finish**. Skip the remaining steps in this procedure.
6. If auto-configuration is not successful, click **Next** so that the wizard can attempt to establish an unencrypted connection to the server. If the auto-configuration and server logon are successful this time, click **Finish** and then skip the remaining steps in this procedure. You must restart Outlook.

> **NOTE** You may be prompted to confirm the user's credentials. If so, type the user's password, select the Remember My Credentials checkbox, and then click OK.

7. If auto-configuration fails twice, you can try to configure settings manually. Select the manual setup option, and then click Next.

8. Use the fields provided to update the mail account configuration. If you need to configure additional settings beyond the user, server, and logon information, click the More button (•••), and then use the Properties dialog box to configure the additional required settings. When you are finished, click **OK** to close the Properties dialog box.

9. To check the new settings, click **Test Account Settings**.

10. Click **Next**, and then click **Finish**.

In some cases, if you've incorrectly configured Exchange, you might not be able to start Outlook and access the Account Settings dialog box. In this case, you can repair the settings using the following procedure:

1. Start the Mail utility. In Control Panel, click **Small Icons** on the View By list and then start the Mail app by clicking its icon or by double-clicking its icon.

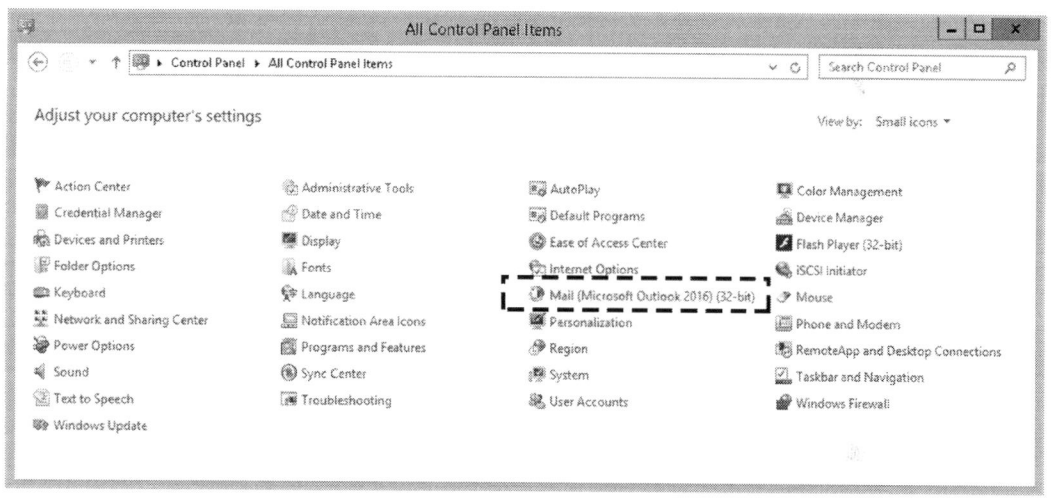

2. In the Mail Setup–Outlook dialog box, click **E-Mail Accounts**. The Accounts Settings dialog box appears.

3. In the Account Settings dialog box, the E-Mail tab is selected by default. Click the incorrectly configured Exchange account and then do one of the following:

- Click Change to modify the Exchange settings using the techniques discussed previously.
- Click Remove to remove the Exchange settings so that they are no longer used by Outlook.

4. When you are finished, close the Mail Setup–Outlook dialog box, and then start Outlook.

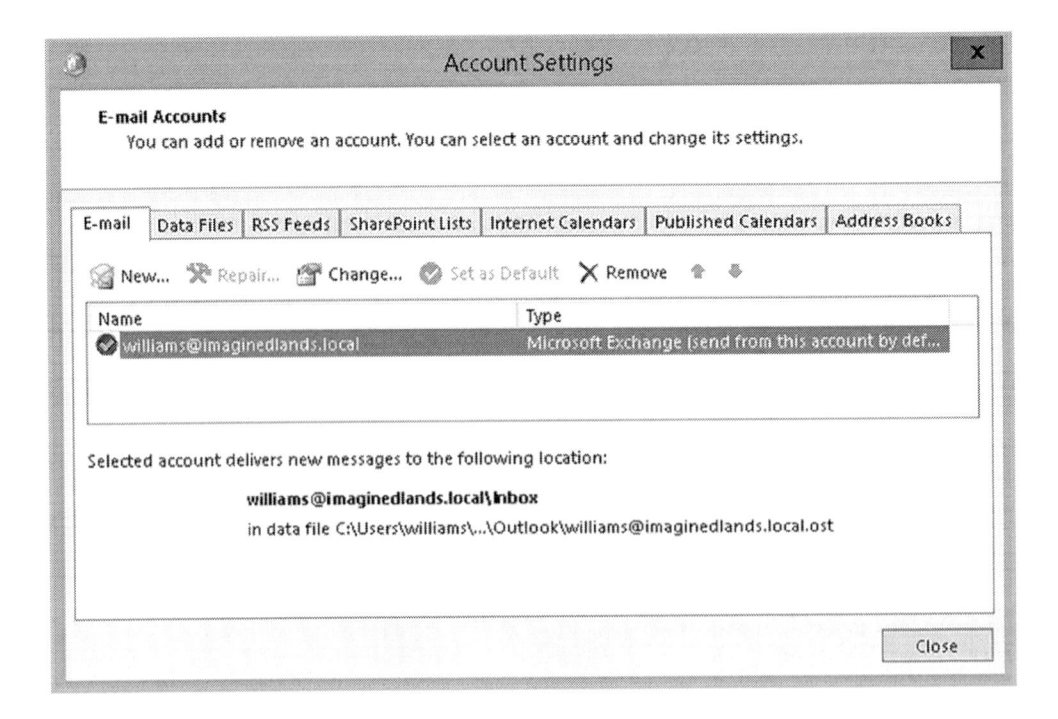

For POP3 or IMAP4, you can change a user's email configuration at any time by completing the following steps:

1. In Outlook 2010, click the Office button, click **Account Settings**, and then select the **Account Settings** option. In Outlook 2013 or Outlook 2016, on the File pane, click **Account Settings**, and then select the **Account Settings** option.

2. In the Account Settings dialog box, the E-Mail tab lists all currently configured email accounts by name. Select the account you want to work with, and then click **Change**.

3. Use the fields provided to update the mail account configuration. If you need to configure additional settings beyond the user, server, and logon information, click the More button (•••), and then use the Properties dialog box to configure the additional required settings. When you are finished, click **OK** to close the Properties dialog box.

4. To check the new settings click **Test Account Settings**.

5. Click **Next**, and then click **Finish**.

Leaving Mail on the Server with POP3

If the user connects to an Internet e-mail server, an advantage of POP3 is that it lets a user leave mail on the server. By doing this, the user can check mail on a home computer and still download it to an office computer later.

With Outlook, you can configure POP3 accounts to leave mail on the server by completing the following steps:

1. In Outlook 2010, click the Office button, click **Account Settings**, and then select the **Account Settings** option. In Outlook 2013 or Outlook 2016, on the File pane, click **Account Settings**, and then select the **Account Settings** option.
2. In the Account Settings dialog box, select the POP3 mail account you want to modify and then click **Change**.
3. Click the More button (•••) to display the Internet E-Mail Settings dialog box.
4. In the Internet E-Mail Settings dialog box, click the **Advanced** tab, as shown in Figure 9-5.
5. Use the options below Delivery to configure how and when mail should be left on the server. To enable this option, select the **Leave A Copy Of Messages On The Server** check box. The additional options depend on the client configuration. Options you might see include the following:

- **Remove From Server After *N* Days**   Select this option if the user will be connecting to an Internet service provider (ISP) and you want to delete messages from the server after a specified number of days. By deleting ISP mail periodically, you ensure that the mailbox size doesn't exceed the limit.
- **Remove From Server When Deleted From "Deleted Items"**   Select this option to delete messages from the server when the user deletes them from the Deleted Items folder. You'll see this option with Internet-only Outlook configurations.

6. Click **OK** when you've finished changing the account settings.
7. Click **Next**, and then click **Finish**. Click **Close** to close the Account Settings dialog box.

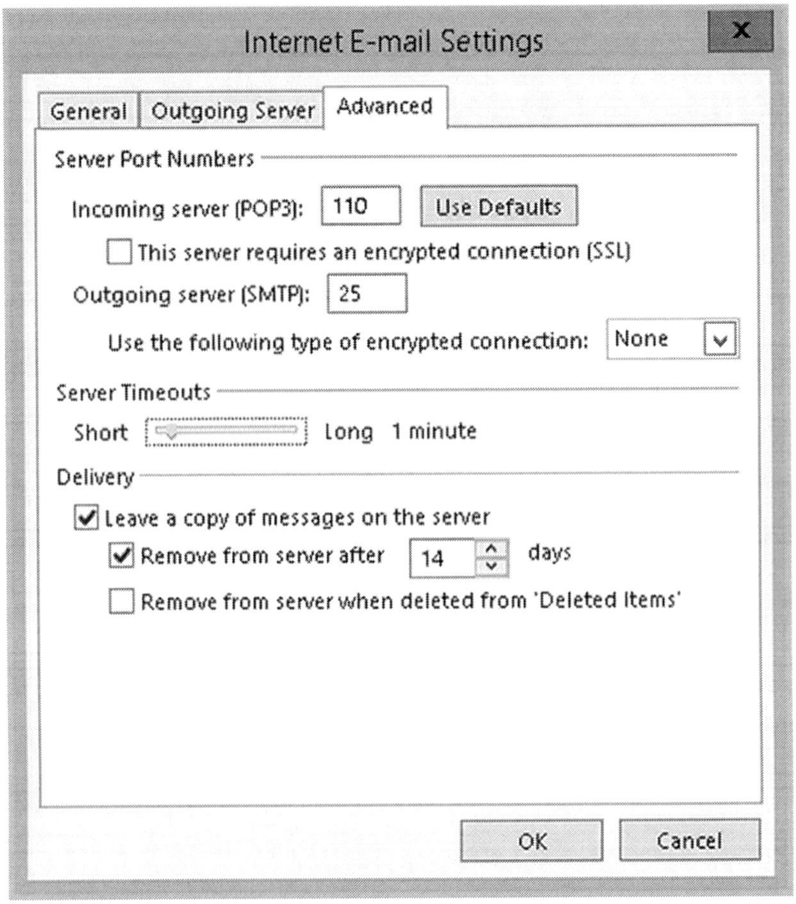

FIGURE 9-5 Using the Advanced tab to configure how and when mail should be left on the server.

Checking Private and Public Folders with IMAP4 and UNIX Mail Servers

With IMAP4, you can check public and private folders on a mail server. This option is enabled by default, but the default settings might not work properly with UNIX mail servers.

With Outlook, you can check or change the folder settings used by IMAP4 by completing the following steps:

1. Start Outlook. In Outlook 2010, click the Office button, click **Account Settings**, and then select the **Account Settings** option. In Outlook 2013, on the File pane, click **Account Settings**, and then select the **Account Settings** option.

2. In the Account Settings dialog box, select the IMAP4 mail account you want to modify and then click **Change**.

3. Click the More button (•••) to display the Internet E-Mail Settings dialog box.

4. In the Internet E-Mail Settings dialog box, click the **Advanced** tab, as shown in Figure 9-6.

5. If the account connects to a UNIX mail server, enter the path to the mailbox folder on the server, such as **~williams/mail**—don't end the folder path with a forward slash (/)—and then click **OK**.

6. Click **Next**, and then click **Finish**.

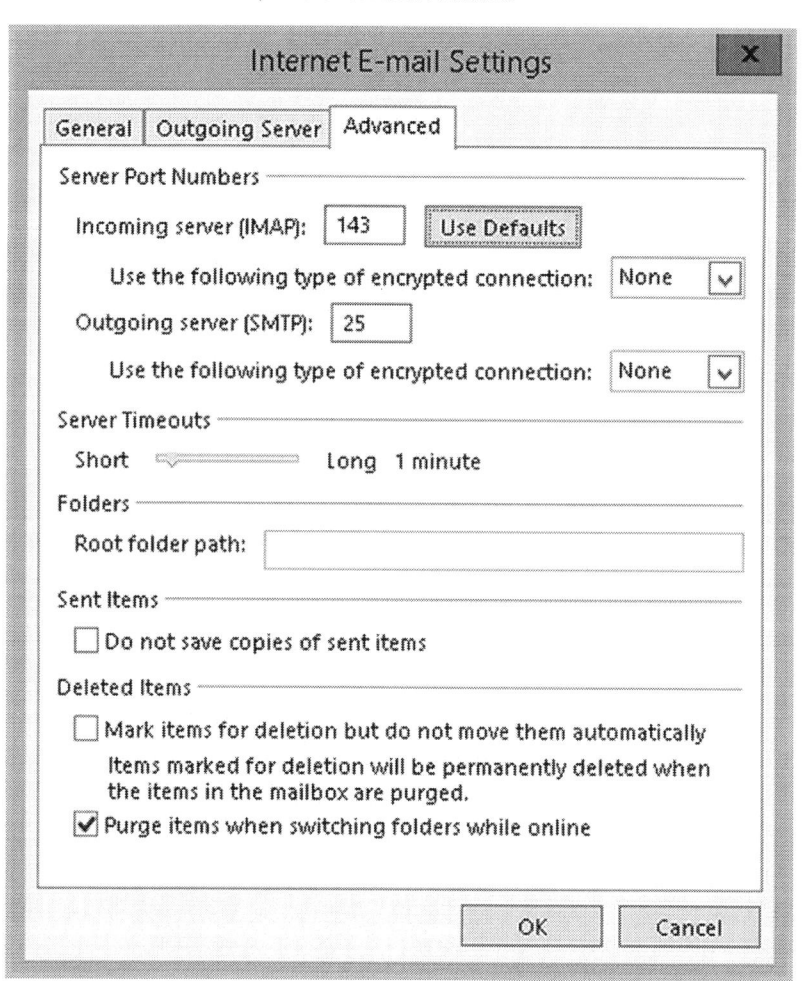

FIGURE 9-6 Using the Advanced tab to configure how folders are used with IMAP4 mail accounts.

Managing the Exchange Configuration in Outlook

Whenever you use Outlook to connect to Exchange, you have several options for optimizing the way mail is handled. These options include the following:

- Email delivery and processing
- Remote mail
- Scheduled connections
- Multiple mailboxes

Each of these options is examined in this section.

Managing Delivery and Processing Email Messages

When Outlook uses Exchange, you have strict control over how email is delivered and processed. Exchange mail can be delivered in one of two ways:

- To server mailboxes with local copies
- To personal folders

Exchange mail can be processed by any of the information services configured for use in Outlook. These information services include the following:

- Microsoft Exchange
- Internet email

Let's look at how you use each of these delivery and processing options.

Using Server Mailboxes

When you are using Outlook 2010 or later with Exchange Online, server mailboxes with local copies are the default configuration option. With server mailboxes, new email is delivered to a mailbox in the Exchange organization, and users can view or receive new mail only when they're connected to Exchange. When users are connected to Exchange, Outlook retrieves their mail and stores a local copy on their computer in addition to the email stored on Exchange.

The local copy of a user's mail is stored in an offline folder .ost file. With Windows 7 and later, the default location of a .ost file is *%LocalAppData%*\Microsoft\Outlook, where *%LocalAppData%* is a user-specific environment variable that points to a user's local application data. Using server mailboxes offers users protected storage and the ability to have a single point of recovery in case something happens to their computer.

Using Personal Folders

An alternative to using server mailboxes is to use personal folders. Personal folders are stored in a .pst file on the user's computer. With personal folders, you can specify that mail should be delivered to the user's inbox and stored on the server or that mail should be delivered only to the user's inbox. Users have personal folders when Outlook is configured to use Internet email or other email servers. Users might also have personal folders if the auto-archive feature is used to archive messages.

> **REAL WORLD** With Windows 7 and later, the default location of a .pst file is *%LocalAppData%*\Microsoft\Outlook, where *%LocalAppData%* is a user-specific environment variable that points to a user's local application data. Personal folders are best suited for mobile users who check mail through dial-up connections and who might not be able to use a dial-up connection to connect directly to Exchange.
>
> Users with personal folders lose the advantages that server-based folders offer—namely, protected storage and the ability to have a single point of recovery in case of failure. In addition, .pst files have many disadvantages. They get corrupted more frequently and, on these occasions, you must use the Inbox Repair Tool to restore the file. If the hard disk on a user's computer fails, you can recover the mail only if the .pst file has been backed up. Unfortunately, most workstations aren't backed up regularly (if at all), and the onus of backing up the .pst file falls on the user, who might or might not understand how to do this.

Determining the Presence of Personal Folders

You can determine the presence of personal folders by following these steps:

1. Start Outlook. In Outlook 2010, click the Office button, click **Account Settings**, and then select the **Account Settings** option. In Outlook 2013 or Outlook 2016, on the File pane, click **Account Settings**, and then select the **Account Settings** option.
2. In the Account Settings dialog box, click the **Data Files** tab.
3. The location of the data file associated with each email account is listed. If the file name ends in .pst, the account is using a personal folder.

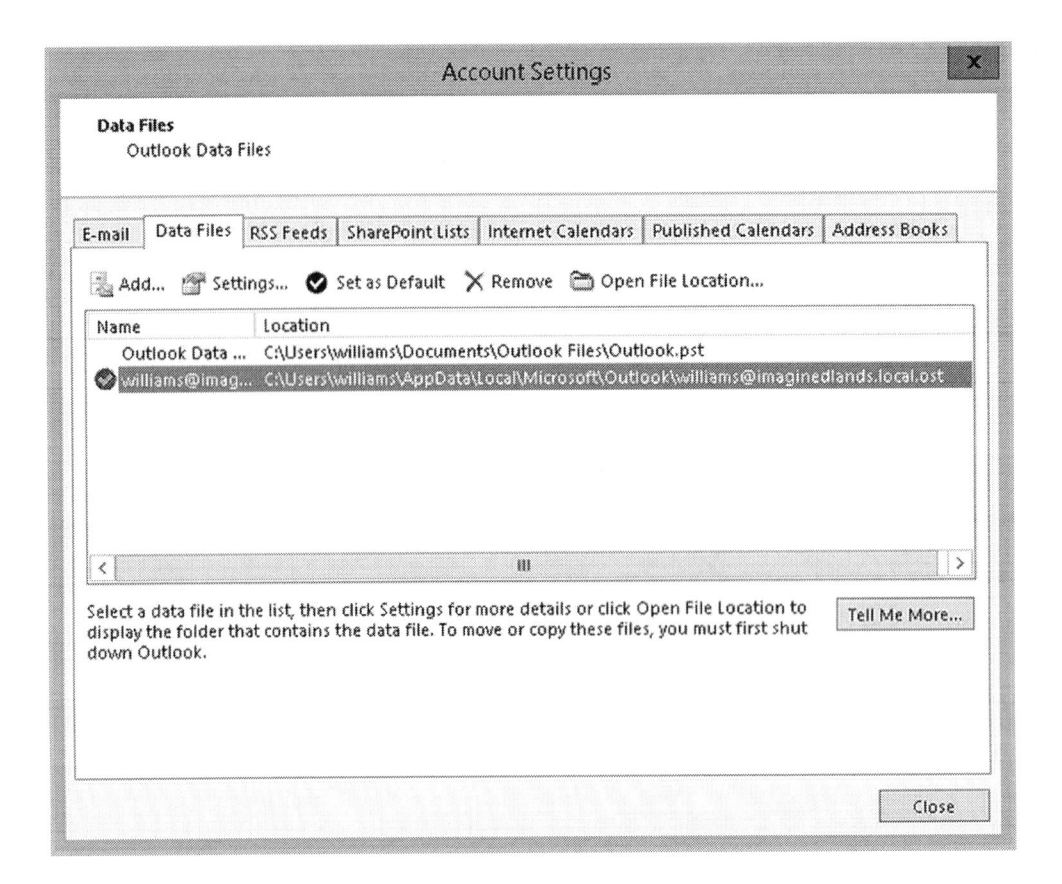

Creating New or Opening Existing Personal Folders

If personal folders aren't available and you want to configure them, follow these steps:

1. Start Outlook. In Outlook 2010, click the Office button, click **Account Settings**, and then select the **Account Settings** option. In Outlook 2013 or Outlook 2016, on the File pane, click **Account Settings**, and then select the **Account Settings** option.
2. In the Account Settings dialog box, click the **Data Files** tab.
3. Click **Add**. If the New Outlook Data File dialog box appears, Office Outlook Personal Folders File (.pst) should be selected by default. Click **OK**.
4. Use the Create Or Open Outlook Data File dialog box, as shown in Figure 9-7, to create a new .pst file or open an existing .pst file:

[Screenshot of the Create or Open Outlook Data File dialog box]

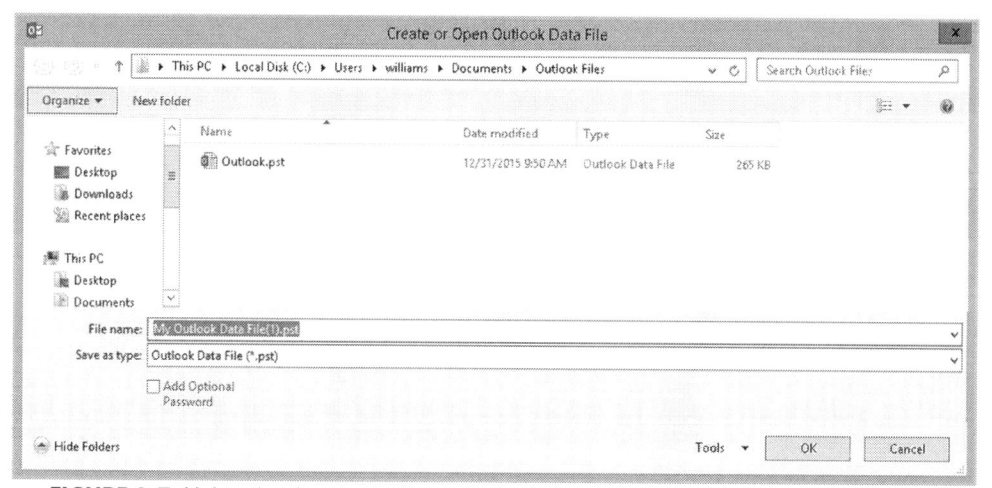

FIGURE 9-7 Using the Create Or Open Outlook Data File dialog box to search for an existing .pst file or to create a new one.

- To create a new .pst file in the default folder, type a name for the Outlook data file in the text box provided or accept the default value. To secure the file and ensure only a person with this password can access the file, select the Add Optional Password checkbox. In the Create Microsoft Personal Folders dialog box, specify a password, verify a password for the .pst file, and click OK.
- To create a new .pst file in a nondefault folder, click Browse Folders to show the folder view if it is hidden. Browse for the folder you want to use, type the file name in the text box provided or accept the default value, and then click OK. Optionally, select the Add Optional Password checkbox. In the Create Microsoft Personal Folders dialog box, specify a password, verify a password for the .pst file, and click OK.
- To open an existing .pst file, click Browse Folders to show the folder view if it is hidden. Browse to the folder containing the .pst file. Select the .pst file, and then click OK. In the Personal Folders dialog box, use the options provided to change the current password or compact the personal folder, and then click OK.

> **NOTE** It is important to be aware that password recovery utility for .pst files aren't available. If a user sets a password on a .pst file and forgets it, the Exchange administrator has no way to reset it. You might find third-party vendors who make password-cracking or recovery tools, but they are not guaranteed to work and they are not supported by Microsoft.

5. Click **Close**. The personal folder you've selected or created is displayed in the Outlook folder list. You should see related subfolders as well.

Delivering Mail to Personal Folders

When you configure mail to be delivered to a personal folder, Outlook saves email messages only locally on the computer. As a result, Outlook removes the messages from Exchange after delivery and you can access the messages only on the currently logged-on computer.

If you want mail to be delivered to a personal folder, complete the following steps:

1. Start Outlook. In Outlook 2010, click the Office button, click **Account Settings**, and then select the **Account Settings** option. In Outlook 2013 or Outlook 2016, on the File pane, click **Account Settings**, and then select the **Account Settings** option.
2. In the Account Settings dialog box, click the **Data Files** tab.
3. Select the .pst file to use in the list of data files provided, and then click **Set As Default**.
4. When prompted to confirm, click **Yes** and then click **Close**.
5. Exit and restart Outlook. Outlook will now use personal folders.

If you want mail to resume using server-stored mail, complete the following steps:

1. Start Outlook. In Outlook 2010, click the Office button, click **Account Settings**, and then select the **Account Settings** option. In Outlook 2013 or Outlook 2016, on the File pane, click **Account Settings**, and then select the **Account Settings** option.
2. In the Account Settings dialog box, click the **Data Files** tab.
3. Select the .ost file to use in the list of data files provided, and then click **Set As Default**.
4. When prompted to confirm, click **OK** and then click **Close**.
5. Exit and restart Outlook. Outlook will now use personal folders.

Repairing .pst data files

When Outlook uses personal folders, you can use the Inbox Repair tool (scanpst.exe) to analyze and repair corrupted data files.

- With Office 2010 and Office 2013, this tool is stored in the %SystemDrive%\Program Files\Microsoft Office\Office*Version* folder, where *Version* is the internal version of Office you are using, such as Office15 for Outlook 2013.
- With Office 2016, this tool is stored in the %SystemDrive%\Program Files\Microsoft Office\root\Office16 folder, such as c:\program files (x86)\Microsoft Office\root\Office16.

If a .pst file won't open or is damaged, you can use the Inbox Repair tool to repair it by completing the following these steps:

1. Exit Outlook. Open the Office folder in File Explorer and then double-click the Inbox Repair tool (scanpst.exe).

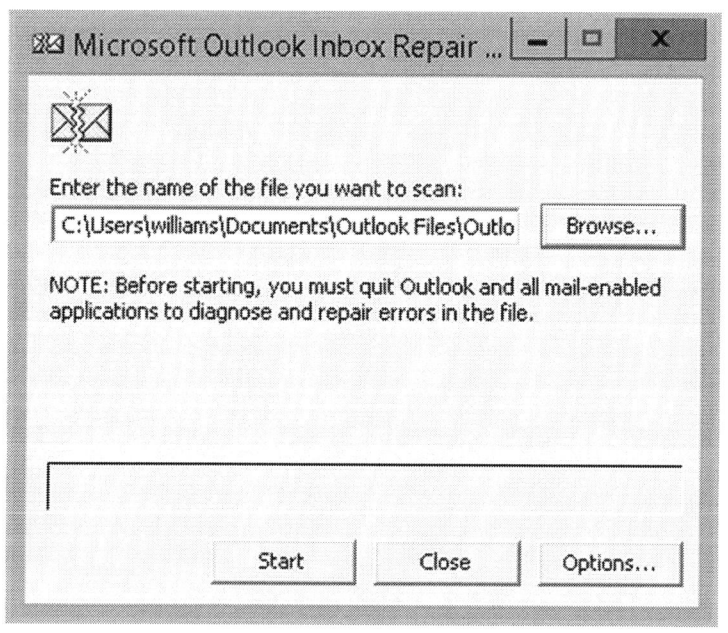

2. Click **Browse**. In the Select File To Scan dialog box, browse to the folder where .pst files are stored, select the .pst file you want to work with, and then click **Open**. Generally, .pst files are either stored in *%LocalAppData%*\Microsoft\Outlook, where *%LocalAppData%* is a user-specific environment variable that points to a user's local application data, or in the %UserProfile%\Documents\Outlook Files folder, where %UserProfile% is a user-specific environment variable that points to the user's local profile data.

3. Click **Start**, and the Inbox Repair tool will begin analyzing the file. The larger the file the longer the analysis will take.

4. If errors are found, click **Repair** to start the repair process. The Inbox Repair tool will create a copy of the .pst file before attempting the repair operation. During the repair, the Inbox Repair tool will rebuild the .pst file. This backup will be stored in the same folder as the original .pst file.

5. Start Outlook with the profile that contains the .pst file that you repaired. Press Ctrl+6 to display the Folder List view and look for a folder named Recovered Personal Folders. This folder contains the default Outlook folders as well as a Lost And Found folder, which contains any items recovered by the Inbox Repair tool.

> **NOTE** You can also display the Folders List view by clicking the More button (•••) in the Navigation menu and then selecting Folders.

6. Create a new .pst data file to store your mail items. Drag the items from the Lost And Found folder into the appropriate folder under the new Personal folders. When you've moved all the items, you can remove the Recovered Personal Folders .

7. The Inbox Repair tool creates a backup of the original .pst file and names it with the .bak file extension. By default this file is stored in the same location as the original .pst file. If you make a copy of this file and name it with a .pst extension, you may be able to recover additional items. To do this, add the .pst file to the mail profile and then move any additional mail items from this old .pst file to the new data file created in step 6.

Repairing .ost data files

When Outlook uses server mailboxes, .ost data files contain copies of information saved on the server. If an .ost file won't open or is damaged, you can re-create the file by completing the following these steps:

1. Exit Outlook. Start the Mail utility. Press the Windows key +I and then click **Control Panel**. In Control Panel, click **Small Icons** on the View By list and then start the Mail app by double-clicking its icon.

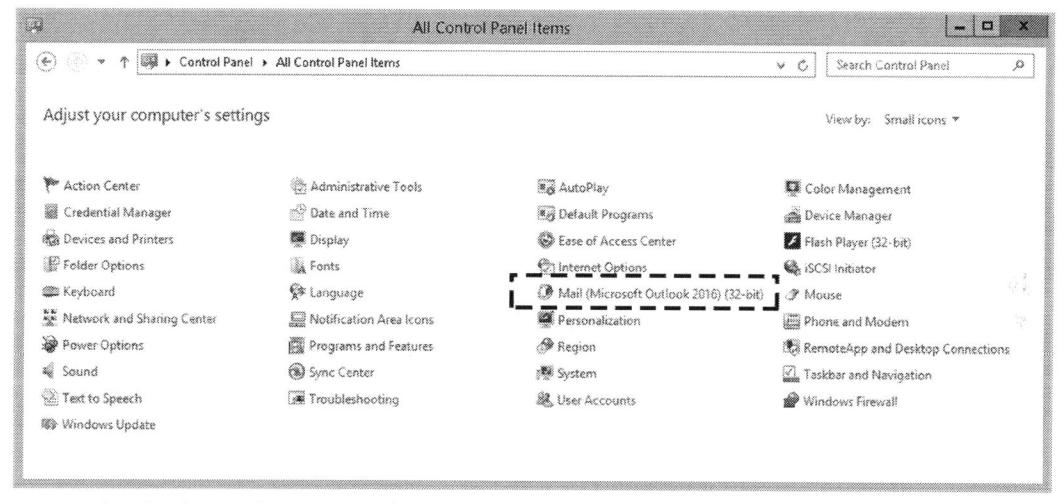

2. In the Mail Setup–Outlook dialog box, click **Data Files**. This opens the Account Settings dialog box with the Data Files tab selected.

3. Select the Exchange account and then click **Open File Location**. This opens File Explorer to the location of the data file. Note this location. By default, .ost files are stored in %*LocalAppData*%\Microsoft\Outlook, where %*LocalAppData*% is a user-specific environment variable that points to a user's local application data.

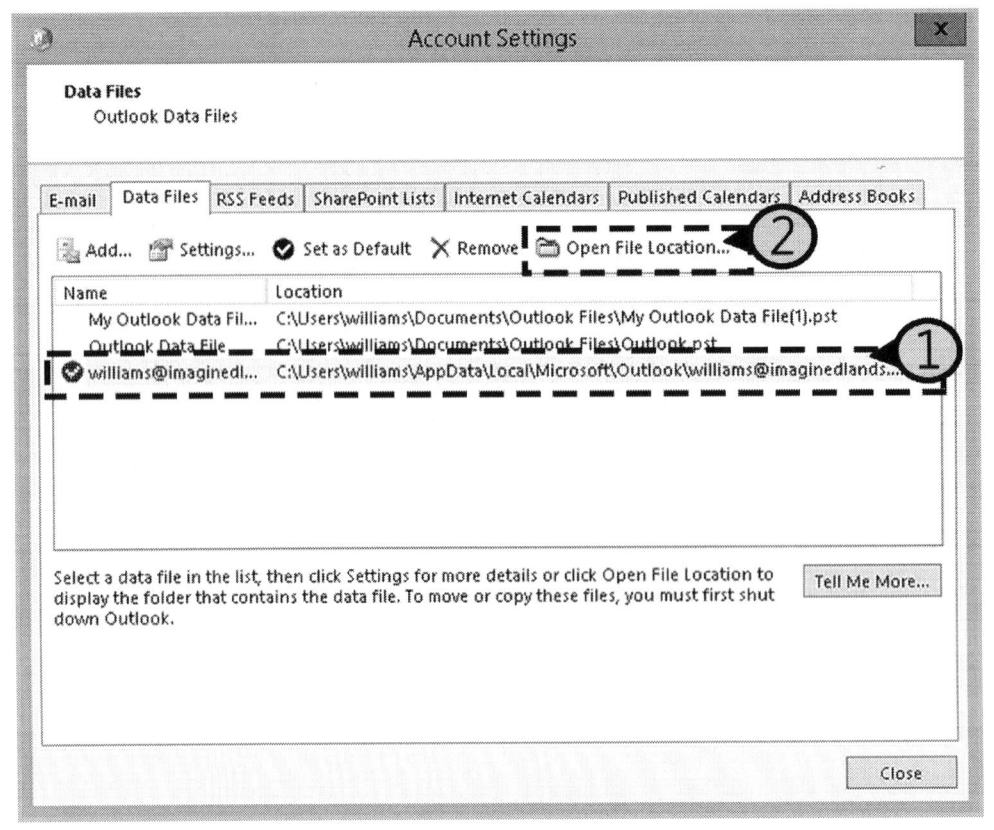

4. Close the Account Settings and Mail Setup dialog boxes. In File Explorer, right-click the .ost file and then click **Delete**. If you are unable to delete the file, make sure all mail and Office windows are closed.

5. Start Outlook. Download a copy of the mail items again to automatically re-create the .ost file.

Accessing Multiple Exchange Mailboxes

Earlier in the chapter, I discussed how users could check multiple Internet mail accounts in Outlook. You might have wondered whether users could check multiple Exchange mailboxes as well—and they can. Users often need to access multiple Exchange mailboxes for many reasons:

- Help desk administrators might need access to the help desk mailbox in addition to their own mailboxes.
- Managers might need temporary access to the mailboxes of subordinates who are on vacation.
- Project team members may need to access mailboxes set up for long-term projects.

- Resource mailboxes might need to be set up for accounts payable, human resources, corporate information, and so on.

Normally, a one-to-one relationship exists between user accounts and Exchange mailboxes. You create a user account and add a mailbox to it; only this user can access the mailbox directly through Exchange. To change this setup, you must change the permissions on the mailbox. One way to change mailbox access permissions is to do the following:

1. Log on to Exchange as the owner of the mailbox.
2. Delegate access to the mailbox to one or more additional users.
3. Have users with delegated access log on to Exchange and open the mailbox.

The sections that follow examine each of these steps in detail.

Logging on to Exchange as the Mailbox Owner

Logging on to Exchange as the mailbox owner allows you to delegate access to the mailbox. Before you can do this, however, you must complete the following steps:

1. Log on as the user or have the user log on for you.
2. Start Outlook. Make sure that mail support is configured to use server mailboxes. If necessary, configure this support, which creates the mail profile for the user.
3. After you configure Outlook to use Exchange, you should be able to log on to Exchange as the mailbox owner.

> **TIP** With multiple mailbox users, you should configure the mailbox to deliver mail to the server rather than to a personal folder. In this way, the mail can be checked by one or more mailbox users.

Delegating Mailbox Access

After you've logged on as the mailbox owner, you can delegate access to the mailbox by completing these steps:

1. Start Outlook. Open the Delegates dialog box by doing one of the following:

- In Outlook 2010, click the Office button, click **Account Settings**, and then select the **Account Settings** option. On the Delegates tab or in the Delegates dialog box, click **Add**.

- In Outlook 2013 or Outlook 2016, on the File pane, click **Account Settings**, and then select the **Delegate Access** option. In the Delegates dialog box, click **Add**.

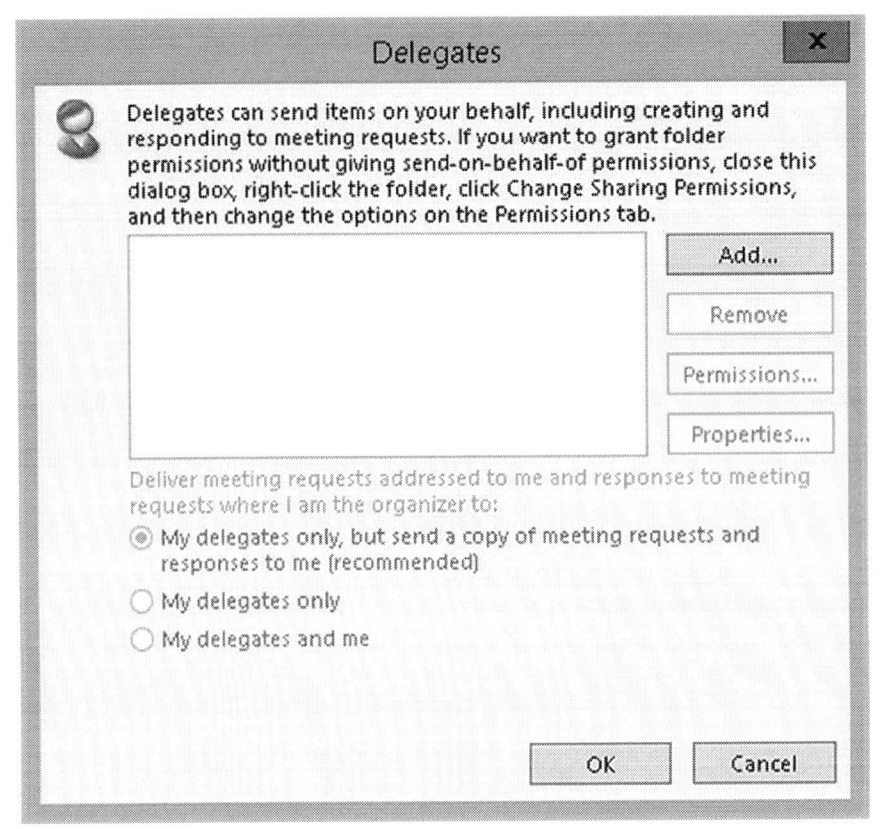

[Delegates dialog box screenshot]

Delegates can send items on your behalf, including creating and responding to meeting requests. If you want to grant folder permissions without giving send-on-behalf-of permissions, close this dialog box, right-click the folder, click Change Sharing Permissions, and then change the options on the Permissions tab.

Deliver meeting requests addressed to me and responses to meeting requests where I am the organizer to:
- ● My delegates only, but send a copy of meeting requests and responses to me (recommended)
- ○ My delegates only
- ○ My delegates and me

2. The Add Users dialog box appears. To add users, double-click the name of a user who needs access to the mailbox. Repeat this step as necessary for other users, and then click **OK** when you're finished.

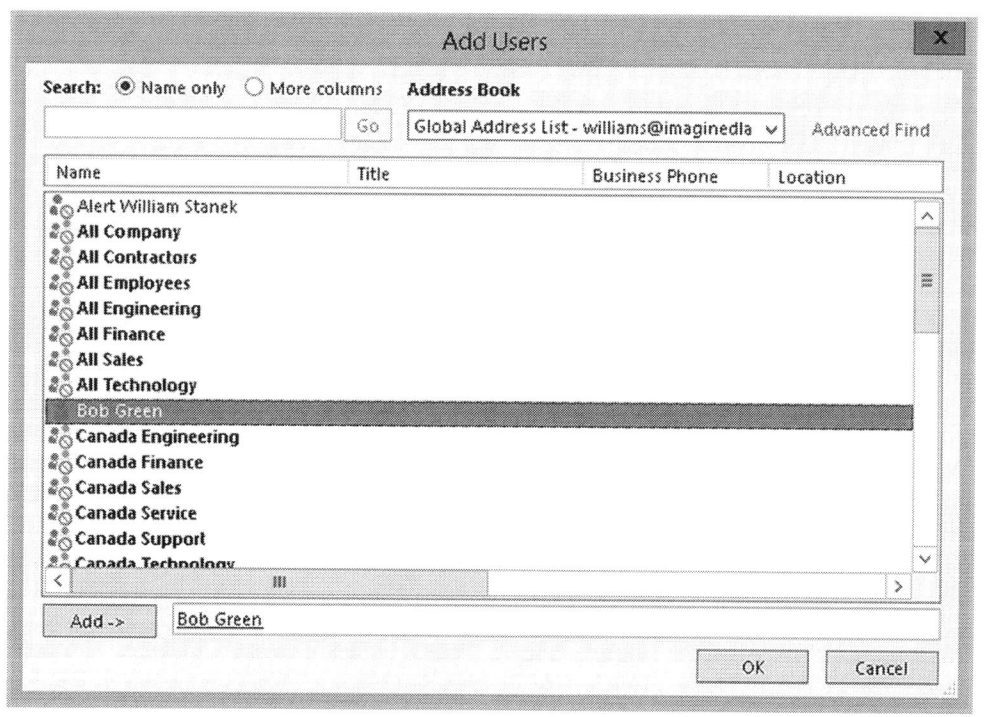

3. In the Delegate Permissions dialog box, assign permissions to the delegates for the Calendar, Tasks, Inbox, Contacts, and Notes. The available permissions include

- **None**   No permissions
- **Reviewer**   Grants read permission only
- **Author**   Grants read and create permissions
- **Editor**   Grants read, create, and modify permissions

> **NOTE**   If the user needs total control over the mailbox, you should grant the user Editor permission for all items.

4. Click **OK** twice. These changes go into effect when the user restarts Outlook.

Delegated users can access the mailbox and send mail on behalf of the mailbox owner. To change this behavior, set folder permissions as described later in the "Granting Permission to Access Folders Without Delegating Access" section.

Delegate Permissions: Bob Green

This delegate has the following permissions:

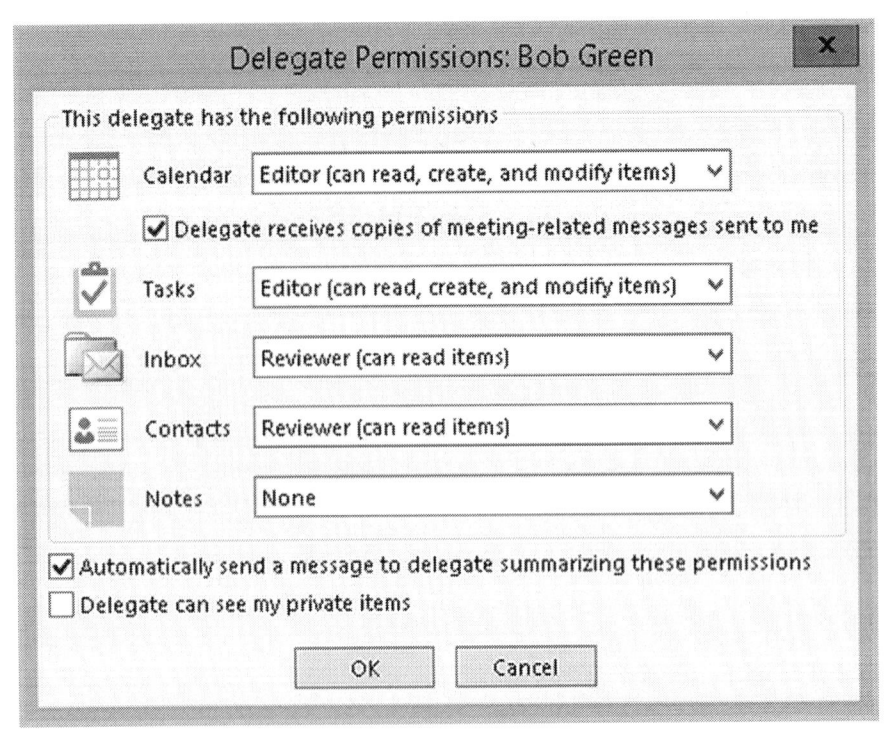

- Calendar: Editor (can read, create, and modify items)
  - ☑ Delegate receives copies of meeting-related messages sent to me
- Tasks: Editor (can read, create, and modify items)
- Inbox: Reviewer (can read items)
- Contacts: Reviewer (can read items)
- Notes: None

☑ Automatically send a message to delegate summarizing these permissions
☐ Delegate can see my private items

[OK] [Cancel]

Opening Additional Exchange Mailboxes

The final step is to let Exchange know about the additional mailboxes the user can open. To do this, follow these steps:

1. Have the user who will be accessing additional mailboxes log on and start Outlook.
2. In Outlook 2010, click the Office button, click **Account Settings**, and then select the **Account Settings** option. In Outlook 2013 or Outlook 2016, on the File pane, click **Account Settings**, and then select the **Account Settings** option.
3. Select the Microsoft Exchange account, and then click **Change**.

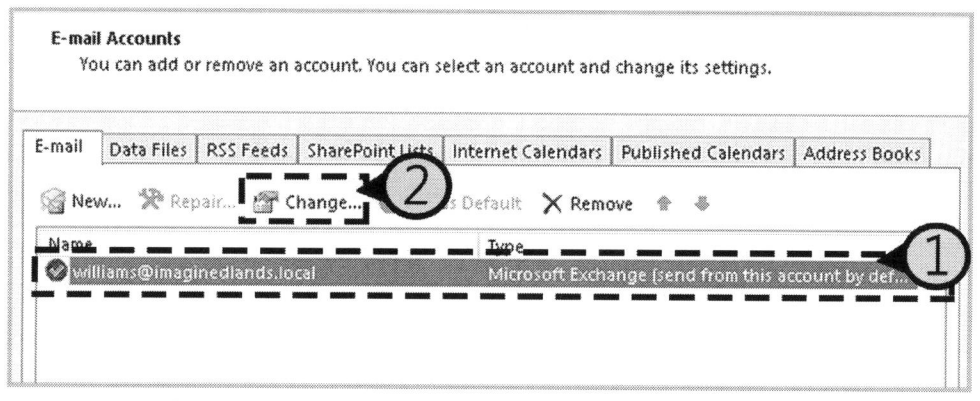

[Screenshot: E-mail Accounts dialog showing the E-mail tab with williams@imaginedlands.local selected (1) and the Change... button highlighted (2).]

4. In the Change Account dialog box, click **More Settings**.
5. In the Microsoft Exchange dialog box, on the Advanced tab, click **Add**.

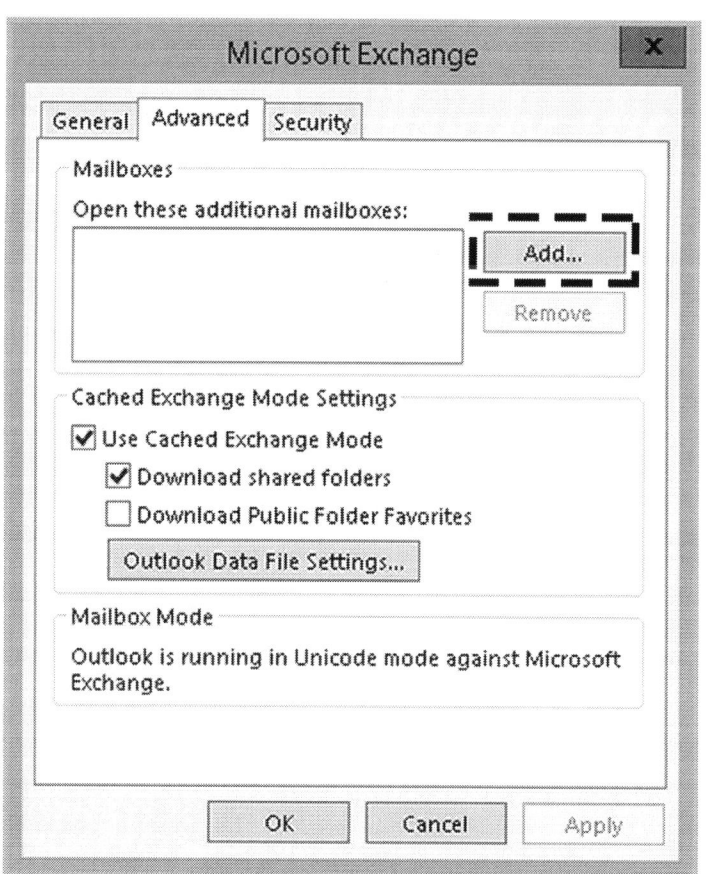

[Screenshot: Microsoft Exchange dialog, Advanced tab, with the Add... button highlighted. Cached Exchange Mode Settings shows "Use Cached Exchange Mode" and "Download shared folders" checked; "Download Public Folder Favorites" unchecked. Mailbox Mode: "Outlook is running in Unicode mode against Microsoft Exchange."]

6. Type the name of a mailbox to open. Generally, this is the same name as the mail alias for the user or account associated with the mailbox. Click **OK**. Repeat this step to add other mailboxes.

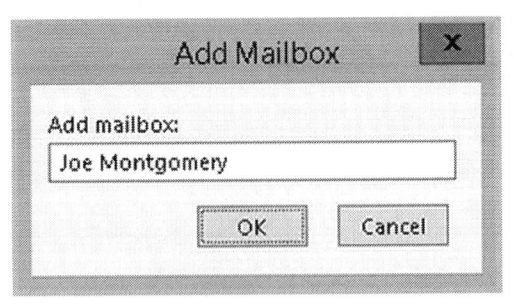

7. Click **Next**, and then click **Finish**.
8. Click **Close**. The additional mailboxes are displayed in the Outlook folder list.

Granting Permission to Access Folders Without Delegating Access

When a mailbox is stored on the server, you can grant access to individual folders in the mailbox. Granting access in this way allows users to add the mailbox to their mail profiles and work with the folder. Users can perform tasks only for which you've granted permission.

To grant access to folders individually, follow these steps:

1. Right-click the folder for which you want to grant access, and then select **Properties**. In the Properties dialog box, select the **Permissions** tab, as shown in Figure 9-8.
2. The Name and Permission Level lists display account names and their permissions on the folder. Two special names might be listed:

- **Default**   Provides default permissions for all users.
- **Anonymous**   Provides permissions for anonymous users, such as those who anonymously access a published public folder through the web.

3. To grant permission that differs from the default permission, click **Add**.

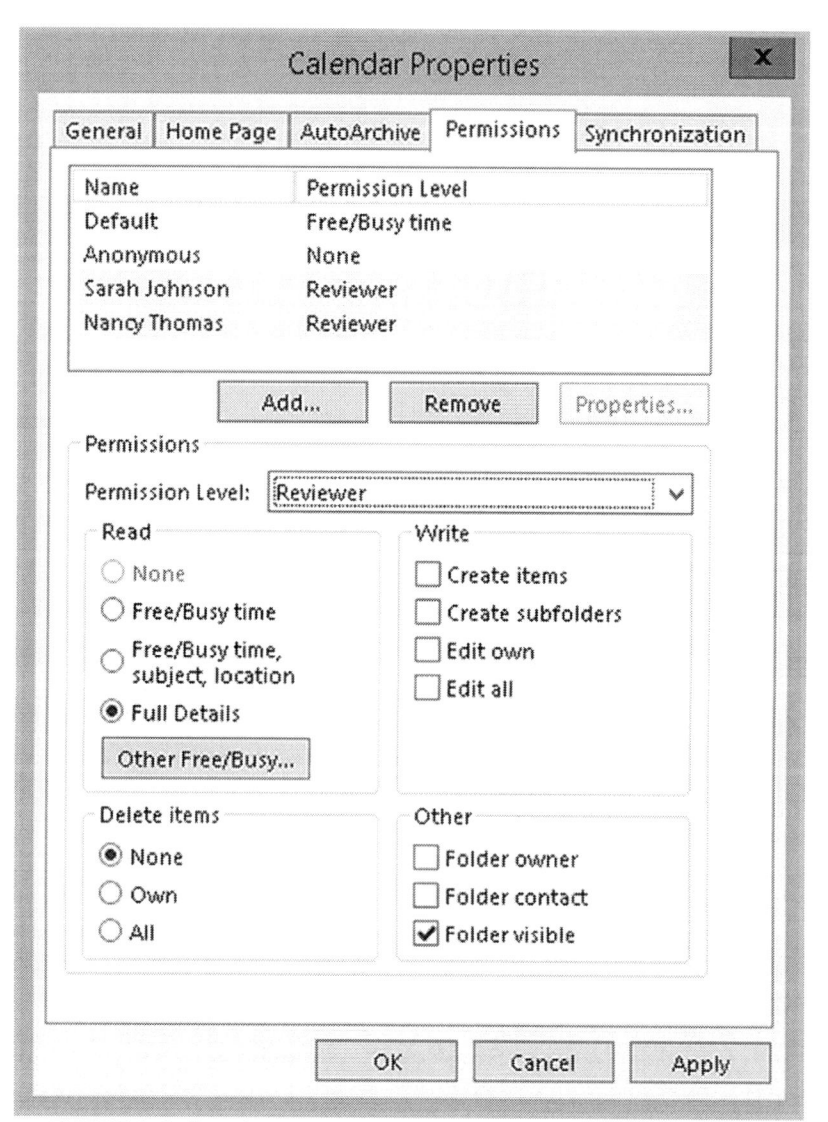

FIGURE 9-8 Granting access to a folder through the Permissions tab.

4. In the Add Users dialog box, double-click the name of a user who needs access to the mailbox. Repeat this step as necessary for other users, and click **OK** when finished.

5. In the Name and Role lists, select one or more users whose permissions you want to modify. Then use the Permission Level list to assign permissions or select individual permission items. The roles are defined as follows:

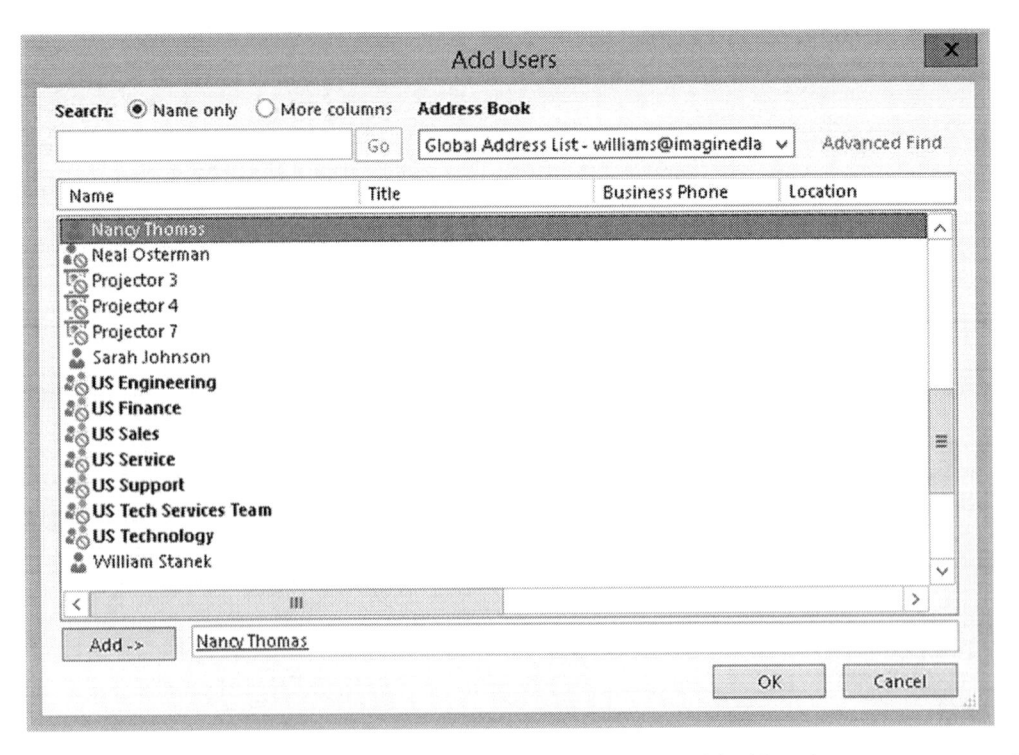

- **Owner** Grants all permissions in the folder. Users with this role can create, read, modify, and delete all items in the folder. They can create subfolders and change permissions on folders as well.
- **Publishing Editor** Grants permission to create, read, modify, and delete all items in the folder. Users with this role can create subfolders as well.
- **Editor** Grants permission to create, read, modify, and delete all items in the folder.
- **Publishing Author** Grants permission to create and read items in the folder, to modify and delete items the user created, and to create subfolders.
- **Author** Grants permission to create and read items in the folder and to modify and delete items the user created.
- **Nonediting Author** Grants permission to create and read items in the folder.
- **Reviewer** Grants read-only permission.
- **Contributor** Grants permission to create items but not to view the contents of the folder.
- **None** Grants no permission in the folder.

6. When you're finished granting permissions, click **OK**.

Using Mail Profiles to Customize the Mail Environment

The mail profile used with Outlook determines which information services are available and how they are configured. A default mail profile is created when you install and configure Outlook for the first time. This mail profile is usually called Outlook.

The active mail profile defines the mail setup for the user who is logged on to the computer. You can define additional profiles for the user as well. You can use these additional profiles to customize the user's mail environment for different situations. Here are two scenarios:

- A manager needs to check the Technical Support and Customer Support mailboxes only on Mondays when she writes summary reports. On other days, the manager doesn't want to see these mailboxes. To solve this problem, you create two mail profiles: Support and Standard. The Support profile displays the manager's mailbox as well as the Technical Support and Customer Support mailboxes. The Standard profile displays only the manager's mailbox. The manager can then switch between these mail profiles as necessary.
- A laptop user wants to check Exchange mail directly while connected to the LAN. When at home, the user wants to use remote mail with scheduled connections. On business trips, the user wants to use SMTP and POP3. To solve this problem, you create three mail profiles: On-Site, Off-Site, and Home. The On-Site profile uses the Exchange service with a standard configuration. The Off-Site profile configures Exchange with scheduled connections. The Home profile uses the Internet mail service instead of the Exchange information service.

Common tasks you'll perform to manage mail profiles are examined in this section.

Creating, Copying, and Removing Mail Profiles

You manage mail profiles through the Mail utility. To access this utility and manage profiles, follow these steps:

1. Exit Outlook. Start the Mail utility. In Control Panel, click **Small Icons** on the View By list and then start the Mail app by clicking its icon or by double-clicking its icon.
2. In the Mail Setup–Outlook dialog box, click **Show Profiles**.

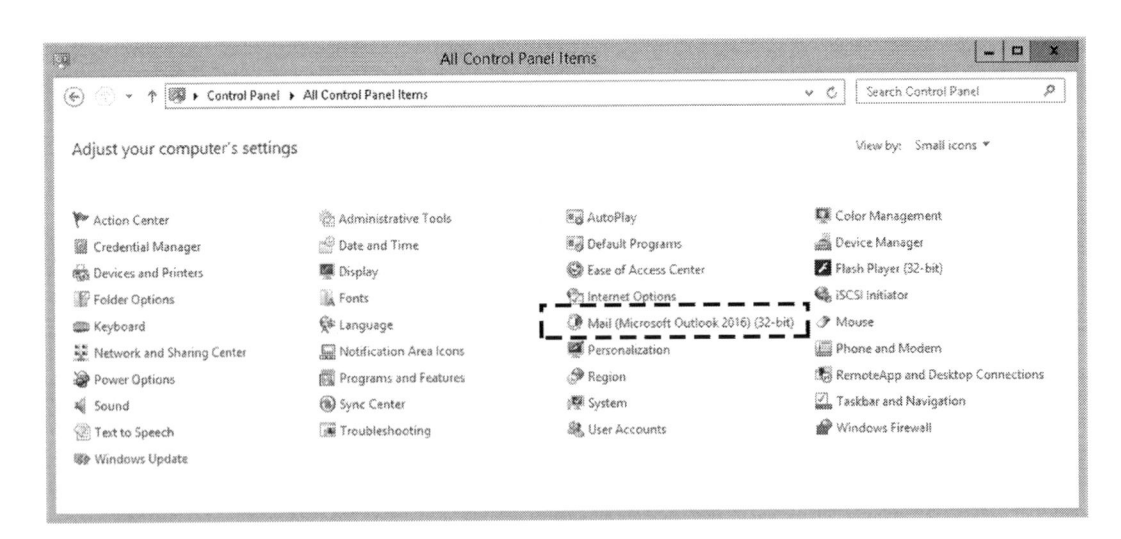

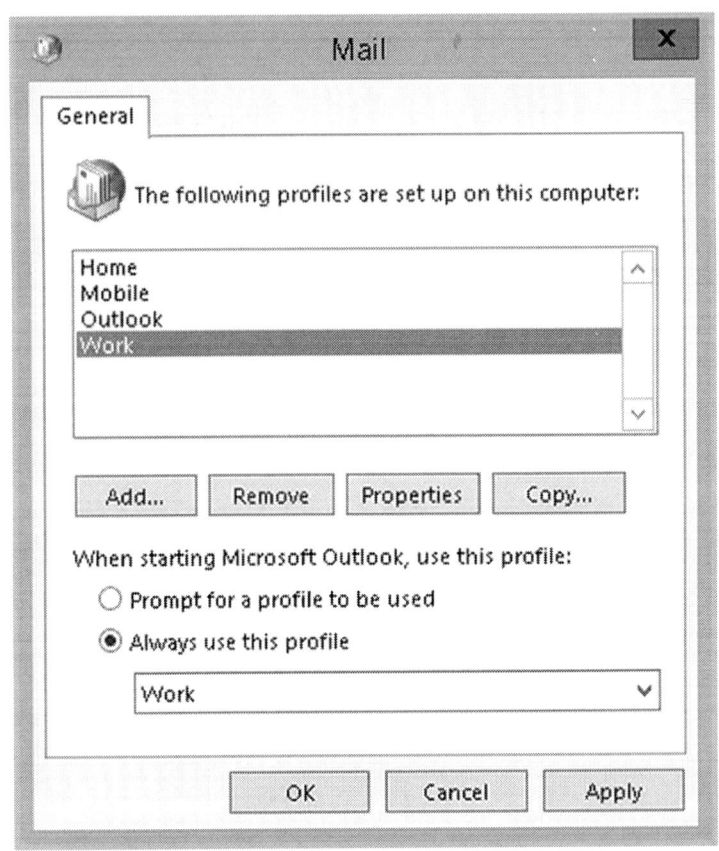

FIGURE 9-9 Using the Mail dialog box to add, remove, or edit mail profiles.

3. As Figure 9-9 shows, you should see a list of mail profiles for the current user. Mail profiles for other users aren't displayed. You can now perform the following actions:

- Click Add to create a new mail profile using the Account Settings Wizard.
- Delete a profile by selecting it and clicking Remove.
- Copy an existing profile by selecting it and clicking Copy.
- View a profile by selecting it and clicking Properties.

Selecting a Specific Profile to use on Startup

You can configure Outlook to use a specific profile on startup or to prompt for a profile to use.

To start with a specific profile, follow these steps:

1. Start the Mail utility. Press the Windows key +I and then click **Control Panel**. In Control Panel, click **Small Icons** on the View By list and then start the Mail app by clicking its icon or by double-clicking its icon.

2. In the Mail Setup–Outlook dialog box, click **Show Profiles**.

3. Select **Always Use This Profile**, and then use the drop-down list to choose the startup profile. Click **OK**.

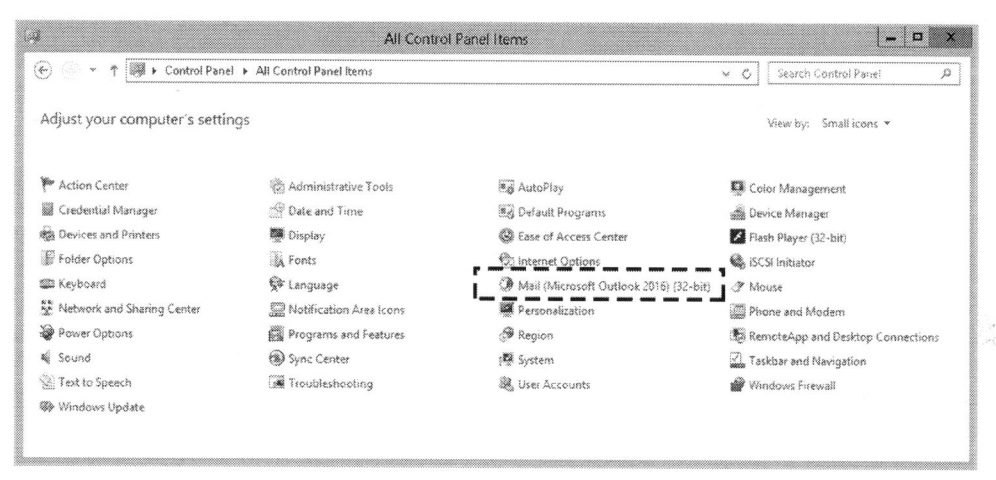

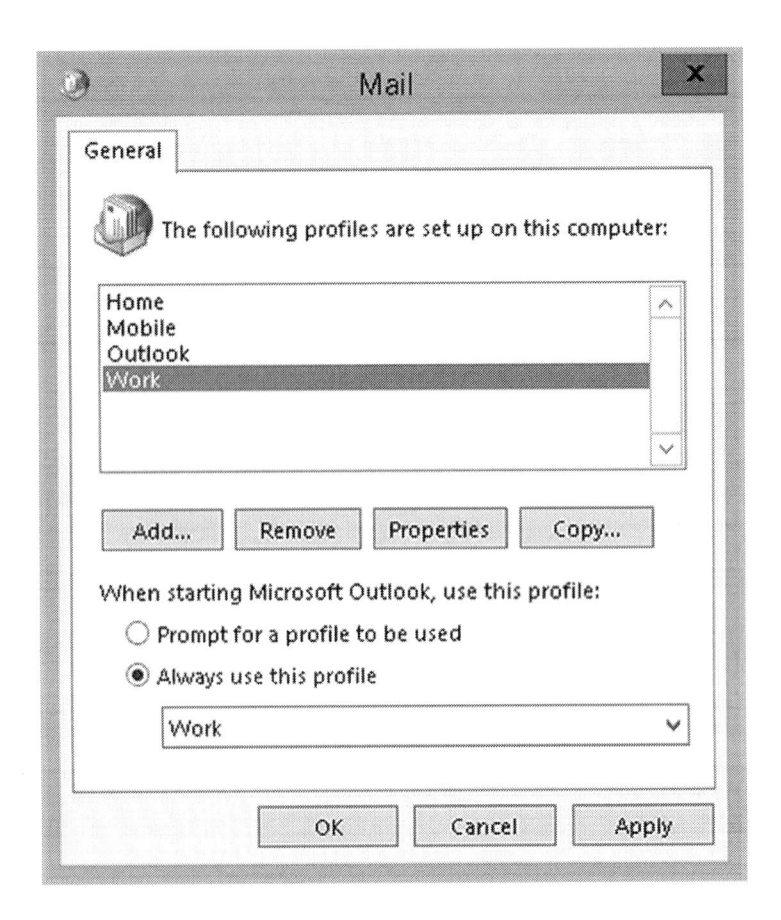

To prompt for a profile before starting Outlook, follow these steps:

1. Start the Mail utility. Press the Windows key +I and then click **Control Panel**. In Control Panel, click **Small Icons** on the View By list and then start the Mail app by clicking its icon or by double-clicking its icon.

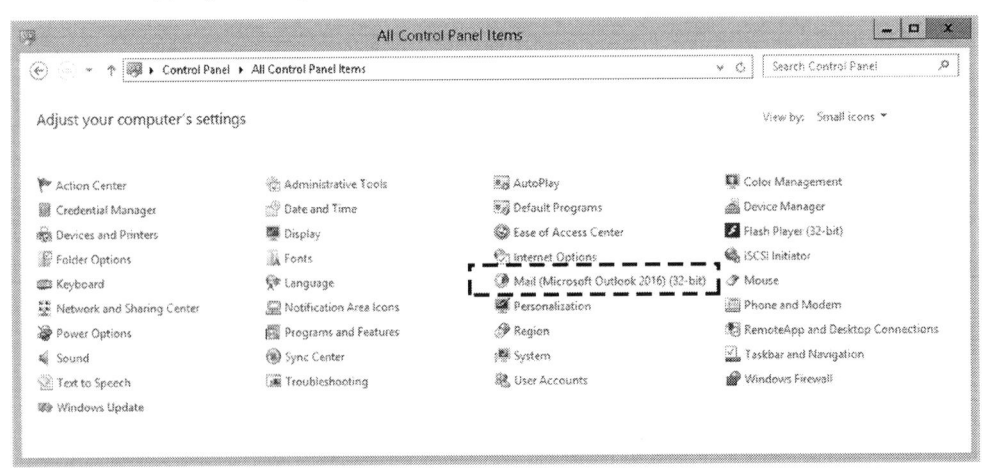

2. In the Mail Setup–Outlook dialog box, click **Show Profiles**.
3. Select **Prompt For A Profile To Be Used**, and then click **OK**.

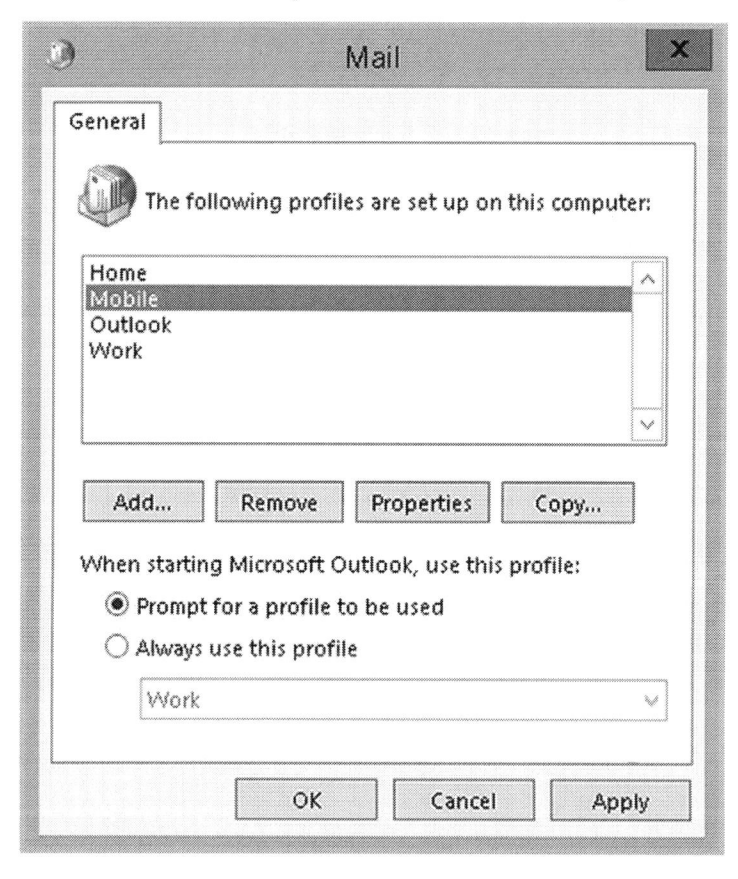

Chapter 10. Customizing & Configuring Exchange Security

You manage Exchange security using either the Windows Azure Active Directory tools or the Exchange management tools. In Windows Azure Active Directory, you manage security using permissions. Users, contacts, and security groups all have permissions assigned to them. These permissions control the resources that users, contacts, and groups can access and the actions they can perform. You use auditing to track the use of these permissions, as well as log ons and log offs. In addition to the standard permissions, Exchange also supports *role-based access control* (RBAC), which are unique to Exchange.

Configuring Standard Exchange Permissions

Windows Azure Active Directory is the central repository for information in hosted domains. Because Windows Azure Active Directory also stores most Exchange information, you can use the features of Windows Azure Active Directory to manage standard permissions for Exchange across the organization.

Assigning Permissions

Users, contacts, and security groups are represented in Windows Azure Active Directory as objects. These objects have many attributes that determine how they are used. The most important attributes are the permissions assigned to the objects. Permissions grant or deny access to objects and resources. For example, you can grant a user the right to create public folders but deny that same user the right to create mail-enabled contacts.

Permissions assigned to an object can be applied directly to the object, or they can be inherited from another object. Generally, objects inherit permissions from *parent objects*. A parent object is an object that is above another object in the object hierarchy. However, you can override inheritance. One way to do this is to assign permissions directly to an object. Another way is to specify that an object shouldn't inherit permissions.

Permissions are inherited through the organizational hierarchy. The root of the hierarchy is the hosted domain. All other containers in the tree inherit the permissions of the hosted domain container.

For the management of Exchange information, Exchange uses several predefined groups. These predefined security groups have permissions to manage the Exchange organization and Exchange recipient data in Windows Azure Active Directory.

When you are working with Exchange Online, you can view the Exchange Management groups by, connecting to Windows Azure and Microsoft Online Services in Windows PowerShell and then entering the Get-Group command. For more information on using Windows PowerShell to work with the online service, see Chapter 1 "Working with Office 365 & Exchange Online."

Understanding Exchange Management Groups

Table 10-1 lists predefined groups created in Windows Azure Active Directory for Exchange Online. As the table shows, each group has a slightly different usage and purpose. Several of the groups are used by Exchange itself. You use the other groups for role-based access control and assigning management permissions.

TABLE 10-1 Security groups created for Exchange Online

GROUP	DESCRIPTION
Compliance Management	A role group. Members of this universal security group have permission to manage compliance settings.
Discovery Management	A role group. Members of this universal security group can perform mailbox searches for data that meets specific criteria.
Help Desk	A role group. Members of this universal security group can view any property or object within the Exchange organization and have limited management permissions.

GROUP	DESCRIPTION
Hygiene Management	A role group. Members of this universal security group can manage the anti-spam and antivirus features of Exchange.
Organization Management	A role group. Members of this universal security group have full access to all Exchange properties and objects in the Exchange organization with some exceptions, such as Discovery Management.
Recipient Management	A role group. Members of this universal security group have permission to modify Exchange user attributes in Windows Azure Active Directory and perform most mailbox operations.
Records Management	A role group. Members of this universal security group can manage compliance features, including retention policies, message classifications, and transport rules.
UM Management	A role group. Members of this universal security group can manage all aspects of unified messaging (UM), including the Unified Messaging service configuration and UM recipient configuration.
View-Only Organization Management	A role group. Members of this universal security group have read-only access to the entire Exchange organization tree in the Windows Azure Active Directory configuration container and read-only access to the hosted domain container.

Table 10-2 lists predefined groups and administrative roles used with Exchange Online and Office 365. These groups and roles are used for role-based access controls and assigning management permissions. However, HelpDeskAdmins and

TenantAdmins aren't managed in Exchange Online. Instead, you add users to the related Office 365 role to get the desired permissions.

TABLE 10-2 Security groups and administrative roles for the Exchange Online and Office 365

GROUP/ROLE	DESCRIPTION
Billing Administrator	Used with Office 365. Members of this role are responsible for managing subscriptions and making purchases. They also can manage support tickets and monitor service health.
Exchange Administrator	Used with Office 365. Members of this role have full access to Exchange Online.
Global Administrator	Used with Office 365. Members of this role have full access to all Office 365 features and are the only ones who can assign other admin roles. Except for password admins, they also are the only ones who can reset passwords for other admins.
HelpDeskAdmins	Used with Exchange Online. Members of this group have the Password Administrator role in the Office 365 organization.
Password Administrator	Used with Office 365. Members of this role are responsible for managing passwords for standard users and other password admins. They also can manage service requests and monitor service health.
Service Administrator	Used with Office 365. Members of this role are responsible for managing service requests and monitoring service health.
SharePoint Administrator	Used with Office 365. Members of this role have full access to SharePoint.
Skype for Business Administrator	Used with Office 365. Members of this role can manage Skype for Business.

GROUP/ROLE	DESCRIPTION
TenantAdmins	Used with Exchange Online. Members of this group have the Global Administrator role in the Office 365 organization.
User Management Administrator	Used with Office 365. Members of this role are responsible for managing standard users and groups. They can reset passwords for standard users, manage service requests, and monitor service health.

When working with Exchange-related groups, keep in mind that Organization Management grants the widest set of Exchange management permissions possible. Members of this group can perform any Exchange management task, including organization, server, and recipient management. Members of the Recipient Management group, on the other hand, can manage only recipient information, and Public Folder Management can manage only public folder information. View-Only Organization Management can view Exchange organization, server, and recipient information, but this group cannot manage any aspects of Exchange.

The TenantAdmins group is a member of the Organization Management role group and inherits its permissions from this role group. Rather than add members directly to TenantAdmins, you add members to this role by granting the Global Administrator role to users in Office 365 Admin Center.

Similarly, the HelpDeskAdmins group is a member of the View-Only Organization Management role group and inherits its permissions from this role group. Rather than add members directly to HelpDeskAdmins, you add members to this role by granting the Global Administrator role to users in Office 365 Admin Center.

Assigning Management Permissions

You use Exchange Admin Center to manage membership in Exchange role groups. When you are managing the organization, select Permissions in the Navigation menu and then select Admin Roles to work with Exchange role groups. When you select a role, the right-most pane provides a description of the role, lists the assigned roles, and also shows the current members (see Figure 10-1). While working with this view, you can double-click a group entry to view and manage its membership.

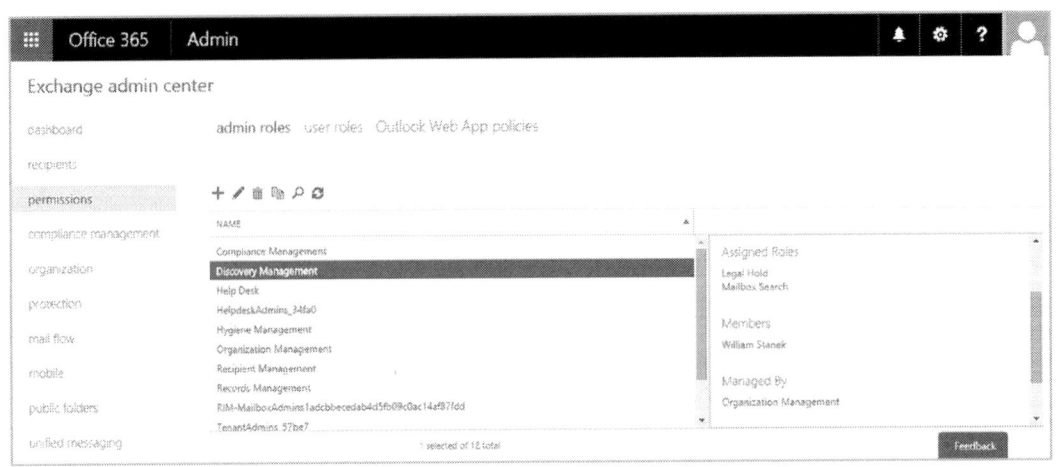

FIGURE 10-1 Using Exchange Admin Center to work with Exchange role groups.

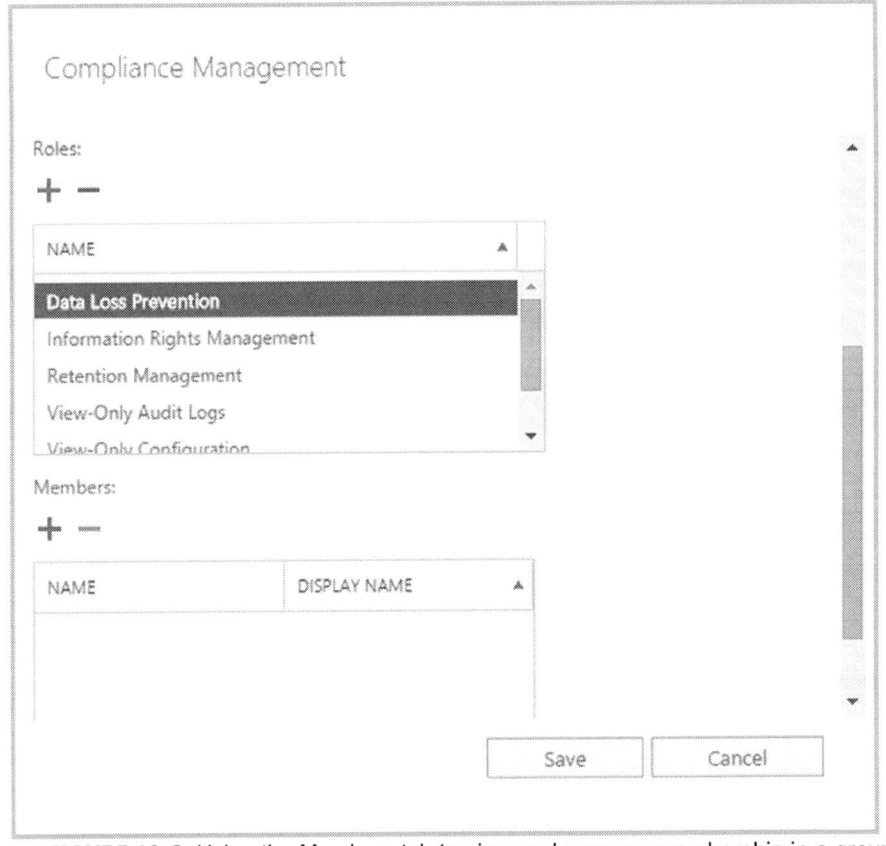

FIGURE 10-2 Using the Members tab to view and manage membership in a group.

To grant Exchange management permissions to a user or group of users, all you need to do is make the user or group a member of the appropriate Exchange management group by completing the following steps:

1. In Exchange Admin Center, select **Permissions** in the Navigation menu and then select **Admin Roles**.

2. Double-click the Exchange management group you want to work with. This opens the group's Properties dialog box, shown in Figure 10-2.

3. Scroll down until you can see the Members panel.

4. On the Members panel, click Add (![+]). The Select Members dialog box appears, as shown in Figure 10-3.

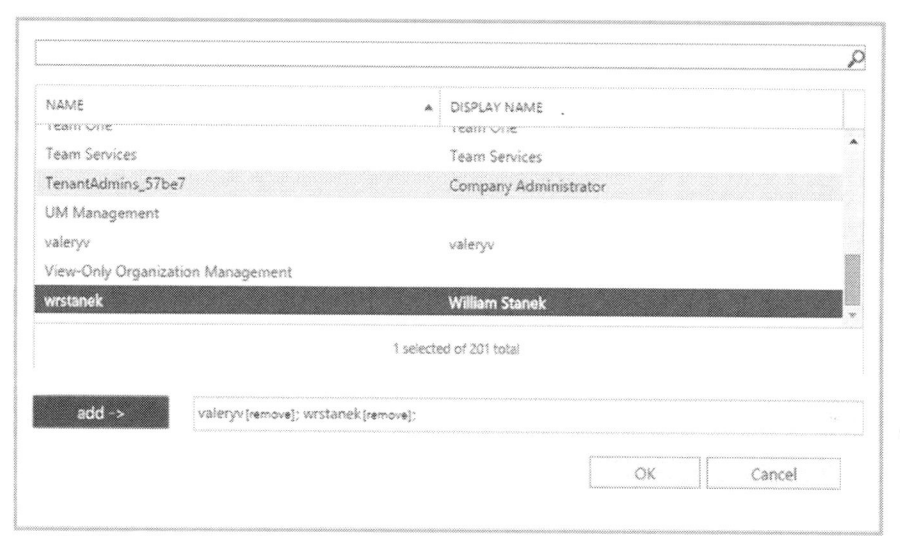

FIGURE 10-3 Specifying the name of the user, contact, computer, service account, or group to add.

5. Click a user or group to add as a member and then click **Add**. Repeat this step as necessary. Click **OK**.

You can remove a user or other group from an Exchange management group by completing the following steps:

1. In Exchange Admin Center, select **Permissions** in the Navigation menu and then select **Admin Roles**.

2. Double-click the Exchange management group you want to work with. This opens the group's Properties dialog box.

3. Scroll down until you can see the Members panel.
4. On the Members panel, click the user or group you want to remove and then click Remove (![]).
5. Click **Save**.

You use Office Admin Center to manage membership in Office 365 role groups. When you are managing the Office 365 service, select **Users** in the Navigation menu and then select **Active Users** to view a list of all active users in the organization.

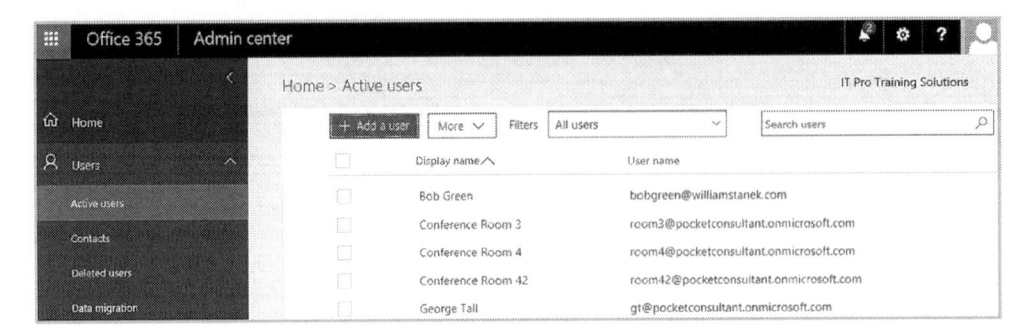

When you select a user, the properties page for the user is displayed. Next, select **Edit** in the Roles pane.

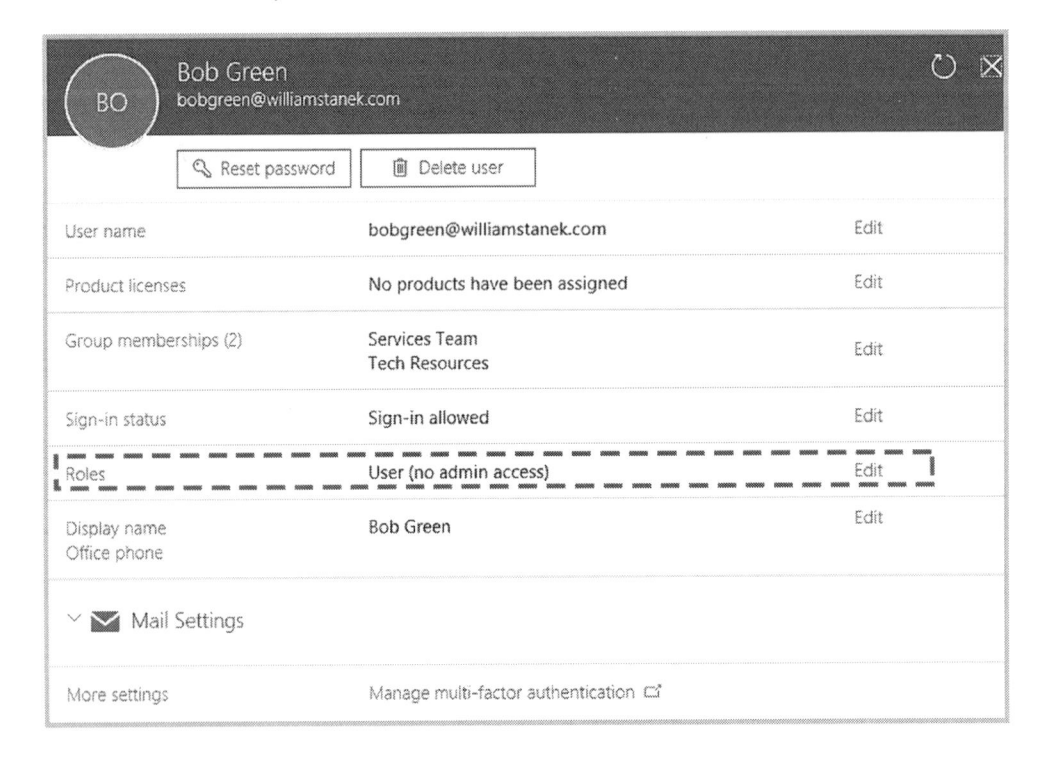

256 | IT Pro Solutions

If you want the user to have administrator privileges, complete the following steps:

1. Choose the role to assign. For example, choose Global Administrator to make the user a member of TenantAdmins or Password Administrator to make the user a member of HelpDeskAdmins in the Exchange Online organization.

2. As necessary, enter an alternative email address for the user. Every Office 365 admin must have an alternate email address.

3. Click **Save** to apply the changes and then click **Close**.

Configuring Role-Based Permissions for Exchange

Exchange Online implements role-based access controls that allow you to easily customize permissions for users in the organization. You use role-based access controls to do the following:

- Assign permissions to groups of users

- Define policies that assign permissions
- Assign permissions directly to users

Before I discuss each of these tasks, I'll discuss essential concepts related to role-based permissions. Because the permissions model is fairly complex, I recommend reading this entire section to understand your implementation options before starting to assign permissions.

Understanding Role-Based Permissions

Role-based access control is a permissions model that uses role assignment to define the management tasks a user or group of users can perform in the Exchange organization. Exchange defines many built-in management roles that you can use to manage your Exchange organization. Each built-in role acts as a logical grouping of permissions that specify the management actions that those assigned the role can perform. You also can create custom roles.

You can assign roles to role groups or directly to users. You also can assign roles through role policies that are then applied to role groups, users, or both. By assigning roles, you grant permission to perform management tasks.

At the top of the permissions model is the role group, which is a special type of security group that has been assigned one or more roles. Keep the following in mind when working with role-based permissions:

- You can assign role-based permissions to any mailbox-enabled user account. Assigning a role to a user grants the user the ability to perform a specific management action.
- You can assign role-based permissions to any universal security group. Assigning a role to a group grants members of the group the ability to perform a specific management action.
- You cannot assign role-based permissions to security groups with the domain local or global scope.
- You cannot assign role-based permissions to distribution groups regardless of scope.

As Table 10-1 showed previously, Exchange Online includes a number of predefined role groups. These role groups are assigned fixed management roles by default. As a result, you do not need to explicitly add roles to these groups to enable management, nor can you add or remove roles associated with the built-in groups.

You can, however, manage the members of the predefined role groups using the procedures discussed previously. You can also create your own role groups and manage the membership of those groups.

When you assign a role to a group, the management scope determines where in the directory hierarchy that objects can be managed by users assigned a management role. The scope is either implicitly or explicitly assigned. Implicit scopes are the default scopes that apply based on a particular type of management role.

Table 10-3 lists key management roles with an organization scope. A role with an organization scope applies across the whole Exchange organization. Table 10-4 lists key management roles with a user scope. A role with a user scope applies to an individual user.

TABLE 10-3 Management roles with an organization scope

MANAGEMENT ROLE	ENABLES MANAGERS TO...
Address Lists	Manage address lists, the global address list, and offline address lists in an organization.
Audit Logs	Manage audit logs in an organization.
Data Loss Prevention	Configure data loss prevention settings in an organization.
Distribution Groups	Create and manage distribution groups and distribution group members in an organization.
Information Rights Management	Manage the Information Rights Management (IRM) features of Exchange in an organization.
Journaling	Manage journaling configuration in an organization.
Legal Hold	Configure whether data within a mailbox should be retained for litigation purposes in an organization.
Mail Enabled Public	Configure whether individual public folders are mail

MANAGEMENT ROLE	ENABLES MANAGERS TO...
Folders	enabled or mail disabled in an organization.
Mail Recipient Creation	Create mailboxes, mail users, mail contacts, distribution groups, and dynamic distribution groups in an organization.
Mail Recipients	Manage existing mailboxes, mail users, mail contacts, distribution groups, and dynamic distribution groups in an organization. This does not enable administrators to create these recipients.
Mail Tips	Manage mail tips in an organization.
Mailbox Search	Search mailboxes in an organization.
Message Tracking	Track messages in an organization.
Organization Configuration	Manage basic organization-wide settings. This role type doesn't include the permissions included in the Organization Client Access or Organization Transport Settings role types.
Organization Transport Settings	Manage organization-wide transport settings, including system messages, SMTP email address configuration, and so forth.
Public Folders	Manage public folders in an organization. This role type doesn't enable administrators to manage whether public folders are mail enabled or to manage public folder replication.
Recipient Policies	Manage recipient policies, such as provisioning policies, in an organization.
Remote and Accepted Domains	Manage remote and accepted domains in an organization.

MANAGEMENT ROLE	ENABLES MANAGERS TO...
Reset Password	Reset users' password in an organization.
Retention Management	Manage retention policies in an organization.
Role Management	Manage management role groups, role assignment policies, management roles, role entries, assignments, and scopes in an organization. Users assigned roles associated with this role type can override the Managed By property for role groups, configure any role group, and add or remove members to or from any role group.
Security Group Creation and Membership	Create and manage security groups and their memberships in an organization.
Team Mailboxes	Define site mailbox provisioning policies and manage site mailboxes.
Transport Agents	Manage transport agents in an organization.
Transport Hygiene	Manage antivirus and anti-spam features in an organization.
Transport Rules	Manage transport rules.
UM Mailboxes	Manage the unified messaging (UM) configuration of mailboxes and other recipients.
UM Prompts	Create and manage custom UM voice prompts.
Unified Messaging	Manage Unified Messaging settings. This role doesn't enable administrators to manage UM-specific mailbox configuration or UM prompts.
User Options	View the Microsoft Outlook Web Access options for

MANAGEMENT ROLE	ENABLES MANAGERS TO...
	users.
View-Only Audit Logs	Search the administrator audit logs and view results.
View-Only Configuration	View all of the nonrecipient Exchange configuration settings.
View-Only Recipients	View the configuration of recipients, including mailboxes, mail users, mail contacts, distribution groups, and dynamic distribution groups.

TABLE 10-4 Management roles for user scope

MANAGEMENT ROLE	ENABLES INDIVIDUAL USERS TO...
MyBaseOptions	View and modify the basic configuration of their own mailboxes and associated settings.
MyContactInformation	Modify their contact information. This information includes their addresses and phone numbers.
MyDiagnostics	Perform basic diagnostics on their mailboxes.
MyDistributionGroupMembership	View and modify their membership in distribution groups in an organization, provided that those distribution groups allow manipulation of group membership.
MyDistributionGroups	Create, modify, and view distribution groups and modify, view, remove, and add members to distribution groups they own.
MyProfileInformation	Modify their names.
MyRetentionPolicies	View their retention tags and view and

	modify their retention tag settings and defaults.
MyTeamMailboxes	Create and connect site mailboxes.
MyTextMessaging	View and modify their text messaging settings.
MyVoiceMail	View and modify their voice mail settings.

Role assignment policies grant users permissions to configure their Outlook Web App options and perform limited management tasks. When you install Exchange Online, the setup process creates the Default Role Assignment Policy and sets this as the default for all new mailboxes. This policy grants users the MyBaseOptions, MyContactInformation, MyDistributionGroupMembership, and MyVoiceMail roles, but it does not grant users the MyDistributionGroups and MyProfileInformation roles.

Exchange Online has a Default Role Assignment policy as well. This default policy, assigned to all Exchange Online users, grants all of the management roles. You can create other role assignment policies as well.

Working with Role Groups

By default, members of the Organization Management group can manage any role group in the Exchange organization. Anyone designated as a manager of a role group can manage the role group. You assign a user as a manager of a role group using the -ManagedBy parameter, which can be set when you create or modify a role group.

To view the currently available role groups and the roles they've been assigned, select **Permissions** in the Navigation menu and then select **Admin Roles**. As shown in Figure 10-4, when you select a role group, the details pane lists the assigned roles and members.

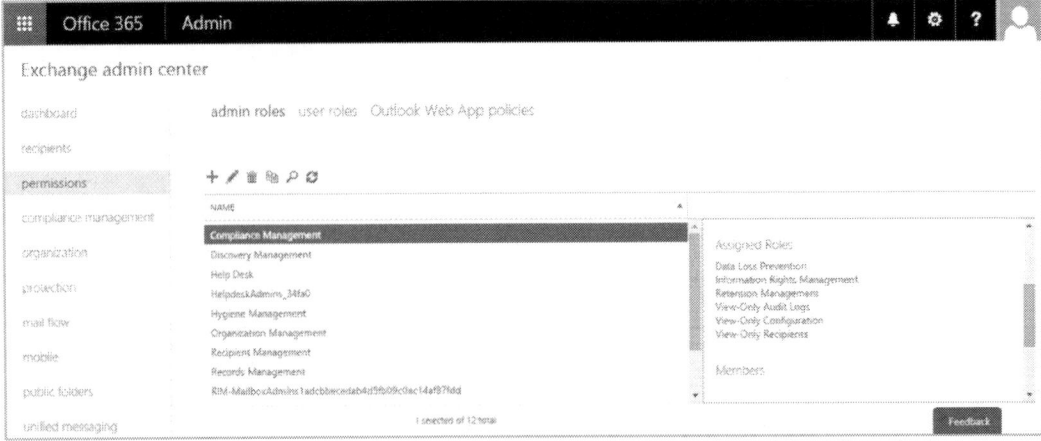

FIGURE 10-4 Viewing the role groups and the assigned roles and members of a selected group.

To create a role group, complete the following steps:

1. In Exchange Admin Center, select **Permissions** in the Navigation menu and then select **Admin Roles**.

FIGURE 10-5 Creating a new role group.

264 | IT Pro Solutions

2. Click **New** (➕). In the New Role Group dialog box, shown in Figure 10-5, type a descriptive name for the role group. By default, the role group will use the implicit write scope.

3. Under Roles, click Add (➕). In the Select A Role dialog box select roles to assign to the role group and then click **Add**. You can select multiple roles using the Shift or Ctrl key, or you can simply select and add each role individually. When you are finished adding roles, click OK.

4. Under Members, click Add (➕). In the Select Members dialog box select members to add to the role group and then click **Add**. You can select multiple members using the Shift or Ctrl key, or you can simply select and add each member individually. When you are finished adding members, click OK.

5. Click **Save** to create the role group.

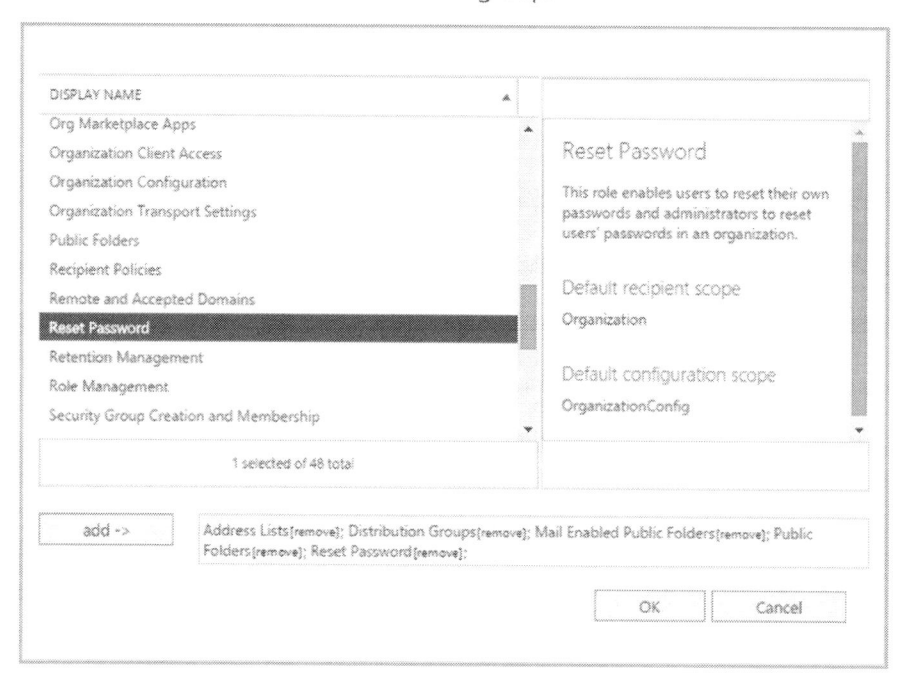

Office 365 & Exchange Online | 265

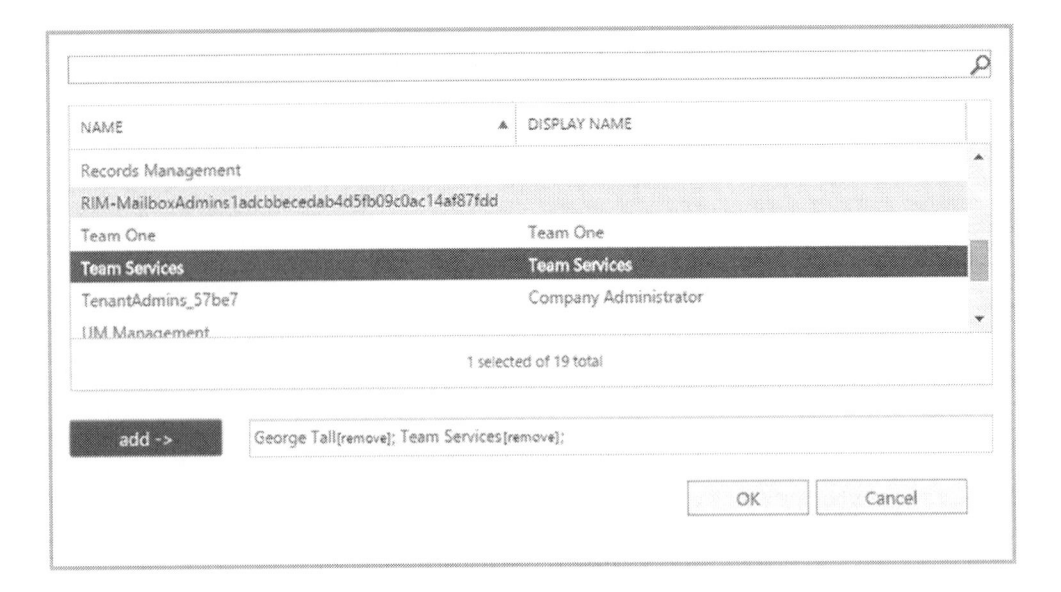

NAME	DISPLAY NAME
Records Management	
RIM-MailboxAdmins1adcbbecedab4d5fb09c0ac14af87fdd	
Team One	Team One
Team Services	**Team Services**
TenantAdmins_57be7	Company Administrator
UM Management	

1 selected of 19 total

add -> George Tall[remove]; Team Services[remove];

OK   Cancel

In the shell, commands you use to work with role groups include the following:

- **Get-RoleGroup**   Displays a complete or filtered list of role groups. When specifying filters, use parentheses to define the filter, such as **–Filter { RolegroupType –Eq "Linked" }**.

```
Get-RoleGroup [-Identity RoleGroupName] {AddtlParams}


{AddtlParams}
[-AccountPartition PartitionID] [-Filter { ManagedBy | Members | Name |
RoleGroupType | DisplayName}] [-Organization OrganizationID]
[-ResultSize Size] [-SortBy {ManagedBy | Members | Name | RoleGroupType |
 DisplayName}] [-UsnForReconciliationSearch Num]
```

- **New-RoleGroup**   Creates a new role group. When specifying roles, you must use the full role name, including spaces. Enclose the role names in quotation marks and separate each role with a comma, such as "**Mail Recipient Creation**", "**Mail Recipients**", "**Recipient Policies**".

```
New-RoleGroup -Name RoleGroupName [-Roles Roles]
[-ManagedBy ManagerIds] [-Members MemberIds] {AddtlParams}


{AddtlParams}
[-CustomConfigWriteScope Scope] [-CustomRecipientWriteScope Scope]
[-Description Description] [-DisplayName DisplayName]
```

```
[-ExternalDirectoryObjectId Objid] [-Organization OrganizationID]
[-PartnerManaged {$True|$False}] [-SamAccountName PreWin2000Name]
[-ValidationOrganization OrgId] [-WellKnownObjectGUID GUID]
```

- **Remove-RoleGroup** Removes a role group. If a role group has designated managers, you must be listed as a manager to remove the role group or use the -BypassSecurityGroupManagerCheck parameter and be an organization manager.

```
Remove-RoleGroup -Identity RoleGroupName {AddtlParams}
```

```
{AddtlParams}
[-BypassSecurityGroupManagerCheck {$True|$False}]
[-ForReconciliation {$True|$False}]
[-RemoveWellKnownObjectGUID {$True|$False}]
```

- **Set-RoleGroup** Configures role group properties. If you specify managers, you must provide the complete list of managers because the list you provide overwrites the existing list of managers. To manage role assignment, see the "Assigning Roles Directly or Via Policy" section later in the chapter.

```
Set-RoleGroup -Identity RoleGroupName [-ManagedBy ManagerIds]
[-Name NewName] {AddtlParams}
```

```
{AddtlParams}
[-BypassSecurityGroupManagerCheck {$True|$False}]
[-Description Description] [-DisplayName DisplayName]
[-ExternalDirectoryObjectId Objid]
```

You use New-RoleGroup to create role groups. When you create a role group, you must specify the group name and the roles assigned to the group. You should also specify the managers and members of the group. The managers and members can be individual users or groups identified by their display name, alias, or distinguished name. If you want to specify more than one manager or member, separate each entry with a comma. The following example creates the Special Recipient Management role group to allow members of the group to manage (but not create) recipients:

```
New-RoleGroup -Name "Special Recipient Management"
-Roles "mail recipients", "recipient policies"
```

```
-ManagedBy "juliec", "tylerk", "ulij"
-Member "mikeg", "lylep", "rubyc", "yus"
```

Role groups are created as universal security groups in the directory database. In Exchange Admin Center, you'll find role groups under Permissions > Admin Roles. After you create a role group, you can manage it using Exchange Admin Center or a remote session with Exchange Online.

The management tasks you can perform depend on which tool you are using. In Exchange Admin Center, you can manage group membership, rename the group, modify file assignments or delete the group. Additional tasks you can perform when you use a remote session with Exchange Online include setting managers.

You can list available role groups using Get-RoleGroup. If you type Get-RoleGroup at the remote session prompt, you see a list of all role groups defined in the Exchange organization to which you are connected. You can filter the output in a variety of ways using standard PowerShell filtering techniques. Get-RoleGroup also has a -Filter parameter that you can use to filter the output according to specific criteria you set. The following example looks for a role group named CS Recipient Management and lists all its properties:

```
Get-RoleGroup -filter {Name -eq "CS Recipient Management"} |
format-list
```

You can use Set-RoleGroup to change the name of a role group or to define a new list of managers. To delete a role group, use Remove-RoleGroup.

Managing Role Group Members

By default, members of the Organization Management group can manage the membership of any role group in the Exchange organization. Anyone designated as a manager of a role group can manage the membership of that role group as well.

In the shell, commands you use to configure role group membership include the following:

- **Add-RoleGroupMember**   Adds a user or universal security group as a member of a role group. If a role group has designated managers, you must be listed as a manager to add role group members or use the -BypassSecurityGroupManagerCheck parameter and be an organization manager.

```
Add-RoleGroupMember -Identity RoleGroupName -Member MemberIds
[-BypassSecurityGroupManagerCheck {$True|$False}]
```

- **Get-RoleGroupMember**   Lists the members of a role group.

```
Get-RoleGroupMember -Identity RoleGroupName
[-ResultSize Size]
```

- **Remove-RoleGroupMember**   Removes a user or universal security group from a role group. If a role group has designated managers, you must be listed as a manager to remove role group members or use the -BypassSecurityGroupManagerCheck parameter and be an organization manager.

```
Remove-RoleGroupMember -Identity RoleGroupName -Member MemberIds
[-BypassSecurityGroupManagerCheck {$True|$False}]
```

- **Update-RoleGroupMember**   Replaces the current group membership with the list of members you provide.

```
Update-RoleGroupMember -Identity RoleGroupName -Members NewMemberIds
[-BypassSecurityGroupManagerCheck {$True|$False}]
```

You add members to a role group using Add-RoleGroupMember. When you add a member to a role group, the member is given the effective permissions provided by the management roles assigned to the role group. If the role group has designated managers, you must be a role group manager or use the -BypassSecurityGroupManagerCheck parameter to override the security group management check. The following example adds a user to the LA Recipient Management role group:

```
Add-RoleGroupMember -Identity "LA Recipient Management"
-Member "joym"
```

When you are working with Exchange Online at the shell prompt, don't forget that all the features of PowerShell are at your disposal. The following example lists all users with mailboxes in the Technology department and adds them to the Technology Management role group:

```
Get-User -Filter { Department -Eq "Technology" -And -RecipientType
-Eq "UserMailbox" } | Get-Mailbox | Add-RoleGroupMember
"Technology Management"
```

You can list members of a particular role group using Get-RoleGroupMember. Members are listed by name and recipient type as shown in the following example and sample output:

```
Get-RoleGroupMember -Identity "CS Recipient Management"

Name                              RecipientType
----                              -------------
Riis Anders                       UserMailbox
Darren Waite                      UserMailbox
```

You can delete role group members using Remove-RoleGroupMember. When you remove a member from a role group, the user or group of users can no longer perform the management tasks made available by that role group. However, keep in mind that the user or group of users might be a member of another role group that grants management permissions. If so, the user or group of users will still be able to perform management tasks.

Assigning Roles Directly or Via Policy

You can assign built-in or custom roles to users, role groups, and universal security groups in one of two ways:

- Directly using role assignment
- Via assignment policy

Directly assigning roles is accomplished using role assignment commands. By adding, removing, or modifying role assignments, you can control the management tasks that users can perform. Although you can assign roles directly to users or universal security groups, this approach increases the complexity of the permissions model in your Exchange organization. A more flexible solution is to assign roles via assignment policy. Assigning roles via assignment policy requires you to do the following:

1. Create assignment policies.

2. Assign roles to these policies.
3. Assign policies to users or groups as appropriate.

Management roles define the specific tasks that can be performed by the members of a role group assigned the role. A role assignment links a management role and a role group. Assigning a management role to a role group grants members of the role group the ability to perform the management tasks defined in the management role. Role assignments can use management scopes to control where the assignment can be used.

In the shell, commands you use to work with role assignment include the following:

- **Get-ManagementRoleAssignment**   Displays a complete or filtered list of role assignments for a role group. You can examine role assignments by name, assignment type, or scope type as well as whether the assignment is enabled or disabled.

```
Get-ManagementRoleAssignment [-Identity RoleAssignmentToRetrieve]
{AddtlParams}


Get-ManagementRoleAssignment [-Role RoleID] [-RoleAssignee IdentityToCheck]
[-AssignmentMethod {Direct | SecurityGroup |
RoleAssignmentPolicy}] {AddtlParams}


{AddtlParams}
[-ConfigWriteScope <None | NotApplicable | OrganizationConfig |
CustomConfigScope | PartnerDelegatedTenantScope |
 ExclusiveConfigScope>] [-CustomConfigWriteScope ManagementScopeId]
[-CustomRecipientWriteScope ManagementScopeId] [-Delegating <$true
| $false>] [-Enabled <$true | $false>] [-Exclusive <$true | $false>]
[-ExclusiveConfigWriteScope ManagementScopeId]
[-ExclusiveRecipientWriteScope ManagementScopeId]
[-GetEffectiveUsers <$true | $false>]
[-GetEffectiveUsers <$true | $false>]
[-Organization OrganizationId] [-RecipientWriteScope <None | NotApplicable
| Organization | MyGAL | Self | MyDirectReports | OU |
CustomRecipientScope | MyDistributionGroups | MyExecutive |
ExclusiveRecipientScope>] [-RoleAssigneeType <User |
```

SecurityGroup | RoleAssignmentPolicy | MailboxPlan |
ForeignSecurityPrincipal | RoleGroup>] [-WritableRecipient **GeneralRecipientId**]

- **New-ManagementRoleAssignment** Creates a new role assignment, and assigns it directly to a user or group or assigns it via an assignment policy.

New-ManagementRoleAssignment –Name **RoleAssignmentName**
-SecurityGroup **Group** -Role **Roles** {AddtlParams}

New-ManagementRoleAssignment –Name **RoleAssignmentName**
-Policy **Policy** -Role **Roles** {AddtlParams}

New-ManagementRoleAssignment –Name **RoleAssignmentName**
-User **User** -Role **Roles** {AddtlParams}

New-ManagementRoleAssignment –Name **RoleAssignmentName**
-Computer **Computer** -Role **Roles** {AddtlParams}

{AddtlParams}
[-CustomConfigWriteScope **Scope**] [-CustomRecipientWriteScope **Scope**]
[-Delegating {$True|$False}] [-ExclusiveConfigWriteScope **Scope**]
[-ExclusiveRecipientWriteScope **Scope**] [-Organization **OrganizationId**]
[-RecipientRelativeWriteScope <None | NotApplicable | Organization
| MyGAL | Self | MyDirectReports | OU |CustomRecipientScope |
MyDistributionGroups | MyExecutive | ExclusiveRecipientScope>]
[-UnscopedTopLevel {$True|$False}]

- **Remove-ManagementRoleAssignment** Removes a role assignment.

Remove-ManagementRoleAssignment –Identity **RoleAssignmentName**

- **Set-ManagementRoleAssignment** Configures role assignment properties.

Set-ManagementRoleAssignment –Identity **RoleAssignmentName**
[-Enabled {$True|$False}]
{AddtlParams1 | AddtlParams2 | AddtlParams3 | AddtlParams4}

{AddtlParams1}
[-CustomConfigWriteScope **Scope**] [-RecipientRelativeWriteScope <None |
NotApplicable | Organization | MyGAL | Self | MyDirectReports | OU |

CustomRecipientScope | MyDistributionGroups | MyExecutive | ExclusiveRecipientScope>]

{AddtlParams2}
[-CustomConfigWriteScope **Scope**]
[-CustomRecipientWriteScope **Scope**]

{AddtlParams3}
[-CustomConfigWriteScope **Scope**]

{AddtlParams4}
[-ExclusiveConfigWriteScope **Scope**]
[-ExclusiveRecipientWriteScope **Scope**]

You can list role assignments using Get-ManagementRoleAssignment. You use New-ManagementRoleAssignment to assign roles. The following example assigns the Retention Management role to the Central Help Desk group:

```
New-ManagementRoleAssignment -Name "Central Help Desk_Retention"
-Role "Retention Management" -SecurityGroup "Central Help Desk"
```

The following example assigns the Mail Recipients role to members of the Marketing Help Desk group:

```
New-ManagementRoleAssignment -Name "Marketing_Options"
-Role "Mail Recipients" -SecurityGroup "Marketing Help Desk"
```

This allows users who are members of the Marketing Help Desk group to manage existing mailboxes, mail users, mail contacts, distribution groups, and dynamic distribution groups. This does not enable these users to create recipients. To create recipients, the users need to be assigned the Mail Recipient Creation role.

You can modify role assignment using Set-ManagementRoleAssignment. The following example disables the Central Help Desk_Retention role assignment:

```
Set-ManagementRoleAssignment -Identity "Central Help Desk_Retention"
-Enabled $False
```

When you disable a role assignment, the users assigned the role can no longer perform the management tasks granted by the role. However, keep in mind that a user might have been granted the permission in another way. By disabling a role assignment rather than removing it, you can easily enable the role assignment again as shown in the following example:

```
Set-ManagementRoleAssignment -Identity "Central Help Desk_Retention"
-Enabled $True
```

However, if you are sure you no longer want to use a particular role assignment, you can remove it using Remove-ManagementRoleAssignment as shown in the following example:

```
Remove-ManagementRoleAssignment -Identity "Central Help Desk_Retention"
```

When you create a new assignment policy, you can assign it to users using the New-Mailbox, Set-Mailbox, or Enable-Mailbox cmdlet. If you make the new assignment policy the default assignment policy, it's assigned to all new mailboxes that don't have an explicitly designated assignment policy. After you create an assignment policy, you must assign it at least one management role for permissions to apply to a mailbox. Without any roles assigned to it, users assigned the policy won't be able to manage any of their mailbox configurations. To assign a management role, use New-ManagementRoleAssignment.

In the shell, commands you use to work with role assignment policy include the following:

- **Get-RoleAssignmentPolicy** Lists all policies or a specified role assignment policy.

```
Get-RoleAssignmentPolicy [-Identity AssignmentPolicyName]
[-Organization OrganizationId]
```

- **New-RoleAssignmentPolicy** Creates a new role assignment policy.

```
New-RoleAssignmentPolicy -Name AssignmentPolicyName
[-Description Description] [-IsDefault {$True|$False}]
[-Organization OrganizationId]
```

- **Remove-RoleAssignmentPolicy** Removes a role assignment policy.

```
Remove-RoleAssignmentPolicy -Identity AssignmentPolicyName
```

- **Set-RoleAssignmentPolicy** Changes the name of a role assignment policy, or sets a role assignment policy as the default.

```
Set-RoleAssignmentPolicy -Identity AssignmentPolicyName
[-Description Description] [-IsDefault {$True|$False}] [-Name NewName]
```

You can list role assignment policies using Get-RoleAssignmentPolicy. Rather than view all available assignment policies, you can easily filter the output to look for default assignment policies. Here is an example:

```
Get-RoleAssignmentPolicy | Where { $_.IsDefault -eq $True }
```

You use New-RoleAssignmentPolicy to create role assignment policies. The following example creates the Standard User Policy and assigns it as the default:

```
New-RoleAssignmentPolicy -Name "Standard User Policy"
```

When you create a new assignment policy, you can assign it to users using New-Mailbox, Set-Mailbox, or Enable-Mailbox as shown in the following example:

```
Set-Mailbox -Identity "tommyj" -RoleAssignmentPolicy "Standard User Policy"
```

If you make the new assignment policy the default assignment policy, it's assigned to all new mailboxes that don't have an explicitly designated assignment policy. You can specify that a policy is the default when you create it using -IsDefault. You can also designate a policy as the default using Set-RoleAssignmentPolicy as shown in this example:

```
Set-RoleAssignmentPolicy -Identity "Standard User Policy" -IsDefault
```

After you create an assignment policy, you must assign at least one management role to it for it to apply permissions to a mailbox. Without any roles assigned to it, users assigned the policy won't be able to manage any of their mailbox configuration. To assign a management role, use New-ManagementRoleAssignment.

You can remove policies using Remove-RoleAssignmentPolicy. The assignment policy you want to remove can't be assigned to any mailboxes or management roles.

Also, if you want to remove the default assignment policy, it must be the last assignment policy. Because of this, you need to use Set-Mailbox to change the assignment policy for any mailbox that's assigned the assignment policy before you can remove it. If the assignment policy is the default assignment policy, use Set-RoleAssignmentPolicy to select a new default assignment policy before you remove the old default policy. You don't need to do this if you're removing the last assignment policy. Additionally, keep in mind that you can use Remove-ManagementRoleAssignment to remove any management role assignments assigned to a policy.

With this in mind, the following series of examples show how you can modify and remove assignment policy. The first example removes the assignment policy called "Standard User Policy" by finding all of the mailboxes assigned the policy and then assigning a different policy:

```
Get-Mailbox | Where {$_.RoleAssignmentPolicy -Eq "Standard User Policy"}
 | Set-Mailbox -RoleAssignmentPolicy "New User Policy"
```

Next, you can remove all the role assignments assigned to an assignment policy:

```
Get-ManagementRoleAssignment -RoleAssignee "Standard User Policy" |
Remove-ManagementRoleAssignment
```

Afterward, you can remove the assignment policy by entering the following:

```
Remove-RoleAssignmentPolicy "Standard User Policy"
```

Configuring Account Management Permissions

User roles control the settings that users can configure on their own mailboxes and on distribution groups they own. These settings determine whether users can:

- Change the display name, contact information, text messaging settings, voice mail settings, and more.
- View and modify apps, mail subscriptions, and retention policies.
- Modify the basic configuration of the mailbox.
- Create and connect site mailboxes.
- Manage text messaging and voice mail settings
- Create, modify, and view distribution groups
- Manage membership of distribution groups they own.

- Manage their membership in distribution groups.

The Exchange organization has a default role assignment policy that grants users permission to configure all user-manageable settings. You can create one or more additional role assignment policies and assign them to users at any time using Exchange Admin Center. To view the currently available policies, select **Permissions** in the Navigation menu and then select **User Roles** as shown in Figure 10-6.

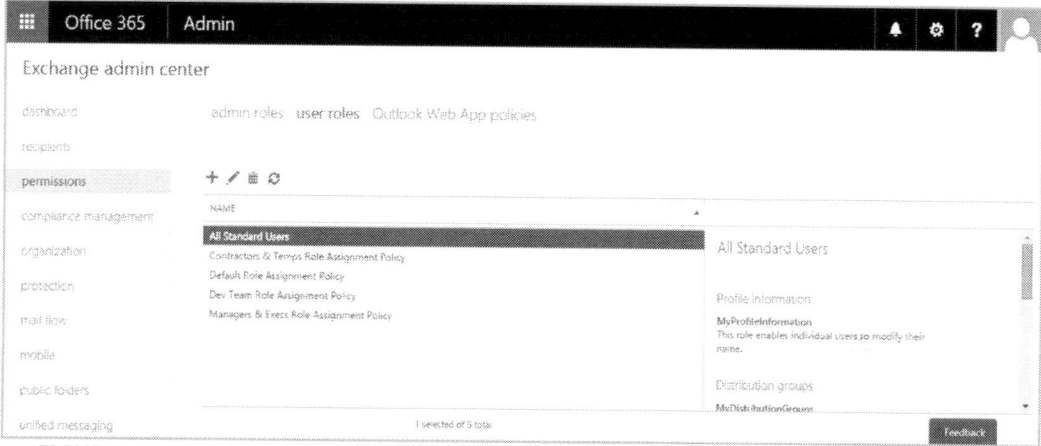

FIGURE 10-6 Configuring user roles to manage permissions.

To create a policy, click **New** (   ). In the Role Assignment Policy dialog box, type a descriptive name for the policy, such as All Standard Users. To grant a role to users, select the related check box. To not grant a role to users, clear the related check box. At a minimum, be sure to grant MyBaseOptions to the policy so that those assigned the policy can access their mailbox and basic settings.

role assignment policy

*Name:

Contractors & Temps Role Assignment Policy

Description:

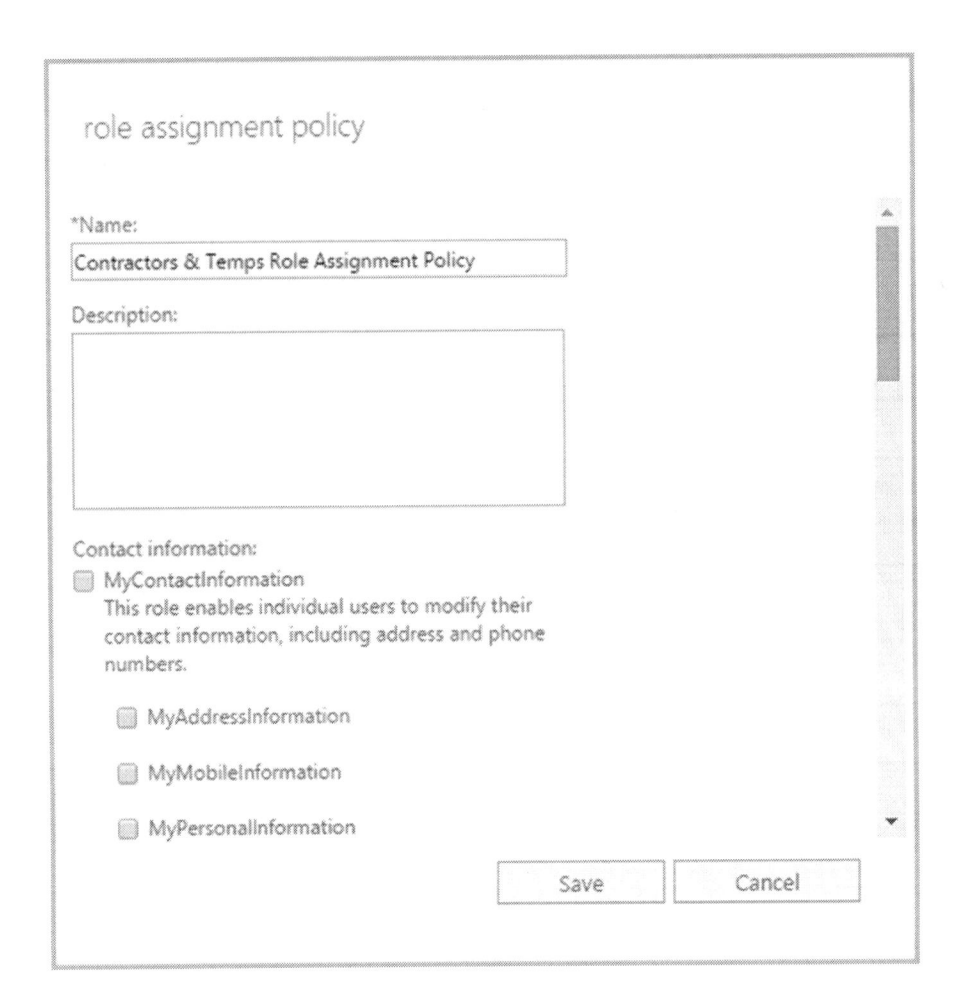

Contact information:
- ☐ MyContactInformation
  This role enables individual users to modify their contact information, including address and phone numbers.
  - ☐ MyAddressInformation
  - ☐ MyMobileInformation
  - ☐ MyPersonalInformation

[Save]   [Cancel]

Finally, click **Save** to create the policy and update the organization settings. It may take several minutes to update the organization settings. If an error occurs, try to create the policy again before you begin any troubleshooting. Sometimes, a complex process won't be completed fully the first time and retrying will resolve the problem.

To assign a policy to a user, follow these steps:

1. In Exchange Admin Center, select **Recipients** in the Navigation menu and then select **Mailboxes**. Double-click the entry for the user.
2. On the Mailbox Features page, use the Role Assignment Policy selection list to choose the policy that you want to apply.
3. Click **Save**.

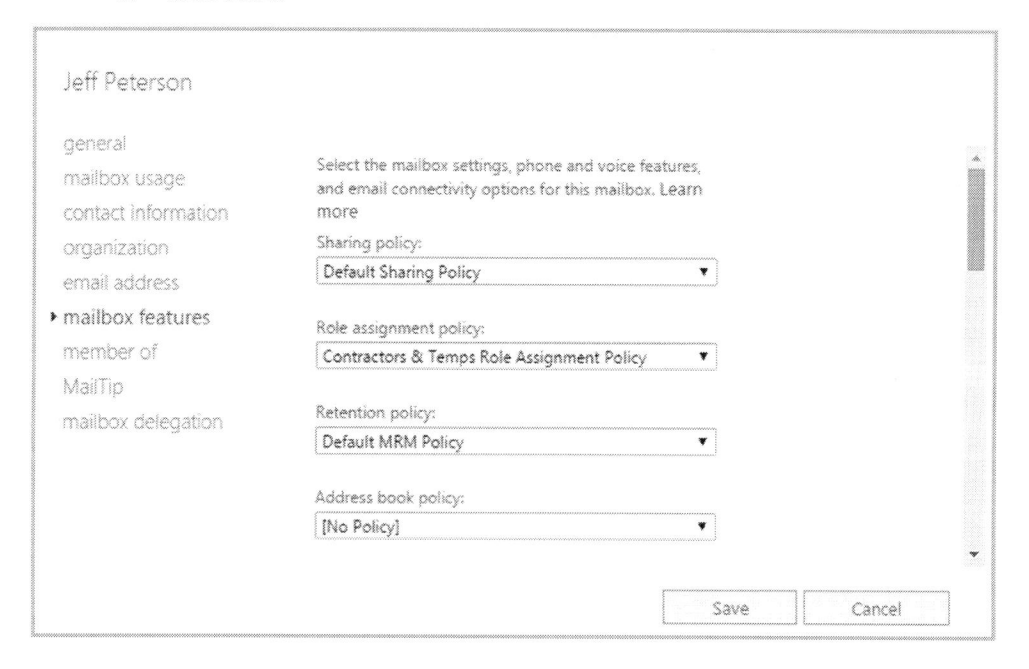

Index

.

.ost file
  repairing 233
.pst file
  repairing 231

A

Add commands and cmdlets
  Add-ADPermission 129
  Add-DistributionGroupMember152, 189
  Add-MailboxPermission 128
  Add-RoleGroupMember................. 268
address lists
  global address list 118
Address lists... 118
apps
  app status 116
Arbitration mailboxes 104
archive mailbox
  bulk editing.. 98
  disabling 101
archive mailboxes
  storage restrictions 132

B

booking options
  configuring 94

C

cmdlet
  Disable-Mailbox 72
  New-MailContact.............................. 76
  Remove-Mailbox............................... 73
  Set-User 71
Connect commands and cmdlets
  Connect-PSSession............................ 28
contacts
  understanding................................... 39

D

Delete commands and cmdlets
  Delete-DistributionGroup 182
Disable commands and cmdlets
  Disable-DistributionGroup 151, 181
  Disable-Mailbox 103
Disconnect commands and cmdlets
  Disconnect-PSSession 27
Discovery search 105
distribution group
  creating 146
distribution groups
  creating 145
  member restrictions 156
  moderating 157

281

distribution lists
    creating in Office 365 184
    Exchange aliases 185
    managing membership 187
    managing membership remotely ... 189
    ownership 189
    remotely adding owners 190
    remotely removing owners 190
    removing 187
    SMTP address 185
dynamic distribution group
    creating 158
    recipients 166
dynamic distribution groups
    filter conditions 163
    using 139

E

Enable commands and cmdlets 106
    Enable-DistributionGroup 150, 181
    Enable-Mailbox 97, 104
    Enable-MailContact 77
Enter commands and cmdlets
    Enter-PSSession 24
Exchange
    assigning management permissions 255
    contact restrictions 124
    creating role groups 264
    custom attributes 118
    custom attributes, defining 118
    delegating mailbox access 235
    group naming policy 143
    individual delivery restrictions 123
    mail restrictions 172
    mailbox access permissions 235
    mailbox apps 114
    management roles 259

Outlook Web App 202
Permissions 250
role groups 253
security groups 250
storage restrictions 131
viewing currently available policies 277
Exchange Admin Center
    addings apps 115
    archive mailbox 95
    archive settings 99
    assigning OWA mailbox policies 198
    assigning user policy 279
    associating mailbox plans 15
    booking options 90
    creating distribution and security groups
    146
    customize the view 15
    discovery and hold settings 105
    discovery searches 105
    distribution lists 178
    features and options 12
    features pane 12
    group moderation 174
    mailbox access permissions 126
    managing apps 115
    managing membership 253
    member restriction 155
    membership 151
    navigation bar 13
    Office 365 Group type 178
    Option buttons 14
    public folders 109, 111
    removing groups 175
    room mail boxes 90
    select multiple items 15
    usage restriction 173
    viewing groups 138

Exchange Admin Center for Exchange Online
    dashboard 12
    starting 12
Exchange alias
    understanding 39
Exchange Management
    creating distribution groups 149
Exchange Management Shell
    How remote sessions work 23
Exchange Online
    booking options 88
    cmdlets 32
    connecting using PowerShell 22
    licensing 7
    logon domain 63
    logon ID 63
    mailbox apps 114
    mailboxes for Office 365 59
    message restrictions 124
    message size restrictions 123
    remote sessions 25
    retention settings 133
    security groups 252
    SMTP address 66
    specific commands and cmdlets 32
    user types 48
    using 7
    using cmdlets 36
    using with Exchange Admin Center .. 11
    viewing current mailboxes, users,
        contacts, groups 45
    with Windows Azure 7

G

Get commands and cmdlets
    get-command 21
    Get-Contact 48

Get-Credential 25
Get-DistributionGroup 154, 170, 190
Get-DistributionGroupMember152, 189
Get-Exbanner 23
Get-Exblog 23
Get-Excommand 23
Get-Group 48
Get-Help 21
Get-Mailbox 36, 99
Get-MailUser 57
Get-ManagementRoleAssignment . 271
Get-MsolUser 121
Get-OwaMailboxPolicy 196
Get-Pscommand 23
Get-RoleAssignmentPolicy 274
Get-RoleGroup 266
Get-RoleGroupMember 269
Get-Tip 23
Get-User 37, 47
Get-DynamicDistributionGroup
    Get-DynamicDistributionGroup 164
group naming policy
    blocked words 144
    using 141
groups
    changing name 195
Groups
    group types 137

I

Import commands and cmdlets
    Import-PSSession 26

M

mail forwarding
    configuring 130
mailbox-enabled user accounts

mailboxes (continued)
    default email addresses 66

mailboxes
    access permissions 126, 240
    archive 95
    bulk editing 113
    display name 64
    equipment 85, 93
    Exchange alias 64
    global settings 68
    hiding 117
    managing 113
    permissions 126
    repairing 122
    restrictions 123
    room 85
    special purpose 85
    viewing storage size 131

mail-enabled contact
    defined 75

mail-enabled contacts
    creating 75
    email addresses 80
    naming 78

mail-enabled group
    configuring email addresses 168
    configuring information 167

mail-enabled users
    creating 57
    removing 59

Mail-enabled users
    creating 54

moderated groups
    creating 173

N

New commands and cmdlets
    New-DynamicDistributionGroup ... 162

New-Mailbox 92, 105, 106
New-MailboxRepairRequest 122
New-MailUser 57
New-ManagementRoleAssignment 272
New-RoleAssignmentPolicy 274
New-RoleGroup 266

New commands or cmdlets
    New-Mailbox 94

O

Office 365
    activate, license synced users 17
    administrative roles 252
    administrator privilege 257
    creating users 59
    distribution list membership 187
    distribution lists 184
    dynamic distribution groups 178
    group mailboxes 190
    licensing 15
    mobile group access 179
    planning user mailbox creation 39
    plans 7
    prerequisites for PowerShell access . 28
    purchase and assign licenses 16
    security groups 252
    security-enabled distribution groups 138
    supported groups 177

Office 365 Admin Center
    changing logon information for online
        users 63
    creating online user accounts 59
    deleting online user accounts 72
    licensing 43
    removing user licenses 72
    restoring users 119

Office 365 groups
    allowing outside emails 194
    changing naming 195
    collaboration 190
    controlling creation 196
    creating 190
    deleting 198
    finding 178
    mail-enabling 181
    member email subscriptions 192
    membership 182
    modifying membership 195
    modifying ownership 194
    private vs public 191
    properties 193
    removing Exchange features 181
    removing Exchange features remotely 182
    setting group ownership 186
    viewing 178
    working with 177
Office 365 Policy
    user passwords 70
Office Admin Center 178
    accessing 7
    accessing Exchange Admin Center ... 12
    changing group naming details 196
    creating security groups 179
    dashboard 11
    deleting groups 199
    group properties 193
    Groups 178
    managing distribution list ownership 189
    managing Office 365 role group
        membership 256
    navigation and options 8
    removing distribution lists 187
    removing security groups 181

    security groups 178
    using 7
online user account
    deleting 72
online users
    restoring 119
Outlook
    additional profiles 243
    address lists 211
    configuring POP3 accounts 223
    configuring remote users 216
    connecting to Exchange Online 213
    first time configuring 212
    internet mail accounts 219
    mail profiles 243
    mailboxes 86
    managing mail profiles 243
    offline address books 211
    repairing mail accounts 220
    scheduling 87
    startup profile 245
Outlook Web App 201
    configuring offline mode 208
    configuring offline users 207
    configuring ports 202

P

personal folder
    delivering mail 229
personal folders 227
    configuring 228
    locating 227
PowerShell
    execution policy 20
    identifying version 18
    setting execution policy 20
    setting the version 18

starting 18
stopping execution............................ 19
public folder mailbox
    creating 110
public folders....................................... 109

R

remote session
    adding or removing group managers 154
    archive mailbox................................ 97
    distribution group settings.............. 156
    dynamic distribution groups 164
    main commands................................ 41
    role assignment............................... 271
    role group membership 268
    role groups 266
remote sessions
    connecting to Exchange Online........ 24
    creating and importing 26
    defined... 22
    ending session................................... 25
    establishing 24
    start interactive session 24
Remove commands and cmdlets
    Remove-ADPermission 129
    Remove-DistributionGroup............. 176
    Remove-DistributionGroupMember 153, 189
    Remove-DynamicDistributionGroup 176
    Remove-MailboxPermission 128
    Remove-MailContact 83
    Remove-MailUser 59
    Remove-ManagementRoleAssignment
        272
    Remove-PSSession 28
    Remove-RoleAssignmentPolicy...... 274
    Remove-RoleGroup......................... 267

Remove-RoleGroupMember 269
role groups
    current 263
    deleting group members 270
    listing available 268
    listing members 270
Role-based access control
    defined...258

S

security group
    creating..146
    mail-enabling 150
security groups
    creating..145
    creating in Office 365 179
    managing 181
Set commands and cmdlets
    Set-CASMailbox 197
    Set-DistributionGroup 170, 190
    Set-DynamicDistributionGroup 165
    Set-Mailbox..99
    Set-ManagementRoleAssignment ..272
    Set-OwaMailboxPolicy.....................196
    Set-RoleAssignmentPolicy 275
    Set-RoleGroup 267
    Set-User 37
shared mailbox
    creating..107
Shared mailboxes.................................106

U

Update commands and cmdlets
    Update-Help 21
    Update-RoleGroupMember 269
user account
    deleting..72

naming 53
removing license 71
reseting password 70
User Account
default reply address........................ 67
user accounts
contact information 67
defined 39
user accounts, mailbox-enabled
understanding 39
user accounts, mail-enabled
usage 39
user objects
defined 39

W

Windows Azure
Active Directory module 28
cmdlets 29
connecting to online services 29
understanding.................................. 28
Windows PowerShell
console... 17
default working environment 19
getting help documentation 21
graphical environment..................... 17
loading profiles 19
using with Exchange Online............. 17

About the Author

William R. Stanek (*http://www.williamrstanek.com*) has more than 20 years of hands-on experience with advanced programming and development. He is a leading technology expert, an award-winning author, and a pretty-darn-good instructional trainer. Over the years, his practical advice has helped millions of programmers, developers, and network engineers all over the world. In 2013, William celebrated the publication of his 150th book.

William has been involved in the commercial Internet community since 1991. His core business and technology experience comes from more than 11 years of military service. He has substantial experience in developing server technology, encryption, and Internet solutions. He has written many technical white papers and training courses on a wide variety of topics. He frequently serves as a subject matter expert and consultant.

William has an MS with distinction in information systems and a BS in computer science, magna cum laude. He is proud to have served in the Persian Gulf War as a combat crewmember on an electronic warfare aircraft. He flew on numerous combat missions into Iraq and was awarded nine medals for his wartime service, including one of the United States of America's highest-flying honors, the Air Force Distinguished Flying Cross. Currently, he resides in the Pacific Northwest with his wife and children.

William recently rediscovered his love of the great outdoors. When he's not writing, he can be found hiking, biking, backpacking, traveling, or trekking in search of adventure with his family! In his spare time, William writes books for children, including *The Bugville Critters Explore the Solar System* and *The Bugville Critters Go on Vacation*.

Find William on Twitter at http://www.twitter.com/WilliamStanek and on Facebook at http://www.facebook.com/William.Stanek.Author.

Windows Server 2016
Essentials for Administration

William R. Stanek
Author & Series Editor

William R. Stanek, Jr.
Contributor

IT Pro Solutions

Exchange Server 2016
Server Infrastructure

William R. Stanek
Author & Series Editor

William R. Stanek, Jr.
Contributor

IT Pro Solutions